A CASEBOO
REPAIR

A CASEBOOK ON REPAIRS

by

D. W. WILLIAMS, B.A., LL.B., M.C.D., M.R.T.P.I.

Principal Lecturer and Course Director
Department of Surveying
Liverpool Polytechnic

1987
THE ESTATES GAZETTE LIMITED
151, WARDOUR STREET, LONDON W1V 4BN

First Edition 1987

ISBN 0 7282 0103 8

Typeset and printed in Great Britain at The Bath Press, Avon

I Mam a'n Nhad
ac i gofio am
Richard Owen Parry

PREFACE

The idea for a casebook on the law of repairs flowed naturally from the publication of "Landlord and Tenant Casebook" published by the Estates Gazette in 1985. The area of repairs and dilapidations is of great importance to the student of surveying, land management, housing and law yet the number of books on the subject are few and far between and, certainly, there is no casebook on this subject area.

This casebook brings together 118 of the leading cases on the subject of repairs and dilapidations and, yet, these cases do not cover the whole subject area. Indeed the casebook concentrates on the landlord and tenant aspects of disrepair and only touches upon any potential tortious liability for disrepair. Neither are the more specific rights under the housing legislation (for example, standards of unfitness etc) covered. The casebook is offered to the surveying and land management student as a source of material for seminars and tutorials but it is also hoped to appeal to the wider range of practitioners practising in this field.

My thanks go to Michael R. Farrell ARICS, senior lecturer at Liverpool Polytechnic for continually discussing with me the more elusive and intricate points of the law of dilapidations. John R. Eaton BSc MBA ARICS ASVA, Director of Estate Management Studies at the same department, assisted me with the initial stages of proof reading. Steven Jennings, of Gorna & Co, Solicitors of Manchester, also made useful comments on some parts of Chapter 6, and for which I am grateful.

It is to be noted that this casebook has no index because the text has been subdivided so as to form its own type of index. Indeed, the casebook has been compiled to be read in sections and not to be consulted for a "quick" answer—there are no easy answers to questions of repair and dilapidations.

I acknowledge the kind permission of the following to reproduce material from their law reports; the Incorporated Council of Law Reporting for England and Wales; Butterworth & Co (Publishers) Ltd and Sweet and Maxwell Ltd. Case 30 is reproduced from Knight's Local Government Reports by kind permission of the Incorporated Council of Law Reporting for England and Wales and the publishers, Charles Knight Publishing, Croydon.

Lastly, but by no means least, my thanks, gratitude and apologies go to my very supportive wife and two year old daughter for their kindness and support not only during the writing of the casebook but also at the proof reading stage. As, at last, I put my pen down I must keep my promise and go and play in the doll's house in the hope that it, too, is not in need of repair!

The law is stated, on the materials before me, as it stood on 1st November 1986, but it has been possible to incorporate the decision in *Elite Investments Ltd* v *T I Bainbridge Silencers Ltd* [which appears in the pages following this preface]. The decision in *Post Office* v *Aquarius Properties* [Case 42] was affirmed by the Court of Appeal on different grounds and that decision is extracted following the *Elite Investments* extract.

Delyth. W. Williams
Department of Surveying
Liverpool Polytechnic

Case 118 Elite Investments Ltd v T I Bainbridge Silencers Ltd
[1986] 2 EGLR 43; (1986) 280 EG 1001. HH Judge Paul Baker
QC (sitting as a High Court judge)

The premises in question consisted of one large and one small industrial unit held by the tenants under separate leases but all under one roof. Whilst the action concerned the two industrial units the main issue related to the larger unit, the lease of which had terminated. The tenants had covenanted, in a general repairing covenant, well and substantially to repair, replace etc. the demised premises including the roof. At the date of the grant the roof was already deteriorating and bitumastic coating had not been applied until the galvanising had to a large extent worn off and by the date of the action the roof was beyond patching and needed to be replaced. The replacement of the roof was estimated to cost £84,364 and in its dilapidated condition the unit had virtually no value for letting purposes but its value as repaired would be about £140,000 or £150,000. As the cost of repairs was less than the diminution in the value of the reversion, section 18 of the Landlord and Tenant Act 1927 did not apply and the only question in regard to the larger unit was whether the replacement of the roof constituted a repair. The lease of the smaller unit was still running and contained a covenant by the tenants to allow the landlords to enter and carry out repairs on the tenant's default and recover the cost. The landlords sought relief in anticipation of the works being undertaken and assistance in them being undertaken.

Held (1) The arguments based upon inherent defect, giving back to the landlords an entirely different thing, disproportionate cost of repair and the test of what a reasonable landlord would do were to be rejected as this was a repair or replacement of part within the meaning of the tenant's covenant. It was not a different thing but merely an industrial building with a new roof. The claim for damages of £84,364 in relation to the larger unit had been established.

(2.) The claim in relation to the smaller unit failed on the facts.

(3.) On the application of the Leasehold Property (Repairs) Act 1938 the decisions in *Colchester Estates (Cardiff)* v *Carlton Industries plc* and *Hamilton* v *Martell Securities Ltd* were to be preferred to that in *Swallow Securities* v *Brand*.

HH Judge Paul Baker QC said (in part)

[Counsel], in his very forceful argument before me (and I am much indebted to him for the range and interest of it), took five points, all of which he said, when you take it as a whole, lead to the conclusion that this is a replacement and not a repair within the repairing covenant. He said, first of all, that the roof was inherently defective; it ought to have been painted at the beginning and was not. It had a limited life expectancy, the building was coming to the end of its life. I do not find that to be so in regard to the rest of the building. Most of the building, as I find, seems to be still good. There were defects in the bricks but they are not more than normal, and it is quite plain that the rest of the building has quite a good life in front of it yet. As to its being an inherent defect, as we have seen going along, that of itself is not fatal to the idea that nevertheless when it fails there is a repair. Over and above that I do not regard such failure to paint galvanised sheeting at the outset as an inherent defect. It may have heightened the need to repair and to do further paintings later, but that is not, in my judgment, any sort of inherent defect in the roof.

Then [counsel] pointed out to me the size of the matter in dispute. The roof and the side cladding was indeed 80% of the surface. What was left really was just a space. So replacing that is really replacing substantially the whole of the building. That goes to assist one, in assessing a matter of degree, but it is not conclusive in this case. In the first place no one is suggesting that the side cladding should be changed, and therefore it is far less than 80% of the surface which is involved in replacing the roof; and it is not right to say that what is inside is just a space, because there is 10% or so of offices, and so on. It is nowhere near justifying one saying that putting on a new roof comes to substantially replacing the whole of the building.

Then [counsel] said, third, that what is now proposed is completely different from the roof that is there at present and it is quite different from what there was before. That is going to be a completely different material. he also called attention to the points that Mr Roberts [witness] had made of the consequential effects of the new material.

As I see that, it is not that the roof is going to be very different. It is a new material, but that is just taking advantage of better materials that are now on the market. It does not really alter the basic structure of the building and, after all, this is quite a simple building, it is not some complex structure such as Hoffmann J had to consider [in *Post Office* v *Aquarius Properties*]. This is a relatively simple building and the roof will not be largely changed simply because it has got a roof looking similar to the existing roof but made of modern materials. Further, it seems largely irrelevant, because the old material is available and costs the same. [Counsel] placed the greatest emphasis on the cost; it is totally disproportionate, he said, to the value of the building in repair. I have already dealt with that going through the cases, and in my judgment that is a false point. What has to be compared in this connection in determining whether you have got a repair or not, is not the value of the resulting building with the new roof but what it will cost you to do away with the building altogether and build a new one, or substantially build a new one. Then he said, having looked at the factors no reasonable landlord would do it. That again is not the test, if I may respectfully say so; it is a question of whether the tenants have undertaken to do what is done and what is the true meaning of the covenant.

So my conclusion on that, as is evident from now, is that this is a repair or replacement of part within the meaning of the covenant. It is not a different thing. It will simply be an industrial building with a new roof. The consequence is that I find that the case for damages in relation to Unit 1 in the sum I mentioned of £84,364 is established.

I must now deal with the claim which is based on the covenant to allow the landlord to enter and do the repairs and recover the cost from the tenant. This raises some matters of a little complexity, and particularly with regard to Unit 7. In view of what I have found, that the full cost is recoverable and it is not diminished by the operation of section 18 of the Landlord and Tenant Act 1927, any claim based on this covenant in relation to Unit 1 does not arise.

To put this into context, a covenant of this type has been found in leases apparently since the beginning of the century, but there is a body of recent authority which has been concerned with the impact on it of the restrictions on the landlord's right to recover damages for repairs imposed by the 1938 Act. The most important case now is that of Vinelott J in *Hamilton* v *Martell Securities Ltd* [1984] Ch 266. There was in that case a claim to recover the cost of repair. The landlord had done repairs and now he was claiming the cost of them pursuant to some such covenant as we have got in this case, to permit the landlord to do repairs and look to the tenant for the costs. Vinelott J held that that claim amounted to a debt and was not damages and as such was outside the scope of the Act of 1938. In taking that view he differed from a decision of McNeil J in *Swallow Securities Ltd* v *Brand* (1981) 45 P&CR 328. The same point was presented to Nourse J (as he then was) in *Colchester Estates (Cardiff)* v *Carlton Industries plc* [1986] Ch 80. McNeill J took the view that the sums claimed were damages and therefore caught by the Act of 1938. Nourse J, when the matter came before him, followed Vinelott J. In the case before him the landlord had not expended any moneys, but the learned judge made a declaration that the leave of the court is not required by the plaintiffs to commence proceedings for the recovery of costs incurred by the landlord of making good defects, decays and wants of repair under the relevant covenant. Nourse J, as I said, followed Vinelott J. He did so on three grounds. First of all, he thought the decision of Vinelott J was right; second, he noted that a number of authorities, one in the Court of Appeal on a related point in relation to recovering the costs of surveyor's fees, had not been cited to McNeill J but had been cited to Vinelott J, and were very persuasive; third, he decided that when a judge of co-ordinate jurisdiction is presented with two decisions of brother judges he should for preference follow the later one unless there is a very good reason, such as that the later one was *per incuriam*, for not following it. I take the same attitude to this and accept the decision of Vinelott J in preference to that of McNeill J without further examination of the merits of the argument.

Note (i) This case should be read as if inserted in the text after Case 42.

Case 42A *Post Office v Aquarius Properties Ltd* (1986) 281 EG 799 Court of Appeal

The facts are stated in Case 42

Held (1) A repairing covenant in standard form contained in a lease of commercial premises did not impose liability on the tenant to remedy defects in the original construction of a building. As the building in this particular case was throughout in the same physical condition, no want of repair had been proved by the landlord for which the tenant could be liable under the covenant.

Ralph Gibson LJ said (in part)

For my part I am unable to accept the submission made for the appellant landlords by [counsel]. The facts of this case seem to me to be, as I have said, highly unusual. I found it at first to be a startling proposition that, when an almost new office building lets groundwater into the basement so that the water is ankle deep for some years, that state of affairs is consistent with there being no condition of disrepair under a repairing covenant in standard form whether given by the landlord or tenant. Nevertheless, as was pointed out in the course of argument, the landlord of such a building gives no implied warranty of fitness merely by reason of letting it; and neither a landlord nor a tenant who enters into a covenant to repair in ordinary form, thereby undertakes to do work to improve the demised premises in any way. I see no escape from the conclusion that, if on the evidence the premises demised are and at all times have been in the same physical condition (so far as concerns the matters in issue) as they were when constructed, no want of repair has been proved for which the tenants could be liable under the covenant.

When the water entered by reason of the original defects damage might have been done to the premises, whether to plaster on walls, or to the flooring, or to electrical or other installations. But no such damage was proved. If such damage is done, the authorities show that the resulting state is a condition of disrepair: see *Ravenseft Properties Ltd* v *Davstone (Holdings) Ltd* [1980] QB 12 and *Elmcroft Developments ltd* v *Tankersley-Sawyer* (1984) 270 EG 140. As to the submission that the court in *Quick's* case was not considering a defect which had been caused by defective work, I accept that such were the facts in that case—the house was built in accordance with the regulations in force and standards accepted at the time (see [1986] 1 QB 816). In my judgment, however, the reasoning of the court in *Quick's* case is equally applicable whether the original defect resulted from error in design, or in workmanship, or from deliberate parsimony or any other cause. If on the letting of premises it were desired by the parties to impose on landlord or tenant an obligation to put the premises into a particular state or condition so as to be at all times fit for some stated purpose, even if it means making the premises better than they were when constructed, there would be no difficulty in finding words apt for that purpose.

Neither [counsel] for the landlord nor [counsel] for the Post Office could refer the court to any reported case in which a defect, whether of design or workmanship, and present unaltered since construction of the premises, and which had caused or permitted entry of water into the premises, had nevertheless caused no damage to the premises demised. It seems to me that the unusual facts of this case are covered by the plain meaning of the word "repair" and by the decision of the court in *Quick's* case. It is not possible to hold that the wetting of the basement floor or the presence of the water upon the floor, coupled with the inconvenience caused thereby to the tenant, constitutes damage to the premises demised. There is, accordingly, no disrepair proved in this case and therefore no liability under the tenant's covenant to repair has arisen.

So to hold is not, in my judgment, to depart from, or to cast doubt upon, the principles established by the decision of the Court of Appeal in *Proudfoot* v *Hart*. Upon examination of the judgment of Lord Esher in that case, it is apparent that he was only directing his observations to premises of which the condition has deteriorated from a former better condition. [Counsel] accepted that that was so. It might be said that there is no difference in principle between, on the one hand, imposing a liability on a tenant to put premises into a better condition than they were at the date of the demise by reference to an earlier state before deterioration had occurred, and, on the other hand, imposing on a tenant, as [counsel] asks the court to do, liability to put premises into a better condition than ever they were in by reference to a state in which they ought to have been if they are to be in some state of fitness or suitability. That, however, in my judgment is not the point. This court in this case is not laying down rules to govern the relationships and mutual responsibilities of landlords and tenants of office buildings. Our task is to construe a repairing covenant in a particular underlease. The decision may be of some general importance, despite the unusual set of facts, because the covenant so far as concerns the words upon which reliance is placed is in common form. But landlords and tenants of such premises are free to modify the repairing covenants as they think appropriate and can agree. There is no basis to be found in the decision in *Proudfoot* v *Hart* for holding that the tenant can be held liable under an ordinary repairing covenant to carry out work merely to improve premises so as to remove a defect present since construction of the building.

That conclusion, if right, is sufficient to dispose of this appeal. The questions considered by the learned judge as to whether, as a matter of degree, any of the schemes of work qualified as "repair", as contrasted with works of improvement or alteration, do not arise. These issues were, however, argued before us and I think it is appropriate to make some comments upon them.

The main criticism advanced by [counsel] was that the learned judge had failed to have due regard to, or to apply correctly the test enunciated by, Forbes J in *Ravenseft Properties Ltd* v *Davstone (Holdings) Ltd*, namely that it was a question of degree whether work carried out on a building was repair or work that so changed the character of the building as to involve giving back to the landlord "a wholly different thing" from that which he demised. It was said that if the judge had given sufficient force to the fact that the necessary work in this case was directed to a subordinate part only of the building he must have reached a different conclusion. For my part I do not accept that the learned judge is shown to have misapprehended or misapplied in this way the appropriate test. The relationship of the part upon which work is required to the whole of the subject-matter of the demise is also, in my judgment and as Slade LJ suggested in argument, a question of proportion and degree. At one end of the scale there has never been any doubt that a party liable under a covenant to repair may have to renew in effect a whole part such as a floor, or a door, or a window. An example of a substantial part is the stone cladding of the building in the *Ravenseft Property* case. I do not accept, however, that it is only open to the court to hold that work involves giving back a wholly different thing if it is possible to say that the whole subject-matter of the demise, or a whole building within the subject-matter of the demise, will by the work be made different.

CONTENTS

	Page
Preface	vii
Table of Cases	xix
Table of Statutes	xxvii
List of Cases from which extracts are taken	xxix

1   THE PREMISES AND THE COVENANT   **1**

   1.1 The premises demised   1

2   EXPRESS REPAIRING OBLIGATIONS   **27**

   2.1 Common repairing obligations   27
   2.2 Extent and type of repair   37
   2.3 Repairs at a specific time   41
   2.4 Covenant to paint   43
   2.5 Fair wear and tear   46
   2.6 Standard of repair   53
   2.7 Landlord's covenant: the requirement for notice   56
   2.8 Implied licence to enter and carry out repairs   70

3   REPAIR—RENEWAL—IMPROVEMENT   **79**

   3.1 Repair—renewal—improvement dichotomy   79
   3.2 Repair—renewal—improvement: works within
        the covenant   106

4   IMPLIED REPAIRING OBLIGATIONS   **123**

   4.1 Houses at low rents   123
   4.2 Repairing obligations in short leases   126
   4.3 The interpretation of sections 11–14 of the 1985 Act   140
   4.4 Works held to be outside the implied covenant   152
   4.5 Damages for breach of the implied covenant
        under the 1985 Act   167
   4.6 Implied covenant of tenant-like user   175
   4.7 Other implied obligations   176

5   DAMAGES FOR DISREPAIR   **185**

   5.1 Damages for breach of tenant's repairing
        covenant at common law   185
   5.2 The operation of the Landlord and Tenant Act
        1927   189

5.3 Section 18 and the relevance of reletting 210
5.4 Date of assessment of damages 219
5.5 Covenants outside the scope of section 18(1) 222
5.6 Other heads of damage 226
5.7 Damages and subtenancies 232
5.8 No damages because of demolition or alteration 239
5.9 Leasehold Property (Repairs) Act 1938 251
5.10 Damages for breach of landlord's repairing covenant 253

6 REMEDIES FOR DISREPAIR **265**
6.1 Other remedies for disrepair 265
6.2 Landlord's remedy: Forfeiture and the section 146 notice 265
6.3 Contents and service of the section 146 notice 276
6.4 Landlord's remedy: Relief for the tenant or waiver 290
6.5 Leasehold Property (Repairs) Act 1938 297
6.6 Relief in respect of internal decorative repairs 316
6.7 Landlord's self-help 317
6.8 Tenant's remedy: Set-off against rent 332
6.9 Tenant's remedy: Specific Performance 340
6.10 Tenant's remedy: Appointment of a receiver of rents 348
6.11 Tenant's remedy: the "Right to Repair" 354

7 OTHER RIGHTS, OBLIGATIONS AND REMEDIES **357**
7.1 Tenant's duty not to commit waste 357
7.2 Landlord's liability under the Defective Premises Act 1972 364
7.3 Occupiers' Liability Acts 1957 and 1984 369
7.4 The operation of the Public Health Act 1936 373

TABLE OF CASES

[Extracts are taken from those cases in bold type.]

A

Page

Adelphi Hotel (Brighton) Ltd (Re) [1953] 1 WLR 955 208
American Cynamid Co v Ethicon Ltd [1975] AC 396 321
Apex Supply Co Ltd (Re) [1942] Ch 108 324
Arden v Pullen (1842) 10 M & W 319 .... 27, 31
Asco Developments Ltd v Gordon [1978] EGD 376 340
Associated Deliveries Ltd v Harrison (1984) 272 EG 321 .... **270**
Ayling v Wade [1961] 2 QB 229 11

B

Bader Properties Ltd v Linley Property Investments Ltd (1967)
   19 P & CR 62 .... 315, 329
Bailey v De Crespigny LR 4 QB 180 45
Baker v Sims [1959] 1 QB 115 .... **303**
Ball v Plummer (1879) 23 So Jo 656 1
Barker v Barker [1829] 3 C & P 557 318
Baylis v Le Gros (1858) 4 CB (NS) 537 .... **43**
Beasley v D'Arcy (1800) 2 Sch & Lef 403 340
Birch v Clifford (1891) 8 TLR 103 .... **226**
Birch v Wright (1786) 1 TR 378 275
Birmingham & District Land Co v London and North Western
   Railway Co (1888) 40 ChD 268 240
Blundell v Obsdale [1958] EGD 145 .... **18**
Borthwick-Norton v Romney Warwick Estates Ltd [1950] 1 All
   ER 798 284
Boswell v Crucible Steel Co [1925] 1 KB 119 .... 7, **8**, 10
**Bradley v Chorley Borough Council [1985] 2 EGLR 49; (1985) 275
   EG 801** **172**
Bradshaw v Pawley [1980] 1 WLR 10 134
Brew Bros Ltd v Snax (Ross) Ltd [1970] 1 QB 612
   .... **92**, 102, 104, 115, 118, 119
Brikom Investments Ltd v Seaford [1981] 1 WLR 863 .... **133**
**British Anzani (Felixstowe) Ltd v International Marine Manage-
   ment (UK) Ltd [1979] 2 All ER 1063** **334**
Brown v Liverpool Corporation [1969] 3 All ER 1345 .... 15, **140**, 369

C

Calabar Properties v Stitcher [1983] 3 All ER 759 .... 170, **255**
Calthorpe v McOscar [1924] 1 KB 716 .... **53**, 58, 91

Campden Hill Towers Ltd *v* **Gardner (1976) 242 EG 375** 12, 13, **146,** 163
Canas Property Co Ltd *v* K. L. Television Services Ltd [1970] 2 QB
    433 271
Carlisle Cafe Co *v* Muse Brothers & Co 77 LT 515 2
Central Estates (Belgravia) Ltd *v* **Woolgar (No. 2) [1972] 1 WLR 1048** 293
Church Commissioners for England *v* **Ve-Ri-Best Manufacturing**
    Co Ltd [1957] 1 QB 238 .... **306**
Citron *v* Cohen (1920) 36 TLR 560 50
Clare *v* Dobson [1911] 1 KB 35 230
Clarke *v* Grant [1950] 1 KB 104 295
Cockburn *v* **Smith [1924] 2 KB 119** **3,** 12, 124
Colchester Estates (Cardiff) *v* Carlton Industries plc [1984] 2 All ER
    601 332
Collins *v* **Flynn [1963] 2 All ER 1068** **91,** 97, 102, 115
Cove *v* Smith (1886) 2 TLR 778 64
Creery *v* Summersell & Flowerdew & Co Ltd [1949] Ch 751 295
Cremin *v* Barjack Properties Ltd (1984) 273 EG 299 297
Cunliffe *v* **Goodman [1950] 2 KB 237** **245**
Cusack-Smith *v* Gold [1958] 1 WLR 611 305

D

Daiches *v* **Bluelake Investments Ltd [1985] 2 EGLR 67; (1985) 275 EG**
    462 .... **349**
Davies *v* Underwood (1857) 2 H & N 570 237
Davis Contractors Ltd *v* Fareham U.D.C. [1956] AC 696 343
Dendy *v* Evans [1910] 1 KB 263 273
Department of Transport *v* Egoroff (1986) 278 EG 1361 140
Devine *v* London Housing Society Ltd [1950] WN 550 146
Dodd Properties (Kent) Ltd *v* Canterbury City Council [1980] 1 All
    ER 928 258
Doe d. Cheny *v* Batten (1775) 1 Cowp 243 295
Doe *v* Rowlands 9 C & P 734 318
Douglas-Scott *v* **Scorgie (1984) 269 EG 1164** **11,** 140
Driscoll *v* Church Commissioners for England [1957] 1 QB 330 273
Drummond *v* **S & U Stores Ltd (1981) 258 EG 1293** **198**
Dumptor's Case (1603) 4 Co Ref 119b 294
Dunster *v* Hollis [1918] 2 KB 795 .... 18, 124

E

Earl Cadogan *v* Guinness [1936] Ch 515 134
Ebbetts *v* **Conquest [1895] 2 Ch 377** 229, 230, **232**
Edmonton Borough Council *v* **W. H. Knowles & Son Ltd (1962)**
    60 LGR 124 .... **74**
Egerton *v* Esplanade Hotels, London Ltd [1947] 2 All ER 88
    .... 283, 286, 296
Egerton *v* Jones [1939] 2 KB 702 307

Elite Investments *v* T I Bainbridge Silencers Ltd [1986] 2 EGLR 43;
  (1986) 280 EG 1001 .... ix, 332
Elmcroft Developments Ltd *v* Tankersley-Sawyer (1984) 270 EG 140
  .... 104, **120**, 157, 159
Espir *v* Basil Street Hotel Ltd [1936] 3 All ER 91 .... 200, 229, **236**
Expert Clothing Service and Sales Ltd *v* Hillgate House Ltd [1985]
  2 EGLR 85; (1985) 275 EG 1011 .... **286**
Eyre *v* Johnson [1946] 1 KB 481 .... **44**
Eyre *v* Rea [1947] 1 All ER 415 .... **223**

F

Family Management *v* Gray (1979) 253 EG 369 .... **216**
Farimani *v* Gates (1984) 271 EG 887 .... **290**
Ferguson *v* Anon 2 Esp 590 358
Fisher *v* Walters [1926] 2 KB 315 .... 58, 60
Francis *v* Cockrell LR 5 QB 501 382
Francis *v* Cowcliffe Ltd (1976) 33 P & CR 368 .... **342**

G

Gardner *v* London Chatham and Dover Railway Co [1867] 2 Ch App
  Cas 201 354
Glass *v* Kencakes Ltd [1966] 1 QB 611 284
Goldfoot *v* Welch [1914] 1 Ch 213 .... **1**
Gooderham & Worts Ltd *v* Canadian Broadcasting Corporation
  [1947] AC 66 .... **34**
Gordon *v* Selico Co Ltd [1986] 1 EGLR 71; (1986) 278 EG 53 .... **346**
Granada Theatres Ltd *v* Freehold Investment (Leytonstone) Ltd
  [1959] 1 WLR 570 .... **20**
Green *v* Eales (1841) 2 QB 225 .... 169, 259
Greg *v* Planque [1936] 1 KB 669 .... **31**
Graystone Property Investments Ltd *v* Margulies (1984) 269 EG 538 **4**
Griffin *v* Pillett [1926] 1 KB 17 .... 61, **64**
Gutteridge *v* Munyard (1834) 7 C & P 129 .... 47, 48, 80, 84, **85**

H

Hack *v* Leonard (1724) 9 Mod 91 341
Hadley *v* Baxendale (1854) 9 Ex 341 .... 234, 235
Halliard Property Co Ltd *v* Nicholas Clarke Investments Ltd (1983)
  269 EG 1257 .... **101**
Hamilton *v* Martell Securities Ltd [1984] 1 All ER 665 .... **327**
Hanak *v* Green [1958] 2 QB 9 340
Hanson *v* Newman [1934] Ch 298 ...... 193, 194, 198, 199, 215, **219**, 225
Harbutt's "Plasticine" Ltd *v* Wayne Tank and Pump Co Ltd [1970]
  1 QB 447 169
Hargroves, Aronson & Co *v* Hartopp [1905] 1 KB 472 124

Harris *v* Beauchamp [1894] 1 QB 801 354
Hart *v* Elmkirk Ltd (1982) 267 EG 946 .... **348**, 350
Hart *v* Rogers [1916] 1 KB 646 .... 333, 340
Hart *v* Windsor (1844) 12 M & W 68 .... 125, 362
Haskell *v* Marlow [1928] 2 KB 45 .... **46**, 53
Haviland *v* Long [1952] 2 QB 81 .... 202, **210**
Hewitt *v* Rowlands [1924] All ER 344 .... **253**
Heyting *v* Foreman [1934] EGD 174 4
**Hibernian Property Co Ltd *v* Liverpool Corporation [1973] 1 WLR
  751** **248**
Hill *v* Barclay (1810) 16 Ves 402 .... 320, 341
Hoffman *v* Fineberg [1949] Ch 245 .... 283, 287, 296
Holiday Fellowship Ltd *v* Hereford [1959] 1 WLR 211 .... **6**
Hope Brothers Ltd *v* Cowan [1913] 2 Ch 312 2
Hopwood *v* Cannock Chase D.C. (1974) 29 P & CR 256 14, 140, 368, 369
Horsefall *v* Mather Holt NP 7 .... 175, 358
Horsey Estate Ltd *v* Steiger [1899] 2 QB 79 269
Howe *v* Botwood [1913] 2 KB 387 .... **33**
Huggett *v* Miers [1908] 2 KB 278 146
Hyman *v* Rose [1912] AC 623 357

I

Inderwick *v* Leech 1 TLR 95 189
Industrial Properties (Barton Hill) Ltd *v* Associated Electrical Industries
  Ltd [1977] QB 580 272

J

James *v* Hutton [1950] KB 9 200
Jaquin *v* Holland [1960] 1 WLR 259 .... **213**, 229, 259, 272, 275
Jeune *v* Queens Cross Properties Ltd [1974] 1 Ch 97 ...... 320, **340**, 344
Jones *v* Carter (1846) 15 M & W 718 217
Jones *v* Herxheimer [1950] 2 KB 107 .... **193**, 200
Joyner *v* Weeks [1891] 2 QB 31 .... **186**, 190, 192, 210, 215, 220

K

Kanda *v* Church Commissioners for England [1958] 1 QB 332 304
Keats *v* Graham [1959] 3 All ER 919 .... **243**
King (Re) [1963] 1 Ch 459 .... 292, 293
Kirklington *v* Wood [1917] 1 KB 333 .... **41**

L

**Land Securities PLC *v* Receiver for the Metropolitan Police District
  [1983] 1 WLR 439** **308**
Landeau *v* Marchbank [1949] 2 All ER 172 .... 196, 197, 200

Lee-Parker *v* Izzet [1971] 1 WLR 1688 .... **332,** 337, 339
Lister *v* Lane and Nesham [1893] 2 QB 212
    79, 82, 84, 85, 87, 88, 92, 97, 102, 104, 107, 112, 115, 118, 153, 254
Lister *v* Romford Ice and Cold Storage Co Ltd [1957] AC 555 178
Liverpool City Council *v* Irwin (1976) 32 P & CR 43
    .... **141,** 152, 177, 180, 182
Lloyds Bank Ltd *v* Lake [1961] 1 WLR 884 .... **227**
London Borough of Newham *v* Patel [1978] 13 HLR 77 .... **164**
London & South Western Railway Co *v* Flower 1 CPD 77 362
Lurcott *v* Wakely and Wheeler [1911] 1 KB 905
    .... 34, 47, 54, 87, 91, 97, 102, **106,** 116, 117, 118, 153, 254

M

McCarrick *v* Liverpool Corporation [1947] AC 219 .... 59, 60, **130**
McCoy & Co *v* Clark [1982] 13 HLR 87 .... **260**
McGreal *v* Wake (1984) 269 EG 1254 .... **167,** 173
Maclenan *v* Segar [1917] 2 KB 325 .... 182, 183
Makin *v* Watkinson (1870) LR 6 Ex 25 .... 62, 67, 362
Manchester Bonded Warehouse Co *v* Carr (1880) 5 CPD 507 ... 50, **361**
Manor House Drive Ltd *v* Shahbazian [1965] EGD 228 .... **37**
Mantz *v* Goring (1838) 4 Bing NC 451 48
Marenco *v* Jacramel Co Ltd [1964] EGD 349 .... **262**
Marsden *v* Edward Heyes Ltd [1927] 2 KB 1 .... 176, **357**
Mathews *v* Smallwood [1910] 1 Ch 777 295
Mathey *v* Curling [1922] 2 AC 180 45
Maud *v* Sandars [1943] WN 246 231
Meadows *v* Clerical, Medical and General Life Assurance Society
    [1981] Ch 70 273
Melles *v* Holme [1918] 2 KB 100 66
Melville *v* Grapelodge Developments Ltd (1978) 254 EG 1193 ...... **338**
Metropolitan Film Studios Ltd's Application (In Re) [1962] 1 WLR
    1315 312
Middlegate Properties Ltd *v* Gidlow-Jackson (1977) 34 P & CR 4
    .... **312,** 330
Middlegate Properties Ltd *v* Messimeris [1973] 1 WLR 168 302
Miller *v* Burt (1918) 63 SoJo 117 50
Miller *v* Hancock [1893] 2 QB 177 124
Mills *v* Guardians of the Poor of the East London Union (1872)
    LR 8 CP 79 .... **185**
Mint *v* Good [1951] 1 KB 517 76
Moorcock (The) (1889) 14 PD 64 .... 76, 143, 181–3
Monk *v* Noyes (1824) 1 Car & P 265 46
Morcom *v* Campbell-Johnson [1956] 1 QB 106 .... **112**
Morgan *v* Hardy (1886) 17 QBD 770 55
Morgan *v* Liverpool Corporation [1927] 2 KB 131 .... 56, 132
Moss Empires Ltd *v* Olympia (Liverpool) Ltd [1939] 3 All ER 460
    .... **222,** 324, 326

Murphy *v* Hurley [1922] 1 AC 369 .... 62, 63, 132
Myers *v* Oldschool [1928] EGD 167 .... **281**

N

Nicholas *v* Ingram [1958] NZLR 972 344

O

O'Brien *v* Robinson [1973] 1 All ER 583 .... **56**
O'Mahoney *v* Dickson (1805) 2 Sch & Lef 400 340
Oak Property Co Ltd *v* Chapman [1947] 1 KB 886 295
Official Custodian of Charities *v* Parway Estates Developments Ltd
   (1984) 270 EG 1077 293
**Old Grovebury Manor Farm Ltd *v* W. Seymour Plant Sales Ltd
   (No. 2) (1979) 38 P & CR 374** **268**
Openshaw *v* Evans (1884) 50 LT 156 32

P

Parker *v* London Borough of Camden [1985] 17 HLR 380 .... **352**
Parker *v* O'Connor [1974] 1 WLR 1161 .... **136**
Payne *v* Haine (1847) 16 M & W 541 .... 28, 72, 80
Pembery *v* Lamdin [1940] 2 All ER 435
   .... **35,** 92, 115, 118, 121, 153, 155, 157, 159
Peninsular Maritime Ltd *v* Padseal Ltd (1981) 259 EG 860 ...... 274, 345
Penley *v* Watts (1841) 7 M & W 601 230
Perry *v* Sidney Phillips & Son (a firm) [1982] 3 All ER 705 258
Photo Productions Ltd *v* Securicor Transport Ltd [1980] AC 827 271
Plummer *v* Ramsey (1934) 78 SoJo 175 325
Portman *v* Latta [1942] WN 97 197
**Post Office *v* Aquarius Properties Ltd [1985] 2 EGLR 105; (1985) 276
   EG 923; Court of Appeal (1986) 281 EG 799** .... xii, **103**
Proudfoot *v* Hart [1890] QB 42 .... **27,** 44, 55, 84, 108, 118, 214

Q

Quick *v* Taff-Ely Borough Council [1985] 2 EGLR 50; (1985) 276 EG
   452 .... **155**

R

**Ravenseft Properties Ltd *v* Davstone (Holdings) Ltd [1979] 1 All
   ER 929** 102, 104, **114,** 120, 157, 158
Rawlings *v* Morgan (1865) 18 CB (NS) 776 189
Read *v* Wotton [1893] 2 Ch 171 275
**Regional Properties Ltd *v* City of London Real Property Co Ltd
   (1979) 257 EG 64** **317**

Regis Property Co Ltd *v* **Dudley [1959] AC 370** **52,** 338
Reigate *v* Union Manufacturing Co (Ramsbottom) Ltd [1918] 1 KB
592 182
Riches *v* Owen (1868) 3 Ch App 820 349
Roberts *v* Church Commissioners for England [1972] 1 QB 278
.... 134, 135, 138
Rugby School (Governors) *v* Tannahill [1935] 1 KB 525 ... 284, 286, 296

S

Salisbury (Marquess) *v* **Gilmore [1942] 2 KB 38** 195, 197, **239,** 244
Samuels *v* **Abbints Investments Ltd [1963] EGD 543** **39**
Sandom *v* Webb [1951] 1 Ch 808 76
Saner *v* **Bilton (1878) 7 ChD 815** 70, 75, 169, 362, 363
Scala House and District Property Co Ltd *v* **Forbes [1974] 1 QB 573 282**
Scales *v* **Lawrence (1860) 2 F & F 289** **45,** 48
SEDAC Investments Ltd *v* **Tanner (1982) 44 P & CR 319 277,** 328, 331
Segal Securities Ltd *v* Thoseby [1963] 1 QB 887 295
Sheldon *v* **West Bromwich Corporation (1973) 25 P & CR 360** **68**
Shelfer *v* City of London Electric Lighting Co [1895] 2 Ch 388 320
Sidnell *v* Wilson [1966] 2 QB 67 .... 302, 309, 311, 331
Skinners Company *v* Knight [1891] 2 QB 542 .... 231, 330
Sleafer *v* **Lambeth Metropolitan Borough Council [1959] 3 All ER
378** **123**
Smedley *v* **Chumley and Hawke Ltd (1981) 44 P & CR 50** **116,** 159
Smiley *v* **Townshend [1950] 2 KB 311** 190, 199, 200, 216, 219, 276
Smith *v* **Bradford Metropolitan Council (1982) 44 P & CR 171** **366**
Smith *v* Marrable (1843) 11 M & W 5 362
Smith *v* Metropolitan City Properties Ltd [1986] 1 EGLR 52; (1986) 277
EG 753 297
Sotheby *v* **Grundy [1947] 2 All ER 761** 87, 92, 102, 118
Stanley *v* Towgood (1836) 3 Bing NC 4 48
Starrokate Ltd *v* **Burry (1982) 265 EG 871** **300**
Stocker *v* Planet Building Society [1879] 27 WR 877 318
Strood Estate Ltd *v* Gregory [1936] 2 KB 605 113
Sturge *v* Hackett [1962] 1 WLR 1257 4
Suffield *v* Brown (1864) 34 De GJ & S 185 75
Summers *v* Salford Corporation [1943] AC 283 59
Surplice *v* Farnsworth (1844) 7 Man & G 576 333
Sutton *v* Temple (1843) 12 M & W 52 .... 182, 362
Swallow Securities Ltd *v* **Brand (1981) 260 EG 63** **322,** 328, 330

T

Taylor *v* Beal (1591) Cro Eliz 222 .... 333–4, 337, 339
Taylor *v* **Knowsley Borough Council [1985] 17 HLR 316** **170**
Taylor *v* **Webb [1937] 2 KB 283** 8, **9,** 53, 334, 338

Terrell *v* Murray (1901) 17 TLR 570 49–51
Terroni *v* Corsini [1931] 1 Ch 515 .... **208**
Torrens *v* Walker [1906] 2 Ch 166 .... **83,** 107
Tredway *v* Machin (1904) 91 LT 310 67

U

Uniproducts (Manchester) Ltd *v* Rose Furnishers Ltd [1956]
1 WLR 45 .... **62**

W

Wainwright *v* Leeds City Council (1984) 270 EG 1289 .... **152,** 157
Warren *v* Keen [1954] 1 QB 15 .... 162, 175
Waters *v* Weigall (1795) 2 Anst 575 .... 333, 338
Wates *v* Rowland [1952] 2 QB 12 .... **89,** 105, 113
West Ham Central Charity Board *v* East London Waterworks Co
[1900] 1 Ch 624 357
West Midland Baptist (Trust) Association Inc *v* Birmingham
Corporation [1970] AC 874 250
Westminster (Duke of) *v* Guild (1983) 267 EG 762 .... **176**
Wettern Electric Ltd *v* Welsh Development Agency [1983] 2 WLR
897 .... **180**
Wheeler *v* Keeble Ltd [1920] 1 Ch 57 274
White and Carter (Councils) Ltd *v* McGregor [1962] AC 413 324
Whitham *v* Kershaw (1886) 16 QBD 613 .... 237, **359**
Wilson *v* Finch-Hatton (1877) 2 Ex D 336 362
Windmill Investments (London) Ltd *v* Milano Restaurant Ltd [1962]
2 QB 373 295
Woods *v* Pope (1835) 6 Car & P 1461 227
Wright *v* Lawson [1903] WN 108 .... **81,** 92
Wycombe Area Health Authority *v* Barnett (1982) 264 EG 619 161, 176

Y

Yanover *v* Romford Finance and Development Co Ltd (unreported)
29 March 1983 .... **98**
Yates *v* Morris [1951] 1 KB 77 296

TABLE OF STATUTES EXTRACTED

		Page
1	Landlord and Tenant Act 1985. Section 8	125
2	Landlord and Tenant Act 1985. Sections 11–14	127
3	Landlord and Tenant Act 1927. Section 18(1)	189
4	Leasehold Property (Repairs) Act 1938. Section 1	251
5	Law of Property Act 1925. Section 146	265
6	Law of Property Act 1925. Section 196	288
7	Landlord and Tenant Act 1927. Section 18(2)	289
8	Leasehold Property (Repairs) Act 1938	298
9	Law of Property Act 1925. Section 147	316
10	Landlord and Tenant Act 1985. Section 17	345
11	Housing Act 1985. Section 96	354
12	Defective Premises Act 1972. Section 4	364
13	Occupiers' Liability Act 1957. Sections 1–3	369
14	Occupiers' Liability Act 1984. Section 1	372
15	Public Health Act 1936. Sections 92–95, 99	373

LIST OF CASES FROM WHICH EXTRACTS ARE TAKEN

Page

1 Goldfoot *v* Welch 1
2 Cockburn *v* Smith 3
3 Graystone Property Investments Ltd *v* Margulies 4
4 Holiday Fellowship Ltd *v* Hereford 6
5 Boswell *v* Crucible Steel Co 8
6 Taylor *v* Webb 9
7 Douglas-Scott *v* Scorgie 11
8 Hopwood *v* Cannock Chase District Council 14
9 Blundell *v* Obsdale 18
10 Granada Theatres Ltd *v* Freehold Investment (Leytonstone) Ltd 20
11 Proudfoot *v* Hart 27
12 Greg *v* Planque 31
13 Howe *v* Botwood 33
14 Gooderham and Worts Ltd *v* Canadian Broadcasting
      Corporation 34
15 Manor House Drive Ltd *v* Shahbazian 37
16 Samuels *v* Abbints Investments Ltd 39
17 Kirklington *v* Wood 41
18 Baylis *v* Le Gros 43
19 Eyre *v* Johnson 44
20 Scales *v* Lawrence 45
21 Haskell *v* Marlow 46
22 Regis Property Co Ltd *v* Dudley 52
23 Calthorpe *v* McOscar 53
24 O'Brien *v* Robinson 56
25 Uniproducts (Manchester) Ltd *v* Rose Furnishers Ltd 62
26 Griffin *v* Pillett 64
27 Melles *v* Holme 66
28 Sheldon *v* West Bromwich Corporation 68
29 Saner *v* Bilton 70
30 Edmonton Borough Council *v* W. H. Knowles & Son Ltd 74
31 Lister *v* Lane and Nesham 79
32 Wright *v* Lawson 81
33 Torrens *v* Walker 83
34 Gutteridge *v* Munyard 85
35 Pembery *v* Lamdin 86
36 Sotheby *v* Grundy 87
37 Wates *v* Rowland 89
38 Collins *v* Flynn 91
39 Brew Brothers Ltd *v* Snax (Ross) Ltd 92
40 Yanover *v* Romford Finance and Development Co Ltd 98

41 Halliard Property Co Ltd *v* Nicholas Clarke Investments Ltd 101
42 Post Office *v* Aquarius Properties Ltd xii, 103
43 Lurcott *v* Wakely and Wheeler 106
44 Morcom *v* Campbell-Johnson 112
45 Ravenseft Properties Ltd *v* Davstone (Holdings) Ltd 114
46 Smedley *v* Chumley and Hawke 116
47 Elmcroft Developments Ltd *v* Tankersley-Sawyer 120
48 Sleafer *v* Lambeth Metropolitan Borough Council 123
49 McCarrick *v* Liverpool Corporation 130
50 Brikom Investments Ltd *v* Seaford 133
51 Parker *v* O'Connor 136
52 Brown *v* Liverpool Corporation 140
53 Liverpool City Council *v* Irwin 141
54 Campden Hill Towers Ltd *v* Gardner 146
55 Wainwright *v* Leeds City Council 152
56 Quick *v* Taff-Ely Borough Council 155
57 Wycombe Area Health Authority *v* Barnett 161
58 London Borough of Newham *v* Patel 164
59 McGreal *v* Wake 167
60 Taylor *v* Knowsley Borough Council 170
61 Bradley *v* Chorley Borough Council 172
62 Warren *v* Keen 175
63 Duke of Westminster *v* Guild 176
64 Wettern Electric Ltd *v* Welsh Development Agency 180
65 Mills *v* Guardians of the Poor of the East London Union 185
66 Joyner *v* Weeks 186
67 Smiley *v* Townshend 190
68 Jones *v* Herxheimer 193
69 Drummond *v* S & U Stores Ltd 198
70 Terroni *v* Corsini 208
71 Haviland *v* Long 210
72 Jaquin *v* Holland 213
73 Family Management *v* Gray 216
74 Hanson *v* Newman 219
75 Moss Empires Ltd *v* Olympia (Liverpool) Ltd 222
76 Eyre *v* Rea 223
77 Birch *v* Clifford 226
78 Lloyds Bank *v* Lake 227
79 Ebbetts *v* Conquest 232
80 Espir *v* Basil Street Hotel Ltd 236
81 Salisbury (Marquess) *v* Gilmore 239
82 Keats *v* Graham 243
83 Cunliffe *v* Goodman 245
84 Hibernian Property Co Ltd *v* Liverpool Corporation 248
85 Hewitt *v* Rowlands 253
86 Calabar Properties Ltd *v* Stitcher 255
87 McCoy & Co *v* Clark 260
88 Marenco *v* Jacramel Co Ltd 262

89 Old Grovebury Manor Farm Ltd *v* W. Seymour Plant Sales
    Ltd (No 2) 268
90 Associated Deliveries Ltd *v* Harrison 270
91 SEDAC Investments Ltd *v* Tanner 277
92 Myers *v* Oldschool 281
93 Scala House and District Property Co Ltd *v* Forbes 282
94 Expert Clothing Services and Sales Ltd *v* Hillgate House Ltd . 286
95 Farimani *v* Gates 290
96 Central Estates (Belgravia) Ltd *v* Woolgar (No. 2) 293
97 Starrokate Ltd *v* Burry 300
98 Baker *v* Sims 303
99 Church Commissioners for England *v* Ve-Ri-Best Manufac-
    turing Co Ltd 306
100 Land Securities PLC *v* Receiver for the Metropolitan Police
    District 308
101 Middlegate Properties Ltd *v* Gidlow-Jackson 312
102 Regional Properties Ltd *v* City of London Real Property Co Ltd 317
103 Swallow Securities Ltd *v* Brand 322
104 Hamilton *v* Martell Securities Ltd 327
105 Lee-Parker *v* Izzet 332
106 British Anzani (Felixstowe) Ltd *v* International Marine
    Management (UK) Ltd 334
107 Melville *v* Grapelodge Developments Ltd 338
108 Jeune *v* Queens Cross Properties Ltd 340
109 Francis *v* Cowcliffe Ltd 342
110 Gordon *v* Selico Co Ltd 346
111 Hart *v* Elmkirk Ltd 348
112 Daiches *v* Bluelake Investments Ltd 349
113 Parker *v* London Borough of Camden 352
114 Marsden *v* Edward Heyes 357
115 Whitham *v* Kershaw 359
116 Manchester Bonded Warehouse Company Ltd *v* Carr 361
117 Smith *v* Bradford Metropolitan Council 366
118 Elite Investments Ltd *v* T I Bainbridge Silencers Ltd ix

1   THE PREMISES AND THE COVENANT

1.1 The premises demised

In attempting to determine legal liability of either a landlord
or a tenant for disrepair of the premises it is essential not only
to determine whether in fact the premises are in a state of disrepair but also the physical scope of the repairing covenant. There
have been a number of judicial decisions on the scope of particular repairing covenants, for example in *Ball v Plummer* (1879)
23 So Jo 656 external windows were held to be part of the "skin
of the house."

Case 1   *Goldfoot v Welch* [1914] 1 Ch 213 Eve J

In 1913 the defendant agreed to let and the plaintiff to
take "all those rooms situate on the first and second floors
of the business premises ... for a term of one year from
March 1, 1913 at an annual rent." The tenant agreed, inter
alia, as follows:

"(2.) to leave the interior of the demised rooms in a
reasonable state of repair and condition (fair wear and
tear and accidental damage by fire and tempest excepted)
and so deliver up at the expiration of the said tenancy,
(3.) to use the premises only for the profession of a dental
surgeon or if the tenant should at any time desire to let
one room the undertenant shall carry on no objectionable
trade or business that may in any way form a breach of
the covenants of the lease under which the premises are
held,
(4.) to permit the landlord at reasonable times of the
day by himself or with his agent or workmen to enter
and inspect the state of repair and condition of the
premises and to execute any structural repairs that may
be necessary,
(5.) not to assign or underlet the premises without consent from the landlord,
(6.) not to exhibit upon the premises any form of advertisement other than those relative to the profession of a
dental surgeon,"

The plaintiff took possession of the premises on March 1, 1913, and practised dentistry there as the Anglo-American Dental Company. He advertised by means of adhesive white letters and figures attached to the windows of the premises facing the High Street. He claimed to be entitled to the possession and use of the outside walls of the rooms subject only to the restrictions as to advertising of clause 6 of the agreement, and that the defendant was not entitled to them except for purposes connected with maintenance and repair.

On or about April 24, 1913, the defendant in derogation, as the plaintiff alleged, of his own grant affixed or authorised to be affixed to the outside wall facing the High Street two large boards on either side of the plaintiff's window on the second floor, upon each board being an advertisement of Lipton's tea or cocoa. The plaintiff requested the defendant to remove the advertisements, but he refused.

The plaintiff thereupon brought this action claiming an injunction to restrain the defendant from interfering with his possession of the external walls, and a mandatory injunction to remove the advertisements.

Held (1) That in the absence of context to the contrary a demise in writing of the "rooms situate on the first and second floors" of business premises included the external walls of the two floors.

Eve J said (in part)

I think on the authorities apart from anything in the document itself to limit or control the demise, it includes the external walls of the first and second floors. I say that because, although in *Hope Brothers Ltd v Cowan* [1913] 2 Ch 312 Joyce J was dealing with an office and not with a "room" so described, in *Carlisle Café Co v Muse Brothers & Co* 77 LT 515. Byrne J had to construe a demise of a studio and a reception room. It is true that in the latter case there were circumstances outside the question of construction which led Byrne J to the decision at which he arrived, but it is clear from the arguments as reported that the point was raised whether the demise of the room included only so much cubic space as the walls enclosed or whether it included also the external walls, and I read the judgment of Byrne J as determining that in the absence of any context to the contrary the demise of a room includes the external walls enclosing the room. Before considering how far anything outside the agreement itself can be looked at to control the effect of the demise, it must first be ascertained whether there is anything in the agreement itself to limit—I will not say its "prima facie" construction—but the construction which it properly bears in the absence of a contrary intention to be gathered from the context. [Counsel] on behalf of the defendant has laid hold of every conceivable point to support his argument that the external walls are not here included—amongst other observations he says that one cannot conceive the landlord entering upon the external walls to view their condition or the plaintiff exercising his profession of a dentist upon the external walls. But in my opinion all those arguments are more than counterbalanced by the sixth clause of the agreement by which the tenant agrees "not to exhibit upon the premises any form of advertisement other than those relative to the profession of a dentist." So far from there being anything in the context to limit or control the demise, it seems to me to go a long way in support of the contention that the parties throughout intended and contemplated that the external walls would be included.

Case 2 *Cockburn v Smith* [1924] 2 KB 119 Court of Appeal

The owner of a block of flats let one of the top flats to a tenant, but kept the roof of the building and the guttering appurtenant thereto in his own possession and control. The guttering became defective, and rainwater which should have been carried away escaped and flowed upon the wall of the tenant's flat and made the flat so damp that the tenant suffered injury to her health and sustained damage. The landlord had notice of the defect, but was dilatory and negligent in remedying it. In an action by the tenant against the landlord:

Held (1) That the defendant was under an obligation to take reasonable care to remedy defects in the roof and guttering of which he had notice and which were a source of damage to the plaintiff; and that even if this duty was purely contractual it was not modified or excluded by the fact that the landlord had expressly agreed in the contract of tenancy to keep the staircases, passages, and landings in good repair.

Bankes LJ said (in part)

... It is said that the landlords have expressly agreed to do certain repairs—namely, to keep the entrance hall, staircases, passages and landings in good repair—and that this must be the full extent of their liability on the principle that "Expressio unius exclusio alterius" or, as the learned judge has held, by an application of the maxim "Expressum facit cessare tacitum."

I cannot agree that either maxim applies in this case. No doubt if a landlord demises premises to a tenant there is ground for arguing that the tenant expressly agreeing to do certain repairs to the demised premises is not liable to do other repairs. In the present case the landlords have demised the suite of rooms with the usual fittings and appurtenances; and although they have not expressly granted any licence to use stairs or passages, they have, by restricting the user of them, impliedly granted such a licence; and they have expressly undertaken a corresponding obligation to keep them in a condition in which they can be used. But the roof of the building, the means of excluding rain and water and of keeping the flat habitable, is not among the premises expressly or impliedly demised or granted. In my opinion express agreements concerning premises demised or granted do not exclude tacit agreements concerning matters which are neither demised nor granted, and I cannot think either party contemplated that because the landlords had agreed to keep the entrance hall, staircases, passages, and landings sufficiently lighted and in good repair, they should therefore be relieved of all duty to take reasonable care that the roof and gutters should not be in such a condition as to render the demised premises uninhabitable.

Note:

(i)   In *Sturge v Hackett* [1962] 1 WLR 1257 the Court of Appeal held that in the absence of provisions to the contrary in a lease a demise of a part of a building divided horizontally or vertically includes the external walls enclosing the part so demised.

(ii) In *Heyting v Foreman* [1934] EGD 174 the tenant occupied an upper ground-floor flat with a projecting greenhouse. Below him was another flat and under the floor of the greenhouse was another room, so that the roof of the greenhouse served as a common roof for the upper ground-floor flat and the semi-basement flat. The Court of Appeal held that the glass walls and roof of the greenhouse were not part of the demised premises.

Case 3 Graystone Property Investments Ltd v Margulies (1984) 269 EG 538 Court of Appeal

The demised premises was a Victorian house with lofty rooms which had been converted into flats. On conversion some of the ceilings were lowered to give the rooms more acceptable proportions. The tenant proposed to remove some of the false ceilings using the space thus produced to construct mezzanine floors. The existence of the false ceilings was obvious since not all ceilings had been lowered with the result that various ceilings were at different heights. The parcels clause in the underlease of the flat referred to it as "formed on the first floor of the block." The landlords argued that the void spaces did not pass with the demise.

Held (1) Unless there are cogent reasons to assume otherwise a demise includes all the space between the floor of the flat and the underside of the flat above.

(2) It was improbable that the landlords would wish to retain ownership of a number of irregularly shaped spaces to which they had no access and for which they had no use.

(3) In the circumstances of the case, the void spaces passed to the tenant with the demise.

Griffiths LJ said (in part)

I now turn to the wording of the underlease. The parcels clause reads as follows:

"The Lessors hereby demise unto the Lessees First all that self-contained residential flat shewn within the pink edging on the plan numbered 1 annexed hereto known or intended to be known as Flat H Hyde Park Gardens London W2 (hereinafter called 'the demised premises') formed on the first floor of the block of Flats there known as Nos 18 to 21 Hyde Park Gardens aforesaid (hereinafter called 'the building') the situation of which said building is for the purpose of identification only more particularly delineated on the plan numbered 2 annexed hereto and thereon coloured pink Secondly all that the Locker No 4 situate in the Basement of the Building (hereinafter called 'the Locker')."

The principal submission on behalf of the appellant is founded on the inclusion of the word "formed" where it appears in this parcels clause. [Counsel], in an admirably succinct and clear argument, has pointed out that in the ordinary conveyancing precedents the word "formed" does not appear, and he submits that that word must have been intentionally inserted by the draftsman to make it quite clear that the intention was to demise only that which the eye could see, namely those parts of the flat bounded by the ceilings that could be observed, and that therefore the limits of the demise were bounded in the vertical dimension by the false ceilings in those passages and rooms which were fitted with false ceilings; he relied upon the dictionary definition of "formed" as meaning "shaped" or "constructed", and he says that the shape of the flat was as it was, with the false ceiling. The learned judge considered that argument, but it did not impress him and he came to the conclusion that the use of the word "formed" was neutral.

For my part, I am unable to attach the significance to the use of the word "formed" which [counsel] urges me to do. I think that far clearer words would be required if it was the intention to exclude the void space above a false ceiling. To my mind, a quite sufficient explanation is to be found for the use by the draftsman of the word "formed" when one considers that this was a flat created out of the first floors of, not one house but of two houses, which would clearly have required a considerable amount of reconstruction work, and I read it as no more than saying that this flat has been constructed out of what were two houses. As I understand [counsel's] argument, he would concede that if the word "formed" had not appeared in the parcels clause, but that it had merely read "the flat known as flat H Hyde Park Gardens London W2 on the first floor of the block of flats", then a conveyancer would read that as conveying the space in the flat in the vertical dimension up to the bottom of the floor of the flat above. As I am unable to attach the significance that he wishes to attach to the word "formed" it seems to me that the words of the parcels clause do, in their natural meaning, convey the vertical space up to the bottom of the floor above.

Case 4 *Holiday Fellowship Ltd v Hereford* [1959] 1 WLR 211
Court of Appeal

The lessee's covenants in a lease of a dwelling-house included a covenant to maintain the demised buildings and the fixtures and fittings therein "(except the roofs and main walls of the said dwelling-house)" in good repair and condition. By a complementary covenant of the lease the landlord covenanted "to keep the main walls roofs . . . in good repair and condition." The tenants sought a declaration that under those covenants the landlord was liable to paint and repair the windows:

Held, (1) That the question in each case was one of degree and, on the true construction of the lease, the windows of the demised premises were not part of the "main walls."

Lord Evershed MR said (in part)

I wish to be a little careful in the meaning that I am attaching to the word "windows." I have described the bays or similar structures, which are, at any rate to judge from the photograph, made of the same material as the walls, in the ordinary sense of that term. We are not concerned with any question of repair to the brick or stone structures containing the actual windows. For the purposes of this case and of the question raised in the originating summons, I take "windows" to mean, and to be confined to, the glass panels and the wooden framework and apparatus in which the glass is placed; and the question is whether, for the purposes of this lease, "main walls" ought to be treated as including the windows as I have defined them.

I must confess that, if I looked at this matter without any guidance (or possibly the reverse) from authority, I should unhesitatingly say, in ordinary language, that the windows, as I have defined them, are distinct from the walls. No doubt they are *in* the walls. Walls may have eyes as well as ears. But I would say that they are, as physical things, distinct from the walls in which they are inserted; and that was the view, plainly, of Harman J. Various illustrations from ordinary conversational usage have been cited; and, to my mind, it is plain that, apart (again) from the effect of any authority, the windows in the walls would be treated as something distinct from the walls themselves.

But it has been argued, with force, by [counsel] that certain authorities binding upon us, being authorities of this court, put a different light upon the matter. The first case, decided in 1925, is *Boswell v Crucible Steel Co* [1925] 1 KB 119. The question in that case arose out of the obligation on the part of the tenant to repair "landlord's fixtures." It was said that by virtue of that obligation he was bound to repair the windows, which had been broken—I gather by mischievous persons throwing stones through them. The premises were shop premises; and (as was pointed out in the judgment of Bankes LJ) far the greater part of what was called (and the phrase was taken from an earlier case that I will mention in a moment) the "skin" of the premises consisted of the shop windows. In the county court it had been held that these shop windows were in truth "landlord's fixtures" and, therefore, within the express language of the tenant's covenants; and the Divisional Court affirmed that view.

... So this court held in *Boswell v Crucible Steel Co* (supra) on the facts of that case, that the windows could not be regarded as "landlord's fixtures" because, in truth, they were part of the structure of the building, and in that sense part of the skin of the house—of the walls of the house.

... So far, therefore, I am unable to hold (and I agree entirely with Harman J that *Boswell's* case does not bind us to hold) that these windows are part of the main walls of this edifice for the purposes of this lease.

A further case was cited of *Taylor v Webb* [1937] 2 KB 283 in which a somewhat similar problem arose. There was an obligation to keep "outside walls and roofs in good and tenantable repair"; and the question was: What of skylights: were they part of the roof? The building was a somewhat unusual one. It appears that there had been at some time an addition to the original structure: a passage had been built over the roof of the back ground floor premises leading to some upper storey behind. The passage and the upper storey behind were only lit from above; and the facts seem to show that the so-called "skylights" constituted a very substantial part of the roof—certainly of the passage. It was said by du Parcq J: "I have no doubt that the skylights are part of the building, and I also think that they are part of the roofs, and that that was the intention of the parties." But once again it is, to my mind, a fallacy to suggest that that case (and du Parcq J's view on this matter was affirmed) leads to the proposition that all skylights for all purposes are part of the roofs in which they appear.

I conclude, therefore (with Harman J), that these cases do not have a binding and conclusive effect. In any case, I would add that there is in truth no evidence whether the windows, as I see them, were or were not part of the original structure of this house. But that is, perhaps, neither here nor there.

If I am right so far in thinking that the matter is not concluded by these authorities, then the question comes back to that of the construction of this lease and of asking and answering the question: Are these windows as limited by my definition, part of the main walls, within the meaning of clause 2 (3) and clause 3 (1)?

Applying, to the best of my ability, the ordinary standards of common sense and interpretation of language, I conclude, unhesitatingly, that they are not; and taking that view (which was the view of Harman J) it follows that this appeal must fail.

Case 5 *Boswell v Crucible Steel Co* [1925] 1 KB 119 Court of Appeal

By a lease made in May, 1912, the plaintiffs let the ground floor of the premises known as 31 and 32 Borough Road and 69 Lancaster Street, Southwark, for a term of years. The premises were let for the purpose of being used as a warehouse and offices for the lessees' trade, and practically the whole of the sides fronting the streets in question consisted of plate-glass windows. The windows were of the

usual kind, and were not made to open. The tenant covenanted to repair the "inside of the demised premises
including all landlord's fixtures."

Held (1) That as the windows formed part of the structure
of the house the covenant did not extend to them.

Scrutton LJ said

In this case the question is whether the landlord or the tenant
is to replace certain broken windows. The premises consist of
a ground floor used as a warehouse and offices, and it appears
from the photograph and plan which were put in that the greater
part of the outer sides of the building consists of plate-glass windows, so that the premises are practically enclosed in a wall
of glass. In the lease the tenant covenanted to repair the inside
of the demised premises, "including all landlord's fixtures," and
the landlord covenanted to repair "the demised premises,"
except so far as the tenant had covenanted to repair them. Some
of the plate-glass windows having been broken, the landlord
claims that they are landlord's fixtures and that the liability to
repair them falls on the tenant. The meaning of the term "tenant's
fixtures" is well understood, but I have always had a difficulty
in understanding what is meant by "landlord's fixtures." But
at all events it seems to me clear that that expression cannot
include a thing which forms part of the original structure of the
building. It must be regarded as confined to things which have
been brought into the house and affixed to the freehold after
the structure is completed. If these windows could be treated
as landlord's fixtures, the whole house would be a landlord's
fixture. Then, if they are not landlord's fixtures, the landlord
is bound to repair them, for they were plainly part of the demised
premises. The county court judge held that the windows were
not part of the wall of the house. Therein I think he was wrong.

Case 6 *Taylor v Webb* [1937] 2 KB 283 du Parcq J

A landlord covenanted in an underlease to keep the outside walls and roofs in tenantable repair as he was required
by the head lease to do. The covenant in the head lease
contained an exception of damage by fire and fair wear and
tear. The tenant complained that the landlord had not in
accordance with such covenant repaired certain glass roofs
and skylights. The landlord contended that: (*a*) the want
of repair complained of was within the exception; (*b*) the
glass roofs were fixtures and therefore within a covenant

by the tenant to repair the interior and all fixtures; (c) the tenant being in arrear with his rent could not sue upon the covenant to repair:

Held (1) The repair here was not within the exception. Where there is a failure to repair defects due to fair wear and tear, the consequences which ensue because the defects grow and spread cannot always be said to be due to fair wear and tear.

(2) The glass roofs were not fixtures but part of the building itself. A fixture is something brought on to a completed building.

(3) The covenant to repair and the covenant to pay rent are independent and a breach of one is no defence to a claim in respect of a breach of the other.

du Parcq J said (in part)

The landlord's obligation to keep the outside walls and roofs properly repaired is subject to the exception that he is not liable for defects produced by fair wear and tear. It has been proved that the walls and roofs were not properly repaired, and it lies on the landlord to show that the lack of repair comes within the exception. In considering whether that has been proved, one has to remember that it is his duty to prevent consequences flowing from wear and tear which would not have occurred if the original defects had been attended to. If he fails to attend to them, it cannot be said that the consequences which ensue because the defects grow and spread and others come into existence are due to fair wear and tear. In this case the plaintiff fails to show that he is protected by the exception, because, whether he misunderstood his liability under the covenant or whether he did not choose to spend the money, he has done no more than tinker with the defects. They have been allowed to go from bad to worse. I think, therefore, that the exception only protects him to the very limited extent which I have mentioned. I have now to consider whether the skylights are part of the roofs, and therefore repairable by the landlord. [Counsel] says that they are not, and that they are fixtures which the tenant is bound to keep in repair. I get some assistance on that point from *Boswell v Crucible Steel Co* [1925] 1 KB 119. There a tenant had covenanted to repair landlord's fixtures. The outside of the premises mainly consisted of plate-glass windows, and it was held that they were part of the structure of the building and were not included in the term "fixtures." I agree with what was said in that case, that fixtures are something brought on to a completed building, and which may belong either to the landlord or the tenant, but do not include something which is part of the building itself. I have no doubt that the skylights are part of the building, and I also think that they are part of the roofs, and that that was the intention of the parties. If they were not, it would mean that over part of the building there would be no roof.

Note:
(i) In *Ayling v Wade* [1961] 2 QB 229 the Court of Appeal doubted the acceptance by the parties that a window did not include a skylight.

Case 7 Douglas-Scott v Scorgie (1984) 269 EG 1164 Court of Appeal

The appellant was the tenant of a top floor flat and held the demised premises under a tenancy agreement clause 1 of which provided

"The Landlord shall let and the Tenant shall take—ALL that suite of rooms or flat consisting of one room kitchen and bathroom on the 3rd floor forming part of the messuage or buildings known as 47 Crawford Street W1. Together with the use of the entrance hall and lift (if any) staircase outer door and vestibule of the said buildings in common with the other tenants and occupiers thereof And together with the fixtures furniture and effects now in and upon the premises hereby agreed to be demised and more particularly specified in the inventory thereof signed by the parties hereto for the term of 7 months from the 1st day of March 1967 . . ."

By another clause the tenant agreed to keep the interior of the premises in repair but it was also agreed that the tenancy was covered by section 32 of the Housing Act 1961 [now the Landlord and Tenant Act 1985]. When the roof fell into a state of disrepair the tenant contended that the landlord was liable to repair under the 1961 Act even though it was conceded that the roof was not part of the demised premises.

Held (1) The mere fact that the roof was not part of the demised premises did not conclude the matter. Whilst it could not be said that the roof of every top-floor flat fell within the 1961 Act everything depended upon the particular facts of the case.

Slade LJ said (in part)

It is perhaps convenient to begin by considering whether the roof of the premises, 47 Crawford Street, actually forms part of the premises let to the plaintiff. This point can be dealt with very shortly. In this context we have been referred to the decision of this court in the case of *Cockburn v Smith* [1924] 2 QB 119, and to the observations of Bankes LJ at p 128 of the report, and of Sargant LJ at p 134 of the report. In the face of this decision Mr Hamilton, [counsel], has not attempted to argue that the roof actually forms part of the demised premises in the present case. Since this point has not been argued before us, I will proceed on the assumption that this concession is a correct one.

However, the mere fact that the roof does not, in conveyancing terms, form part of the demised premises by no means concludes the matter, as is shown by the recent decision of this court in *Campden Hill Towers Ltd v Gardner* [1977] QB 823. That case concerned an underlease of a third-floor flat comprised in a block of flats, not on the top floor of the building in question. The county court judge had taken the view that in applying the provisions of section 32(1) of the 1961 Act to a flat comprised in a block of flats, the whole shell of the building had to be regarded as the exterior of the dwelling-house. The Court of Appeal rejected this very broad construction of paragraph (a) of section 32(1). On the other hand, it likewise rejected a very narrow construction submitted on behalf of the landlords to the effect that paragraph (a) cannot apply to anything, with the exception of drains, gutters and external pipes, which is not a part of the property demised.

Megaw LJ, in the course of delivering the judgment of the court, said this

> "We do not accept the lessors' contention in so far as it would limit 'the structure and exterior of the dwelling-house' to that which, in the conveyancing meaning, is included in the particular terms of the demise in the lease. Anything which, in the ordinary use of words, would be regarded as part of the structure, or of the exterior, of the particular 'dwelling-house', regarded as a separate part of the building, would be within the scope of paragraph (a). Thus, the exclusion by the words of clause 2 of the underlease of 'any part of the outside walls' would not have the effect of taking outside the operation of paragraph (a) that which, in the ordinary use of language, would be regarded as the exterior wall of the flat—an essential

integral part of the flat, as a dwelling-house; that part of the outside wall of the block of flats which constitutes a wall of the flat. The paragraph applies to the outside wall or walls of the flat; the outside of inner party walls of the flat; the outer sides of horizontal divisions between flat 20 and flats above and below; the structural framework and beams directly supporting floors, ceilings and walls of the flat. We do not accept the lessees' contention so far as it goes further."

The assistant recorder himself appears to have regarded the passage which I have cited from the *Campden Hill Towers* case, which he himself cited, as authority for the proposition that a roof above the top-floor flat of premises can *never* form part of the structure and exterior of a dwelling-house in relation to that top-floor flat, within the meaning of paragraph (a) of section 32(1), unless the roof actually forms part of the demised flat. For my part, I think this involves a misunderstanding of what Megaw LJ said. In my opinion, for present purposes the crucial sentence in Megaw LJ's judgment in the *Campden Hill Towers* case is this:

"Anything which, in the ordinary use of words, would be regarded as part of the structure, or of the exterior, of the particular 'dwelling-house' regarded as a separate part of the building, would be within the scope of paragraph (a)."

Following this guidance given by the Court of Appeal, the crucial question to which the assistant recorder should have directed his mind was, in my opinion, whether the roof of the premises would, in the ordinary use of words, be regarded as a part of the structure or of the exterior of the plaintiff's top-floor flat, when that flat is regarded as a separate part of the building, 47 Crawford Street. If on the evidence the proper answer to this question is in the affirmative, I can see no reason why the roof should not fall within the scope of paragraph (a).

It is true that in his judgment Megaw LJ, having enunciated the relevant test, proceeded to enumerate a number of particular items to which, on the particular facts of that case, paragraph (a) would apply, that is to say:

". . . the outside wall or walls of the flat; the outside of inner party walls of the flat; the outer sides of horizontal divisions between flat 20 and flats above and below; the structural framework and beams directly supporting floors, ceilings and walls of the flat."

This enumeration thus did not include the roof of the building in that case. The assistant recorder, as I read his judgment, appears to have attached much importance to this omission. However, he apparently did not appreciate that there was one obvious reason for it, and one crucial distinction between the facts of that case and the facts of this. The flat in question in the *Campden Hill Towers* case was not a top-floor flat. Presumably, therefore, in the ordinary use of words there would have been no question of the roof in that case being regarded as a part of the structure or of the exterior of that particular flat, viewed as a separate part of the building. It seems to me that quite different considerations may apply where the subject of a tenancy is a top-floor flat. I can see no reason in principle why the roof above such a flat should not be capable in some circumstances of falling within the scope of paragraph (a).

To take the simplest case by way of example, if the ceiling and roof of a particular top-floor dwelling all formed part of one flat, inseparable, structural unit, it would seem to me *prima facie* that in the ordinary use of words, the roof and ceiling would be regarded as part of the structure or exterior of that dwelling, as much as its outside walls, inner party walls, and so forth. On the other hand, I do not think one can go so far as to say that the roof, or part of the roof, which lies above *any* so-called top-floor flat necessarily will fall within the definition in paragraph (a) of the subsection. Borderline cases, for example, might arise where one found a void space or an uninhabited loft between the flat and the roof. Everything must depend on the particular facts of the case.

Case 8 Hopwood v Cannock Chase District Council [1974] 29 P & CR 256 Court of Appeal

The plaintiff was the widow of a tenant of a dwelling-house owned by the defendants to which section 32 of the Housing Act 1961 applied. At the rear of the house was an area of concrete and paving consisting of two concrete strips with a row of paving slabs between them. The level of the slabs was about one-and-a-half inches below that of the strips. The ordinary access to the house was from the front, but there was a way out from the rear of the house across the strips and slabs into an alley or lane and also into the yard of an adjoining house. The plaintiff was injured when she tripped on one edge of the paving slabs, and she brought an action against the defendants for damages, relying on the provisions of section 32 (1) (*a*) of the Housing Act 1961 and section 4 (1) of the Occupiers' Liability Act 1957. The deputy circuit judge found that the defendants had known of the condition of the slabs, but held that the concrete and paved area did not form part of the exterior of the house within section 32 (1) (*a*) of the Act of 1961, and that, accordingly, there had been no obligation on the defendants to keep it in repair.

On appeal by the plaintiff:

Held (1) Dismissing the appeal, that section 32 (1) (*a*) of the Act of 1961 could not be construed so as to extend to a yard of the kind in question which was not necessary to the house as a means of access to it.

Cairns LJ said (in part)

In reaching his decision, he [the judge at first instance] founded himself on the only reported case, so far as we know, that has been decided under this provision; it is the decision of the Court of Appeal in *Brown v Liverpool Corporation* [1969] 3 All ER 1345. That was a case in which the house had a path running to steps which went up to the road, the house being at a lower level than the road, and the plaintiff met with an accident on those steps. The question was whether the landlords had a duty under section 32 of the Act of 1961 to keep those steps in repair, and the question that had to be considered in that case, as in this, was: did the steps form part of the structure or exterior of the building?

Danckwerts LJ, giving the first judgment, first easily reached the conclusion that they did not form part of the structure, and then went on in this way:

"On the other hand it seems to me equally clear that the seven feet of flagstones and the steps up do form part of the exterior of the dwelling-house. They are attached in that manner to the house for the purpose of access to this dwelling-house, and they are part of the dwelling-house which is necessary for the purpose of anybody who wishes to live in the dwelling-house enjoying that privilege. If they have not means of access of some sort they could not get there, and these are simply the means of access. The steps are an outside structure, and therefore, it seems to me they are plainly part of the building, and, therefore, the covenant implied by section 32 of the Act of 1961 fits and applies to the obligations of the landlords in this case."

Salmon LJ agreed. He said:

"I do not think that this case is by any means free from difficulty or, indeed, from doubt. I do not wish to lay down any general principle of law or any general proposition as to the construction of the Housing Act 1961, or as to the meaning of the words 'building' or 'dwelling-house.' I base my judgment on the particular facts of this case."

Then, after referring to the main facts and quoting section 32 (5) of the Act of 1961, he went on:

"In the particular circumstances of this case I think it proper to regard the house, with the short concrete path and steps leading to it, as being one unit. Together they formed one building and were, therefore, 'the dwelling-house.' It is conceded by the defendant corporation that the steps and the path were demised with the house. It seems to me that the path and steps must be an integral part of the building, otherwise it would be impossible for the building to be used as a dwelling-house for it would have no access. On that narrow ground I think that the judgment of the learned county court judge can be supported. I also think that an alternative way of putting the matter would be to say that, on the facts here, that short concrete path and those four steps were part of the exterior of the dwelling-house. Whichever way it is put— whether it is put in that way or whether one says that, looking at the facts, the path, steps and house are all part of the building which was let as a private dwelling-house—it would follow that the plaintiff is entitled to succeed."

Sachs LJ, after quoting section 32 (5), went on:

"For my part I have no doubt but that, as counsel for the plaintiff has correctly conceded, the definition given to 'the dwelling-house' was intended to and does exclude from the ambit of the landlord's liability those parts of the demise that are not part of the building itself. In particular, to my mind, there would normally be excluded from the ambit of those liabilities a garden or a pond, and likewise the fences round or a gate leading to such a garden or pond. Similarly, there would normally be excluded the steps leading into a garden from a road. . . . The question, accordingly, is whether, in this particular case, the seven feet approach with the steps at the end of it really was part of the exterior of the terrace building or whether that seven feet pathway and the steps down into it were simply part of a means of traversing a garden. That seems to me—as, indeed, counsel for the plaintiff rightly contended—to be a question of degree, and a very close run thing at that.''

Then, after quoting a clause of the conditions of tenancy, he said:

"In the end, however, I have come to the conclusion that the learned county court judge adopted the right approach and did treat this question as one of degree and fact. He referred specifically to the point that this concrete path was 'only seven feet long,' and it seems to me that on the evidence he was entitled to come to the conclusion which he reached on this question of fact, *i.e.* that in all the circumstances the steps formed part of the building.''

One matter on which all three members of the court founded their judgments was that in that case the path and steps formed an essential part of the means of access to the house, in that it was the only way in. In this case that certainly was not so; the ordinary means of access to the house was from the front of the house and to my mind it is very doubtful whether this yard could be regarded as a means of access to the house at all. It is true that there was a way out from one side of the yard, apparently into an alley or lane, this house being at the end of the terrace of houses, and there was also a way through from the yard into the corresponding yard of the adjoining house. That, however, is very far from saying, as could be said in *Brown's* case, that the yard was necessary to the house as the means of access to it.

Sachs LJ in *Brown's* case went no further than to say that there were materials on which it was open to the county court judge to reach the conclusion which he did reach. Here, the deputy county court judge has reached the opposite conclusion; he did, I think, approach it as a question of degree and of fact, and it appears to me that the facts were such as entitled him to reach that conclusion. I should be prepared to go still further and say that, treating it as Danckwerts LJ and Salmon LJ did, as a matter of law and construction of section 32, in my view section 32 cannot be extended beyond what was held in *Brown's* case so as to include a yard of this kind.

Note:
(i) In *Dunster v Hollis* [1918] 2 KB 795 the court held that an implied undertaking by the landlord that the house shall be "kept by the landlord in all respects reasonably fit for human habitation" did not impose on the landlord of part of a house an obligation to keep a common flight of steps in repair.

Case 9 *Blundell v Obsdale Ltd* [1958] EGD 144. Harman J

The defendant company was the tenant of a house under an underlease for a term of 21 years expiring in 1963 and the plaintiffs were the leaseholders for a term expiring in 1983. The underlessors brought an action against the assignees of the underlease claiming possession and damages for breach of repairing obligations. The underlease contained a covenant by the underlessee.

"And also will at her expense during the said term well and substantially repair uphold support maintain and reinstate where necessary the foundations and party walls of the said messuage or tenement buildings and premises hereby demised (damage by fire excepted) but the lessee shall not be responsible for structural repairs to the foundations roof main walls and drains. And also will well and effectually repair lead paint paper cleanse amend and keep the demised premises with their appurtenances and all fixtures additions and improvements which shall during the said term be erected or made in or upon the said premises with all necessary reparations and amendments whatsoever when where and as often as occasion shall require except structural repairs to the foundations roof main walls and drains."

In the action, two breaches were relied upon as grounds of forfeiture namely (i) the defendant's failure to repair a balustrade forming the boundary of a balcony to a first floor front room and (ii) a failure to repair a lead roof on the fourth floor at the rear of the premises. The defendant counterclaimed that it had repaired another larger lead flat with a lantern over the back room of the first floor which was the landlord's liability.

Held (1) The balustrade was not a wall and to describe its restoration as a repair to a main wall was quite wrong. The repairs were not structural repairs within the covenant.

(2) The repair to the lead in the flat roof was a structural repair within the exception to the lessee's repairing covenant. However, merely to redress the lead and solder the cracks would not amount to structural repair and would fall within the defendant's liability.

(3) The work undertaken on the larger lead flat and lantern amounted to structural repair outside the defendant's liability.

Harman J said (in part)

In the action, two breaches are relied upon as grounds of forfeiture, first, the defendant's failure to repair a balustrade forming the boundary of a balcony to the first floor front room, and, secondly, a failure to "solder and repair" a lead roof on the fourth floor at the back. As to the balustrade, the defendant maintains that to repair it constitutes a structural repair to a main wall. I can deal with this shortly. In my judgment, the balustrade in question is not a wall at all; still less is it a main wall. It is or was an ornamental feature over the front door consisting of half-a-dozen balusters in sandstone or terra-cotta supporting a coping about 2 ft. 6 in. up. These balusters have decayed by the action of time, but to describe their restoration as repairs to a main wall seems to me to be quite wrong. Apart from this, these repairs were not in my judgment structural, for this piece of decoration is not part of the structure of the house. This balustrade has in the course of the action, and with the acquiescence of the head landlord, been replaced by a brick structure at an expense of about £10, and with this all concerned seem to be content.

The second breach relied on is nearer the line. There is a flat roof over an extension at the rear of the fourth floor. It is made of lead laid on boards. It seems to me that the lead is part of the structure of the house, and that, if it were necessary to strip off the lead and still more so to repair the boards below, that would be a structural repair to the roof within the exception to the lessee's repairing covenant. There was, however, a dispute as to whether it was necessary to strip the lead. The surveyor called by the plaintiffs was of opinion that the lead merely required redressing, an operation costing perhaps £15, and, if that were done and some solder applied, he thought the repair would be satisfactory . . .

. . . On the other hand, . . . a director of the building firm who did some soldering repairs to the lead flat, was of the opinion that the lead had reached the end of its life and needed stripping, and that, moreover, two of the supporting boards were rotten, and would require replacing. A surveyor called by the defendant said the lead was in a bad condition and near the end of its life. Now the notice served on the defendant prior to the action is in the following form: "to solder and repair the lead roof at the rear of the said premises." This, in my judgment, merely required the defendant to do the repairs which the plaintiffs' surveyor thought necessary, that is to say, to redress the lead and solder the cracks. This, in my judgment, was not a structural repair, and was therefore a liability of the defendant. If the advice given to the defendant was right and a bigger job was required, then that was not the tenants' liability. It may have been that of the landlord; and, if so, the proper notice should have been served, but this was not done. Accordingly, I hold that both the breaches alleged by the plaintiffs had been committed, and that there was a legal right to claim forfeiture . . .

Case 10 *Granada Theatres Ltd v Freehold Investment (Leytonstone) Ltd* [1959] 1 WLR 570 Court of Appeal

By clause 2 (3) of a lease made in 1941 of a cinema the tenant covenanted to keep the demised premises "in good and substantial repair and condition and properly decorated . . . but nothing in this clause contained shall render the [tenants] liable for structural repairs of a substantial nature to the main walls roofs foundations or main drains of the demised building." By clause 3 (2) the landlords covenanted, except so far as the tenants were liable under their covenants, to "repair maintain and keep the main structure walls roofs and drains of the demised premises in good structural repair and condition." On December 13, 1954, the lease was assigned to the plaintiffs (the tenants).

The roof being in disrepair and the cement rendering and brickwork of the front main elevation being defective, the tenants, on January 31, 1955, served a schedule of dilapidations on the landlords in respect of these. Long negotiations followed. The tenants contended that the roofs required re-roofing at a cost of £961, the landlords, on the other hand, alleged that they had obtained a tender of £130 10s. for the work, and that £961 was excessive. The landlords further contended that the repairs were the liability of the tenants, being due to the failure of the tenants' predecessors in title to keep the premises in good repair in accordance with their repairing covenants. The tenants required the landlords to furnish their surveyor with a written specification of the repairs the landlords proposed to do. The landlords failed to do so but, after a long correspondence, on September 19, 1955, on their instructions, a builder with his men entered on the premises and started to repair the roof. They were ordered off the premises by the tenants, who subsequently did the repairs themselves at a cost of £961 and in this action claimed damages for breach of the landlords' covenant to repair the roof, and a declaration that the landlords were liable to repair the front elevation:

Held (1) That making good the rendering and brickwork of the front elevation were structural repairs of a substantial nature and fell within the landlords' covenant to repair.

(2) That the repairs to the roof also fell within the landlords' covenant.

(3) That an assignee of a term is not liable for particular breaches of a tenant's repairing covenants committed by his predecessor, though he is liable for the disrepair of the premises as they stand when he takes over so far as their then state of disrepair falls within the scope of the tenant's repairing covenants; but that particular breaches committed before the assignment to him, as distinct from the state of the premises when he takes over, are matters, generally speaking, with which he is not concerned; and that, in the short time which elapsed between the assignment of the premises to the plaintiffs and the service of the notice of dilapidations, no appreciable part of the disrepair could be attributed to breach of the lessees' covenant by the plaintiffs as tenants; accordingly, the accumulated breaches of the lessees' repairing covenants could not be set off against the claim against the landlords for breach of covenant.

(4) (Jenkins LJ dissenting), that, assuming that the repairs which the landlords proposed to do to the roof would have constituted a sufficient performance of their covenant under clause 3 (2) of the lease, the landlords had, on the facts, given to the tenants a sufficient warning of their intention to do the repairs, and of the nature of the work they proposed to do, and that the tenants having prevented the landlords from doing the work, the landlords were not in breach of their repairing covenants in regard to the roof and the tenants had no cause of action in respect of the landlords' failure to repair the roof.

(5) That the case must be remitted back to the trial judge to determine whether the landlords' proposed repairs would

have, if completed, have complied with the landlords'
repairing covenant.

Jenkins LJ said (in part)

As to the specific items of disrepair upon which the dispute
turns, I may deal first with the front elevation of the premises.
The competing views are, on the one hand, that you have here
a wall, which no doubt is part of the structure, coated with a
cement rendering, which can be regarded for this purpose as
equivalent to paint. The cement rendering is merely, one might
say, decorative, perhaps to some extent protective, but is no
more part of the structure than a coat of paint would be. On
the other hand, it is said that the front elevation of the cinema
consists not of a wall with the incidental application of cement
rendering, but it consists of a 9-inch wall rendered in cement.
The bricks and the cement should be taken together, and they
together constitute the front elevation. In my view, the latter
way of regarding this cement rendering and the wall behind
it is correct ... I do not think that a matter of 350 to 500 slates
out of a total of 12,000 slates on a roof could be regarded as
a mere trifle. The question, when one is dealing with such things
as slates, is necessarily to some extent one of degree. It was
put in the course of the argument that if a gale blew off two
slates, for example, the work of replacing them could hardly
be said to be a structural repair of a substantial nature. But
obviously different considerations must apply if there were a
hurricane stripping the house of all its slates, and I would add
that, if somebody "bought blind" a house represented to be
"structurally complete," and he went there and found the rafters
with no slates on them, he could, I apprehend, complain with
justification that his vendor had been guilty of misrepresentation. There are, of course, two ways of putting this ..., while
admitting that a roof is a part of the structure and, accordingly,
that repairs to the roof would be in the nature of repairs to the
structure, says that in this case there is not enough substance
in the structural aspect of the repairs. I think that fairly puts
his position, and his reason for so submitting is that, although
no doubt slates would have to be replaced and renewed, there
would be no interference with the rafters or roof beams of the
cinema; it would merely be a matter of replacing the protective
skin or layer in the form of slates which formed part of the roof
but which could be removed and replaced without interfering
with the structure of the roof.

Paying the best attention I can to the arguments and the evidence, I see no sufficient reason here for differing from the view taken by the judge that the roof repairs also fell within the landlords' repairing covenant . . .

Then there was the interesting point to which I have already referred to the effect that these dilapidations did not occur overnight, but occurred, as it were, slate by slate, as slates got loose or fell off over the years, and inch by inch as the rain gradually seeped down the cement rendering or chemical reaction began to do its work. On this basis it is said that the alleged breaches of the landlords' repairing covenant are no more than an accumulation of individual breaches of the lessees' repairing covenant, and, consequently, that the tenants here cannot recover. It is said that, in view of their liability under their covenant for the individual wants of repair making up the totality of disrepair they must be liable for the totality of disrepair made up of these individual items, and that can be expressed as a set-off or cross-claim for an amount sufficing to wipe out the claim under the landlords' covenant. It appears to me that this contention fails for a number of reasons. First, it is clear, in view of the very short time which elapsed between the assignment to the tenants and the service of the schedule of dilapidations, that no appreciable part of the disrepair could have been attributable to breaches of the lessees' covenant to repair committed by the plaintiffs as tenants themselves. It seems to me that this in itself is sufficient to dispose of the argument. An assignee of a term is not liable for particular breaches of tenant's repairing covenants committed by his predecessors. He is, of course, liable for the disrepair of the premises as they stand when he takes over, so far as their then state of disrepair falls within the scope of the tenant's repairing covenants, but particular breaches committed before the assignment to him, as distinct from the state of the premises when he takes over, are matters, generally speaking, with which he is not concerned. Over and above that, it is to be observed that this part of the landlords' case is pleaded so as to apply only to the acts of the tenants themselves and not of their predecessors in title, and it appears that, when it was sought to amend the defence by bringing in this point, the inclusion of a reference to the predecessors in title of the present tenants was expressly disallowed, the proposed amendment being objected to by the tenants.

Finally, it seems to me, if this point were otherwise sound, it could only operate by way of counterclaim; each side would have their claim to damages for breach of covenant, and if one of them wanted to pursue his claim after a claim had been made against him by the opposite party, I should have thought his proper course would have been to do so by an appropriate counterclaim in the action, and, as I understand it, there is no question of any such counterclaim here.

... It does remain to consider with respect to the repairs to the main roof of the cinema, the landlords' contention to the effect that the landlords were, and had at all material times been, ready and willing to carry out the requisite repairs in accordance with the landlords' covenant in clause 3 (2) of the lease, but were prevented from doing so by the tenants.

On this aspect of the case we were invited by both parties to assume that the repairs to the main roof, which the landlords engaged their builder, Tidey, to carry out, would, if carried out, have constituted a sufficient performance by the landlords of their obligations under clause 3 (2) of the lease so far as this roof was concerned, and to decide whether, on that assumption, the tenants' conduct was such as to destroy their claim to damages under this head. This question turns almost entirely on the correspondence, to which I have already referred. Rusha, the landlords' architect, was cross-examined at considerable length on the correspondence, and he made it quite clear that he gave the tenants' architect, Coles, no particulars at all of the work the landlords intended to do on the main roof, apart from the last paragraph of his letter of July 7, 1955:

> "Subject to my client's approval, I recommend that a reputable firm of builders should be employed to overhaul both the roofs, replacing broken and cracked slates and refixing where slipped."

That statement clearly did not commit Rusha or the landlords to anything. Thereafter Rusha, acting on instructions, repeatedly either refused, or simply did not answer, Coles' request for information as to the work to be carried out, and the only information Coles ever got from Rusha as to the work proposed seems to have been that the roof was to be made "watertight."

As to the law to be applied to the facts emerging from the correspondence and from Rusha's evidence:

(1) It is well settled that a landlord's covenant to repair is a covenant to repair on notice.

(2) It is further well settled that under such a covenant the landlord has an implied licence to enter on the premises for the purpose of performing it.

(3) Where, as here, the covenant is to "keep" in repair, failure to perform it after notice constitutes a continuing breach in respect of which a fresh cause of action arises from day to day so long as the requisite repairs remain undone.

(4) In the event of the landlord failing to do the requisite repairs within a reasonable time after notice, the tenant is entitled to sue him in damages without first incurring expense by doing the repairs himself.

(5) The covenant is clearly not specifically enforceable, but I apprehend that, in the event of the landlord failing to do the repairs in a reasonable time, the tenant can, at his option, do the requisite repairs himself and claim the proper cost of so doing as damages flowing from the breach.

(6) If the landlord attempts within a reasonable time to do the work but is prevented from so doing by the tenant refusing him entry on the premises in accordance with the implied licence, the tenant cannot, I apprehend, maintain his action for damages so long as he persists in such refusal, because, in such circumstances, the landlord is not in breach of his covenant, or, at all events, has only been put in breach of it by the tenant's own conduct.

(7) The parties are under a duty to each other to act reasonably. It behoves the landlord, who is in breach of his covenant, to be diligent in the remedying of such breach. He is not entitled to keep the tenant waiting indefinitely and then complain if the tenant ultimately decides to do the work himself. On the other hand, he must be reasonable in the exercise of his licence to enter and (as I think) give the tenant sufficient notice of his intention to enter, and information as to the nature and extent of the work he proposes to carry out. On his part, the tenant must not unreasonably obstruct the landlord in the exercise of his right of entry for the purpose of doing the work, or take the matter out of the landlord's hands by doing the work himself before the landlord has had a reasonable opportunity of doing so.

Ormerod LJ said (in part)

In my judgment, it appears sufficiently from the correspondence between the parties that the landlords were prepared to do such work in the repair of the roof as would have complied with the tenants' original notice of want of repair.

2 EXPRESS REPAIRING OBLIGATIONS

2.1 Common repairing covenants

Most modern leases of either business or residential property contain a covenant by the tenant to keep the demised property in repair during the term. The classical phrases used by the draftsman are "to keep in repair"; "to put in repair"; "to leave in repair" and "good, habitable and tenantable repair". By far the most commonly used is "to keep in repair" which obliges the tenant to keep the demised premises in a state of repair throughout the term and, *a fortiori*, put them into repair if they are in a state of disrepair at the commencement of the term. In determining whether a "defect" falls within the covenant to repair regard should be had to the true construction of the covenant in the context and this will involve a consideration of the meaning of "repair". In the absence of any express undertaking (or one implied by statute) the landlord will not be under an obligation to repair the premises. It was held in *Arden v Pullen* (1842) 10 M & W 319 that where a tenant of a house undertakes by his agreement to keep it in as good repair as when he took it (fair wear and tear excepted) he is not entitled to quit upon it becoming uninhabitable for want of other repairs during the term and the landlord is under no implied obligation to do any repairs in such a case.

Case 11 *Proudfoot v Hart* [1890] QB 42 Court of Appeal

The house and premises in question were let by the plaintiff to the defendant under an agreement in writing dated November 11, 1885, for a term of three years from November 12, 1885, and the defendant thereby agreed that he would "during the said term keep the said premises in good tenantable repair, and so leave the same at the expiration thereof". The official referee awarded damages in respect of the cost incurred by the plaintiff after the termination of the tenancy in repapering the walls of rooms, where the paper which was upon them when the tenancy commenced had become worn out; in repainting the internal woodwork, where the paint which was on such woodwork when the tenancy commenced had worn off; in whitewashing and cleaning the staircases and ceilings; and in replacing with a new floor

27

a kitchen floor which had existed when the tenancy commenced.

Held (1) Under an agreement to keep a house in "good tenantable repair", and so leave the same at the expiration of the term, the tenant's obligation is to put and keep the premises in such repair as, having regard to the age, character, and locality of the house, would make it reasonably fit for the occupation of a tenant of the class who would be likely to take it.

Lord Esher MR said (in part)

What is the true construction of a tenant's contract to keep and deliver up premises in "tenantable repair"? Now, it is not an express term of that contract that the premises should be *put* into tenantable repair, and it may therefore be argued that, where it is conceded, as it is in this case, that the premises were out of tenantable repair when the tenancy began, the tenant is not bound to put them into tenantable repair, but is only bound to keep them in the same repair as they were in when he became the tenant of them. But it has been decided—and, I think, rightly decided—that, where the premises are not in repair when the tenant takes them, he must put them into repair in order to discharge his obligation under a contract to keep and deliver them up in repair. If the premises are out of repair at any time during the tenancy the landlord is entitled to say to the tenant, "you have now broken your contract to keep them in repair"; and if they were out of repair at the end of the tenancy he is entitled to say, "you have broken your contract to deliver them up in repair". I am of opinion that under a contract to keep the premises in tenantable repair and leave them in tenantable repair, the obligation of the tenant, if the premises are not in tenantable repair when the tenancy begins, is to put them into, keep them in, and deliver them up in tenantable repair. ... In *Payne v Haine* (1847) 16 M & W 541 the contract was to keep the premises, and at the expiration of the tenancy deliver up the same, in "good repair," which is much the same thing as "tenantable repair." This was the case which decided that in order to satisfy the tenant's obligation under his contract it was not sufficient for him to deliver up the premises in the same condition of repair as when he took them; he must deliver them up in good repair, even if they were not in good repair when the tenancy began. Parke B, in the course of his judgment, said:

> "This is a contract to keep the premises in good repair *as old premises*, but that cannot justify the keeping them in bad repair

because they happened to be in that state when the defendant took them. The cases all shew that the age and class of the premises let, with their general condition as to repair, may be estimated in order to measure the extent of the repairs to be done. Thus a house in Spitalfields may be repaired with materials inferior to those requisite for repairing a mansion in Grosvenor Square; but this lessee cannot say he will do no repairs, or leave the premises in bad repair, because they were old and out of repair when he took them. He was to keep them in good repair, and in that state, with reference to their age and class, he was to deliver them up at the end of the term."

Alderson B said:

"A contract to 'put' premises in good repair cannot mean to furnish new ones where those demised were old, but to put and keep them in good tenantable repair with reference to the purpose for which they are to be used ..."

With regard to the papering ... Take a house in Grosvenor Square. If when the tenancy ends, the paper on the walls is merely in a worse condition than when the tenant went in, I think the mere fact of its being in a worse condition does not impose upon the tenant any obligation to repaper under the covenant, if it is in such a condition that a reasonably-minded tenant of the class who take houses in Grosvenor Square would not think the house unfit for his occupation. But suppose that the damp has caused the paper to peel off the walls, and it is lying upon the floor, so that such a tenant would think it a disgrace, I should say then that the tenant was bound, under his covenant to leave the premises in tenantable repair, to put up new paper. He need not put up paper of a similar kind—which I take to mean of equal value—to the paper which was on the walls when his tenancy began. He need not put up a paper of a richer character than would satisfy a reasonable man within the definition.

The same view applies as to painting. If the paint is in such a state that the woodwork will decay unless it is repainted, it is obvious that the tenant must repaint. But I think that his obligation goes further than that. A house in Spitalfields is never painted in the same way as one in Grosvenor Square. If the tenant leaves a house in Grosvenor Square with painting only good enough for a house in Spitalfields, he has not discharged his obligation. He must paint it in such a way as would satisfy a reasonable tenant taking a house in Grosvenor Square. As to whitewashing, one knows it is impossible to keep ceilings in the same condition as when they have just been whitewashed. But if, though the ceilings have become blacker, they are still in such a condition that a reasonable man would not say, "I will not take this house because of the state of the ceilings," then I think that the tenant is not bound, under his covenant to leave the house in tenantable repair, to whitewash them. Take, again, the case of a house in Grosvenor Square having an ornamental ceiling, which is a beautiful work of art. A tenant goes in and finds such a ceiling in the house, and in course of time the gilding becomes in such a bad condition, or so much worn off, that the ceiling is no longer ornamental. I should think that a reasonable tenant taking a house in Grosvenor Square would not require a gilded ceiling at all. If that be so, on the mere covenant to leave the premises in tenantable repair, I should think that the tenant who has entered into that convenant was not bound to regild the ceiling at all. As to the floor, it may have been rotten when the tenancy began. If it was in such a state when the tenancy began that no reasonable man would take the house with a floor in that state, then the tenant's obligation is to put the floor into tenantable repair. The question is, what is the state of the floor when the tenant is called upon to fulfil his covenant? If it has become perfectly rotten he must put down a new floor, but if he can make it good in the sense in which I have spoken of all the other things—the paper, the paint, the whitewashing—he is not bound to put down a new floor. He must satisfy his obligation under the covenant by repairing it. If he leaves the floor out of repair when the tenancy ends, and the landlord comes in, the landlord may do the repairs himself and charge the costs as damages against the tenant; but he is only entitled to charge him with the necessary cost of a floor which would satisfy a reasonable man taking the premises. If the landlord puts down a new floor of a different kind, he cannot charge the tenant with the cost of it. He is entitled to charge the cost of doing what the tenant had to do under his covenant; but he is not entitled to charge according to what he has himself in fact done.

Lopes LJ said (in part)

What is the meaning of "good tenantable repair"? That expression appears to me to mean such repair as, having regard to the age, character, and locality of the house, would make it reasonably fit for the occupation of a reasonably-minded tenant of the class who would be likely to take it.

Note:

(i) In *Arden v Pullen* (1842) 10 M & W 319 the court held that where the tenant of a house undertakes by his agreement to keep it in as good repair as when he took it (fair wear and tear excepted) he is not entitled to quit upon its becoming uninhabitable for want of other repairs during the term; and the landlord is under no implied obligation to do any repairs in such a case.

Case 12   Greg v Planque [1936] 1 KB 669 Court of Appeal

The ground floor of a larger building was demised to the appellant, who carried on business therein as a court dressmaker. Through the part so demised, but not forming part of the demise, there ran a flue which served the other parts of the building. The lease provided that the appellant would "permit the lessor or his ... agents and workmen ... to enter the said premises ... for executing repairs and alterations of or upon the other parts of the said messuage ... making good all damage thereby occasioned." During the currency of the lease the lessor by his agents entered the demised premises for the purposes of cleaning the flue, and as a consequence of the work that was done a quantity of soot was scattered over the appellant's stock of dresses, thereby damaging them. On a claim in respect of this damage:

Held (1) That the cleaning of the flue was "executing repairs" within the meaning of the lease;

(2) That the words "making good all damage thereby occasioned" were not to be restricted to structural damage to the premises but were wide enough to cover damage to the appellant's stock-in-trade;

(3) That in assessing the quantum of damage regard must be had to the question whether the appellant had taken reasonable precautions for minimizing the amount of damage.

Greer LJ said (in part)

... I have had some hesitation in coming to the conclusion that the word "repair" is wide enough to include the cleaning of the flue, but as between these parties I feel bound to treat the word as covering the maintenance of the flue in the condition in which it ought to be to carry out the purposes for which it was placed where it was—namely, to provide heat to the other parts of the building which were let out as flats. If that be so, then the permission to go to the premises to do that work was subject to the other terms of sub-clause 5—namely, that the landlord would make good all damage thereby occasioned. It has been argued, however, that "damage" in that clause is limited to damage to the structure. That argument carried no weight to my mind when it is remembered what it was that was let and the purpose for which it was let. There is an undertaking by the lessee to use the premises for the business of dressmaking and millinery or for such purpose or purposes as may from time to time be authorised by the previous consent of the landlord. It was, I think, intended that if the landlord took advantage of the permission given by sub-clause 5 he should be responsible for all the damage thereby occasioned, which would include damage to the defendant's stock-in-trade, and if he could not make it good by restoring the frocks to the condition in which they were before the operations began, he would have to pay for having failed to do that which he had undertaken to do— namely, make good all damage thereby occasioned. [Counsel] contended that we ought not to hold that there was any damage thereby occasioned, because the lessee might have prevented the damage by moving her goods from the position in which they were to some other part of the premises. I agree that she was under an obligation to take all reasonable steps to see that damage would not be occasioned by the landlord's operations, but it is a question of fact still to be determined whether by removing her frocks from the showroom to the office she did all that reasonably could be expected of her in the circumstances. I think the learned judge came to a wrong conclusion on the construction of this clause, being persuaded by [counsel] that it referred only to structural damage to the premises. With that view I disagree. I think the sub-clause is wide enough to cover damage to the stock-in-trade on the premises. The quantum of damage remains to be determined, and in deciding that the referee will have to consider whether or not the defendant could, at reasonable expense, which she would have been entitled to recover, have prevented the damage which occurred.

Note:

(i) In *Openshaw v Evans* (1884) 50 LT 156 an agreement for the letting of a farm and mill provided that the tenant should "keep and leave the messuages and buildings in good and substantial repair". In an action by the landlord to recover damages for non-repair of a demised mill wheel the Court of Appeal held that the tenant was liable.

Case 13 *Howe v Botwood* [1913] 2 KB 387. Channell J

A lease of a dwelling-house contained a covenant by the lessee to "pay and discharge all rates, taxes, assessments, charges, and out-goings whatsoever which now are or during the said term shall be imposed or charged on the premises or the landlord or tenant in respect thereof (land tax and landlord's property tax only excepted)." The lessor covenanted to "keep the exterior of the said dwelling-house and buildings in repair." The sanitary authority served notice during the term of the lessor under the Public Health Act, 1875, stating that a nuisance existed on the premises arising from an outside defective drain and requiring him to do certain work which involved the renewal and reconstruction of the drainage system outside the house; and an order of justices was made directing him to do the work. The lessor accordingly did the work required, and claimed to recover from the lessee the cost thereof so far as it exceeded mere repair:

Held (1) That the lessee's covenant to pay "all outgoings imposed on the landlord in respect of the premises" must be read as being subject to the performance by the lessor of his covenant to keep the exterior of the buildings in repair, and that, as the work of renewal and reconstruction was necessary in order to enable the lessor to perform his covenant to repair, he was bound to bear the cost thereof.

Channell J said (in part)

There is ... in this case ... a covenant by the plaintiff to keep the exterior of the dwelling-house and buildings in repair. Without doubt the drains in question are part of the buildings and are outside the dwelling-house; and they are in fact out of repair. The plaintiff under his covenant had to keep them in repair, and as the drains were out of repair he had to repair them. The law, however, did not allow him to do the repairs to the drains unless he fulfilled certain requirements of the sanitary authority which were in the nature of improvements upon the then existing drainage system. Suppose that a drain was laid in mortar, and the law required, when the landlord came to repair it, that it should be laid in concrete, it is clear that the landlord would have to lay it in concrete, the only way in which the law would allow him to effect the necessary repairs. The law only allowed him to repair the drains upon the terms of his constructing inspection chambers and carrying up the soil pipe, and therefore he became unable to perform his covenant to repair without executing work which was in the nature of improvements to the drainage system. It is like the case of the wall in *Lurcott v Wakely* [1911] 1 KB 905, which was so out of repair that it could not have been repaired without being rebuilt, and the tenant was held liable, under his covenant to repair, to pay the cost of taking down and rebuilding the wall. If it was impossible to repair the drains without effecting improvements to the drainage system, the plaintiff would have to effect the improvements in order to perform his obligation under his covenant to repair. The law gives the sanitary authority the right, where a nuisance exists, to require by notice certain work to be executed which may be in the nature of improvements, and to apply to a Court of summary jurisdiction to enforce the requirements of the notice. The expense of executing the work would under this covenant fall on the plaintiff. If therefore that covenant by the plaintiff had stood alone without the covenant by the defendant, that is how I should construe it. That covenant, however, has to be read with the earlier covenant by the tenant to pay and discharge all outgoings. There are thus two covenants, one placing the burden on the tenant and the other placing it on the landlord. We must construe the lease as a whole so as to make it consistent in both its parts. In my opinion the covenant by the tenant must be read as if it contained the words "except such as are by this lease imposed upon the landlord." By reading that exception into the covenant by the tenant the two covenants can be read together. If it were not so read in, the cost of ordinary repairs to the outside drains might come within the tenant's covenant.

Case 14   *Gooderham and Worts Ltd v Canadian Broadcasting Corporation* [1947] AC 66 House of Lords (Privy Council)

By an indenture of lease "as of May 15, 1933" the appellants, the owners of a private radio station, leased to the Canadian Radio Broadcasting Commission their land and premises and all plant and equipment "2, for and during the term of three years ... to be complete and ended on May 15, 1936," at a rent of £12,000 yearly, payable in advance in equal quarterly instalments. It was provided by cl. 4 of the lease that "the lessee covenants with the lessor to keep the whole of the demised premises modern and up-to-date and in good repair and operating condition," and by cl. 12 that "at the expiration of the term hereby granted by the lessor to the lessee as hereinafter provided the lessor will . . . grant a new lease for a further term of three years from the determination of the present or then existing lease . . . and if no such new lease be entered into as aforesaid the present or then existing lease, as the case may be, and all the terms and conditions thereof shall continue until terminated by the lessor upon one month's notice in writing to the lessee . . .".

The necessary statutory approval of the lease by the Governor in Council under s. 9 of the Canadian Broadcasting Act, 1932, as amended by s. 2 of c. 35 of the Statutes of 1932–33, was explicitly stated to be of a lease "for a period of three years at a price of £12,000 per annum," and no reference was made to any conditions. On the expiry of the term of three years on May 15, 1936, no new lease was entered into, but the Commission remained in occupation and continued to pay the rent quarterly. On January 20, 1938, the Canadian Broadcasting Corporation, the respondents, which were constituted under the Canadian Broadcasting Act, 1936, and took over thereunder all the obligations and liabilities of the Commission, gave notice to terminate the lease at May 15, 1938. Thereupon, the appellants, in April, 1938, instituted the present proceedings claiming, inter alia, a declaration that the lease was valid and subsisting and for specific performance; alternatively, they claimed a declaration that the respondents were tenants under a yearly tenancy expiring on May 15 in each year on the terms of the lease so far as applicable; they also claimed damages in respect of the respondents' alleged failure to keep the demised premises modern and up-to-date and in good repair and operating condition.

Held (1) That cl. 12 of the lease, which modified cl. 2 by providing that in the absence of a month's notice the parties were to remain indefinitely in the relation of landlord and tenant, was unauthorised by the Order in Council, which had approved a lease for a period of three years only, and was invalid ab initio, and ineffectual to extend the relation of tenancy beyond May 15, 1936. Clause 12 was, however, severable, and its elimination left an effective three years' lease. The payment and acceptance of rent and the continuance of the respondents possession after May 15, 1936, had in law the result that from and after that date the relation of the parties was by presumption of law that of landlord and tenant under a year to year tenancy terminable by six months' notice on either side before May 15 in any year, and all the terms of the original lease, so far as consistent with a yearly tenancy, were thenceforth by law binding on the respondents, including the obligations of cl. 4. The notice to the appellants to terminate the lease as from May 15, 1938, being dated less than six months before that date, was accordingly bad, and was ineffective to all intents and purposes.

(2) That the respondents were at the time the action was brought in breach of the covenant contained in cl. 4, and the matter must be referred to the Master of the Supreme Court at Toronto to determine the amount of the damages in accordance with the law and practice of the court. The terms of the covenant were unusual and of very wide scope, but having regard to the nature of the premises and the purpose for which they were designed and used it was enforceable as a condition of the respondents' yearly tenancy and must receive a fair and reasonable interpretation. While it was not possible to devise a precise formula for the instruction of the referee, the covenant must be construed in a business sense. The obligations of the lessee were to be construed as being obligations to keep the whole of the demised premises modern and up-to-date in so far as the thing demised was capable of being kept modern and up-to-date, so that if the existing site of the station was inadequate for the accommodation of the plant necessary for a modern station the respondents were under no obligation to acquire additional land, and the duty imposed on them by the covenant did not extend to the substitution of an installation involving the use of higher power than that of the station demised. The damages for breach must depend on the loss suffered by the appellants from the respondents' failure to fulfil the covenant.

Lord Macmillan said (in part)

It now only remains to consider the question of the interpretation of the covenant "to keep the whole of the demised 'premises modern and up-to-date and in good repair and operating condition." The terms of the covenant are unusual and of very wide scope, but having regard to the nature of the premises and the purpose for which they were designed and used their Lordships are of opinion that it is enforceable as a condition of the respondents' yearly tenancy. It was suggested in the Court of Appeal that if an extreme interpretation were placed on the covenant the result might be to render it inapplicable altogether, first as being originally unauthorised by the approval of the Governor in Council, and second, as not being such a provision as the law would import into a yearly tenancy. In their Lordships' opinion, however, the covenant is binding on the respondents and must receive a fair and reasonable interpretation . . .

The interpretation and application of the covenant to keep the whole of the demised premises modern and up-to-date was the subject of much debate before their Lordships, as it had been in the courts in Ontario. The appellants complained that too narrow a construction had been placed on it, while the respondents sought to restrict its scope. In their Lordships' view it is not possible to devise a precise formula for the instruction of the referee, and they think it undesirable by anticipation to fetter unduly the business judgment which it will be his province to exercise. They agree, however with many of the general observations made by Greene J. and the learned judges of the Court of Appeal in so far as they emphasise that it is the demised premises, that is, the station, studio and offices as let, that are to be kept modern and up-to-date, and that if the existing site of the station is inadequate for the accommodation of the plant necessary for a modern station the respondents are under no obligation to acquire additional land. Again, Henderson J. well expresses it when he says:

"The obligations of the lessee are to be construed as being obligations to keep the whole of the demised premises modern and up-to-date, in so far as the thing demised is capable of being kept modern and up-to-date."

Applying this, their Lordships note that the station demised is a five kilowatt station, and the duty imposed on the respondents by the covenant does not extend to the substitution of an installation involving the use of higher power. The damages for breach must, of course, depend on the loss suffered by the appellants from the respondents' failure to fulfil the covenant. The covenant must be construed in a business sense.

2.2 Extent and type of repair

Case 15 Manor House Drive Ltd v Shahbazian [1965] EGD 228
Court of Appeal

The maisonnette in question was let to the tenant on April 14, 1960, on a 99-year lease at a premium of £3,700 and rent of £50 a year. The landlords covenanted to "maintain, repair and decorate the main structure and roof of the building," and the tenant was under an obligation to pay a proportion of the cost of works. In the winter of 1961–62 there was a great deal of trouble with the roof and water came through, damaging some of the tenant's belongings. The landlords took advice from a surveyor who said that certain zinc below a covering of canvas and bitumen was old and had defects. He advised the removal of the existing temporary coverings and the old zinc, and replacement by new zinc. If the work was carried out as soon as possible there should be no further trouble for another 25 to 30 years, but temporary treatment would be a waste of money and not likely to be effective for more than a few months. On the advice of this qualified surveyor the landlords employed builders to put in a new zinc roof at a cost of £401 11s. 6d. They then called on the tenants to pay their proportions of the cost of the works. The respondent tenant disputed the claim, and evidence was given at the county court that instead of the new zinc roof, first-aid repair could have been done of a further coat of heavy bitumen or Aquaseal at a cost of £100. This would last only three years, and would have to be replaced by bitumen every two years at a cost of £25; however, such work would cost only about £300 every 20 years as against the £400 for the new zinc roof. In argument it was put to the judge that it might have been reasonable in a sense to put in a zinc roof, but that it was not really necessary. The judge accepted this and held it was not necessary to do all the repair work with zinc, and he rejected the landlords' claim altogether.

Held (1) The works undertaken were a reasonable and proper way of maintaining the roof and "patching up" was not reasonable in view of the surveyor's advice.

Lord Denning MR said (in part)

However, the repair that was done was not just renewal or improvement; it was a repair to the entire structure. It was part of the work of maintaining the roof, and was reasonable, and a proper fulfilment of the repairing covenant. On the evidence before the judge there was only one finding, that it was a reasonable and proper way of maintaining the roof to put in zinc as advised. Patching up by bitumen or Aquaseal was not reasonable or even proper in view of the surveyor's advice. If water had come through after temporary repair there would have been no possible answer to a claim by the tenant that the work had not been done properly.

Case 16 Samuels v Abbints Investments Ltd [1963] EGD 543, Ungoed-Thomas J

The lease of the demised premises was dated February 21, 1962, and was for 99 years, at £50 a year, and it included a covenant by the landlords binding them ". . . to keep the main structure of the block in tenantable repair provided nevertheless that the landlords shall not be liable for any breach of this covenant unless the landlords shall fail to take reasonable steps to remedy such breach after written notice thereof is given to the landlords by the tenant." Before entering into her contract, the plaintiff obtained a surveyors' report, and this referred to evidence of dampness and rot in parts of the flat. When the matter was referred to the defendants' solicitors they replied that defects in the flat would be the plaintiff's responsibility. The plaintiff accepted this. The position therefore was that the plaintiff had taken over the flat knowing that there had been damp and rot there. She had disclaimed any claim in respect of rot existing before the lease was granted, and the liability for repairs clearly was governed by the lease.

The plaintiff had said in evidence that when she took over the flat in June, 1962, she was horrified to find damp in a toilet external wall and the wall next to the kitchen, and immediately got into touch with the defendants' surveyors, who advised that the wall should be given time to dry out. In July, 1962, the plaintiff first noticed dry rot. She contacted the defendants' surveyors, who called in a dry rot expert. In September the defendants' surveyors informed the plaintiff that under the terms of the lease she was responsible for the eradication of the dry rot. The plaintiff instructed a firm to deal with the dry rot, and her solicitors wrote to the defendants' surveyors claiming that the dry rot had been caused by defects in the building's structure, and stating that the plaintiff would hold the defendants responsible for the repair. There was substantial agreement among the expert witnesses about the cause of the rot. As a result of a defective waste pipe the external wall had become wet, resulting in the removal of mortar, infiltration of water through the brickwork, and dry rot. This dry rot had been dealt with, and had not reappeared. The flat was defined as including "the internal and external walls . . . but exclud-ing the outside brick, steel or concrete work."

Held (1) At the date of the lease the tenant became liable for the state of disrepair of the flat. Therefore she was liable for the dry rot in the flat at that date.

(2) The landlords were liable for the disrepair of the main structure and also, apart from considerations of notice and the construction of the covenant, for the saturation of the wall and for making good any damage by dry rot due to saturation of the wall after the date of the lease.

Ungoed-Thomas J said (in part)

The evidence clearly established that defective pointing of itself, apart from its association with the leaking pipe, had not caused dry rot in the interior wall of the flat, and he (his Lordship) was also satisfied that although from time to time water had come out of the overflow pipes against the wall it had not caused the trouble complained of. Any trouble subsequent to the lease being granted must have been due to the wet condition of the walls when the lease was granted.

The next question was liability for that state of disrepair—the saturation of the wall resulting in dry rot spreading—under the provisions of the lease. At the date of the lease the plaintiff became liable for the state of disrepair of the flat under the les-see's covenant, however the disrepair was caused. Therefore she was liable for the dry rot in the flat at that date, and for any dry rot resulting from that which existed at that date. The defendants, however, were liable for the disrepair of the main structure and, also, apart from considerations of notice and the construction of the covenant, for the saturation of the wall and for making good any damage by dry rot due to saturation of the wall after the date of the lease. The question was how far under the landlords' repair covenant the defendants were liable for the saturation of the external brick wall as it existed after the granting of the lease. If on the true construction of the lease the flat was defined to include—as *prima facie* it would—the exter-nal walls, and if the walls were specifically mentioned, there would be a very strong case for giving these words a meaning that would prevail over the *prima facie* meaning of "main struc-ture" in the covenant.

The first schedule to the lease defined the flat as including "the internal and external walls . . . but excluding the outside brick, steel or concrete work." It seemed to him (his Lordship) that "but excluding the outside brick, steel or concrete work" applied to the external walls, so that the outside bricks of the external walls would not come within the definition of the flat for which the plaintiff was responsible. If that were so, the outside bricks would come within "the main structure of the block." The position therefore was that the plaintiff was responsible for the inside part of the external walls and the defendant for the external part. This might seem an odd arrangement, but the evidence was that there was a recognisable distinction between the two parts.

So subject to the question of notice, the defendants' responsibility was limited to the outside bricks and any damage resulting from them, and to dry rot which had spread from the outside bricks since the date of the lease.

On the facts, he (his Lordship) had come to the conclusion that proper and adequate notice of the saturation had been given by the plaintiff by letter. The defendants' liability dated from that notice. However, before even that degree of liability could operate, it was provided in the covenant that the landlord should not be liable for any breach unless he had failed to take reasonable steps to remedy such breach. It had been suggested that it had not been possible to take reasonable steps. What reasonable steps could have been taken? He (the judge) had been told that although heat treatment could dry the inside of the wall it would not be effective in the outside part. But it would have been possible to dispose of the saturation by taking out the bricks and treating or replacing them, and in his opinion the defendants were liable for damage resulting from their failure to take those or other appropriate steps. That left the question of damages, limited to damage caused after the receipt of the notice. The firm employed by the plaintiff had treated the inside of the flat with a fluid, the effect of which was to put down a toxic barrier that shut out the possibility of dry rot damage being caused by reason of the wet condition of the outside walls. That seemed to him (his Lordship) to have been a proper course to have taken in mitigation of any damage that might have occurred, and presumably was cheaper than having the bricks replaced. It was an expense for which the defendants were liable, and to that limited extent, therefore, the plaintiff succeeded.

2.3 Repairs at a specific time

Case 17   Kirklington v Wood [1917] 1 KB 333 Lush J

A lease contained (inter alia) the following covenant by the lessee:

"And will in the year 1909, and also in the year 1916, if this lease shall so long last paint varnish and grain all the inside wood and iron work usually painted varnished or grained of the said demised premises with three coats of good oil and white lead paint in a proper and workmanlike manner."

The lessee died in 1915, and his executors, under a power in that behalf contained in the lease, gave six months' notice to the lessor to determine the lease on March 1, 1916. On the determination of the term, the covenant not having been performed, the lessor claimed damages for the breach of it:

Held (1) That the executors were liable.

(2) Where a lease contains a covenant to execute specific repairs in a particular year, if the lease shall be then subsisting, the obligation to perform the covenant attaches as soon as the year begins, and the fact that the lease is determined by the lessee by notice expiring before the end of the year does not relieve the lessee of his obligation to perform the covenant.

Lush J said (in part)

... It is quite true that if the lease had not been determined there would have been no breach on the part of the executors of the lessee on the date in question, namely, March 1, 1916; but none the less there was an obligation on the executors of the lessee, as soon as the year 1916 commenced, to perform that covenant, and inasmuch as the executors of the lessee, by giving that notice, put it out of their power to perform the covenant after March 1 they cannot contend that they were not under an obligation to perform it during the period that intervened between January 1 and March 1. The executors, by giving the notice, shortened the period during which they had the opportunity of doing the painting and performing the covenant. It seems to me quite impossible for them, having taken that course, to say that they had the whole of the year 1916 in which to perform it, and that therefore there was no breach on March 1. The case was put in argument as to what would have happened if the lessor had given the notice. I do not think it is necessary for me to consider what would have been the case if that had happened. It is not what did happen. The lessee's executors gave the notice, and in my opinion, the obligation having attached to them as soon as the year 1916 commenced, they were bound to perform it or to show some excuse for their non-performance. They have not performed it; they have given no excuse for their non-performance.

Case 18 Baylis v Le Gros (1858) 4 CB (NS) 537

The lease of the demised premises contained a covenant by the tenant to repair, uphold, support, amend and keep the premises when, where and as often as required. The lease also contained a separate covenant to repair within three months upon notice by the landlord.

Held (1) A general covenant to repair and further to repair within three months after notice from the lessor are separate and independent covenants. A right of re-entry, therefore, may attach to the former though no notice has been given under the latter.

Cockburn CJ said

I am clearly of opinion that a forfeiture has been incurred here. The lease in question contains a general covenant by the lessee, his executors, &c., to repair and keep the premises in repair; and also a covenant that it should be lawful for the lessor, his executors, &c., to enter at all convenient times to view the condition of the premises, and to give the lessee notice of any want of repair, requiring him to do such repairs within three months, and that the lessee, his executors, &c., should within that period repair accordingly. These two covenants are quite separate and independent. The authorities are all clear to that effect; and they coincide with the common sense of the thing. It would indeed be monstrous, if, giving credit to his tenant that he will duly perform his engagement, the landlord abstains from harassing him with continual inspection, and then should find himself debarred of his remedy for a breach of a positive covenant. I cannot entertain the slightest doubt that there has been a forfeiture here. As to the entry also, my mind is equally free from doubt. Finding the premises in a dilapidated state, the landlord comes upon them and enters into an agreement with a man he finds in possession, to become his tenant,—intending thereby to act upon the forfeiture and to oust the lessee. I think that was quite sufficient to constitute an entry by the landlord so as to put an end to the lease.

2.4 Covenant to paint

A lease may contain a covenant by the tenant to paint the premises (either internally, externally or both) which is separate from the repairing obligation. Alternatively the obligation to paint may be part of the main repairing covenant. The main authority on the subject is *Proudfoot v Hart* [1890] QB 42 [Case 11].

Case 19 *Eyre v Johnson* [1946] 1 KB 481 Denning J

In 1930, a landlord let a house for twenty-one years, the lease containing covenants by the tenant to keep and yield up the premises in repair. The tenant having given six months' notice, pursuant to the terms of the lease, to determine the tenancy in December, 1944, applied to the Minister of Health for licences to effect repairs, but these were refused and the premises were yielded up to the landlord unrepaired. In an action for damages for breach of the covenants to repair, the tenant pleaded that performance of the covenants became illegal by reason of the Defence (General) Regulation, 1939, No. 56A, and that therefore he was not liable. The judge found that, since the outbreak of war in 1939 very little had been done to the premises by the tenant by way of repair. There was no regulation restricting the tenant from effecting repairs until 1941 and from 1941 to 1944 the limit of work which could be done without licence was at first £500 and then £100.

Held, That (1) the condition of non-repair of the house was due to a series of breaches of covenant to keep in repair.

(2) The landlord having performed his obligations under the lease, the fact that it had become difficult or even impossible for the tenant to perform certain of his obligations under the lease, did not amount in any sense of the word to frustration and did not relieve the tenant from the payment of damages for his breaches of covenant.

Denning J said (in part)
The first answer to that is that I think this condition of non-repair was really brought about by a series of breaches of the covenant to keep in repair. If the lessee had performed his covenants from 1939 to 1941 when there was no regulation on the matter, or even from 1941 to 1944 when there was a regulation, but the limit was at first £500 and then £100, I do not think there would have been any difficulty in keeping these premises in proper repair and there would have been nothing to prevent him performing his covenant. He cannot rely, as a defence to this action, on a condition of things which his own breaches have brought about.

That really is a sufficient answer to this defence, but I go further. It seems to me that although illegality which completely forbids the performance of a contract may give rise to frustration in some cases, illegality as to the performance of one clause which does not amount to frustration in any sense of the word, does not carry with it the necessary consequence that the party is absolved from paying damages. Take this case. The landlord has performed all his part of the bargain. The tenant has had the premises all this time. The fact that it has become difficult, or even impossible, for the tenant to perform the covenants does not relieve him from the obligation of paying damages. The case of *Baily v De Crespigny* LR 4 QB 180 was cited to me on behalf of the tenant. When that case was considered in the House of Lords in *Matthey v Curling* [1922] 2 AC 180, Lord Buckmaster said (at p. 228):

> "I find myself unable to think that this has any application to a covenant entered into by a lessee, either to pay rent or to deliver up the premises. He has bound himself to do these definite acts, and it is no excuse that circumstances which he could not control have happened and have prevented his compliance."

In that case the tenant was held liable on his repairing covenant, although circumstances which he could not control had happened and prevented his compliance. So that here, even assuming circumstances beyond the tenant's control which prevented his compliance, I am satisfied they do not establish a defence to this action for damages.

Case 20 Scales v Lawrence (1860) 2 F & F 289 Willes J

The demised premises was a house comprising three sitting-rooms and four-bedrooms with stables, outhouses and a large garden which had been let to the defendant in 1852 for a term of seven years. The tenant had covenanted so often as need should require, well and sufficiently to repair, uphold, sustain, paint, glaze, cleanse, scour the premises (with all needful reparations and cleansings) and to leave the premises in such repair, reasonable wear and tear excepted.

Held (1) On a covenant, as often as necessary well and sufficiently to repair, cleanse, etc, and keep and leave in such repair, reasonable wear and tear excepted, the tenant, if he has repaired within a reasonable time before leaving, is only bound, in addition to the repair of actual dilapidations, to clean the old paint, etc, and not to repaint.

Willes J said (in part)

By the covenant the defendant was bound to do the things specially mentioned, and also all that was necessary to leave the house in a good condition, with reference to the obligation of a tenant. As to that, you must consider the character and condition of the house; thus, if he takes an old house, he must not let it tumble down, he must keep it up; but only as an old house. No tenant is bound to leave, for his landlord, a new house; but the house which he took, 'in a state of fit repair, as such house. And if he has painted the outside in three years and the inside within seven years, he is not bound to do it again when leaving, unless so far as is required by actual dilapidations or destruction of the paint; and so of other repairs. He may, if he likes, have the benefit of his repairs, so as he leaves the premises in a fit state, reasonable wear and tear excepted. If he painted and papered within seven years, and there is no damage in the way of breaking down or tearing off, then the reasonable construction of the covenant is, that he should "cleanse" the old paint, &c. (or renew it only where destroyed), and give up the house in a clean and fair condition, and for fair wear and tear he would not be liable. Questions of this sort are questions of fact for you, to be decided on what are the substantial merits of the case rather than on strict or extreme law. The landlord is not to claim for every crack in the glass or every scratch on the paint. The reasonable rule probably would be not to charge for a pane of glass merely with one crack in it, and so forth. Such covenants must not be strained, but reasonably construed, on the principle of "give and take."

Note: (i) In *Monk v Noyes* (1824) 1 Car & P 265 the court held that under a covenant that the tenant "should and would substantially repair, uphold, and maintain" a house he was bound to keep up the inside painting.

2.5 Fair wear and tear

Most leases contain a proviso to the effect that the convenantor's liability under the repairing covenant does not include liability for disrepair through fair wear and tear of the premises.

Case 21 Haskell v Marlow [1928] 2 KB 45 King's Bench Division

A testator devised a dwelling-house to his wife for her life, she insuring the same against loss by fire, "and also keeping the same in good repair and condition (reasonable wear and tear excepted)," and after her death he directed that the same should fall into his residuary estate, which was to be divided among his children in equal shares. The testator's widow occupied and devised premises until her death, a period of forty-two years. She did nothing actively to injure the premises, but did nothing substantially to counteract the natural process of decay. The plaintiffs, the trustees of the will, alleged that she had neglected to keep the premises in good repair and condition in conformity with the terms of the will, and claimed from the defendants, her executors, the cost of the necessary repairs:

Held (1) That the testator's widow, having accepted and occupied the premises, was bound by the terms of the devise, that the words of the exception were not to be treated as mere surplusage, and that a reasonable meaning must be given to them, but that having regard to the length of time during which no substantial repairs had been done to the premises, and to the extent of the damage thereby caused, the widow, as tenant for life, was not protected by the words of the exception, and that her executors were liable for the damage arising from the natural process of decay.

Salter J said (in part)

Turning to the authorities, there are many cases in which the net liability imposed by a covenant of this kind has been considered, but only two which have dealt—and those perhaps rather slightly—with the exception of fair wear and tear considered alone and the effect that such an exception has upon the liability to repair under the covenant. The first case that is often referred to in cases of this kind is *Gutteridge v Munyard* (1834) 7 C & P 129. That was a case between landlord and tenant. There was a covenant to keep and leave in a certain condition of repair, "reasonable use and wear thereof in the mean time only excepted," and upon that covenant Tindal CJ thus directed the jury:

"The main subject of the demise is an old house. Now, when a very old building is demised, it is not meant that it should be restored in an improved state, nor that the consequences of the elements should be averted: but the tenant has the duty of keeping it as nearly as may be in the state in which it was at the time of the demise by the timely expenditure of money and care."

That direction was the subject of some criticism in the Court of Appeal in *Lurcott v Wakely and Wheeler* [1911] 1 KB 905. In that case, however, there was no exception of fair wear and tear.

Mantz v Goring (1838) 4 Bing NC 451 was an action by landlord against tenant for damages for breach of the covenant to repair. The covenant was to keep "in tenantable repair, reasonable wear and tear excepted." The buildings were old. There was a verdict for the plaintiff. A rule nisi for a new trial was obtained on the ground of exclusion of evidence. The rule was discharged, and in giving judgment Tindal CJ, presiding over the Court, said:

> "Every one knows what such a covenant means, and the tenant must fulfil it according to the nature of the premises: for it is established by *Stanley v Towgood* (1836) 3 Bing NC 4 and other cases that the same nicety of repair is not exacted for an old building as for a new one. It is clear, however, that justice has been done here according to that principle, for it was proved that it would have cost £155 to put these premises in complete repair, and the jury threw off the £100, probably because they were old."

That judgment, like the summing up in *Gutteridge v Munyard* (*supra*), seems to deal mainly with the application of a covenant of this kind to an old house.

The next case referred to was *Scales v Lawrence* (1860) 2 F & F 289 also a landlord and tenant case. There there was a covenant so often as need should require, well and sufficiently to repair, uphold, sustain, paint, glaze, cleanse, etc., a house and premises, and to leave the premises in such repair, "reasonable wear and tear excepted." It was held that if at the expiration of the lease the tenant had repaired within a reasonable time before leaving, he was only bound, "in addition to the repair of actual dilapidations, to clean the old paint, etc., and not to repaint, etc." Upon that covenant Willes J directed the jury:

> "No tenant is bound to leave, for his landlord, a new house; but the house which he took, in a state of fit repair, as such house. And if he has painted the outside in three years, and the inside within seven years, he is not bound to do it again when leaving, unless so far as is required by actual dilapidations or destruction of the paint; and so of other repairs. He may, if he likes, have the benefit of his repairs, so as to leave the premises in a fit state, reasonable wear and tear excepted. If he painted and papered within seven years, and there is no damage in the way of breaking down or tearing off, then the reasonable construction of the covenant is, that he should

'cleanse' the old paint, etc. (or renew it only where destroyed), and give up the house in a clean and fair condition, and for fair wear and tear he would not be liable. Questions of this sort are questions of fact for you, to be decided on what are the substantial merits of the case rather than on strict rights or extreme law. The landlord is not to claim for every crack in the glass or every scratch on the paint. The reasonable rule probably would be not to charge for a pane of glass merely with one crack in it, and so forth. Such covenants must not be strained, but reasonably construed, on the principle of 'give and take.'"

I think that the point to be made for the present purpose from those three cases is that in all of them very little stress is laid on the exception of reasonable wear and tear. The covenant is construed in those cases not quite, no doubt, as it would have been construed, but very much as it would have been construed if that exception had not been present. Those three cases I think go strongly to show that this exception is not to be construed as making any great or grave inroad on the general liability to repair.

... *Terrell v Murray* (1901) 17 TLR 570 ... was an action by landlord against tenant for breach of contract in failing to deliver up the demised house in the agreed state of repair. The covenant was to deliver up "at the expiration or sooner determination of the said term in as good repair and condition as it is now in, reasonable wear and tear ... excepted." There was no covenant to repair during the term. At the expiration of the term the lessor claimed for dilapidations including three items, one for painting the outside woodwork of the house, another for repointing the brickwork, and the third for repairing parts of the kitchen floors which had become affected by dry rot. It was held that the lessee was not liable for those three items. The official referee had found the liability at £39, which included £12 for painting the outside woodwork of the building, £2 for repointing certain brickwork, and £5 for repairing parts of the kitchen floor. On appeal the Divisional Court gave judgment for the appellant, the defendant. [Counsel for the plaintiff], went so far as to argue that the words in the exception were mere surplusage, and did not, at any rate, apply to the outside of the house. Bruce J said that it was a little curious that there was no very satisfactory authority as to the meaning of the words "fair" or "reasonable" wear and tear. He could not agree with [counsel] when he said that no meaning ought to be given to the words at all, nor could he agree that they had no operation in regard to the outside of the premises.

The meaning of the covenant in his opinion was that the tenant was bound at the end of the tenancy to deliver up the premises in as good condition as they were in at the beginning, subject to the following exceptions, that was to say, dilapidations caused by the friction of the air, dilapidations caused by exposure, and dilapidations caused by ordinary use. As he was of opinion that outside painting was not a thing the tenant was bound to do under that covenant, and as the amount due to the plaintiff would thus be reduced to the amount paid into court, he gave judgment for the defendant. Phillimore J felt some difficulty, but on the whole he concurred. The only points decided in that case were that an exception of reasonable wear and tear is not to be regarded as mere surplusage, and that a proper meaning must be given to it, and that there was no liability cast upon the tenant to do outside painting. That case was much relied upon by the appellants but I find nothing in it to alter the view which I have formed. The next case is *Citron v Cohen* (1920) 36 TLR 560. In that case Sankey J accepted the definition or explanation of "reasonable wear and tear" given in *Terrell v Murray* (*supra*) but the case was decided on other grounds.

The next case is *Miller v Burt* 63 SoJo 117. In that case the house was old, and was in bad repair at the beginning of the term. The covenant was to keep the house in the same state of repair, that is to say, it amounted to a covenant not to allow the house to go from bad to worse, "fair wear and tear excepted." The court pronounced a formula for the guidance of the arbitrator in these words:

> "The tenant is responsible for repairs necessary to maintain the premises in the same state as when he took them. If, however, wind and weather have a greater effect on the premises, having regard to their character, than if the premises had been sound, the tenant is not bound so to repair as to meet the extra effect of the dilapidations so caused."

That appears to be nothing more than a statement that in dealing with a covenant to keep old premises in the same state of repair as they were in at the date of the lease, the age of the premises and their condition at the beginning of the tenancy must be taken into consideration, but that would equally have been so if there had been no exception of fair wear and tear, and it appears to me that that formula throws no light at all upon the meaning and effect of a fair wear and tear exception.

The last case referred to was *Manchester Bonded Warehouse Co. v Carr* (1880) 5 CPD 507. There the plaintiffs had demised certain floors in a warehouse to the defendant, and the defendant had covenanted to repair, maintain and keep the inside of the premises in good and tenantable repair and condition and to deliver them up at the end of the term, damage by fire, storm, or tempest, or other inevitable accident, and reasonable wear and tear only excepted. Five points were discussed, but the only one which is now material was the extent of the liability of the defendant under his covenant. Lord Coleridge CJ, delivering the judgment of the court, said:

> "It only remains to consider whether reasonable wear and tear can include destruction by reasonable use. These words, no doubt, include destruction to some extent, e.g., destruction of surface by ordinary friction, but we do not think they include total destruction by a catastrophe which was never contemplated by either party."

That case and *Terrell v Murray* (*supra*) are the only cases in which the exception has been separately considered, where wear and tear was defined as meaning the dilapidations caused by certain destructive agencies rather than those agencies themselves. In my opinion, such words as "fair" and "reasonable" in an exception of this kind qualify both the destructive agencies and also the dilapidation which they bring about. Such words can be used no doubt to qualify human user, but they could not be used to qualify forces of nature. It would be impossible to speak of an "unfair rain" or an "unreasonable frost." To bring dilapidations within the protection of such an exception as that in this case, I think that two things must be shown: First, that the dilapidations for which exemption is claimed were caused by normal human use or by the normal action of the elements, and, secondly, that they are reasonable in amount, having regard to the terms of the contract to repair the premises and the other circumstances of the case.

Talbot J said (in part)

The meaning is that the tenant (for life or years) is bound to keep the house in good repair and condition, but is not liable for what is due to reasonable wear and tear. That is to say, his obligation to keep in good repair is subject to that exception. If any want of repair is alleged and proved in fact, it lies on the tenant to show that it comes within the exception. Reasonable wear and tear means the reasonable use of the house by the tenant and the ordinary operation of natural forces. The exception of want of repair due to wear and tear must be construed as limited to what is directly due to wear and tear, reasonable conduct on the part of the tenant being assumed. It does not mean that if there is a defect originally proceeding from reasonable wear and tear the tenant is released from his obligation to keep in good repair and condition everything which it may be possible to trace ultimately to that defect. He is bound to do such repairs as may be required to prevent the consequences flowing originally from wear and tear from producing others which wear and tear would not directly produce.

For example, if a tile falls off the roof, the tenant is not liable for the immediate consequences; but, if he does nothing and in the result more and more water gets in, the roof and walls decay and ultimately the top floor, or the whole house, becomes uninhabitable, he cannot say that it is due to reasonable wear and tear, and that therefore he is not liable under his obligation to keep the house in good repair and condition. In such a case the want of repair is not in truth caused by wear and tear. Far the greater part of it is caused by the failure of the tenant to prevent what was originally caused by wear and tear from producing results altogether beyond what was so caused. On the other hand, take the gradual wearing away of a stone floor or staircase by ordinary use. This may in time produce a considerable defect in condition, but the whole of the defect is caused by reasonable wear and tear, and the tenant is not liable in respect of it.

Case 22 *Regis Property Co Ltd v Dudley* [1959] AC 370 House of Lords

The landlords of a block of flats in London applied to the county court to determine the increase of rent permissible under the Act in respect of one of the flats let unfurnished at an inclusive rent of £139 16s. 9d. a year, which, owing to an increase of rates, had been increased to £145 12s. 5d. The tenant's obligations to repair under the lease were to keep the interior of the flat in good and substantial repair and clean sanitary condition, fair wear and tear and damage by accidental fire excepted. The judge fixed the appropriate factor at 1⅔, holding that the liability of the landlords and of the tenant for repairs was about equal:

Held (1) (Lord Keith of Avonholm and Lord Denning dissenting) That the judge had not erred in principle in fixing the appropriate factor. Even though some items of repair might be made necessary by the act of the tenant for which he could be made liable at common law, yet, if he was also liable for it under the terms of the tenancy, he was to be regarded as responsible for it for the purpose of determining the appropriate factor, since the court was concerned only with his responsibility expressed by the terms of the tenancy. For the purpose of the determination a hypothetical tenant was to be assumed who was reasonably careful in his user of the premises, but that did not import a tenant who was never gulity of any act of negligence.

(2), (unanimously), That the judge did not err in crediting the tenant with more than a nominal amount in respect of his liability to repair, in view of the "fair wear and tear" exception. The exemption covered no more than the reme- dying of things which wear out in the course of reasonable use; if did not cover other damage which flowed from the wear and tear.

Lord Denning said (in part)

... The next question is what is the effect of the exception of "fair wear and tear" in a repairing covenant. I find myself in full agreement with what Talbot J. said on this subject in *Haskell v Marlow* [1928] 2 KB 45. I think the Court of Appeal in *Taylor v Webb* [1937] 2 KB 283 were wrong in overruling *Haskell v Marlow (supra)*. I have never understood that in an ordinary house a "fair wear and tear" exception reduced the burden of repairs to practically nothing at all. It exempts a tenant from liability for repairs that are decorative and for remedying parts that wear out or come adrift in the course of reasonable use, but it does not exempt him from anything else. If further damage is likely to flow from the wear and tear, he must do such repairs as are necessary to stop that further damage. If a slate falls off through wear and tear and in consequence the roof is likely to let through the water, the tenant is not responsible for the slate coming off but he ought to put in another one to prevent further damage.

2.6 Standard of repair

The standard of repair is the same throughout the term. One of the leading authorities on the subject is *Proudfoot v Hart* [1890] QB 42 [Case 11]. The matter was considered further in *Calthorpe v McOscar*.

Case 23 *Calthorpe v McOscar* [1924] 1 KB 716 Court of Appeal

A lease of three newly erected houses made in 1825 for a term of ninety-five years contained a covenant by the lessee in very wide terms, the effect of which was, put shortly, that he would during the term well and sufficiently repair the premises with all manner of necessary reparations and would yield up at the end of the term the said premises so being in all things well and sufficiently repaired.

At the end of the term the assignee of the reversion brought an action against the assignees of the lease for breach of the above covenant. By an order of the court the assessment of the damages was referred to an arbitrator. At the beginning of the term the houses were country houses; at the end of the term the only tenants likely to occupy the houses or parts of them would be tenants on short terms. The arbitrator assessed the damages at two alternatives sums. He computed the smaller sum on the basis that the defendants were liable to execute such repairs only as in view of the age, character, and locality of the premises would make them reasonably fit to satisfy the requirements of reasonably minded tenants of the class that would then be likely to occupy them. He found that tenants of this class would require only such repairs as would keep out wind and water:

Held (1) That this was not the proper measure of liability; but that the defendants were liable for the cost of doing all necessary acts well and sufficiently to repair the premises in the words of the covenant, that is to say, for the cost of putting them into that state of repair in which they would be found if they had been managed by a reasonably minded owner, having regard—to their age; (per Banks LJ); to their character and ordinary uses, or the requirements of tenants of the class likely to take them, at the time of the demise or at the commencement of the term; (per Atkin and Scrutton LJJ).

Scrutton LJ said (in part)

... In my view the matter can be dealt with as if the covenant were one to "keep and yield up at the end of the term in repair." I do not think there is any substantial difference in construction between "repair," which must mean "repair reasonably or properly" and "keep in good repair," or "sufficient repair" or "tenantable repair," or most of the various phrases cited to us. There is an analysis of the meaning of "repair" by Buckley LJ in *Lurcott v Wakely* [1911] 1 KB 905 with which, as far as it goes, I agree. The tenant must when necessary restore by reparation or renewal of subsidiary parts the subject matter demised to a condition in which it is reasonably fit for the purposes for which such a subject matter would ordinarily be used. The question in dispute seems to be whether, as the purposes for which such a subject matter is ordinarily used may vary from time to time, the standard of repair is to vary from time to time, or remains as it was when the subject matter was demised. For instance, where a fashionable mansion let for a long term of years has fallen to the position of a tenement house for the poorer classes, is the standard of repair to become less onerous than when the house is let? To take an illustration of Bankes LJ, if the sub-tenants of a tenement house do not want a front door, is the tenant to be excused from keeping a properly repaired front door on the premises?

In my view this question has been decided, as far as this court is concerned, by the decision in *Morgan v Hardy* (1886) 17 QBD 770. In that case the referee had to decide between the claim that the premises and the neighbourhood had deteriorated, and in consequence of such deterioration a great portion of the repairs required "were not suited to the said premises and were unnecessary for their use and enjoyment" they need not be considered in awarding damages. This court, affirming Denman J, said very summarily that it was a wholly untenable proposition to say that the depreciation of the neighbourhood ought to lower the amount of damages for breach of a covenant to repair. This can only mean that the fact that the class of persons who would use the house at the end of the term had deteriorated, so that their requirements in the way of repairs were less, was immaterial in ascertaining the repairs that the tenant was bound to execute. *Morgan v Hardy* was the case of a fifty years' lease.

In *Proudfoot v Hart* [1890] QB 42 the lease was for three years only, and the covenant was to keep in good tenantable repair. There was no suggestion of any change in character of the house or its probable tenants between the beginning and the end of the term. Lopes LJ framed a definition which Lord Esher adopted as follows:

> "Such repair, as having regard to the age, character, and locality of the house, would make it reasonably fit for the occupation of a reasonably-minded tenant of the class who would be likely to take it."

I do not think there was any intention of suggestion that a deterioration in the class of tenants would lower the standard or repairs; the point was not before the court, and had been decided the other way by the court four years previously. Therefore in my view we are bound to look to the character of the house and its ordinary uses at the time of the demise. It must then be put in repair and kept in repair. An improvement of its tenants or its neighbourhood will not increase the standard of repair, nor will their deterioration lower that standard.

2.7 Landlord's covenant: the requirement for notice

In those cases where the landlord has covenanted to repair part, or all, of the demised premises (or where statute implies such an obligation) it is a condition precedent of the landlord's liability that he has notice of the disrepair.

Case 24 O'Brien v Robinson [1973] 1 All ER 583 House of Lords

The first plaintiff was the lessee of a dwelling-house consisting of the basement and ground floor of a house which belonged to the defendant. The lease was one to which s. 32 of the Housing Act 1961 applied and in consequence, under s. 32 (1), there was implied in the lease a covenant that the defendant, as lessor, would keep the structure of the dwelling-house in repair. The first plaintiff and his wife, the second plaintiff, were in bed one night when the ceiling of their bedroom fell in causing them injuries. The fall was caused by a latent defect in the ceiling of which neither the plaintiffs nor the defendant were aware until the fall took place. The plaintiffs, contending that the defendant was in breach of his implied covenant to keep the structure of their dwelling-house in repair, brought an action against him in respect of the injuries and damage which they had suffered.

Held (1) Under the covenant implied by s. 32 of the 1961 Act a lessor's obligation to start carrying out any work of repair to premises occupied by his lessee did not arise until he had information about the existence of a defect in the premises such as would put a reasonable man on enquiry whether works of repair were needed. That was the case even where, because the defect was latent, the lessee was not in a position to bring it to the attention of the lessor. Accordingly, since the defendant had no knowledge of the defect in the ceiling he could not be held liable for the damage which the plaintiffs had sustained.

Lord Morris of Borth-y-Gest said (in part)

In *Morgan v Liverpool Corpn* [1927] 2 KB 131 one basis of claim was that there had been a failure to perform the statutory undertaking that the house would be 'kept in all respects reasonably fit for human habitation'. As I have shown, there was at that date a statutory right in a landlord to enter for the purposes of inspection. The accident which gave rise to the claim was that when the upper portion of a window was being opened one of the cords of the window sash broke with the result that the top part of the window slipped down and caught and injured the plaintiff's hand. In the argument on behalf of the plaintiff in the Court of Appeal it was admitted that the defect was a latent one (of which the plaintiff did not know and about which accordingly he could not give any notice) but it was contended that there was a statutory obligation on the landlord which was different from that contained in an ordinary covenant and that in the Act (Housing Act 1925) there were no words requiring that any notice should be given to the landlord. Furthermore reliance was placed on the statutory right of the landlord to enter and inspect. Apart from any such statutory right the facts of the case showed that there was a notice posted up in the house containing certain conditions which included a reservation by the landlord of the right of entering the house at any time without previous notice in order to view the state of repair. The Court of Appeal held that the landlord was not liable and that any liability was conditional on his having been given notice of any defects even though they were latent ones and that this result was not affected by the fact that the landlord had a right to enter in order to inspect. There were divisions of opinion on certain points which arose: in particular on the point whether by reason of the breaking of the sash cord the particular dwelling (which was most limited in size) was rendered unfit for human habitation. But all three Lords Justices were of the opinion that the claim failed because the landlord did not have notice and because in such a case as that under consideration notice was required before the liability of the landlord to repair existed. Lord Hanworth MR said that it had long been established that where there is a covenant on the part of a landlord to keep premises in repair the tenant must give notice to the landlord of what is out of repair. He held that notice was required whether or not the landlord had means of access; he said that the fact that the origin of a covenant was statutory did not give the covenant any higher authority than one inserted in a contract by the parties. Atkin LJ said that in ordinary circumstances the obligation of a landlord to do repairs does not come into existence until he has had notice of the defect which his contract to repair requires him to make good. He said:

> "I think the power of access that is given, extensive though it may be, does not take the case away from the principle

from which the courts have inferred the condition that the liability is not to arise except on notice. The position is quite a satisfactory one, because as soon as the tenant is aware of the defect he must then give notice, and if the landlord does not repair it, the landlord will be liable. If in fact the tenant is not able to ascertain the defect, there seems to be no reason why the landlord should be exposed to what remains still the same injustice of being required to repair a defect of which he does not know, which seems to me to be the real reason for the rule. This was a case in which notice was not given to the landlord. As I have said, it appears to me that, as soon as the defect became so known by the fall of the sash, the tenant was able to give notice to the landlord and did give notice. In my view the landlord then became under a liability to repair in the circumstances of this case, because if he did not, the house would be in a state not in all respects fit for human habitation; but as no notice was given, I think the landlord was not liable."

Lawrence LJ said:

"On the question of notice I am in complete agreement with the judgments delivered by the Master of the Rolls and Atkin LJ and have very little to add. In my opinion the established rule is that the obligation of the landlord to keep the premises in repair is not broken unless notice had been given to him of the want of repair, and that mere knowledge is not sufficient to saddle the landlord with liability. The foundation of such rule is that the tenant in occupation is generally in a far better position to know of any want of repair. I am further of opinion that for the reasons stated by Atkin LJ the rule applies to latent as well as to patent defects, and certainly applies to the defect which existed in the present case."

The decision in *Fisher v Walters* [1926] 2 KB 315 (a case where the defects in the ceiling were latent), which counsel for the landlord had submitted had gone too far, was not expressly mentioned in the judgments.

If the decision in *Morgan's* case is correct it would, I think, govern the present case. Although all three Lords Justices agreed as to the necessity for notice it did not become necessary for the court to decide whether such notice had to be given by the tenant of whether knowledge in the landlord of a necessity to do repairs or notice from some other source to him of such necessity would also suffice to create a liability in the landlord to do repairs. There was in that case neither notice to the landlord of the existence of the defective or broken sash-cord nor was there knowledge in the landlord of the state of affairs.

In *Summers v Salford Corpn* [1943] AC 283 a case came to this House in which the tenant did give notice to the landlord's agent that one sash-cord in the only window of a bedroom had broken. No repair was effected and about two months later the second sash-cord broke in circumstances causing injury to the tenant. The issue that arose was whether there was a breach by the landlord of the implied undertaking (see s. 2 (1) of the Housing Act 1936) that the house would be kept by the landlord during the tenancy in all respects fit for human habitation. In his speech Lord Atkin said:

> "In the present case the point upon which the Court of Appeal in *Morgan's* case decided for the defendant does not arise, viz., that notice of the lack of repair complained of must be given to the landlord before his statutory obligation arises. I can see that different considerations may arise in the case of an obligation to repair imposed in the public interest; and I think that this question must be left open, and I reserve to myself the right to reconsider my former decision if the necessity arises."

... Then in *McCarrick v Liverpool Corpn* [1947] AC 219 the question whether *Morgan's* case was correctly decided was presented for consideration in this House. The tenant's wife had fallen by reason of the defective condition of two stone steps leading from the kitchen to the back kitchen. The provisions of the Housing Act 1936 were applicable. It was held that the house was not kept in the state required by s. 2 of that Act. No notice of want of repair was given to the landlords. They had the statutory right of entry to view the state of the premises. The defects would appear to have been patent. The tenant could therefore be aware of them; so also could the landlords have been had they exercised their right of entry. It was argued that *Morgan's* case was wrongly decided, that the Housing Act 1936 contained no provision requiring notice, that the duty imposed on a landlord by the Act (particularly as he was given a right of entry to inspect) was absolute and was analogous to that imposed on a factory occupier by the Factories Acts, and that the effect of the legislation should not be minimised or neutralised by introducing notions inspired by the old law.

Very important questions of principle were therefore raised. The significant previous authorities were considered. It was held that the decision in *Morgan's* case was correct. Lord Thankerton said that the effect of s. 2 (1) of the 1936 Act was to incorporate the prescribed condition in the contract so that it became an integral part of it and the statutory origin of the condition did not differentiate it, in any question of construction, from any of the conventional stipulations in the contract: it followed, therefore, that a condition as to notice of the material defect (established by a long line of authority) fell to be implied. Lord Porter said that whatever view might have been taken of the section if no previous history lay behind it it had to be remembered that similar provisions in earlier Acts had been interpreted as only requiring the landlord to repair after notice: he considered that it was too late to reinterpret its meaning. That was in 1946. Since then there have been the Housing Act 1957, and the Act now being considered. Lord Simonds's speech was concurred in by Lord Thankerton and by Lord Macmillan; after reviewing the authorities he clearly held that the provision which the 1936 Act imported into the contract of tenancy fell to be construed in the same way as any other term would be construed and that the correct construction of the provision was that no obligation was imposed on the landlord unless and until he had notice of a particular defect. Lord Uthwatt said that it was an implied term (resulting from the comprehensiveness of the statutory term and the circumstances necessarily involved in the tenancy) that in a case where the tenant knows the defect and the landlord does not, the obligation to do a specific act directed to repairing the defect does not arise until at least the landlord becomes aware of the need for it.

The decision in *McCarrick's* case must have guided landlords and tenants in their business transactions in the years since 1946. Later legislation has followed. In my view, it would not be within the intendment of the power reserved in 1966 now to disturb a decision which as Lord Porter indicated was given in 1946 "finally to determine" the point first decided in *Morgan's* case in 1927 and then left open in *Summers's* case in 1943. The question does, however, arise whether the decision of this House in *McCarrick's* case governs the present appeal which concerns a latent defect.

In *McCarrick's* case the defects were there to be seen by the tenant. In the present case no defect was visible and so there was no visible defect to which the landlord's attention could be called. In *McCarrick's* case Lord Simonds said that the decision in *Fisher v Walters* could not stand and his speech was concurred in by Lord Thankerton and by Lord Macmillan. Lord Porter said that no question of the latency of the defect came in issue as it did in *Fisher v Walters* and that if it did the decision in that case would require to be "carefully scrutinized". Lord Uthwatt remarked that latent defects were not in question and he expressed no opinion as to their position.

Although there were these reservations, *Morgan's* case was approved and *Morgan's* case must, I think, be regarded as a case in which the defect was latent, even though some defects in a window sash-cord might be visible. I have cited above a passage from the judgment of Atkin LJ. He also said:

> "Here is a case of something which arose quite suddenly. It is possible that a very careful inspection of the window cords might have revealed the state in which they were, but there are many other defects which arise quite suddenly, leaks quite suddenly spring up in joints of water pipes and gas pipes, and so on, and to say that the landlord is responsible for the consequences of those not being in repair in circumstances in which no time could have elapsed between the time when the defect first arose and the time when the injury from it occurred, would certainly be to impose a very harsh obligation upon a landlord which the courts do not impose except subject to a condition that he must receive notice of the defect. To my mind in those circumstances it is clear that, if the landlord gives the exclusive occupation to the tenant, the landlord does not in fact know, and in this case could not know of the defect."

In my view, these and other parts of the judgment of Atkin LJ were based on the reasoning that it is only when defects (although previously latent or invisible) become patent and are made known to the landlord that his liability to repair arises. Furthermore, it seems to me that both the words of Lord Simonds and his reasoning in *McCarrick's* case show that a landlord's obligation to take action only arises when he had notice of a defect. He will not have notice if no one knows that there is a defect.

The question does not now arise for express decision whether a landlord's obligation to repair will arise not only when he receives notice from his tenant of a defect but also if he receives such notice aliunde or if he has knowledge of it: but I observe that in *Griffin v Pillett* [1926] 1 KB 17 where a lessee gave notice that steps to a dwelling-house needed attention but where the lessee did not know that the steps were in fact actually dangerous. Wright J held that a liability rested on the lessor when subsequently he, although not his lessee, did acquire knowledge that the steps were actually dangerous. The purpose of a notice is to impart knowledge that the moment for action under a covenant to repair has or may have arisen. If a lessor who is under an obligation to keep premises in repair acquires knowledge that there is a state of disrepair which may be dangerous then even if such knowledge is not shared by the lessee I would consider that there arises an obligation on the part of the lessor to take appropriate action.

Case 25 Uniproducts (Manchester) Ltd v Rose Furnishers Ltd
[1956] 1 WLR 45 Glyn-Jones J

Landlords covenanted to keep in good tenantable repair the roof, main structure and outside walls of a shop leased to the plaintiffs in February, 1953, for a term of five years. In June, 1953, the plaintiffs themselves carried out limited repairs to make safe the floorboards of a store room on the ground floor at the request of the local authority. On November 10, 1953, while the shop manager was standing on this floor it gave way and he was precipitated therefrom into the basement whereby he sustained serious injuries for which he was compensated by the plaintiffs. No notice of want of repair had been given to the landlords. In an action by the plaintiffs for breach of covenant in which they claimed an indemnity from the landlords to cover the compensation and the costs which they had paid to the shop manager:

Held (1) That although the landlords' covenant to keep in repair included a duty to repair any defect that existed when the premises were let, such obligation did not arise until they had notice thereof; and that as the landlords had not been given notice of the defect and the plaintiffs had not proved that they had actual knowledge of it, they were not in breach of their covenant.

Glyn-Jones J said (in part)

. . . that for a very long-time—certainly since *Makin v Watkinson* (1870) LR 6 Ex Cl 25—there has had to be read into a covenant by a lessor to keep premises in repair an implied condition that the lessor shall have notice of the want of repair before he can be called upon, under the covenant, to make it good.

[Counsel] I think, goes so far as to argue that every covenant by a landlord to keep the demised premises in repair must be read as if there were imported into it in unqualified terms an absolute provision that the landlord's obligation is not to have effect unless and until notice has been given to him by the tenant of the defect. This, I think, goes too far.

I bear in mind what was said in the speeches in the House of Lords in *Murphy v Hurley* [1922] 1 AC 369 to this effect: that the reason for the condition that the landlord must not be held liable unless he has had notice is that, since he is out of possession of the premises and the tenant is in possession of them, it would be wholly unreasonable, and indeed unrealistic, to hold the landlord liable for not having effected repairs if he did not know and could not know that the repairs needed doing. Certainly Lord Buckmaster and Lord Sumner, in their speeches in *Murphy v Hurley*, indicate that the principle laid down in *Makin v Watkinson* is not an absolute and unvarying rule such that every covenant by a landlord must be qualified by a proviso that he is not obliged to repair unless and until he has had notice from the tenant of the want of repair.

Lord Buckmaster, for instance said:

"The principle upon which notice is required to be given to a lessor requiring him to repair demised premises in accordance with his covenant before proceedings are taken to obtain damages for the breach is not inherent in the relationship between landlord and tenant. The doctrine depends upon the actual facts existing in each case and upon the consideration whether the circumstances are such that knowledge of what may be required to be done to comply with the covenant cannot reasonably be supposed to be possessed by one party while it is by the other."

Lord Sumner said:

"The rule requiring a notice of want of repair by the tenant to the landlord, in the case of an ordinary landlord's repairing covenant for dwelling-houses, warehouses and similar structures, is well settled, and no-one proposes to alter or restrict it. The nature and conditions of this rule are, however, equally well settled. As a rule of construction it reads into the covenant words—namely, 'upon notice'—which are not there, its application naturally depends on the existence of those strong circumstances, of necessity, which alone justify the implication of a condition upon an obligation, which is itself expressed unconditionally."

... I have, perhaps, begged the question whether or not a landlord is liable to put right, under a covenant to keep in repair, defects which existed at the time of the letting, which is sometimes expressed as being an obligation not only to keep in repair but also to put into repair. It is, of course, well settled, as is shown by the many cases which have been cited to me, that where a landlord undertakes to keep premises in repair he may not, when a notice is given of a defect, say: "That defect existed at the time when I let the premises. If you make me repair that, you will, in effect, be making me put the premises into repair and I have not covenanted to do so." If he has covenanted to keep premises in repair and notice is given to him of a defect, he is bound as a rule to repair that defect, whether it existed at the time of the original demise or has come since into existence.

That, in my opinion, is the sense in which a covenant by a landlord to keep in repair may be said to be a covenant to put into repair, and I reject [counsel's] argument that, merely because a covenant to keep in repair has been construed as requiring the landlord to put the premises into repair, in the sense that he is as well liable to repair defects which existed at the beginning of the lease as defects which have subsequently come into existence, the obligation to put the premises into repair by curing any defect existing at the start of the term rests upon the landlord at the moment the term begins to run, whether he has notice of the existence of the defect or not and even whether the defect is apparent or concealed. This means, I think, that [counsel] fails in his main contention. I am of opinion that, whether the defect existed at the beginning of the tenancy or not, the obligation of the lessors to repair it did not come into existence until they had notice, and it is conceded that no express notice of this defect was ever given to the lessors.

Note:

(i) In *Cove v Smith* (1886) 2 TLR 778 a lease contained a covenant by the lessee to repair within three months after notice. The lessor gave the lessee the required notice and before the expiration of the three months gave the lessee notice specifying the breach of covenant, requiring the same to be remedied, and compensation to be made, and threatening an action for recovery of possession in case of non-compliance. Wills J held that the second notice was valid under s. 14 of the Conveyancing Act 1881.

Case 26 *Griffin v Pillett* [1920] 1 KB 17 Wills J

In the lease of a dwelling-house the lessor covenanted to keep the exterior of the premises in good and substantial repair. During the currency of the term the lessee wrote to the lessor on April 2, 1924, that "the steps to the front door want attention." Thereupon the lessor communicated with his builders, who on April 8 inspected the premises and reported that "the front steps are in a dangerous condition, and being so defective we have put the matter in hand." The builders obtained an estimate for the work, and on April 16 the steps were repaired. In the meantime, however— namely, on April 14, while the lessee, who was unaware that the steps were dangerous, was leaving the house the steps collapsed and he fell into the cellar below sustaining serious injuries. In an action by the lessee to recover damages for breach of the lessor's covenant to repair:

Held (1) That the letter of April 2 was a sufficient notice of want of repair, although it did not specify the precise degree of non-repair;

(2) That even if that letter could not be relied upon as express notice of non-repair it gave the lessor a right of entry, and the actual knowledge of the condition of the steps acquired by him on April 8 through his agents the builders prevented him setting up the absence of express notice;

(3) That having actual knowledge on April 8 of the dangerous condition of the premises the lessor was bound to take immediate steps to render the premises temporarily safe if the permanent repairs could not be executed at once;

(4) That the lessor had committed a breach of covenant; and

(5) That the lessee having been injured owing to that breach was entitled to recover damages.

Wills J said (in part)

... In the present case the notice given by the letter of April 2 did not treat the non-repair as an urgent matter or a matter of danger, for the simple reason that the lessee was unaware that there was any danger. All that the letter said was that the steps required attention. In my opinion that notice was sufficient to put the lessor upon inquiry and to impose upon him the obligation of ascertaining the extent of the non-repair and of taking the necessary steps to remedy the defect ...

... In the present case there was not only actual knowledge on the part of the lessor, but actual knowledge acquired by a notice from the lessee drawing attention to the fact that a certain part of the structure required attention. Coupled with that, the lessor had a right of entry to examine into the condition of the premises and to do necessary repairs. The difficulty does not therefore seem to me to exist in this case, and I hold as a matter of law, if it be necessary in the circumstances, and assuming that the letter of April 2 cannot be relied upon by the lessee as

express notice of non-repair, that the actual knowledge acquired
by the lessor of the non-repair prevents him on the facts of the
case setting up in answer to the lessee's claim the answer that
express notice of the actual non-repair was not given to him.

Case 27 *Melles v Holme* [1918] 2 KB 100 Salter J

By a lease dated June 24, 1915, the defendants, who were
the owners of a house in Wood Street, Liverpool, demised
the front rooms on the first and second floors of the house
for a term of seven years to the plaintiffs, who carried on
business as dealers in artificial flowers, feathers, and millinery goods. The plaintiffs covenanted that they would use
the demised rooms "only as store or show rooms for the
safe keeping exhibition and sale of goods dealt in by them
in their business." and the defendants covenanted that they
would during the term "keep the outside of the demised
premises and the roof and walls and drains thereof other
than those within the demised rooms in good and tenantable
condition." The top floor was let by the defendants to one
Collinson, a bootmaker, and there was access to the roof
from his premises. On the roof was a parapet wall, and
between the parapet and the sloping roof was a gutter for
carrying off the rainwater. The defendants retained in their
own hands the control of the roof. The downflow pipe from
the gutter became choked, whereby the rainwater rose in
the gutter, flowed down through the roof into the plaintiffs'
premises, and damaged their goods. Inside the pipe which
was stopped up were found, in addition to a small quantity
of ashes, a piece of felt sock from the inside of a boot, some
string, pieces of leather, and a cork lining; and it was suggested that these latter things had been thrown into the
gutter by Collinson's workmen. The plaintiffs sued the
defendants in the county court for breach of their covenant
to keep the roof in good and tenantable condition. The
defendants had received no notice of the defective condition
of the gutter previously to the occurrence of the damage
complained of. They had caused the roof to be inspected
once a quarter. The county court judge found that, apart
from the block caused by the intrusion of foreign matter,
the gutters were in good and tenantable condition, and that
there had been no want of care on the part of the defendants.
He held that if the blocking of the gutter amounted to a
want of tenantable condition within the meaning of the covenant notice to the lessors of the defective condition was

necessary, and in the absence of such notice he gave judgment for the defendants. The plaintiffs appealed.

Held (1) The rule that a landlord who has covenanted with his tenant to keep the premises in tenantable condition is not liable for damage caused to the tenant by the condition of the premises becoming defective unless he had express notice of it has no application to a case in which he demises only a portion of the premises and retains in his own control the portion the defective condition of which causes the damage.

Salter J said (in part)

... I think the matter turns on the express terms of the covenant. It is not necessary to determine whether there also exists an implied covenant to maintain the roof in any particular condition. If such an implied covenant exists, its terms cannot be wider than those of the express covenant. It is said that the plaintiffs cannot enforce that covenant because they gave no notice of the breach. In some cases no doubt there must be read into a covenant by a landlord to repair a condition that the tenant must give him notice of the want of repair before he can be entitled to complain of it. The principle of that rule is thus laid down by Bramwell B in *Makin v Watkinson* (1870) LR 6 Ex 25:

> "When a thing is in the knowledge of the plaintiff, but cannot be in the knowledge of the defendant, but the defendant can only guess or speculate about the matter, then notice is necessary,"

This was also put very clearly by Collins MR in *Tredway v Machin* (1904) 91 LT 310.

> "That rule rests upon the principle that the landlord is not the occupier of the premises, and has no means of knowing what is the condition of the premises unless he is told, because he has no right of access to the demised premises, whereas the occupier has the best means of knowing of any want of repair."

To justify the court in reading into a covenant a condition which is not there, there must be very strong ground for their doing so. Here there are no such grounds. The roof was in the possession and control of the defendants, not of the plaintiffs. Therefore there is no justification for saying that they cannot enforce the covenant in the absence of notice. It only remains to consider whether there was a breach of the covenant to maintain the roof

in a good and tenantable condition. Whether the obstruction
of the downflow pipe amounted to a breach of the covenant
depends upon what was the intention of the parties. When considering that one must bear in mind the purpose of the lease and
the consequent necessity of keeping the demised rooms free from
damp. It must have been contemplated by the defendants that
their obligation under the covenant included the scouring of the
gutter and the keeping the passage of the downflow pipe at
all times free. The defendants having failed to do that were in
my opinion guilty of a breach of the covenant, and the judgment
should have been for the plaintiffs for the amount of the damages
which were found by the judge.

Case 28 Sheldon v West Bromwich Corporation (1973) 25 P & CR 360 Court of Appeal

While investigating complaints by the tenant of a council
house of noises in the water pipes the defendant corporation
discovered that the cold water tank, which was some thirty
to forty years old, was discoloured, though it was not "weeping." They did nothing by way of repair or replacement.
Subsequently, the tank burst, doing damage, and the tenant
brought an action against the corporation alleging breach
of their implied covenant under section 32 (1) of the Housing
Act 1961 to keep the installation for the supply of water
in repair. The county court judge, who heard evidence to
the effect that the discoloration of the tank must have existed
for some years but that it was unusual for a water tank
to burst without first weeping, held that the discoloration
of the tank had not, in the absence of weeping, indicated
that immediate repair was required, and he dismissed the
tenant's action.

On appeal by the tenant:

Held (1) Allowing the appeal, that in view of the time
for which discoloration had existed in this old tank it had
required to be repaired or replaced by the corporation as
soon as they had had notice of the state of discoloration
and, possibly, decay in the metal which it had reached at
the time of their inspection.

Stephenson LJ said (in part)

The question in this case is, I think, a narrow one. On the
admitted facts, was the condition of this tank as regards discoloration on May 28, 1970, such a condition of disrepair as to put
the landlord upon inquiry as to whether works of repair were

needed—in other words, as to require repair, not immediately, not the next day, but within a reasonable time, and within a reasonable time short of the six weeks which elapsed before this tank in fact burst.

I have come to the conclusion that, on the whole of the evidence, the landlords, the defendants, ought, by their plumber who carried out this inspection of the tank on May 28, 1970, to have realised that this tank required repair before July 8. This was an old tank. The evidence of Mr Harper (witness) was that it must have been as old as the house, which was nearly forty years old, that he would expect the life of one of these tanks to be fifty to sixty years but that some tanks started to corrode after twenty years. His evidence was that inspection would not have revealed corrosion, only discoloration. His evidence also was that before a tank burst it usually started to weep, though it is quite true that in cross-examination (as so often happens) he strengthened that and said that a tank which was going to burst would always weep first. But he also made it plain that "weeping comes about" (as he put it) "because a hole has been made."

What the argument for the defendants amounts to is that there is no obligation, in accordance with the statutory covenant, upon a landlord to carry out any repairs to a discoloured tank unless a hole had actually been made so that weeping has begun. Mr Cartwright (witness) the plumber called for the defendants, agreed with Mr Harper that a tank which burst without weeping was unusual, if not unique. He considered this tank to be at least thirty years old and expressed the opinion that there had been discoloring on it "for some years"; that, as I have pointed out, must mean at least two and a half to three years since the first complaints were made about the water hammer. Contrary to the opinion of Mr Harper, he added that there must have been visible some sign of metal decay as well as discolouring. He had known tanks to weep for three months before bursting, and Mr Harper seemed to think that a tank might weep "maybe for a month," from which I conclude that he regarded that as perhaps the maximum time for which one would expect a tank to weep before it became really dangerous.

I have come to the conclusion that the absence of weeping is not fatal to the plaintiff's case. In my judgment, the time for which discoloration had existed in this aging tank did mean that it required to be repaired by the landlords as soon as they had knowledge of the state of discoloration and, possibly, decay in the metal which it had reached by May 28.

It is, of course, extremely difficult to look at the position on May 28 without bearing in mind what happened on July 8. But, in all the circumstances, it does not seem to me to be putting a strained construction upon the statutory covenant or too heavy a burden on the landlords, on the admitted facts of this case, to say that they were bound to take action although there was no weeping and to put this tank in repair, either by re-lining it or by replacing it—there was no evidence about what would be required but I suspect that it would have required a new tank—once it had reached the state in which, on the evidence, it was by May 28.

2.8 Implied right to enter and carry out repairs

Where a landlord has the obligation to repair the premises he has an implied licence to enter to undertake the repairs. This implied licence is also applicable to the carrying out of works under the implied covenant under the Landlord and Tenant Act 1985.

Case 29 *Saner v Bilton* (1878) 7 ChD 815 Fry J

In a lease of a newly constructed grain warehouse there was a covenant by the lessor that he would during the term "keep the main walls and main timbers of the warehouse in good repair and condition." The lessee entered under the lease and stored grain in it, in (as the court held upon the evidence) a reasonable and proper way. After a short time a beam which supported one of the floors broke, and ultimately the external walls sank and bulged outwards, and the lessor spent a large sum in repairing the premises.

The lease contained a proviso that, in case the warehouse, or any part thereof, should at any time during the term "be destroyed or damaged by fire, flood, storm, tempest, or other inevitable accident," the rent, or a just proportion thereof, should cease or abate so long as the premises should continue wholly or partly untenantable or unfit for use or occupation in consequence of such destruction or damage. During the period in which the lessor was executing the repairs the lessee was excluded from the use and occupation of the whole or a part of the premises, and he claimed an abatement of rent under the proviso:

Held (1) That the lessee had not been guilty of waste:

(2) That the lessor was bound under his covenant to put the walls and main timbers in good repair, having regard

to the class of buildings to which the warehouse belonged, and not merely to the condition of the particular building:

(3) That the covenant implied a license by the tenant to the landlord to enter upon the premises for a reasonable time for the purposes of executing the necessary repairs.

(4) That the words "inevitable accident" imported something *ejusdem generis* with what had been previously mentioned, and did not apply to that which, though not avoidable so far as the lessee was concerned, was not in its nature inevitable, but resulted from the default of the lessor, and that the lessee was not entitled to an abatement of rent.

Fry J said (in part)

It is said that if the building was used in any manner which produced injury, although that user might have been a proper and reasonable user of the class of tenement to which the building belonged, nevertheless, if it produced the destruction of the tenement or a serious injury to its stability, waste was committed. It appears to me that this proposition is a very serious one, and cannot be maintained without great difficulty. It would be a very serious thing to hold that if a man chooses to construct a house in such a flimsy manner as that the moment, for instance, a bedstead is put up in it the timbers give way, and the house comes down, that coming down of the house resulting from the putting into it of the ordinary furniture required for its occupation would be, on the part of the tenant, waste. Yet the argument of the plaintiff's counsel has gone to that extent. It is admitted that no authority can be produced for the proposition, but reliance is placed upon the general expressions in which waste has been defined, such as anything which leads to the destruction of the tenement. If it were necessary for me to determine the point, I should be prepared to hold that no user of a tenement which is reasonable and proper, having regard to the class to which it belongs, is waste. But it is not necessary now to determine that question, because there is in the present case an express covenant by the lessor that he will during the term "keep the main walls and main timbers of the warehouse in good repair and condition." Upon that I make two observations. The first is that, in my judgment, the covenant obliges the lessor to put the main walls and main timbers into good repair and condition, if they were in bad condition when the lessee took the warehouse. The second is this, that the question, what is "good repair and condition," is to be viewed having regard to the class to which the demised tenement belongs, and not with regard to that tenement itself alone. If it were not so, I should be landed in this absurdity. Assuming that the main walls and main timbers were in bad repair when the lessee took the warehouse, and assuming that the "good repair" is to be construed with regard to the particular subject-matter, good would mean bad, and the covenant to keep in good repair would be satisfied by keeping the tenement in bad repair. Not only is that opposed to common sense, but, if authority were necessary, it is opposed to the decision in *Payne v Haine* (1847) 16 M & W 541, where it was held with regard to a house in bad condition, that a covenant to keep it in good condition required that it should be put into good condition, which would not be the case if the covenant were read with reference to the condition of the demised tenement itself.

Weighing the evidence as best I can, I come distinctly to the conclusion that the defendant did use the warehouse in a reasonable and proper manner. Nay, I go further, and say that I believe he attended with great propriety to suggestions made by the Plaintiff that the danger was caused by the manner in which he was loading, and did his best to load rather lightly than over much.

If I were bound to come to a conclusion on this conflicting evidence, I should find for the defendant and not for the plaintiff. It is enough, however, for me to say that, reviewing the whole of the evidence, and having given to it the best attention I can, I have come to the conclusion that the injury which the building has sustained may well be attributed to other causes than an improper user by the defendant, and I cannot come to the conclusion that the defendant has used it improperly.

The result is, that the plaintiff, having taken upon himself the burden of showing that the defendant has, by his mode of using the warehouse, committed waste, has in my judgment failed to support the burden, and consequently his action must be dismissed with costs.

There remain two other questions which are raised by the counter-claim. The first of them arises in this way: The plaintiff has done extensive repairs, the execution of which has occupied a considerable time. The result was that for four months the defendant could not take any goods into the warehouse; and besides that, portions of the warehouse which the defendant would otherwise have used, were for a further period occupied by the plaintiff's workmen, and the warehouse therefore could not receive the defendant's goods, and for this he claims an abatement of rent under the proviso in the lease. He says that the injury so happening to the building was an inevitable accident within the meaning of the proviso, and consequently that he is entitled to an abatement of the rent.

Now it is to be observed that the words "inevitable accident" are coupled with the word "other," which seems to show to some extent that they are to be construed by the rule of *ejusdem generis*, that is, the inevitable accident pointed at is one of a kind similar to "flood, fire, storm, or tempest," referred to in the earlier words. In my opinion, the injury sustained by the building was not an inevitable accident within the meaning of those words. I think that the words do not apply to anything arising from the acts or defaults of either of the contracting parties. Those acts and defaults were made the subject of express covenant. I think the words do not apply to things existing at the time of the contract, or to the natural result of things existing, which were known or might have been known to the contracting parties, and further than that, it is obvious from the very words that they do not apply to a thing which is evitable or avoidable. It is to be an "inevitable accident," but here the accident, according to the defendant's own case, might have been avoided if the building had been properly constructed, and consequently it was not an "inevitable accident." It is said that "inevitable accident" includes that which was not evitable by the acts of the defendant. I do not think that is the real meaning. The clause is, I think, intended to apply to matters outside the existing state of things, and outside the acts and defaults of the contracting parties. That being so, I determine that the defendant is not entitled to any abatement of rent in respect of the occupation of the warehouse by the plaintiff for the execution of the repairs.

The second question is this: it is said that, over and above that loss, the defendant has been put to other loss in consequence of the occupation of this warehouse for the repairs done by the plaintiff, and that he is entitled to be paid for it. It is to be borne in mind that there is an express covenant that the lessor shall keep in good repair and condition the main walls and the main timbers. I have construed that covenant to mean that he shall put them into good condition if necessary, and in my judgment that covenant carries with it an implied license to the lessor to enter upon the premises of the lessee, and to occupy them for a reasonable time to do that which he had covenanted to do, and which he has not only covenanted to do, but which he has a right to do, because he has an interest in being allowed to perform his covenant. It is said that the time occupied was reasonable, but of that I have no evidence. It is further said that the construction of the covenant, as carrying with it an implied license to enter, is inconsistent with the lessor's covenant for quiet enjoyment. I do not think it is, and for this reason, that the covenant for quiet enjoyment, if read as absolutely unqualified, is as inconsistent with an entry on the warehouse for a single moment as it is with an occupation for a month or a year. The mere sending a man in to do the repairs would be a technical breach of the covenant, if it was construed as absolute and unconditional. But that, in my opinion, is a thing which the plaintiff has a clear right to do, for otherwise he could not perform that which he has covenanted to do. Therefore I think the covenant for quiet enjoyment must be read as subject to the license which I have held to be implied in the covenant to repair.

Case 30　Edmonton Borough Council v W H Knowles & Son Ltd (1962) 60 LGR 124

By a lease dated 2nd September, 1954, a local authority, landlords of an industrial estate, leased a factory to a company. Under the lease the company covenanted, *inter alia*, by clause 2 (4),

"To pay to the council the cost (as certified by the borough architect for the time being) of painting in a workmanlike manner every third year of the term all outside wood and metal work and other external parts of the demised premises and any addition thereto heretofore or usually painted."

The local authority did not expressly reserve for itself the right of entry although it had done so in respect of other terms in the lease. In September, 1957, the authority, by its employees, entered the premises and painted the exterior. The company refused to pay the sum certified by the borough architect on the grounds that it was excessive and the matter was referred to arbitration. The company denied that the painting was carried out under the terms of the lease, and counterclaimed for damages for trespass. The arbitrator found that the company was liable to pay the sum certified by the borough architect, that there was an implied right for the authority to enter the premises for the purpose of painting and that the company was not entitled to damages for trespass. The company moved to set aside the award on the grounds that there was an error of law on its face in the finding that the authority had an implied licence to enter the premises, and that the arbitrator had not dealt with all the matters referred to him for decision.

Held, Dismissing the motion, (1) that, on the true construction of clause 2 (4), having regard to the company's express obligation to pay to the authority the cost of repairs, there was an implied obligation on the local authority to paint the premises and, of necessity, a licence to enter the premises so to do must be implied.

(2) That, although the arbitrator had not stated in terms that there had been no trespass or that the sum claimed was reasonable, in finding that the company was liable in the sum claimed, he was clearly adjudicating against the company's claims that there had been a trespass and that the cost was unreasonable. Accordingly, the motion must be dismissed.

McNair J said (in part)

The argument starts with an invocation of Coke from Justice Windham's Case, 5 Co Rep 7, at p. 8: "that the grant shall be taken more strong against the grantor, and shall take effect as near as may be according to the intent of the parties." Throughout the cases one finds the reference again and again to "the intent of the parties." The positive high water-mark of the applicants' case is to be found in *Suffield v Brown* (1864) 34 De GJ & S 185, where one finds in the judgment of Lord Westbury, this passage. "It seems to me more reasonable and just to hold that if the grantor intends to reserve any right over the property granted, it is his duty to reserve it expressly in the grant, rather than to limit and cut down the operation of a plain grant (which is not pretended to be otherwise than in conformity with the contract between the parties), by the fiction of an implied reservation." That is the general rule which has been acted upon, and it is suggested before me that it is really only subject to two limitations as illustrated by the cases, the first limitation being that expressed by Fry J in *Saner v Bilton* (1878) 7 ChD 815, which was in fact stated to be authority for the exception to the rule stated in *Suffield v Brown* (*supra*), and where it was said that a right of entry might be implied where there was an express covenant that the lessee shall keep in good repair and condition the "main walls and timbers." Fry J said:

"In my judgment that covenant carries with it an implied license to the lessor to enter upon the premises of the lessee, and to occupy them for a reasonable time."

I do not understand that judgment as in any way intending to say that that was the only exception from *Suffield v Brown* (*supra*), or indeed to say that it is essential, even for this purpose, that there should be an express covenant. There was in the instant case an express covenant, but, if Fry J had been able to find on a proper construction of the lease an implied covenant, I think his conclusion of the implied licence would equally follow.

The second exception is to be found in *Mint v Good* [1951] 1 KB 517 where Somervell LJ was prepared to hold that there was in a weekly tenancy an implied reservation of a right of entry, and it was said that that exception was based upon the fact that it was indeed an implied tenancy. Again, I do not think that is the point of the case. I think that that case, as indeed was the case to which I shall subsequently refer is merely an illustration of this, that, although in dealing with a lease the court will proceed with caution in implying terms not expressed, it is permissible and indeed right for them to imply such terms where the ordinary common law principles which govern the condition of implied terms can be fulfilled.

In *Sandom v Webb* [1951] 1 Ch 808, a case dealing with the alleged implied reservation by the lessor of a right to exhibit advertisements on the wall of the demised premises, Lord Evershed MR gave quite an elaborate review of the the the cases, including *Suffield v Brown* (*supra*), and came to the conclusion at the end that it had not been proved on the evidence that there was such a common intention of the parties as would justify the implication of a term such as the landlords asked for. I think it is clear throughout his judgment that he proceeds on the basis that, if the true construction of the document in the light of the circumstances surrounding it does show a sufficient common intention to justify the implication of a term which is absent from the written words, that term will be implied. Lord Evershed MR said:

"If the court were satisfied that, in order to make the transaction between landlord and tenant sensible and effective according to its terms, they must have intended some particular right to be reserved to the landlord, it might be possible to imply an appropriate reservation."

That seems to me to state, if I may say so with respect, with precision the circumstances in which, on ordinary *Moorcock* principles (1889) 14 PD 64, the term may be implied. In the same case I find in the judgment of Jenkins LJ a statement to the effect that the exceptions to the rule in *Suffield v Brown (supra)*, are not limited to the well-known exceptions but may extend to further matters where some implication is necessary in order to give proper effect to the common intention of the parties.

Note:
  (i) The landlord's remedy of entering and carrying out the repairs is considered in Chapter 6.

3 REPAIR—RENEWAL—IMPROVEMENT

3.1 Repair—renewal—improvement dichotomy

The meaning of "repair" in a repairing covenant is of critical importance in determining the rights and liabilities under such a covenant. When such a word or phrase is called into question it is a matter of the proper construction of the covenant in the light of the factual matrix. The distinction between "repair" and "renewal" has been considered by the courts on many occasions with differing conclusions.

Case 31 Lister v Lane and Nesham [1893] 2 QB 212 Court of Appeal

> The plaintiffs granted to the defendants a lease of a house in Lambeth, containing a covenant by the lessees that they would "when and where and as often as occasion shall require, well, sufficiently, and substantially, repair, uphold, sustain, maintain, amend and keep" the demised premises, and the same "so well and substantially repaired, upheld, sustained, maintained, amended and kept", at the end of the term yield up to the lessors. Before the end of the term one of the walls of the house was bulging out, and after the end of the term the house was condemned by the district surveyor as a dangerous structure and was pulled down. The plaintiffs sought to recover from the defendants the cost of rebuilding the house. The evidence showed that the foundation of the house was a timber platform, which rested on a boggy or muddy soil. The bulging of the wall was caused by the rotting of the timber. The house was at least 100 years old, and possibly much older. The solid gravel was seventeen feet below the surface of the mud. There was evidence that the wall might have been repaired during the term by means of underpinning:
>
> *Held* (1) That the defect having been caused by the natural operation of time and the elements upon a house the original construction of which was faulty, the defendants were not under their covenant liable to make it good.

Lord Esher MR said (in part)
   ... You have to consider not only what the damage is—what
is the amount of repair required—but also whether the covenant
has been broken. That I take to be the right rule, and it is derived
partly from the summing-up of Tindal, CJ, in *Gutteridge v
Munyard* (1834) 7 C & P 129 which is always cited on this point.
The learned Chief Justice said:

> "Where a very old building is demised, and the lessee enters
> into a covenant to repair, it is not meant that the old building
> is to be restored in a renewed form at the end of the term
> or of greater value than it was at the commencement of the
> term. What the natural operation of time flowing on effects,
> and all that the elements bring about in diminishing the value,
> constitute a loss which, so far as it results from time and nature,
> falls upon the landlord".

   You have then to look at the condition of the house at the
time of the demise, and, amongst other things, the nature of
the house—what kind of a house it is. If it is a timber house,
the lessee is not bound to repair it by making a brick or a stone
house. If it is a house built upon wooden piles in soft ground,
the lessee is not bound to take them out and to put in concrete
piles. . . .
   Those cases seem to me to show that, if a tenant takes a house
which is of such a kind that by its own inherent nature it will
in course of time fall into a particular condition, the effects of
that result are not within the tenant's covenant to repair. However large the words of the covenant may be, a covenant to
repair a house is not a covenant to give a different thing from
that which the tenant took when he entered into the covenant.
He has to repair that thing which he took; he is not obliged
to make a new and different thing, and, moreover, the result
of the nature and condition of the house itself, the result of
time upon that state of things, is not a breach of the covenant
to repair.

Kay LJ said (in part)
   In construing such a covenant, regard must be had to the character and condition of the demised property, and, assuming that
this covenant is, as has been argued, expressed in the largest
terms, that it is a covenant to keep in repair and to put in repair,
still *Payne v Haine* (1847) 16 M & M 541 shows that regard must
be had to the character of the house to which the covenant
applies. Here the house was built upon a timber structure laid
upon mud, the solid gravel being seventeen feet below the timber

structure, and the only way in which the effect of time upon the house could be obviated is, according to the surveyor's evidence, by "underpinning" the house. That was the only way to repair it during the tenancy. "Underpinning," as I understand, means digging down through the mud until you reach the solid gravel, and then building up from that to the brickwork of the house. Would that be repairing, or upholding, or maintaining the house? To my mind, it would not; it would be making an entirely new and different house. It might be just as costly to underpin as to pull the house down and rebuild it. No one says, as I judge from the evidence, that you could repair the house by putting in a new timber foundation. The only way, as the surveyor says, to repair it is by this underpinning. That would not be either repairing, or upholding, or maintaining such a house as this was when the lessee took it, and he is not liable under his covenant for damage which accrued from such a radical defect in the original structure.

Case 32 *Wright v Lawson* [1903] WN 108 Court of Appeal

The action was brought by a lessor against a lessee upon a covenant contained in a lease, dated the 24th of February, 1888, of a house and shop in King's Road, Fulham. The covenant was that the lessee

"will, during the said term, when, where, and as often as occasion shall require, and to the satisfaction of the lessor, or her surveyor, for the time being, substantially and effectually repair, uphold, maintain, drain, paint, whitewash, and cleanse the premises for the time being held under this demise."

And there was a further covenant by the lessee to deliver up the premises, at the end of the term, in a condition in accordance with the covenant. On the first floor of these premises there was a bay window, which developed cracks and other symptoms of dilapidation. On the 30th of June, 1900, the defendant was served with a "dangerous structure notice," on behalf of the London County Council, under the London Buildings Acts, 1894 and 1898, to take down or otherwise secure the brickwork of the external walls and bay window, so far as cracked, bulged, loose, sunk, overhanging, out of upright, or otherwise defective; also to shore up the bay window and arch over the back door immediately. The defendant thereupon instructed his builder to comply with the notice, and the window was taken down; and it being impossible, owing to the house being old and badly built, to re-erect the window in the same way in which it was before without its being condemned as dangerous by the county council, the defendant built a new window set back in the main wall of the house. The plaintiff by this action asked that the defendant might be ordered to restore the premises to the condition in which they were when the lease was granted, by replacing the bay window. The evidence showed that practically a new bay window, such as would satisfy the requirements of the county council, could only be erected by supporting it by two columns from the ground to the window; or, at any rate, that supports of a substantial character would be required.

Kekewich J gave judgment for the defendant with costs. His Lordship was of opinion that the defendant was not liable to replace the bay window, since it was impossible to do so consistently with the requirements of the London County Council. His Lordship did not think that erecting a new bay window supported by columns could be regarded as the repair of the old bay window. It would be erecting a new bay window of a totally different character. The defendant had really been prevented from performing his covenant by *vis major* in the shape of the London County Council. The plaintiff appealed.

Held (1) The tenant was not liable to replace the bay window since it was impossible to do so consistently with the requirements of the London County Council.

(2) Erecting a new bay window with columns could not be regarded as repair of the old bay window.

Vaughan Williams LJ said (in part)
It was only necessary to take the words of Lord Esher in *Lister v Lane and Nesham*, [1893] 2 QB 212, 216, where his Lordship, after referring to certain authorities, said this:

"Those cases seem to me to show that, if a tenant takes a house which is of such a kind that by its own inherent nature it will in course of time fall into a particular condition, the effects of that result are not within the tenant's covenant to repair."

That was clearly applicable to this case. Having regard to the nature and condition of the house as found by Kekewich J from the evidence given at the trial, it was impossible to come to any other conclusion than that the learned judge was perfectly right, both upon the law and upon the facts. Accordingly this appeal must be dismissed, with costs.

Case 33 *Torrens v Walker* [1906] 2 Ch 166 Warrington J

In 1890 the three upper storeys of a house in London were demised to the lessee for a term of eighteen years from March 25, 1890, at a rent of £150. The lessor covenanted to keep the outside of the demised premises in good and substantial repair. The lessee covenanted to keep the inside in repair, to permit the lessor to enter and view the state of repair, and to use the premises for the business of a private hotel-keeper. In 1905 the plaintiff was the assignee of this lease and the defendant was the owner of the reversion. On July 13, 1905, the London Country Council served on the premises a notice requiring the owner to take down the front and back walls of the house as being dangerous structures. The plaintiff at once communicated this notice to the defendant and required him to repair the walls. The defendant did nothing, and the London County Council themselves took down the walls from the first floor upwards, propped up the floors with timber, and left the place uninhabitable.

The plaintiff brought this action against the defendant for breach of the covenant to keep the outside in repair. The defendant had no notice before July 13, 1905, of any want of repair. At that date the house, which was about 200 years old, had by the natural effect of time become so worn out and decayed that it was impossible to repair it except by taking it down and rebuilding:

Held (1) That there had been no breach of the lessor's covenant to repair.

(2) A covenant by a lessor to keep the outside walls of the demised premises in repair will be construed as a covenant to repair on notice, and there can be no breach of such a covenant until the lessor has notice of want of repair.

(3) The principles of construction which have been applied to lessees' covenants to repair apply equally to similar covenants by lessors. Regard must be had to the age and condition of the buildings to which the covenant refers. A lessor is not bound by such a covenant to rebuild during the term of the lease premises which have at the date at which he receives notice become worn out by age, and, merely from the action of time on the materials used, been reduced to a state in which repair is impossible.

Warrington J said (in part)

... It will be sufficient to take the law from *Lister v Lane* [1893] 2 QB 212. I admit there is some difference between that case and this, but the principles there laid down substantially govern the law I have to apply. Lord Esher says,

> " 'These cases establish that, when there is a general covenant to repair, the age and general condition of the house at the commencement of the tenancy are to be taken into consideration in considering whether the covenant has been broken; and that a tenant who enters upon an old house is not bound to leave it in the same state as if it were a new one.'

You have to consider not only what the damage is—what is the amount of repair required—but also whether the covenant has been broken. That I take to be the right rule, and it is derived partly from the summing up of Tindal CJ in *Gutteridge v Munyard* (1834) 7 C & P 129, which is always cited on this point. The learned Chief Justice said:

> "Where a very old building is demised, and the lessee enters into a covenant to repair, it is not meant that the old building is to be restored in a renewed form at the end of the term, or of greater value than it was at the commencement of the term. What the natural operation of time flowing on effects, and all that the elements bring about in diminishing the value, constitute a loss, which, so far as it results from time and nature, falls upon the landlord.' "

The judgment of Cave J in *Proudfoot v Hart* (1890) 25 QBD 42 is much to the same effect. He says:

> "So with regard to the walls, the floor, the doors, the windows, and all the different parts of the house, the tenant is bound where there is a breakage—whether arising from his own family or from some external accident—to repair it to the best of his ability; but he is never bound, when a portion of the structure has become absolutely worn out and necessary to be replaced, to substitute a new structure in the place of it. All that he undertakes to do is to patch the thing up so long as it is, in the nature of things, right and reasonable that the thing should be patched up. But, where it has got to such a state that patching up is of no avail—and we all know that things do at last get to that state—then the tenant is not bound to put in anything new, or to pay any proportion of the cost of putting in the new thing, because the old one has become unfit to discharge its duty."

Both those cases were decided on the liability of the lessee in respect of a lessee's covenant, and it is contended that they do not apply to a covenant by the lessor. But, in my judgment, there is no difference in principle. If the lessee is not bound to give back to the lessor at the end of the term a different thing from that which was demised to him, neither, in my judgment, is the lessor bound, by a similar covenant, to give to the lessee during the term a different thing from that which the lessee took from him at the beginning of his tenancy. If that distinction is unsound, every word of Lord Esher's judgment in *Lister v Lane* (*supra*) applies to the present case, and to the state of this house on July 13, 1903. The house had got to the state described by Cave J in the passage I have read when patching up was of no avail. It had by its own inherent nature fallen into the condition in which it was then found to be. Then repairs were impossible, and it was necessary to rebuild the front wall and the greater part of the back wall, to do which was not within the lessor's covenant.

It is said I must put *Lister v Lane* (*supra*) out of account, because the state of the building in that case was stated to have arisen from faulty construction. That is true, and probably the collapse happened sooner than it would have done if the construction had been different. But in this case also the state of the house was the result ultimately of faulty construction. Houses can be built so as to last considerably more than 200 years without becoming dangerous. But the state of this house resulted from the effect of time upon the materials used, and the method of construction adopted. So in this respect also *Lister v Lane* (*supra*) is an authority in the defendant's favour. It is said that this construction will inflict great hardship upon the lessee. But to construe the covenant the other way would inflict an equal hardship on the lessor. I must put aside all questions of hardship, and can only look at the legal construction of the covenant.

Case 34 *Gutteridge v Munyard* (1834) 7 C & P 129 Tindal CJ

The tenant of the demised premises covenanted to "well and sufficiently repair, uphold, support, maintain, glaze . . . and keep the said messuage or tenement . . . in, by, and with all and all manner of needful and necessary reparations . . ." The landlord alleged that the tenant wrongfully suffered and permitted the demised premises to be out of repair and in a bad and dilapidated state.

Held (1) Where a very old house is demised, with the usual covenants to repair and yield up in repair, it is not meant that the house should be restored in an improved state, or that the consequences of the elements should be averted; but the tenant has the duty of keeping the house in the state in which it was at the time of the demise, by the timely expenditure of money and care.

Tindal CJ said (in part)

The great question, however, is, I think, as to the repairs; and you will say whether you think that this covenant has been substantially kept. If it has not, you will find for the plaintiff; but if you find that it has been substantially kept, you will find for the defendant. The main subject of the demise is an old house. Now when a very old building is demised, it is not meant that it should be restored in an improved state, nor that the consequences of the elements should be averted: but the tenant has the duty of keeping it as nearly as may be in the state in which it was at the time of the demise by the timely expenditure of money and care. You will therefore consider whether, making every fair allowance, the Chicken-house was or was not kept in repair.

Case 35 *Pembery v Lamdin* [1940] 2 All ER 435 Court of Appeal

A lessor demised certain old premises not constructed with a damp course or with waterproofing for the outside walls, and covenanted to keep the external part of the demised premises other than the shop front in good and tenantable repair and condition. The tenant claimed that, under the covenant, the landlord was liable to waterproof the outside walls, and so render the place dry:

Held (1) The obligation on the landlord was only to keep the premises in repair in the condition in which they were when demised, and, as they were old premises, he was not liable to do any more than point the brickwork.

(2) An external wall is one forming part of the enclosure of the premises, and is not necessarily exposed to the atmosphere, but may adjoin another building.

Slesser LJ said (in part)

. . . When one comes to construe the repairing covenant, and looks (as directed by the authorities) to the nature of the premises demised, it is clear from the evidence, the judgment, and the surveyor's report that this was a house of the old type, with a cellar for the most part built into the ground, without any precautions against damp oozing through the porous bricks into the cellar. The house above fortunately may have remained dry, but that was the kind of house which was demised.

The repairing covenant on which the defendant sought to recover a considerable sum by way of damages is as follows:

> "The lessor hereby covenants with the lessee as follows that is to say that the lessor will keep the external part of the demised premises in good and tenantable repair and condition. . . ."

The first question which arises in this case is what was the nature of the obligation to repair. In order to ascertain that, it is first necessary to consider the nature of the premises which had to be repaired under the covenant. I think that, for the purposes of this case, the principle, which has never been doubted, is to be found stated in a short passage in a judgment of Lord Esher MR, in *Lister v Lane & Nesham* [1893] 2 QB 212. That is a case which has been subsequently followed and approved in *Lurcott v Wakely & Wheeler* [1911] 1 KB 905. In *Lister v Lane & Nesham* after reviewing the earlier authorities, Lord Esher MR, who was speaking there of a tenant, says, at pp. 216, 217:

> "Those cases seem to me to show that, if a tenant takes a house which is of such a kind that by its own inherent nature it will in course of time fall into a particular condition, the effects of that result are not within the tenant's covenant to repair. However large the words of the covenant may be, a covenant to repair a house is not a covenant to give a different thing from that which the tenant took when he entered into the covenant. He has to repair that thing which he took; he is not obliged to make a new and different thing . . ."

Applying that to a landlord, in the same way as it is in that case applied to a tenant, if the counterclaim here made by Mrs Lamdin be correct, she is entitled to receive at the hands of this landlord "a different thing" from that which she took when she entered into the covenant. She took this old house with a cellar without any waterproof protection, and she is asking the landlord so to repair that house as to give her a cellar which has a waterproof protection and is dry. That is not a right which she can possibly maintain, because the obligation of the landlord is to repair that which is demised, and not to give her something much drier in its nature than that which was demised.

Case 36 Sotheby v Grundy [1947] 2 All ER 761 Lynskey J

A lease of a newly erected house, made in 1861 for a period of 99 years, contained a covenant by the lessee to "repair uphold support maintain . . ." the premises "with all necessary reparations and amendments whatsoever." In 1944 the walls were bulged, fractured and overhanging, and the house was condemned by the London County Council as a dangerous structure under the London Building Acts and was demolished. The expenses incurred by the council were recovered from the landlord who sought to recover them from the tenant as damages for breach of the repairing covenant. The evidence showed that, contrary to the Metropolitan Building Act, 1855, which was then in force, the main walls of the house were built entirely without, or on defective, footings, that, having regard to the defective foundations and the made-up ground on which the house was built, there was every likelihood that what in fact happened would happen as a result of the settling of the foundations, and that the only way in which this could have been avoided would have been by underpinning, which would have meant shoring up the premises, the removal of existing foundations, stage by stage, and the substitution of a new foundation in the way of footings and concrete:

Held (1) The expenses were incurred because of the inherent nature of the defect in the premises, and, therefore, did not come within the terms of the repairing covenant, with the result that the landlord was not entitled to recover them from the tenant.

Lynskey J said (in part)
. . . It may be that the inherent nature of a building may result in its partial collapse. One can visualise the floor of a building collapsing, owing to defective joists having been put in. I do not think *Lister v Lane* [1893] 2 QB 212 would be applicable to such a case. In those circumstances, in my opinion, the damage would fall within the ambit of the covenant to repair, but, as I say, it must be a question of degree in each particular case. I am told here by the two witnesses whose evidence I accept that the only way in which what happened could have been prevented would have been by underpinning. It is suggested that if 15 years ago, when bulging was noticed, the tenant had underpinned, he would have been able to prevent further deterioration taking place. I am told that that would have meant shoring up the premises, the removal of the existing foundations, such as they were, stage by stage, and the putting in of a new foundation in the way of footings and concrete to make the building safe. That, in my view, would, in effect, be asking the tenant

to give the landlord something different in kind from that which had been demised. The premises demised here were premises with insecure foundations. What the tenant would have had to do would be to put in a new foundation which would alter the nature and extent of the property demised, turning a building which, as originally constructed, would not last more than some 80 odd years into a building that would last for probably another 100 years.

In my view, that does not come within the purview of the repairing covenant in question here. If the landlord desired to obtain such rights, he ought to have made it clear in the lease, so that the tenant would know that he was undertaking an obligation, not merely to repair, maintain and support the existing building demised, but also to make good original defects in the premises as erected. The expenses claimed were incurred because of the inherent nature of the defect in the premises and do not come within the terms of the covenant contained in the lease.

Case 37 *Wates v Rowland* [1952] 2 QB 12 Court of Appeal

The water level having for some reason risen, water had seeped in between the concrete foundations on which the floor joists were laid and the floor of a dwelling-house, with the result that the floor had rotted causing a nuisance. The sanitary inspector having served a notice requiring the nuisance to be abated, the landlord laid a further layer of concrete on the original concrete foundation raising the surface by nine inches. On that surface he laid a tiled floor. The house being within the protection of the Rent Restriction Acts, the landlord, on the completion of the works, served a notice on the tenant increasing the rent by eight per cent. of the cost of the work, less an allowance for the cost of reflooring. The tenant refused to pay the increase on the ground that although the works in question might be an "improvement" or "structural alteration" they were "repairs" and accordingly the landlord was not entitled to raise the rent under the power conferred by section 2 (1) (*a*) of the Increase of Rent and Mortgage Interest (Restrictions) Act, 1920, as amended by the Rent and Mortgage Interest Restrictions Act, 1939. The county court judge dismissed the landlord's proceedings to recover the increased rent. On appeal:

Held (1) That work required in order to make a dwelling-house fit for habitation was not necessarily "repairs" within the meaning of the section. It might be an "improvement" or "structural alteration," expenditure on which ranked for increased rent under section 2 (1) (*a*) of the Act of 1920. It was a matter of degree whether such expenditure constituted "an improvement" or "structural alteration."

(2) The expenditure by the landlord on the addition of nine inches of concrete to the substratum of the house was *prima facie* expenditure on an "improvement," since the house was a better house than it had ever been before. There was no sufficient ground for holding that this expenditure was to be excluded from consideration on the ground that it was expenditure on repairs. Up to a point the work done was work of repair. The replacement of the floor would come within the description "repairs" which would not rank for the eight per cent. increase. The landlord had, however, done more than provide a new floor. He had made a structural alteration and an improvement consisting of the laying of the additional concrete bed over the existing concrete. There might be an "improvement" in the way of a "structural alteration" or otherwise which was not "unnecessary" within the meaning of the proviso to the subsection, which could not be regarded as merely "repairs" within the meaning of the definition of that word in section 2 (5) of the Act.

Jenkins LJ said (in part)

Is there, then, any sufficient reason for holding that this expenditure is to be excluded from consideration on the ground that it was expenditure on repairs? In my judgment the answer to that question is: up to a point this work, the totality of the work done, was work of repair. The tenant had a floor in the house when he went in, and clearly the house could not be said to be in good tenantable repair after the floor had become rotten. The replacement of a floor of some kind would, I think, therefore fairly come within the description of "repairs." It would be making good a defect arising from the action of the water underneath the floor which had caused the floor to rot, and to that extent, therefore, the expenditure in my view could not properly rank for the 8 per cent. increase, and it is not contended that it should so rank.

But the landlord did substantially more, in my view, than merely provide a new floor. He did make a structural alteration and an improvement, consisting of the laying of the additional concrete bed over the existing concrete, and that provided the house with a better substratum than it had ever had before, in the shape of a solid concrete bed on to which the new floor could be laid direct, thus getting rid of the disadvantage under which the house had laboured from the time it was built, consisting of the cavity beneath the floor, into which, under the changed conditions brought about by the rise in water level, water could find its way. Accordingly, although this is not an altogether easy case, in my view the appeal should be allowed, to the extent that the expenditure consisting of the structural alteration in the shape of the concrete work should be considered as expenditure on an improvement or structural alteration, and not an expenditure on repairs.

Case 38 Collins v Flynn [1963] 2 All ER 1068 Sir Brett Cloutman QC. Official Referee

The lease of a house contained covenants on the part of the lessee well and substantially to repair, amend, renew, etc., the premises, and on the determination of the term to yield them up so well and substantially repaired, amended and renewed. Owing to an inherent defect, namely inadequate foundations, a pier carrying one end of a girder supporting a considerable part of the back main wall, and indirectly part of the side wall, of the house subsided and this necessitated the rebuilding of the pier and walls with newly designed foundations.

Held (1) The work effected an important improvement of the premises and the lessee's covenants did not impose on the tenant liability to remedy such an inherent defect, which would involve him in rendering up the premises in a different condition from that in which they were demised.

Sir Brett Cloutman QC said (in part)

... First, then, in the construction of the covenant, does the word "renew" add anything to the obligation to "repair"? While I am most anxious to give effect to every word of the covenant, as Atkin LJ, insisted in *Anstruther-Gough-Calthorpe v McOscar* [1923] 2 All ER 198, yet every repair does involve a degree of renewal (except, perhaps, tightening a loose screw, as counsel for the tenant suggested). This was the opinion of Buckley LJ, in *Lurcott v Wakely and Wheeler* [1911] 1 KB 905, and I feel that I can give a separate meaning to the word "renew" only by holding that it includes rebuilding the whole property demised; and I think that if this were intended, much stronger and more specific words would have to be used. However, this is of no importance, since I regard the word "repair" as apt to cover the renewal of a part of the premises, and, therefore, so far as the words of the covenant are concerned I regard the obligation of the defendant lessee as being similar to that in the cases cited where only the word "repair" is used.

I now come to the crucial point. Do the words "repair" and "renew" import a liability to rebuild with newly designed foundations and footings the pier supporting the girder, which in turn carries a great part of the rear wall and a part of the side wall in addition? This is manifestly a most important improvement, which, if executed by the tenant, would involve him in rendering up the premises in different condition from that in which they were demised, and on the authority of Lord Esher MR, in *Lister v Lane and Nesham* [1893] 2 QB 212, I do not think that the tenant is under any such obligation. Furthermore, although a suggestion of liability for removal of an inherent defect in a subsidiary part seems to have been touched on in *Sotheby v Grundy* [1947] 2 All ER 761, I do not think that the obiter remarks of Lynskey J, as to defective joists have any bearing on the present case.

If it is necessary to go beyond *Lister v Lane and Nesham* (*supra*), then I think that the decisions in *Wright v Lawson* [1903] WN 108 (the bay window case) and *Pembery v Lamdin* [1940] 2 All ER 435 (the damp basement case) are ample authority for the view that this doctrine of subsidiary parts does not throw on the lessee an obligation to provide an improvement to eliminate an inherent defect, though affecting only a part of the building; and I so hold.

Case 39　Brew Brothers Ltd v Snax (Ross) Ltd [1970] 1 QB 612
Court of Appeal

On June 30, 1965, the freehold owners demised certain premises to tenants for a term of 14 years. By clause 2 of the lease the tenants covenanted

"(e) to repair uphold support maintain ... and keep in repair the demised premises. ... (f) To pay ... a reasonable share ... of the expense incurred in maintaining repairing ... all party walls ... drains ... used ... by the owners or occupiers of the demised premises in common with the owners or occupiers of any adjoining premises ... (i) To permit the landlords ... twice in every year ... to enter upon and view the condition of the demised premises and to repair and make good all ...

want of repair due to the breach by the tenant of any covenant . . ."

In November, 1966, the flank wall of the demised premises tilted towards the plaintiffs' neighbouring premises and was found to be in a dangerous condition. It was shored up to prevent it falling into the plaintiffs' forecourt but caused an obstruction which continued for 18 months. The condition of the wall was caused by a shift in the foundations which, though adequate when the wall was built, had been affected by seepage of water from certain drains which had been defective for many years and by the removal of a tree from the pavement opposite the wall. The plaintiffs brought an action against both owners and tenants seeking abatement of the nuisance and damages. The tenants did not seriously contest their liability to the plaintiffs, but the owners, in third party proceedings, contended that the tenants were solely responsible for the nuisance on the ground that the damage to the wall had been caused by their failure, in breach of the repairing covenant, to repair the drains, and they claimed to be indemnified by the tenants against their liability (if any) to the plaintiffs. The tenants contended that the covenant to repair drains was impliedly excluded by, *inter alia*, clause 2 (f) of the lease and that the owners had a responsibility to effect repairs under clause 2 (i); further, that the extensive works required to make the premises safe were outside the ambit of the repairing covenant and therefore not their responsibility.

The trial judge found that there was evidence of instability in the wall at the date of the demise of which the owners ought to have known, and that mere repair of the drains (which was the tenants' responsibility) would not at that date have been sufficient to re-establish the wall. He held that the works required to make the premises safe were of such a substantial and costly nature (amounting to some £8,000, almost equal to the cost of a new building) as not to constitute repairs within the repairing covenant and that the tenants were not liable vis-à-vis the owners to carry out the work. He held the owners equally liable with the tenants to the plaintiffs for nuisance; on the ground that they had allowed the tenants to occupy the premises without taking from them a covenant which would oblige the tenants to make them safe; alternatively, if the work required was properly "repairs" for which the tenants were liable under the repairing covenant, the owners were responsible, under clause 2 (i), for making good defects they found on the exercise of their right of entry and inspection, and in failing so to do had authorised them. In 1968, the owners had repaired the drains, rebuilt the flank wall and put in entirely new foundations at a cost of some £5,000.

On appeal by the owners:

Held (1) That the obligation on the tenants to repair drains under clause 2 (e) was not excluded by clause 2 (f) and that, on the true construction of clause 2 (i), the tenants were responsible for repairing defects pointed out by the owners on the exercise of their right of entry and inspection, and the owners were not authorising defects if they failed to make good any they found when exercising their right of entry.

(2) (*Per Sachs and Phillimore LJJ.*) That the owners must be presumed to have known that the state of the premises at the date of the lease was such as to constitute a nuisance, and where an owner had knowledge of the existence of a nuisance at the date when a lease was granted it was his duty, by reason of the control he had over the property before that date, to ensure that the nuisance caused no injury; that he could not divest himself of liability to a third party for any damage which resulted merely by signing a document which, as between himself and a tenant, cast on the latter the burden of executing remedial work; and he remained liable to third parties for the effects of the nuisance if it was not abated unless he was excused by some further fact over and above a repairing covenant taken from the tenant; and since in the present case there was no such further fact the owners were liable to the plaintiffs because they suffered the nuisance to continue from the date of the demise until November, 1966, and, a fortiori, thereafter during the time that the shoring was erected.

(3) (*Per Harman and Phillimore LJJ.*) That the owners were jointly responsible with the tenants for obstructing the plaintiffs' forecourt by the erection of the shoring after the nuisance had become apparent in 1966, since it was in their power to abate the nuisance and they had failed to do so, and accordingly they were jointly responsible with the tenants for any damages resulting from the obstruction and subsequent abatement of the nuisance.

(4) That whether the end-product of work requiring to be done properly constituted "repair" was a question of

degree in every case; that (*Harman LJ* dissenting) the correct approach was for the court to conclude, on a fair interpretation of the precise terms of the lease in relation to the state of the property at the date of the lease whether the work could fairly be called repair or not; and that in coming to its conclusion the court must look at the work as a whole and not at individual component parts thereof.

Per Sachs LJ   I doubt whether there is any general definition which satisfactorily covers the distinction between work which constitutes "repairs" and work which does not, but if "inherent nature" or "inherent defects" have to be considered, they are not confined to a state of affairs due to the age of the premises or to defects that originated when the building was erected.

(5) (*Harman LJ* dissenting) That in the present case the work which the tenants were required to carry out and pay for went far beyond that which any reasonable person would have contemplated under the word "repair," even on the basis that they had only to perform the more limited work which the owners had now done; accordingly, none of the work was within the repairing covenant, and the owners could not recover damages from the tenants in respect thereof; nor were they entitled to be indemnified in respect of the damages for which they were liable to the plaintiffs. Accordingly, the appeal must be dismissed.

Per Harman LJ   The judge was not justified in considering all the work required to be done as a whole. The defective drains were the cause and not the consequence of the defects in the wall and their repair was within the repairing covenant. The wall, though large, was still a subsidiary portion of the demised premises and its character had not been changed after repair in such a way as to make it a different thing from that demised and was similarly within the repairing covenant; but the new foundations had been put in by the owners to protect their freehold and were entirely different from those which previously existed and so were not within the repairing covenant.

Harman LJ said (in part)
   . . . What on the evidence was the state of things at the time of the demise? There were cracks in the wall which according to the judge should have put the landlords on inquiry as to its stability. There was no evidence that anybody knew that the

drains below the tunnel were cracked or defective, and I cannot see how there could have been any duty upon the landlords to inquire into that matter. Still, according to the judge's finding, which I think we must accept, there was evidence of the instability of the wall in 1965 and that in fact at that date the mere repair of the drains would not have been sufficient to re-establish the wall and it would have been necessary at that time to do substantially all the work which has now been done.

Making these assumptions, I still cannot see why the landlords were not justified in taking a repairing covenant sufficient to put on the tenants the obligation to put in repair. It was for the tenants to protect themselves by having a survey made before they entered into the lease, a precaution which they neglected to take.

The judge held that all the work required, namely, the repair of the foundations, the rebuilding of the wall and the repair of the drains, ought all to be considered as one, and that if any of them were outside the repairing covenant all of them were. I can see no justification for this. If the repairs of the drains had been made necessary by the defect in the wall and this latter was outside the covenant, then I can see that the repair of the drains, being consequent upon the other, might likewise be the liability of the landlords; but the exact reverse is the truth of the matter. The defective drains were the cause and not the consequence of the defects in the wall, and I think the three matters must be treated separately. First, then, the drains. The repair of these is, in my judgment, clearly within the repairing covenant and remains the obligation of the tenants. Secondly, the wall. The rebuilding of this is clearly a very large operation, and the question has been said to be one of degree . . .

. . . In the present case the property was not an old property worn out by the course of time, nor were there inherent defects in its structure, and it does not seem to me that the cases which exclude some rebuilding from the ambit of the repairing covenant go as far as this case. The tenants' argument was that the state of the property at the date of the demise was the material matter and that as at that date the property was, as the judge said, doomed, that is to say, it would fall down sooner or later, the necessary work would give the landlords a different thing from that which was demised. So far as the wall is concerned I cannot accept this. The wall was, though large, still a subsidiary portion of the building. After its repair it was just the same kind of wall as it was before and the fact that the lower courses of bricks were, owing to modern building regulations, $13\frac{1}{2}$ inches instead of nine inches in thickness is not such an alteration in the character of the wall as to make it a new thing . . .

. . . There remains the question whether the landlords, if called upon to contribute to the plaintiffs' damages for the nuisance, can recover against the tenants. So far as the work on the house is concerned, the judgment already given covers the matter, but there remain the damages which may be allowed to the plaintiffs for the obstruction of their premises caused by the shoring. For this, in my judgment, the tenants are liable, and must indemnify the landlords. It was their breach of the repairing covenant which caused the wall to lean and necessitated the shoring, and I think they must indemnify the landlords against their contribution to damages thus caused.

Sachs LJ said (in part)

The question whether extensive work involving the rebuilding of walls in whole or in part, of reconstructing foundations, and of underpinning does or does not on the particular facts of an individual case fall within a repairing covenant, has provided much material for the books. In the course of argument we were appropriately and carefully referred to the plethora of authorities from *Lister v Lane & Nestham* [1893] 2 QB 212 (with the much-cited judgment of Lord Esher MR that "however large the words of the covenant to repair may be it is not a covenant to give a different thing from that which the tenant took when he entered into the covenant"); through *Lurcott v Wakely & Wheeler* [1911] 1 KB 905, to *Collins v Flynn* [1963] 2 All ER 1068, with its helpful review of many of the decisions.

In the course of their submissions counsel referred to a number of varying phrases which had been used by judges in an endeavour to express the distinction between the end-product of work which constituted repair and that of work which did not. They included "improvement," "important improvement," "different in kind," "different in character," "different in substance," "different in nature," "a new and different thing," and just "something different." They likewise referred to another set of phrases seeking to define the distinctive quality of the fault to be rectified, such as "inherent nature" (frequently used since *Lister v Lane & Nesham* [1893] 2 QB 212), "radical defect in the structure," "inherent defect" and "inherent vice." Each of these two sets of phrases in turn was discussed in what tended to become an exercise in semantics. Moreover, it is really not much use looking at individual phrases which necessarily deal with only one of the infinitely variable sets of circumstances that can arise.

For my part I doubt whether there is any definition—certainly not any general definition—which satisfactorily covers the above distinctions: nor will I attempt to provide one. Things which can be easily recognised are not always susceptible of simple definition. Indeed the only observation I need offer is to reject the submission that if "inherent nature" or "inherent defects" have to be considered, they are confined to a state of affairs due to the age of the premises or to defects that originated when the building was erected.

It seems to me that the correct approach is to look at the particular building, to look at the state which it is in *at the date of the lease*, to look at the precise terms of the lease, and then come to a conclusion as to whether, on a fair interpretation of those terms in relation to that state, the requisite work can fairly be termed repair. However large the covenant it must not be looked at in vacuo.

Case 40 *Yanover v Romford Finance and Development Co Ltd* (29 March 1983) (unreported) Park J

By a lease dated 17th May 1963, assigned to the plaintiffs by an assignment dated 26th May 1972, the plaintiffs became the lessees of a flat known as 2, Redbridge Court, Ilford, of which premises the defendants were the lessors. The flat was a small modern flat consisting of two bedrooms, lounge, kitchen and bathroom on the ground floor of a nine-storey block of 36 flats, four flats to each floor, built in 1962. Before its purchase by the plaintiffs the flat had been occupied for about 10 years by their predecessors in title. Throughout that period the lessors managing agents had received no complaint in relation to dampness from the lessee or on his behalf. The plaintiffs, who inspected the flat before agreeing to purchase it, observed, on that inspection, that the decorations were in good order. They then decided to buy the flat with a mortgage from a building society, the flat was examined by a surveyor on the building society's behalf, and nothing untoward was brought to the plaintiffs' attention as a result of that inspection.

The plaintiffs went into occupation in about May 1972, and the tenant said that during the following winter dampness first appeared in bedroom No. 2 on the outside wall between the floor and the window. Although the managing agents had no written complaint about dampness until January 1974, the tenant said that an employee of that firm,

looked at the wall and expressed the opinion that the dampness was due to condensation.

In the summer of 1973 the walls appeared to become dry,
but dampness re-appeared in the winter of 1973–74. The
managing agents contended that the problem was one of
condensation, but the plaintiffs' expert contended that the
problem was one of rising damp and that the internal walls
and partitions at floor level required the insertion of damp-
proof courses. The landlords' covenant was to keep in repair
the exterior of the building whilst the tenants' obligations
were to keep clean and in good and substantial repair the
interior of the demised premises, including the walls, floors
and partitions.

Held (1) The work of installing the damp-proof courses
was a major building operation to improve the building and
to enable it to comply with the relevant building regulations,
which could not fairly be termed a repair which either the
landlords or the tenants would be required to undertake
under the terms of the lease.

Park J said (in part)

To prevent further damage from rising damp Mr Brod [the
tenant's surveyor] is of opinion that a silicone injection would
have to be made into the inner leaf of the exterior wall and the
internal partition walls so as to provide a damp-proof course
therein; also that the parquet floors would have to be lifted so
that a bitumen damp-proof membrane could be laid with screed
on top of it, and thereafter the wooden blocks would have to
be replaced. He is of the opinion, therefore, that extensive ancillary work, such as replacing skirting boards, shortening doors,
refitting cupboards, replastering and redecoration would also
have to be carried out. Mr Brod described the work as a major
building operation which would create great disruption and
inconvenience, and would probably require the occupants to
move out during some of the work. He did not cost the work
in detail, but at 1982 prices he put it at between £4,000 and £8,000.

The defendants accept that if rising damp is the cause of the
dampness Mr Brod's opinion as to the work to be done to cure
it is correct.

On these facts the first question to be decided is whether the
works constitute repair. That word, of course, appears in both
the lessees' covenant and in the lessor's covenant.

The lessees' covenant . . . is in these terms:

"(iii) The Lessee will keep clean and in good and substantial repair order and condition the interior of the demised premises and all additions thereto and the water gas and other pipes and the electric wires and the water and sanitary apparatus therein solely installed or used only for the purpose of the demised premises.

And it is hereby agreed and declared without prejudice to and without in any way limiting the generality of the foregoing that the Lessee shall be responsible under the terms of this covenant for the repair of *inter alia* the following parts namely the ceilings the floors all walls and partitions within the said flat and the glass and casements in all windows thereof".

The lessors' covenant, . . . is in these words:

"That the Lessors will at all times during the said term

(i) keep the exterior of the building of which the demised premises form part including the roof gutters down pipes and foundations thereof in repair and (as to such parts as so required) pointed".

The word "repair", in my judgment, in both covenants, must bear the same meaning. . . . I consider first the building in question, that is, flat No. 2. It forms one-quarter of the ground floor of a large block of flats built, as I have earlier said, in 1962 in accordance with building regulations then in force. The damp-proof system complied with those regulations. It still does. All that now has changed has been the regulations. Now it probably does not comply with them. There is no evidence that the occupiers of the flat suffered from any form of dampness in it until the winter of 1972. For the reasons I have given I am not satisfied that dampness, and the dampness which followed at intervals until the winter of 1979, was caused to more than a minimal extent by the inability of the damp-proof system to cope with rising damp. Mr Brod said that the block had been built on land which was at one time marshy, and that under such land there can be long-term changes in the level of the water table. When such changes occur there will be a difference in the moisture content of the soil; and although the matter was not investigated further at the trial it seems to me that rising damp in flat No. 2, and in no other flat in the block, probably occurred owing to a change in the water level affecting only that part of the block in which flat No. 2 is situated, and that but for this change in the water level the damp-proof system for the flat would have been as effective in the 1970s, to prevent rising damp as it had been since 1962. Further, as I understand the evidence of Mr Brod, it does not follow that any change in the water level would produce a permanent increase in the moisture content of the soil.

However, the plaintiffs' complaint is, not that the damp-proof system has fallen out of repair but that for some reason, at some unknown date after 1972, it became and remains less able to cope with rising damp than it had been during the ten years after the flats were built.

It is in these circumstances that the plaintiffs seek an order that the defendants be required, not to repair the existing damp-proof system but, by a major building operation, to improve it so as to cause it to comply with building regulations which came into force three years or so after the block has been built.

I return again to Lord Justice Sachs' guideline. [in *Brew Brothers Ltd v Snax Ross Ltd* [Case 39]] I take into account the state of the flat at the date of the lease and for the first ten years thereafter; I look at the repairing covenant, both the lessors' and the lessees' and, as best I can, try to ascertain the good sense of the agreement.

The conclusion I have reached, on a fair interpretation of the agreement, is that the work to be done cannot fairly be termed "repair" which either the lessor could require the lessee to carry out or the lessee require the lessor to carry out.

Case 41 *Halliard Property Co Ltd v Nicholas Clarke Investments Ltd* (1983) 269 EG 1257 French J

The premises were demised for a term of 14 years from 1979, and were used by the tenants for the purposes of their paint retailing business. In the lease the tenants had covenanted to support, uphold, cleanse, maintain and well and substantially repair and keep in good and substantial repair and good decorative order and working order and renew as often as necessary throughout the term, the demised premises, both externally and internally, all fixtures, fittings and appliances. There was a jerry-built structure at the rear of the demised premises which comprised, *inter alia*, a 4.5 inch thick wall; this wall was virtually unsupported apart from two brick piers. This wall collapsed and the landlords claimed, under the terms of the lease, that the tenants were liable to rebuild the jerry-built structure and reinstate it in accordance with the relevant building by-laws. The landlords claimed damages and forfeiture of the lease.

Held (1) Although the case was close to the borderline, if the premises were reinstated to the landlords' demands it would involve handing back to the landlords an edifice entirely different from the unstable jerry-built structure of which the tenants took possession at the end of the lease. The landlords' claim therefore failed.

French J said (in part)

A number of authorities were cited to me which bear more or less closely on this matter: *Lister v Lane* [1893] 2 QB 212; *Lurcott v Wakely & Wheeler* [1911] 1 KB 905; *Sotheby v Grundy* [1947] 2 All ER 761; *Collins v Flynn* [1963] 2 All ER 1068; *Brew Brothers v Snax* [1970] 1 QB 612; and *Ravenseft Properties v Davstone (Holdings)* [1979] 1 All ER 929. I do not propose to repeat the helpful citations which were given to me from those authorities. The respectful conclusion to which I come is that the matter was summed up both accurately and neatly by Forbes J in *Ravenseft Properties* when he said this:

"The true test is, as the cases show, that it is always a question of degree whether that which the tenant is being asked to do can properly be described as repair, or whether on the contrary it would involve giving back to the landlord a wholly different thing from that which he demised. In deciding this question, the proportion which the cost of the disputed work bears to the value or cost of the whole premises, may sometimes be helpful as a guide."

The conclusion which I come to is one which I reach not without a certain amount of hesitation. It seems to me that this case must be very close to the borderline. There is no doubt that the cost of a proper rebuilding of this utility room would represent rather more than a third of the cost of rebuilding the whole premises, that cost being rather less than the price at which the premises could be sold to a willing purchaser. It seems to me of some significance as to the merits, if in no other way, that there is no evidence to show, or no sufficient evidence to satisfy me having regard to the conflict, that the defendants should have realised that they were leasing premises which the plaintiffs' own expert said were inherently defective. I bear in mind that there was no possible way in which the defendants could have known that the only support which had kept this wall up, perhaps miraculously, for some 30 years was the cantilever effect of the foundations upon that wall and upon the 9 in brick piers on either side of the door. I bear in mind that there was no possible way in which the defendants could have known that the wall was restrained at the top, if by anything worth mentioning, only by 1 in of a wire nail and possibly a little friction imposed by the weight of the roof.

Regarding, as I do, this matter as a borderline case, the conclusion that I come to is that the reinstatement or rebuilding of this utility room is not covered by the obligations imposed upon the defendants by the repairing covenant. In my judgment, that which would be involved in rebuilding the utility room could not properly be described as a repair. While, of course, that which would be handed back on the expiry of the demise would include the intact "two-thirds in area" front part of the premises, it would involve handing back to them, so far as the utility room was concerned, an edifice entirely different from the unstable and jerry-built structure of which the defendants took possession at the start of this lease.

Case 42 Post Office v Aquarius Properties Ltd [1985] 2 EGLR 105; (1985) 276 EG 923. Hoffmann J

> The basement of an office building flooded owing to a rise in the water table combined with certain defects of construction. The basement had been under several inches of water between 1979 and 1984, but owing to a lowering of the water table had been dry from that date. Structural engineers for both parties agreed that there had been a failure of a joint between the floors and the walls caused by poor workmanship which had resulted in weak areas of concrete with a porous texture. The remedial schemes proposed required substantial structural additions to the basement.
>
> *Held* (1) The works required fell outside the repairing covenant as they involved structural alterations and improvements to the basement.

Hoffman J said (in part)

The repairing covenant in the Post Office's underlease is clause 2(3). It is in fairly standard form and I shall not quote it in full because the critical words are "... keep in good and substantial repair the demised premises and every part thereof ..." "Keep in repair" implies, of course, an obligation to put in repair so far as the premises are out of repair at the commencement of the lease, but I do not think that this helps to answer the problem in this case, which is whether the work required to water-proof the basement can be described as "repair".

Counsel have referred me to a number of cases on the meaning of "repair" from *Lister v Lane* [1893] 2 QB 212 to *Elmcroft Developments Ltd v Tankersley-Sawyer* (1984) 270 Estates Gazette 140. I have found most assistance in the judgment of Sachs LJ in *Brew Brothers Ltd v Snax Ross Ltd* [1970] 1 QB 612. This says, in effect, that the whole law on the subject may be summed up in the proposition that "repair" is an ordinary English word. It also contains a timely warning against attempting to impose the crudities of judicial exegesis upon the subtle and often intuitive discriminations of ordinary speech. All words take meaning from context and it is, of course, necessary to have regard to the language of the particular covenant and the lease as a whole, the commercial relationship between the parties, the state of the premises at the time of the demise and any other surrounding circumstances which may colour the way in which the word is used. In the end, however, the question is whether the ordinary speaker of English would consider that the word "repair" as used in the covenant was appropriate to describe the work which has to be done. The cases do no more than illustrate specific contexts in which judges, as ordinary speakers of English, have thought that it was or was not appropriate to do so. [Counsel] for the landlords formulated a number of propositions which he said could be derived from three recent cases, namely *Brew Brothers, Ravenseft Prosperties Ltd v Davstone (Holdings) Ltd* [1980] QB 12, and *Elmcroft*. The most important was that the test for whether or not the work which needed to be done was repair was whether it would give the landlord a wholly different thing from that which he had before. In this case, he said, the landlord would still have essentially the same building and therefore the work was repair. The proposition, in my view, illustrates the wisdom of Sachs LJ's warning, because it does not make sufficient allowance for the range of distinctions embodied in ordinary words. I think [counsel's] proposition does express what is usually implied in the distinction between repair and rebuilding or reconstruction, but these are not the only concepts which border upon repair. There are also words like "improvement", "alteration" and "addition" which are distinguishable from repair in different ways. For example, one usually thinks of an improvement as a fairly substantial and identifiable addition to or change in a building but involving a subsidiary part rather than the building as a whole. Nevertheless, "improvement" is different from repair. It is often said that whether or not something is repair is a question of degree, but the question of degree which has to be answered is not necessarily always the same.

There are different criteria for distinguishing the word "repair" from its various neighbours. These differences can be seen operating in *Brew Brothers*, in which the majority of the court thought that the works taken as a whole were so extensive as to amount to a reconstruction rather than a repair. Harman LJ did not accept that the totality was reconstruction but thought that one part of the work, namely the construction of new foundations, was an improvement. *Wright v Lawson* [1903] WN 108, is also an example of an addition or improvement, the construction of a new bay window, which could not be described as a rebuilding or reconstruction of the premises as a whole.

In this case [counsel] accepts that it would be difficult, except in a somewhat artificial and question-begging sense, to say that the work needed in the basement would make Abbey House a wholly different building from what it was before, but he says he is not bound to submit that the work amounts to a reconstruction of the premises. He says that it is not repair because it should more appropriately be called a substantial improvement to the premises, creating a thoroughly water-proof structure in the basement which was not previously there.

Both counsel agree that the question is one of degree and, to a large extent, one of impression on which different people could reasonably give different answers. I think one is entitled to take into account, first, as part of the context, the commercial relationship between the parties at the time of the demise. This was that the landlords had a head lease of 125 years and the tenants had been given an underlease of about 22 years. Secondly, in considering whether the work was improvement rather than repair, one must have regard to its substantiality. In this case both experts advise that whatever scheme of water-proofing is adopted, there should be a very substantial structural addition to the basement, namely a new concrete slab with reinforcement on the upper side, thicker than the existing slab and laid above it (compare *Wates v Rowland* [1952] 2 QB 12). This has the effect of reducing the head room in the basement and necessitates some degree of repositioning the ducts and services under the ground-floor slab, although the experts are not agreed on how much. In the asphalt schemes of both experts it is also necessary to construct inner concrete skins against the existing walls.

Thirdly, I think I am entitled to take into account the probable cost of the work, which at the lower end of the range of figures mentioned in the evidence is about £100,000. This is twice the likely annual market rent for the whole building with water-proof basement and over 15% of its total capital value. I was not given a separate figure for the total value of the basement but it must be a small fraction of the whole.

Taking these matters into consideration and deploying my ordinary understanding of language, I do not think it would be appropriate to describe any of the three schemes of treatment as work of repair. In my judgment, they involve structural alterations and improvements to the basement. Consequently, they do not fall within the tenant's obligations under the lease and I shall so declare.

Note:
  (i) This decision was affirmed by the Court of Appeal on different grounds: see Case 42A in Preface.
  (ii) See also the decisions on sections 11–16 of the Landlord and Tenant Act 1985 especially *Quick v Taff-Ely Borough Council* [Case 56] and *Wainwright v Leeds City Council* [Case 55].

3.2 Repair—renewal—improvement: works within the covenant

Case 43 Lucrott v Wakely and Wheeler [1911] 1 KB 905 Court of Appeal

A lease of a house in London contained a covenant by the lessee to substantially repair and keep in thorough repair and good condition the demised premises and at the end or sooner determination of the term to deliver up the same to the lessors so repaired and kept. Subsequently the reversion expectant on the lease was assigned to the plaintiff and the lease to the defendants. Shortly before the expiration of the term the London County Council served a notice on the owner and occupiers requiring them to take down the front external wall of the house to the level of the ground floor as being a dangerous structure, and the plaintiff called upon the defendants to comply with this notice, which they failed to do. After the expiration of the term, the plaintiff, in compliance with a demolition order of a police magistrate, took down the wall to the level of the ground floor, and then, in compliance with a further notice of the London County Council, took down, the remainder of the wall and rebuilt it in accordance with modern requirements. The house was very old and the condition of the wall was caused by old age, and the wall could not have been repaired without rebuilding it:

Held (1) That the defendants were liable under the covenant to recoup from the plaintiff the cost of taking down and rebuilding the wall.

Cozens-Hardy MR said (in part)
... When I look at the facts in *Torrens v Walker* [1906] 2 Ch 166, when I see that that was a covenant by the landlord simply to repair the outside of the premises, and when I see that the outside walls in question in that case, which were two sides of a triangle, were in such a condition that they could not be repaired and had to be pulled down from top to bottom, I think that that decision was quite right on the facts, and that the change of circumstances in that case was one which could not have been in the contemplation of the parties when the covenant was entered into, and that the covenant must be construed with reference to that limitation. The same thing is true of *Lister v Lane* [1893] 2 QB 212 where a house, which was rather an old house, was built upon what is called a timber cill and really had no foundation. The timber was put on the top of 17 feet of mud. That timber had rotted. The house could not be repaired. Nothing could be done but to remove it, to pull it down, or to underpin it to a depth of 17 feet, and to build some brick or other structure from the gravel or chalk up to the house. It was there held by the Court of Appeal, and I see no reason to quarrel with their decision, that the change of circumstances which had arisen could not have been in the contemplation of the parties and that it would not be reasonable to construe the covenant to repair as applicable to that change of circumstances. But then when I come to what I should have thought was everyday experience in cases of this kind, when I come to consider what is to happen when by reason of the elements acting on an old building, say, a chimney stack is blown down, is it possible for the tenant to say he is not liable to put that up because the collapse was due merely to age and the elements? I am astonished to hear that such a contention can be raised. So, if a tenant under a repairing lease finds that a floor has become so rotten that it cannot be patched up, that it is in such a condition that it cannot bear the weight of human beings or of furniture upon it, can it be said that the tenant is exempt from the liability of

replacing that floor, and repairing it in the only way in which
it can be repaired in order to make the house habitable, merely
because the state of the floor is due to time and the elements?
I am entirely unable to follow that argument. *Proudfoot v Hart*
25 QBD 42 seems to lay down a perfectly sound and intelligible
proposition on this point, namely, that in such a case it is the
duty of the tenant, if he cannot patch up the floor so as to make
it a floor, to replace that which is no longer a floor by something
which is a floor.

That being so, it seems to me that we are driven to ask in
this particular case, and in every case of this kind, Is what has
happened of such a nature that it can fairly be said that the
character of the subject-matter of the demise, or part of the
demise, in question has been changed? Is it something which
goes to the whole, or substantially the whole, or is it simply
an injury to a portion, a subsidiary portion, to use Buckley LJ's
phrase, of the demised property? In this case the view taken
by the official referee and the Divisional Court is the view which
commends itself to me, that this portion of the wall, 24 feet
in front, is merely a subsidiary portion of the demised premises,
the restoration of this wall leaving the rest of the building, which
goes back more than 100 feet, untouched. The restoration of
this wall will not change the character or nature of the building,
and I am unable to say that the question differs in any way
from that which we should have had to consider if by reason
of the elements and lapse of time, say, some rafters in the roof
had become rotten, and a corner of the roof gave way so that
the water came in. It seems to me that we should be narrowing
in a most dangerous way the limit and extent of these covenants
if we did not hold that the defendants were liable under covenants framed as these are to make good the cost of repairing
this wall in the only sense in which it can be repaired, namely,
by rebuilding it according to the requirements of the county council. In my opinion this appeal fails and must be dismissed with
costs.

Fletcher Moulton LJ said (in part)
    ... The sole duty of the court is to give proper and full effect
to each word used, and the question whether this leads to more
or less overlapping is of no legal importance. I therefore look
upon these as three separate covenants: there is a covenant to
repair, there is a covenant to keep in thorough repair, and there
is a covenant to keep in good condition.

But all these three relate to the demised premises, and we must construe them, not in an abstract sense, but as applied to the subject-matter. I will take the one which, to my mind, is the most important in this case, as enabling us to decide it with the greatest certainty and with the least difficulty. That is the covenant to keep the premises in good condition. In the year 1881 these premises were old. Nearly thirty years have passed since then, and there is no doubt that although they had not then suffered from age as much as was the case at the termination of the lease, even then they were old premises. Now what is the meaning of keeping old premises in good condition? I can see no difficulty in deciding the meaning of that. It means that, considering that they are old premises, they must be in good condition as such premises. Let me take a parallel to which I referred in argument. Suppose the case of a ship. A man who covenants to keep the *Mauretania* in good condition must, of course, keep her in the perfection of condition by reason of the fact that she is a vessel of her class and new. Suppose a man covenants for a year to keep in good condition a tramp that has been at sea for fifteen years, he must perform the covenant just as much as the man who covenanted to keep the *Mauretania* in good condition. But the keeping in good condition in the second case will mean something very different from that which it meant in the former case: it will mean in good condition for a vessel of that age and nature. I desire to state that for my own part I feel no reluctance to give full effect to this consideration in interpreting this covenant. We have to consider what it obliges the lessee to do in the case of an old building. But we must bear in mind that, while the age and the nature of the building can qualify the meaning of the covenant, they never can relieve the lessee from his obligation. If he chooses to undertake to keep in good condition an old house, he is bound to do it, whatever be the means necessary for him to employ in so doing. He can never say "The house was old, so old that it relieved me from my covenant to keep it in good condition." If it was so old that to keep it in good condition would require replacement of part after part until the whole was replaced—if that was necessary—then, by entering into a covenant that he would do it, he took on his own back the burden of doing it with all that this duty might entail. I have looked at all the cases which have been cited in argument, and, with the exception of one to which I shall presently refer, and which I think can be explained on other grounds, I find no case which even suggests that the age and nature of the structure relieve the covenantor from the duty of maintaining it, if he has undertaken to maintain it.

I have dwelt by preference on the covenant to keep in good condition because it seems to me that it is entirely free from any consideration of the means that have to be employed by the lessee to do the work. The duty undertaken is expressed in clear language and must be performed. Supposing there is a house on a plot of land which is let on a lease for eighty years, and the person who takes the lease undertakes to keep that house in good condition for the eighty years, he cannot assert that it is a house which from the nature of the case would under ordinary circumstances last out twenty years, and therefore that he may let it die at the end of twenty years. He must do all that is necessary to keep that house in good condition for the period for which he has covenanted. But, as I have pointed out, the words "keep in good condition" will have a different meaning according to the nature and age of the house. Now of one thing one can be certain: there is a breach of the covenant if the house no longer remains a house. It is quite clear that, however you qualify the meaning of the keeping of a house "in good condition," it implies that there is a house; and in the present case it seems to me that the defendants' contention is that they were justified in allowing the house to get into a state where it was no longer a house at all because they only covenanted to do repairs. The answer to that contention is this: that they covenanted to keep the house in good condition, besides covenanting to do repairs (a point with which I will deal later on), and therefore they could not plead that they had performed their contract if they allowed the house to come into a condition in which it was no longer habitable as a house.

I turn to the facts of the case to see whether the defendants maintained the house and left the house in good condition. It is perfectly obvious that they did not. If a house is in such a condition that it is dangerous to the public, and that a portion of it has to be pulled down and rebuilt at the demand of the authorities on the ground of public safety,—which must be the safety of the people within as well as of the people without— there is a plain breach of the covenant to keep in good condition, and I should be satisfied to decide this case on that ground alone, for in my opinion it would be adequate to support the case for the plaintiff.

Now I will go to the second covenant, which is to keep in thorough repair. Here we get more into the realm of previous decisions by reason of the fact that in some of them it has been treated as a covenant the language of which pointed to the mode in which or the means by which the covenantor is to perform his duty. They leave it, however, a matter on which one is free to express one's opinion, and personally I think that to keep in thorough repair does not in any way confine the duty of the person who is liable under the covenant to the doing of what are ordinarily called repairs. A house is spoken of as being in thorough repair when it is a house to which no repairs have to be done. But it is a description of a state and not of a mode by which that state has been arrived at, and, therefore, in my own mind I draw no wide distinction between keeping in thorough repair and keeping in good condition; they both appear to me to describe the condition of the house. What a surveyor would call in good condition and what a surveyor would call in thorough repair may differ somewhat, but they would be something very like, the one to the other. As I have said, the legal obligation is to keep the house in that state, and I confess that I do not think that from the legal point of view there is much difference between the nature of the two obligations.

I come now to the third covenant, which is to repair. Here there is a duty to perform an operation. No doubt, if you thoroughly repair, it will put the house in a good condition and in a state of thorough repair. But it is plain that the word "repair" refers to the operation to which the defendants bind themselves to have recourse. For my own part, when the word "repair" is applied to a complex matter like a house, I have no doubt that the repair includes the replacement of parts. Of course, if a house had tumbled down, or was down, the word "repair" could not be used to cover rebuilding. It would not be apt to describe such an operation. But, so long as the house exists as a structure, the question whether repair means replacement, or, to use the phrase so common in marine cases, substituting new for old, does not seem to me to be at all material. Many, and in fact most, repairs imply that some portion of the total fabric is renewed, that new is put in place of old. Therefore you have from time to time as things need repair to put new for old. If you properly repair as you go along the consequence will be that you will always get a house which will be in repair and usable as a house, but you will not get a house that does not suffer from age, nor a house which when old is the same as when it was new. I cannot think that there is any case which lays down that if a person has undertaken throughout a term to repair a house he can ever say that he has no longer any duties because, although he has properly repaired, the house no longer exists. So far, however, as the present case is concerned, that is a point that need not be decided. The two other covenants are quite sufficient to decide the case.

Buckley LJ said (in part)

"Repair" and "renew" are not words expressive of a clear contrast. Repair always involves renewal; renewal of a part; of a subordinate part. A skylight leaks; repair is effected by hacking out the putties, putting in new ones, and renewing the paint. A roof falls out of repair; the necessary work is to replace the decayed timbers by sound wood; to substitute sound tiles or slates for those which are cracked, broken, or missing; to make good the flashings, and the like. Part of a garden wall tumbles down; repair is effected by building it up again with new mortar, and, so far as necessary, new bricks or stone. Repair is restoration by renewal or replacement of subsidiary parts of a whole. Renewal, as distinguished from repair, is reconstruction of the entirety, meaning by the entirety not necessarily the whole but substantially the whole subject-matter under discussion. I agree that if repair of the whole subject-matter has become impossible a covenant to repair does not carry an obligation to renew or replace. That has been affirmed by *Lister v Lane*. But if that which I have said is accurate, it follows that the question of repair is in every case one of degree, and the test is whether the act to be done is one which in substance is the renewal or replacement of defective parts, or the renewal or replacement of substantially the whole. It is with such limitations as these that the language in the cases which have been cited to us must be read.

Case 44 *Morcom v Campbell-Johnson* [1956] 1 QB 106 Court of Appeal

The landlords of a 60-year-old block of flats incurred expenditure of some £10,000 on replacing the original old and worn water-borne drainage and cold-water systems by more efficient modern equivalents, and on lowering the area adjacent to the building which had been defective from its origin. On their application to the court for declarations that they were entitled to increase the standard rent of the tenants by an apportioned amount of eight per cent. of the sum expended, as "expenditure on the improvement . . . of the dwelling-house (not including expenditure on . . .

repairs)" within section 2 (1) (*a*) of the Increase of Rent and Mortgage Interest (Restrictions) Act, 1920, as amended:

Held (1) That an "improvement of the dwelling-house" within section 2 (1) (*a*) meant the provision of something new which was beneficial, judged objectively from the point of view of the reasonable tenant; that (i) the replacement of the old drainage and cold-water systems by their modern equivalents, although resulting in making the dwelling-house better than it was before, were not such improvements but repairs only; and (ii) lowering the area, though an improvement per se, was not, in the circumstances, an improvement of any dwelling-house or flat; and that the landlords accordingly were not entitled to increase the rent under the section.

Denning LJ said (in part)

I find great difficulty in framing a definition of what is an "improvement" as distinct from a "repair." Perhaps the most helpful way is to give a few illustrations. In *Strood Estate Ltd v Gregory* [1936] 2 KB 605 there was an old-fashioned privy at the bottom of a garden which was simply a pit which was emptied every month or so by the local authority. The landlords removed that old-fashioned privy, and substituted a modern water closet in which the refuse was taken away by a water-born system. That was, no doubt, an improvement. In *Wates v Rowland* [1952] 2 QB 12 the floor of a house had become rotten by damp. When the floor was made good, instead of putting in a wooden floor, a tiled floor was put in. That was held not to be an "improvement" but a "repair." But in the self-same case a new concrete bed, some nine inches in depth, was put into the house because the water level in the area had risen. That was held to be an "improvement." Jenkins LJ said (in *Wates v Rowland*): "The replacement of a floor of some kind would, I think, therefore fairly come within the description of 'repairs'"—and he held that the tiled floor replacing the old wooden floor was repairs. Evershed MR said (ibid): "In the course of the argument examples were given showing that what was undoubtedly repair might yet involve some degree of improvement, in the sense of the modern substitute being better than that which had gone before."

It seems to me that the test, so far as one can give any test in these matters, is this: if the work which is done is the provision of something new for the benefit of the occupier, that is, properly speaking, an improvement; but if it is only the replacement of something already there, which has become dilapidated or worn out, then, albeit that it is a replacement by its modern equivalent, it comes within the category of repairs and not improvements.

Case 45 *Ravenseft Properties Ltd v Davstone (Holdings) Ltd* [1979] 1 All ER 929 Forbes J

A building erected between 1958 and 1960, consisting of a 16-storey block of maisonettes, was constructed of a reinforced concrete frame with stone claddings. Expansion joints were omitted from the structure because at the date of erection it was not standard practice to include them in such a structure since it was not then realised that the expansion rates of the concrete frame and the stone cladding were different. In 1966 the tenant took an underlease of the building. The underlease contained covenants by the tenant "to repair" the building including the walls, and to repay to the landlord costs incurred in executing works to remedy, *inter alia*, want of reparation. In 1973 part of the stone cladding on the building became loose and in danger of falling because of bowing of the stones caused principally by the defect in design of lack of expansion joints, but also because of defective workmanship in failing properly to tie in the stones. In view of the urgency of securing the cladding the landlord executed the necessary remedial works removing the cladding and reinstating it with expansion joints (which by that date, 1973, it was standard practice to insert) and proper ties. The total cost of the work was £55,000 of which only £5,000 was attributable to the work of inserting the joints. The cost of erecting the building in 1973 would have exceeded £3 million. The landlord brought an action against the tenant claiming repayment of the whole of the cost of the works carried out, under the covenants to repair and to repay the cost of repairs executed by the landlord. The tenant denied liability for the cost of inserting the joints on the grounds that it was caused by an inherent defect in the demised premises and repairs resulting from an inherent defect could not fall within the ambit of a covenant to repair; alternatively he contended that the tenant was not bound to pay for that part of the repairs which remedied an inherent defect.

Held (1) There was no doctrine that want of repair due to an inherent defect in the demised premises could not fall within the ambit of a covenant to repair. It was a question of degree whether that which the tenant was asked to do, or pay for, could properly be described as repair so as to fall within a covenant to repair, or whether it involved giving back to the landlord a wholly different thing from that demised in which case the work would not fall within a covenant to repair or pay for repairs. The insertion of the joints did not amount to changing the character of the building so as to take that work out of the ambit of the covenant to repair or the covenant to pay for repairs, for the joints formed a trivial part only of the whole building, and the cost of inserting them was trivial compared to the value of the building. It followed that the landlord was entitled to repayment of the whole of the cost of the works executed.

Forbes J said (in part)

This necessarily brief review of authorities indicates quite clearly to my mind that apart from *Collins v Flynn* [1963] 2 All ER 1068 which I consider of doubtful authority, the explanation of the ratio in *Lister's case* [1893] 2 QB 212 as giving the tenant a complete defence, if the cause of the want of reparation is an inherent defect, has never been adopted by any court, but on the contrary, in *Pembery v Lamdin* [1940] 2 All ER 435 the court, when dealing with wants of reparation caused by inherent defect, chose to treat the matter as one of degree, and in *Brew Brothers* [1970] 1 QB 612 the court effectively said that every case, whatever the causation, must be treated as one of degree.

I find myself, therefore, unable to accept counsel's contention for the defendants that a doctrine such as he enunciates has any place in the law of landlord and tenant. The true test is, as the cases show, that it is always a question of degree whether that which the tenant is being asked to do can properly be described as repair, or whether on the contrary it would involve giving back to the landlord a wholly different thing from that which he demised.

In deciding this question, the proportion which the cost of the disputed work bears to the value or cost of the whole premises, may sometimes be helpful as a guide. . . . The expansion joints form but a trivial part of this whole building and looking at it as a question of degree, I do not consider that they amount to such a change in the character of the building as to take them out of the ambit of the covenant to repair.

I pass to counsel's second point for the defendants, namely that the tenant is not liable under the repair covenant for that part of any work of repair necessary to remedy an inherent defect. Again it seems to me that this must be a question of degree.

In *Lucrott v Wakely and Wheeler* [1911] 1 KB 905 the wall was defective in the sense that it had no proper footings or damp course. When it was rebuilt, concrete footings and damp course were provided. The court nevertheless found the tenant liable for the whole cost of the work including these improvements. Counsel for the defendants seeks to distinguish that case because he says that in *Lurcott* the improvements were necessary to comply with the requirements of the statute. Here there was no such requirement and the expansion joints were included merely as a matter of moral duty.

. . . Counsel for the defendants urges me not to consider cost and that may, perhaps, in some circumstances, be right. He argues that the result of carrying out this improvement is to give back to the landlord a safe building instead of a dangerous one and this means the premises now are of a wholly different character. Further, he argues that because they are of a wholly different character, the work on expansion joints, the work necessary to cure the inherent defect, is an improvement of a character which transforms the nature of the premises demised, and, therefore, cannot fall within the ambit of the covenant to repair. I cannot accept this. I find myself, therefore, bound to follow the guidance given by Cozens-Hardy MR in *Lurcott's case*.

"It seems to me we should be narrowing in a most dangerous way the limit and extent of these covenants if we did not hold that the defendants were liable under covenants framed as these are to make good the cost of repairing this wall *in the only sense in which it can be repaired*, namely, by rebuilding it according to the requirements of the county council." (Judge's emphasis.)

Case 46 Smedley v Chumley and Hawke Ltd (1981) 44 P & CR 50 Court of Appeal

By covenant 3 (b) contained in a 21-year lease dated December 31, 1971, of a building near a river bank the defendant landlords covenanted

"To keep the main walls and roof in good structural repair and condition throughout the term and to promptly make good all defects due to faulty materials or workmanship in the construction of the premises."

The plaintiff tenant covenanted, *inter alia*, by covenant 2 (e) "well and substantially to repair, maintain and keep the interior and exterior of the premises in good order and condition." The building was to be used as a restaurant. By 1976 defects developed in the walls and floors of the restaurant. It appeared that the building was timber framed and built on a concrete raft supported by piles at the river end but not at the other. The unsupported end of the raft had sunk causing the raft to tilt. The landlords carried out remedial work. In September 1976 the tenant brought proceedings against the landlords claiming a breach of the covenant to repair and damage caused thereby. The landlords denied breach of covenant and pleaded that any defects in the premises were a direct consequence of the design of the building and so outside the scope of covenant 3 (b). Judge Mervyn Davies, QC, sitting as a High Court judge, tried the issue of the landlords' liability and held on the evidence that the landlords were in breach of covenant 3 (b) since the walls were not in good substantial repair and condition.

On appeal by the landlords, the architect supporting them:

Held (1) Dismissing the appeal, that when construing a covenant to repair a particular building, the state in which it was at the date of the lease and the precise terms of the lease should be looked at and then it should be decided whether the work could fairly be termed "repair"; that the two covenants in 3 (b) under which the landlords were responsible for the good structural condition of the walls and roof and for any defects due to faulty materials or workmanship in the construction of the premises were independent of each other so that the responsibility for keeping the walls and roof in good structural condition was unqualified and was placed firmly upon the landlords; that, on the facts, the only way to put the walls and roof in a safe structural condition was to carry out such major work to the foundations as was necessary and there was ample evidence to conclude that the landlords were in breach of their covenant.

Cumming Bruce LJ said (in part)

On the meaning of the words "To keep the main walls and roof in good structural repair and condition throughout the term," I, like Judge Mervyn Davies, derive assistance from the judgment of Fletcher-Moulton LJ in *Lurcott v Wakely* [1911] 1 KB 905. There this court was deciding the extent of a tenant's covenant "to well and substantially repair ... and keep in thorough repair and good condition ... the ...premises ... demised" in a lease for a term of 28 years of a house at least 200 years old, in which a wall had become unsafe through old age and lapse of time so that it had to be rebuilt. Fletcher-Moulton LJ first sought to give full meaning to each word of the covenant. Then he examined the effect of the covenants to keep the premises in good condition and to keep them in thorough repair as compared with the covenant to repair. The first two covenants imposed an obligation to keep the house in a certain state and he drew no wide distinction between keeping in thorough repair and keeping in good condition as both describe the condition of the house. If the house was no longer in that condition, the covenantor was obliged to put it into that condition, as this court had decided in *Proudfoot v Hart* (1890) 25 QBD 42. The covenant to repair by contrast imposed a duty to perform the operation of repair . . .

. . . The judge applied the test propounded in this court in *Lurcott v Wakely*, (*supra*) and concluded:

"The evidence shows that on September 14, 1976, the walls of the Vandyke Restaurant were unstable due to subsidence. That means that the walls were not 'in good substantial repair and condition,' as I understand these words. According, the [landlords] were in breach of covenant 3 (b)."

In my judgment, there was ample evidence to support that finding and conclusion.

The answer of the landlords is that the judge was wrong because the effect of the conclusion was to impose on the landlords an obligation to carry out an improvement and give to the tenant different and better premises than the premises constituting the parcels of the lease. The argument is put in two ways. There is a long line of authority to the effect that where a tenant is liable to keep in repair, he is not liable to do work that has the effect of giving the landlord a different and better house than the house that was let. Counsel for the landlords and the third party relied upon *Lister v Lane & Nesham, Pembrey v Lamdin, Sotheby v Grundy* and *Brew Brothers Ltd v Snax (Ross) Ltd (supra)*.

I make two observations upon those cases. It is important to distinguish the extent of the obligations where the lessor has let to the lessee an old house which has gradually deteriorated, through the inevitable effect of the passage of time, from the extent of the obligations imposed in connection with the lease of premises recently constructed. Many of the old cases are concerned with the former situation and do not assist in the analysis of the latter situation. Secondly, in order to discover whether there is an obligation to do work made necessary in order to correct the effect of defects in design, it is necessary

to examine carefully the whole lease and to decide the intention
to be collected therefrom, and in this lease the intention was
to place upon the landlords an unqualified obligation to keep
the walls and roof in good structural condition.

Then it is contended that the work required to make the walls
and roof safe was such that it involved an improvement to the
premises and rendered the premises different premises from the
parcels demised. Those parcels were, it is said, premises with
defective foundations, so designed that the base on which the
walls were built was bound to tilt over in four or five years.
The work necessarily done to make the walls and roof stable
and safe involved giving the premises a new and different character, namely, a foundation which enabled the house to stand
instead of tumbling down. The landlords rely upon *Brew Brothers
Ltd v Snax (Ross) Ltd (supra)* and in particular the passage in the
judgment of Phillimore LJ where he accepted that the vital question in each case is whether the total work to be done can properly
be regarded as repair since it involves no more than renewal
or replacement of defective parts, or whether it is in effect
renewal or replacement of substantially the whole, a question
of degree in each case.

It was contended on behalf of the landlords that the test
whether the effect of the works was to render the premises something different from the premises conveyed is to be applied by
comparing the physical state of the premises as they were at
the date of the lease with their physical state after the work
had been done.

I prefer to compare the premises contemplated by the parties
at the date of the lease with the premises as changed by the
works actually done. Here the landlords built a complex of
chalets with a restaurant for the use of the public including the
persons occupying the chalets. Having built the restaurant they
let it to the tenant on terms that the tenant would run it as
a restaurant for the use of their licensees. The landlords accepted
the obligation to keep the structure of the walls of the restaurant
in good structural condition. When the work was done, they
returned the restaurant to the tenant in the state it was in at
the date of the lease. The only difference was that the structure
of walls and roof were stable and safe upon foundations made
structurally stable.

I would distinguish the facts in the instant case from the facts
in *Brew Brothers Ltd v Snax (Ross) Ltd*. I compare and contrast
the extent of the obligations imposed by the covenant to keep
in repair in the context of the lease and of the circumstances

in that case with the extent of the obligation, with its emphasis upon structure, in covenant 3 (b). That emphasis upon structure is significant, because the structural condition of walls and roof is likely to depend on their foundations. So here I would hold that after the works were done the difference to the premises was that the walls and roof were in the condition that both parties contemplated as their necessary condition at the date of the lease.

Case 47 *Elmcroft Developments Ltd v Tankersley-Sawyer* (1984) 270 EG 140 Court of Appeal

The appellants were the head-lessors of a late Victorian purpose-built block of flats, and were appealing against three separate actions. In each case the lessors had covenanted to "maintain and keep the exterior of the building and the roof, the main walls, timbers and drains thereof in good and tenantable repair and condition".

The problem in each case consisted of penetrating damp in the ground-floor flat due to the damp-proof course having been positioned below the ground level, with a consequent bridging effect rendering the damp course ineffective. The surveyor estimated that the cost of the remedial work would be approximately £500 in two cases and £200 in the other case. The tenants contended that the work was within the scope of the landlords' covenant to repair in which they covenanted to

"maintain and keep the exterior of the building and the roof, the main walls, timbers and drains thereof in good and tenantable repair and condition."

Held (1) The landlords were in breach of their covenant to repair. The remedial works required did not go beyond "repair" as defined by the authorities as such works did not involve the provision of a wholly different thing from that demised.

Ackner LJ said (in part)

[The] various well-known authorities were all viewed again by Forbes J in the case of *Ravenseft Properties Ltd v Davstone (Holdings) Ltd* [1980] 1 QB 12. The facts are quite irrelevant to this case, but he held—and this was in no way disputed by [counsel] as being a wrong approach—that it was a question of degree whether work carried out on a building was a repair or work that so changed the character of the building as to involve giving back to the landlord a wholly different building to that demised.

In view of the learned judge's findings of fact, I see no problem at all in deciding this matter as one of degree. I fully accept the learned judge's findings, which were these:

"This is not a case, therefore, where the dry condition of the premises can be achieved only by, for example, the reconstruction or renewal of the whole of the subject-matter of the covenant or by making a substantial alteration in the design or structure of the building or the main walls thereof. It does not involve the demolition and rebuilding of any wall nor does it involve any, or any major, structural alterations."

He went on to say that, as a matter of degree,

"the work which the appellants will be required to undertake is not such that will involve the plaintiffs in giving to the defendants a new or a wholly different thing from that demised. That work does not involve a change in the nature and character of the flats, nor do the flats undergo a radical change by the insertion of a damp-proof course; one exists, albeit one which became ineffective by being bridged."

[Counsel's] sheet anchor is a case *Pembery v Lamdin* [1940] 2 All ER 434. That was a case in which there had been let premises known as 62 Blandford Street, Marylebone, consisting of a shop and premises on the ground floor, together with what Slesser LJ referred to as "a cellar for the most part built into the ground, without any precautions against damp oozing through the porous bricks into the cellar". The remedial work necessary was extensive. It involved removing panelling from the walls, cleaning down, asphalting the walls, and building a $4\frac{1}{2}$-inch wall inside to keep the asphalt in position, and laying a new concrete floor to prevent water coming under the walls. It was held that the landlord was not liable under his repairing covenant because otherwise it would have involved ordering him to give the tenant a different thing from that which was demised.

I personally find this case of no assistance at all. It does not involve the letting of a flat. It involved letting of premises that contained this cellar in a building which was built some 100 years before the court considered the problems. That must be round about 1840. We are concerned with a letting a few years ago of what was built as a separate self-contained flat and a flat in a high-class fashionable residential area in the centre of London.

I entirely agree with what Forbes J said in the *Ravenseft* case
. . . that this was a decision arrived at by considering the question
as one of degree. That view was followed by the learned county
court judge, and I consider that he was wholly right in so doing.

Note (i) The decision in *Elite Investments Ltd v T I Bainbridge
Silencers Ltd* [Case 118] [situated at the end of the Preface] should
be read in the context of this section.

4 IMPLIED REPAIRING OBLIGATIONS

4.1 Houses at low rents

At common law there is no implied obligation that an unfurnished house is fit for human habitation at the commencement of the term. Such an obligation exists in the case of a furnished letting.

Case 48 Sleafer v Lambeth Metropolitan Borough Council [1959] 3 All ER 378 Court of Appeal

A local authority let a flat to a tenant on a weekly tenancy under a written tenancy agreement, containing no express stipulation as to the liability to repair but the following conditions:

"(2) The tenant is required to reside in the dwelling which is to be used as a private dwelling only ... (9) The tenant shall not do or allow to be done any decorative or other work to any part of the dwelling without consent in writing. Nails on no account are to be driven into the walls, floors, or any part of the dwelling ... (11) The [landlords] shall be at liberty on production of a written authority under the hand of the town clerk or other authorised officer by [their] agents or workmen to enter the dwelling to inspect the state of repair and to execute repairs therein, or for any other purpose, at all reasonable times of the day ... (15) The tenant shall deliver up the dwelling at the end of the tenancy together with all landlords' fixtures in good and tenantable repair and condition (subject to fair wear and tear) and with all locks, keys and fastenings complete".

In practice the repairs were done by the landlords. The front door of the flat became difficult to close through jamming against the weatherplate fixed inside the threshold and against the upright, and evidence was given that this was the subject of a complaint to the authority but it was not put right. When leaving the flat one evening, the tenant was pulling hard at the handle or knocker when it came away in his hand and he fell heavily against an iron balustrade opposite and was injured.

Held (1) The landlords were not liable to the tenant for damages in respect of his injury because:

(i) there was no duty on the landlords to do such a repair to the demised premises as this, viz., the repair to the door so as to ease its shutting, in the absence of contractual obligation to that effect, and

(ii) no term should be implied in the contract of tenancy, that is to say, (a) (*per Morris* and *Ormerod, LJJ*) no term that the landlords would repair the demised premises of which the door formed part, since condition (9) of the tenancy agreement did not prohibit the tenant from doing work of repair but merely required him to obtain the landlord's consent before he did it, and (b) *per Willmer, LJ*) no term that the landlords would do this repair to the demised premises, viz., the repair of the door by easing its shutting.

Morris LJ said (in part)

... Counsel for the tenant submitted that there was to be implied in the contract of tenancy a term which would make the landlords liable. In his reply, he somewhat modified the term that he originally submitted should be implied. He first submitted that, if a part of the demised premises or access thereto, the use of which was necessary for the tenant, could not reasonably be used by him unless it was kept in repair, and if the right to repair it was solely in the landlords, then there was an implied contractual term that it could be repaired by the landlords provided they knew, or had adequate notice, of the necessity for such repair. Counsel somewhat simplified that contention, for he submitted that, on the facts of this case, it was to be implied that the landlords should make the premises in all respects reasonably fit for human habitation. If there was an implied term to that effect, it would be necessary for counsel for the tenant to assert that, if a door jammed and could only be closed with difficulty, the house was not reasonably fit for human habitation. Counsel for the tenant further submitted that, apart from the implication of a term, in all the circumstances, there was a duty in the landlords to effect repairs.

It is common ground that there is no question of the application of any statutory provisions. Counsel for the tenant in his interesting argument cited a number of cases dealing with the obligations that may lie on landlords in certain circumstances. He began by referring to *Miller v Hancock* [1893] 2 QB 177 and later made a submission as to the extent to which that case still survived. He referred us to such cases as *Hargroves, Aronson & Co v Hartopp*

[1905] 1 KB 472, *Dunster v Hollis* [1918] 2 KB 795, and *Cockburn v Smith* [1924] 2 KB 119 and to several other cases.

If a landlord lets a flat and retains the staircase which gives access to it, questions may arise as to the obligations cast on the landlord. If a landlord lets a flat and retains possession of the premises above the flat, questions may arise as to his obligations if rainwater is allowed to go into the flat. But it seems to me that such questions do not arise in the present case. In the present case, the door was clearly a part of the demised premises.

In regard to the general law concerning premises let on lease, we were referred by counsel for the landlords to several cases, including *Hart v Windsor* (1844) 12 M & W 68. In his judgment in that case, Parke B, said:

"It appears, therefore, to us to be clear upon the old authorities, that there is no implied warranty on a lease of a house, or of land, that it is, or shall be, reasonably fit for habitation or cultivation. The implied contract relates only to the estate, not to the condition of the property."

In *Cockburn v Smith* (*supra*) Bankes LJ, said this:

"I want to make it plain at the outset that this is not a letting of the whole house where, without an express covenant or a statutory obligation to repair the landlords would clearly be under no liability to repair any part of the demised premises whether the required repairs were structural or internal and whether they had or had not notice of the want of repair."

Statute 1: Landlord and Tenant Act 1985. Section 8
Implied terms as to fitness for human habitation

8.—(1) In a contract to which this section applies for the letting of a house for human habitation there is implied, notwithstanding any stipulation to the contrary—

(a) a condition that the house is fit for human habitation at the commencement of the tenancy, and

(b) an undertaking that the house will be kept by the landlord fit for human habitation during the tenancy.

(2) The landlord, or a person authorised by him in writing, may at reasonable times of the day, on giving 24 hours' notice in writing to the tenant or occupier, enter premises to which this section applies for the purpose of viewing their state and condition.

(3) This section applies to a contract if—

(a) the rent does not exceed the figure applicable in accordance with subsection (4), and

(b) the letting is not on such terms as to the tenant's responsibility as are mentioned in subsection (5).

(4) The rent limit for the application of this section is shown by the following Table, by reference to the date of making of the contract and the situation of the premises:

TABLE

Date of making of contract	Rent limit
Before 31st July 1923.	In London: £40 Elsewhere: £26 or £16
On or after 31 July 1923 and before 6th July 1957.	In London: £40 Elsewhere: £26
On or after 6th July 1957	In London £80 Elsewhere: £52

(5) This section does not apply where a house is let for a term of three years or more (the lease not being determinable at the option of either party before the expiration of three years) upon terms that the tenant puts the premises into a condition reasonably fit for human habitation.

(6) In this section "house" includes—

(a) a part of a house, and

(b) any yard, garden, outhouses and appurtenances belonging to the house or usually enjoyed with it.

Note:

(i)   These provisions were formerly contained in section 6 of the Housing Act 1957.

(ii) The application of section 8 of the 1985 Act to certain houses occupied by agricultural workers is contained in section 9 of the 1985 Act.

4.2 Repairing obligations in short leases

The repairing obligation might be borne by the landlord expressly in the lease or it may be imposed on him by virtue of an implied repairing obligation. The repairing obligation most commonly found in leases of dwelling-houses is implied by virtue of sections

11 to 14 of the Landlord and Tenant Act 1985 [formerly sections 32 and 33 of the Housing Act 1961].

Statute 2: Landlord and Tenant Act 1985. Sections 11–14

Repairing obligations in short leases

11.—(1) In a lease to which this section applies (as to which, see sections 13 and 14) there is implied a covenant by the lessor—

  (a) to keep in repair the structure and exterior of the dwelling-house (including drains, gutters and external pipes),

  (b) to keep in repair and proper working order the installations in the dwelling-house for the supply of water, gas and electricity and for sanitation (including basins, sinks, baths and sanitary conveniences, but not other fixtures, fittings and appliances for making use of the supply of water, gas or electricity), and

  (c) to keep in repair and proper working order the installations in the dwelling-house for space heating and heating water.

(2) The covenant implied by subsection (1) ("the lessor's repairing covenant") shall not be construed as requiring the lessor—

  (a) to carry out works or repairs for which the lessee is liable by virtue of his duty to use the premises in a tenant-like manner, or would be so liable but for an express covenant on his part,

  (b) to rebuild or reinstate the premises in the case of destruction or damage by fire, or by tempest, flood or other inevitable accident, or

  (c) to keep in repair or maintain anything which the lessee is entitled to remove from the dwelling-house.

(3) In determining the standard of repair required by the lessor's repairing covenant, regard shall be had to the age, character and prospective life of the dwelling-house and the locality in which it is situated.

(4) A covenant by the lessee for the repair of the premises is of no effect so far as it relates to the matters mentioned in subsection (1)(a) to (c), except so far as it imposes on the lessee any of the requirements mentioned in subsection (2)(a) or (c).

(5) The reference in subsection (4) to a covenant by the lessee for the repair of the premises includes a covenant—

  (a) to put in repair or deliver up in repair,

  (b) to paint, point or render,

  (c) to pay money in lieu of repairs by the lessee, or

  (d) to pay money on account of repairs by the lessor.

(6) In a lease in which the lessor's repairing covenant is implied there is also implied a covenant by the lessee that the lessor,

or any person authorised by him in writing, may at reasonable times of the day and on giving 24 hours' notice in writing to the occupier, enter the premises comprised in the lease for the purpose of viewing their condition and state or repair.

Restriction on contracting out of s. 11

12.—(1) A covenant or agreement, whether contained in a lease to which section 11 applies or in an agreement collateral to such a lease, is void in so far as it purports—

(a) to exclude or limit the obligations of the lessor or the immunities of the lessee under that section, or

(b) to authorise any forfeiture or impose on the lessee any penalty disability or obligation in the event of his enforcing or relying upon those obligations or immunities,

unless the inclusion of the provision was authorised by the county court.

(2) The county court may, by order made with the consent of the parties, authorise the inclusion in a lease, or in an agreement collateral to a lease, of provisions excluding of modifying in relation to the lease, the provisions of section 11 with respect to the repairing obligations of the parties if it appears to the court that it is reasonable to do so, having regard to all the circumstances of the case, including the other terms and conditions of the lease.

Leases to which s. 11 applies: general rule

13.—(1) Section 11 (repairing obligations) applies to a lease of a dwelling-house granted on or after 24th October 1961 for a term of less than seven years.

(2) In determining whether a lease is one to which section 11 applies—

(a) any part of the term which falls before the grant shall be left out of account and the lease shall be treated as a lease for a term commencing with the grant,

(b) a lease which is determinable at the option of the lessor before the expiration of seven years from the commencement of the term shall be treated as a lease for a term of less than seven years, and

(c) a lease (other than a lease to which paragraph (b) applies) shall not be treated as a lease for a term of less than seven years if it confers on the lessee an option for renewal for a term which, together with the original term, amounts to seven years or more.

(3) This section has effect subject to—

section 14 (leases to which section 11 applies: exceptions), and

section 32(2) (provisions not applying to tenancies within Part II of the Landlord and Tenant Act 1954).

Leases to which s. 11 applies: exceptions

14.—(1) Section 11 (repairing obligations) does not apply to a new lease granted to an existing tenant, or to a former tenant still in possession, if the previous lease was not a lease to which section 11 applied (and, in the case of a lease granted before 24th October 1961, would not have been if it had been granted on or after that date).

(2) In subsection (1)—

"existing tenant" means a person who is when, or immediately before, the new lease is granted, the lessee under another lease of the dwelling-house;

"former tenant still in possession" means a person who—

(*a*) was the lessee under another lease of the dwelling-house which terminated at some time before the new lease was granted, and

(*b*) between the termination of that other lease and the grant of the new lease was continuously in possession of the dwelling-house or of the rents and profits of the dwelling-house; and

"the previous lease" means the other lease referred to in the above definitions.

(3) Section 11 does not apply to a lease of a dwelling-house which is a tenancy of an agricultural holding within the meaning of the Agricultural Holdings Act 1948.

(4) Section 11 does not apply to a lease granted on or after 3rd October 1980 to—

a local authority,

a new town corporation,

an urban development corporation,

the Development Board for Rural Wales,

a registered housing association,

a co-operative housing association, or

an educational institution or other body specified, or of a class specified, by regulations under section 8 of the Rent Act 1977 (bodies making student lettings).

(5) Section 11 does not apply to a lease granted on or after 3rd October 1980 to—

(*a*) Her Majesty in right of the Crown (unless the lease is under the management of the Crown Estate Commissioners), or (*b*) a government department or a person holding in trust for Her Majesty for the purposes of a government department.

Meaning of "lease" and related expressions

16. In sections 11 to 15 (repairing obligations in short leases)—
(*a*) "lease" does not include a mortgage term;
(*b*) "lease of a dwelling-house" means a lease by which a building or part of a building is let wholly or mainly as a private residence, and "dwelling-house" means that building or part of a building;
(*c*) "lessee" and "lessor" mean, respectively, the person for the time being entitled to the term of a lease and to the reversion expectant on it.

The obligations under sections 11–14 of the 1985 Act do not arise until the landlord has notice of the disrepair.

Case 49 *McCarrick v Liverpool Corporation* [1947] AC 219 House of Lords

The appellant was at all material times the tenant of a dwelling-house in Liverpool of which the respondents were landlords. The rent was 7s. 6d. and by reason of which the house was subject to the provisions of the Housing Act 1936 s. 2 of which stipulates:

"(1) In any contract for letting for human habitation a house at a rent not exceeding (a) in the case of a house situate in the administrative county of London, forty pounds; (b) in the case of a house situate elsewhere, twenty-six pounds; there shall, notwithstanding any stipulation to the contrary, be implied a condition that the house is at the commencement of the tenancy, and an undertaking that the house will be kept by the landlord during the tenancy, in all respects reasonably fit for human habitation.

. . . (2) The landlord, or any person authorised by him in writing, may at reasonable times of the day, on giving twenty-four hours' notice in writing to the tenant or occupier, enter any premises to which this section applies for the purpose of viewing the state and condition thereof."

By reason of the defective condition of two stone steps leading from the kitchen to the back kitchen the house was not "reasonably fit for human habitation". In consequence of this defect the appellant's wife on June 9, 1943, fell and fractured her leg. The appellant brought an action for

damages against the respondents in the Liverpool Court of
Passage, the damages being agreed at £70. The deputy presiding judge, having held that the house was not kept in
the state required by s. 2 of the Act, nevertheless found
as a fact that no notice of want of repair was received by
the respondents. He accordingly dismissed the action. The
Court of Appeal having affirmed this decision, the appellant
appealed to the House of Lords.

Held (1) The undertaking implied by the section that a
dwelling-house will be kept in all respects reasonably fit
for human habitation is subject to an implied term that the
obligation on the landlord to repair any defect does not arise
until he has notice of it.

Lord Porter said (in part)
    ... in construing this statute its exact terms must be con-
sidered. It does not impose extraneously a duty upon the landlord, it merely inserts a term into the tenancy agreement, and
this term then becomes part of the contract between the parties,
whether they wish it or not. In such a tenancy there is no reason
why any term should not be implied, provided it is necessary
to secure the business efficacy of the contract and it is not contrary
to the provisions of the Act. In determining this question one
must treat the tenancy agreement as if the provision enjoined
by the Act was inserted in it and consider whether an agreement
in that form means that the landlord must keep the premises
habitable though no notice had been given to him that they were
or are not fit for human habitation. My Lords, I cannot see that
the insertion of the words "provided he knows that the premises
are not in habitable repair", or, if you please "provided that
the tenant has given him notice of the want of repair", is contra-
dictory of the wording of the section, though no doubt it limits
its effect. But it still has to be determined whether their insertion
is necessary to give business efficacy to the contract. I think it
is. In an ordinary case where a landlord undertakes to repair
the outside of the main structure of a house it is unusual to
insert an express covenant entitling him to enter and do the
repairs, though where the tenant undertakes to do some repairs
or decoration, it is usual to insert a covenant permitting the
landlord to enter and view in order to ascertain that the tenant
has complied with his covenant. Nevertheless in the former case
a right to enter and repair has, I think been implied, and the
landlord's obligation has been held only to arise if he has knowledge or notice of the want of repair: ... The reasoning in that

case was that it would be impossible for a landlord to carry out his obligations unless he could ascertain whether repairs were required and if they were could enter and do them. If cases under the Act are taken into consideration there are a number of decisions to the same effect. . . .

. . . *Murphy v Hurley* [1922] 1 AC 369 in my view supports the respondents' contention in the present case. In particular the words of Lord Sumner are apposite. He says:

> "The rule requiring a notice of want of repair by the tenant to the landlord, in the case of an ordinary landlord's repairing covenant . . . is well settled, and no one proposes to alter or restrict it. The nature and the conditions of this rule are, however, equally well settled. As a rule of construction, which reads into the covenant words—namely, "upon notice"— which are not there, its application naturally depends on the existence of those strong circumstances of necessity, which alone justify the implication of a condition upon an obligation, which is itself expressed unconditionally. Those circumstances are (1) that the tenant is in occupation and the landlord is not; (2) that the tenant, therefore, has the means of knowledge peculiarly in his possession, while the landlord has no right of access and no means of knowing the condition of the structure from time to time. . . and (3), perhaps I may add, that the repairs of dwelling-houses, however frequently required, are still casual and occasional, and not, as here, such as to demand of the landlord incessant vigilance and almost daily care"

My Lords, I doubt whether it is accurate to say that a landlord who is under an obligation to repair has no right of access but at least the tenant has the means of knowledge peculiarly in his possession and the requirements of repair are casual. In such circumstances, it would, I think, be unreasonable to require of the landlord the incessant vigilance and almost daily care envisaged by Lord Sumner, even though he had under his contract a right to enter and inspect. Particularly do these considerations apply when the duty imposed on the landlord is so stringent as that falling upon him under the Act. For my own part I find myself in agreement with the result arrived at in *Morgan v Liverpool Corporation* [1927] 2 KB 131.

Note:
   (i) If the repairing obligation is borne by the landlord either expressly or by implication the golden rule is that the

tenant must inform the landlord of the disrepair before the obligation becomes operative.
(ii) See para 2.7 for other authorities on the requirement for notice. See also the decision in *McGreal v Wake* [Case 59].

For the repairing obligation to be implied the lease must be for less than seven years.

Case 50 Brikom Investments Ltd v Seaford [1981] 1 WLR 863 Court of Appeal

A lease of a flat expressed to be for a term of seven years from November 1, 1969, contained a tenant's covenant to carry out all internal repairs. The tenant moved into the flat on November 1 and paid rent in advance as from that date. The lease was executed on or about November 12 and was delivered on November 15. In 1975 the landlords applied to the rent officer to determine a fair rent of the flat. The rent officer made his assessment on the footing that the landlords were liable for the repairs specified in section 32 (1) of the Housing Act 1961 and registered a higher rent than if the tenant were liable, and the landlords accepted the rent on that basis. Further assessments by the rent officer, on the same basis, were made in 1977 and 1979. In the event the tenant did the repairs himself and withheld a proportion of the rent to cover the cost.

In November 1979 the landlords brought an action against the tenant for possession and arrears of rent. In his defence the tenant claimed to set off the cost of the repairs against the arrears of rent. The landlords disputed their liability and claimed that the lease was for a term of seven years, and accordingly was not within section 33 (1) of the Act of 1961 and therefore they were not liable for the section 32 repairs. Judge Honig gave judgment for the landlords.

On appeal by the tenant:

Held (1) That on its true construction "lease" in section 33 (1) included an agreement for a lease as well as a lease, and for the purpose of that section the term of any lease as so defined began at the point of time at which the tenant was in a position to say that he was entitled to remain in the premises thereafter as tenant either at law or in equity; that that date was November 1, 1969. since all the terms of the lease had been agreed and there was part performance on that date by entry into possession and payment and acceptance of rent; and accordingly that the tenant's term was one of seven years and the landlords were therefore not in principle liable for section 32 repairs.

(2) But, allowing the appeal, that since the landlords had throughout accepted rent at an enhanced rate on the basis that they were liable for section 32 repairs, they were estopped from subsequently denying responsibility for the repairs while at the same time claiming rent at the enhanced rate, and the tenant could only be made liable for the repairs under his covenant if the registered rent was corrected to reflect the tenant's liability.

Ormrod LJ said (in part)

It has been held in many cases, of which *Earl Cadogan v Guinness* [1936] Ch 515, *Roberts v Church Commissioners for England* [1972] 1 QB 278 and *Bradshaw v Pawley* [1980] 1 WLR 10 are examples (arising, however, in connection with different statutes), that a term defined in a deed as beginning from a date prior to the delivery of the deed, say for 10 years from such date, is not a term of 10 years. It is a shorter term beginning from the date of delivery of the deed and ending 10 years from the earlier date specified in the lease: see *per* Clauson J in *Earl Cadogan v Guiness* [1936] Ch 515, 518, or, as Stamp LJ put it in *Roberts v Church Commissioners for England* [1972] 1 QB 278:

> "It is well settled that the habendum in a lease only marks the duration of the tenant's interest, and that the operation of the lease as a grant takes effect only from the time of its delivery: . . ."

[Counsel] for the tenant in this case, accordingly submits that, although the habendum refers to a term of seven years from November 1, 1969, the actual term created by the lease is two weeks short of seven years, and is, accordingly, a lease for a term of less than seven years and, therefore, falls within section 32.

The question to be decided, however, is what does the phrase "being a lease for a term of less than seven years" mean in the context of section 33. [Counsel] for the landlords, drew attention to section 33 (5), which reads:

> "In the application of this section to a lease granted for a term part of which falls before the grant, that part shall be left out of account and the lease shall be treated as a lease for a term commencing with the grant."

[Counsel] submitted that if section 33 (1) is construed in accordance with the principle laid down in the cases cited, subsection

(5) is wholly unnecessary because in any event the term cannot start before the grant. So, he says, section 33 (1) must refer to the term as described in the habendum, namely, seven years from November 1, 1969; the term in the present case is therefore not a term of less than seven years. This submission, however, does not help him because if he is right such a lease is caught later by the same subsection (5); the part falling before the grant must be left out of account, and the term computed from the date of the grant. So, he is back to square one!

This is obviously an unsatisfactory conclusion. It is difficult to believe that Parliament intended that the application of section 32, which seriously affects the rights of landlords and tenants, should depend on something so essentially fortuitous as the date of the delivery of the lease. Fortunately, there is another way of approaching the problem which the judge in the court below in substance adopted.

This Act (unlike the Acts with which this court was concerned in other cases) contains a definition section which defines the word "lease" in relatively broad terms. Section 32 (5) provides that "lease" includes, *inter alia*, "an agreement for a lease ... and any other tenancy," and the word "term" is to be construed accordingly. In the present case there was, undoubtedly, an agreement for a lease of seven years beginning on November 1, 1969, made by the parties on or before that date, because by that time the terms of the lease as set out in the specimen lease or in the counterpart had been agreed and there had been part performance by entry into possession and payment and acceptance of rent.

In *Roberts v Church Commissioners for England* [1972] 1 QB 278 there was, as Russell LJ emphasised, no agreement for a lease of the length required to satisfy the terms of section 3 (1) of the Leasehold Reform Act 1967, namely, a tenancy for a term of years certain exceeding 21 years. "Tenancy" in that Act means a "tenancy at law or in equity": section 37 (1) (*f*). Russell LJ suggested at p 284 a test which the tenant must pass to fulfil that definition, namely, that he

"must at some point of time be, or have been, in a position to say that, subject to options to determine, rights of re-entry and so forth, he is entitled to remain tenant for the next 21 years, whether at law or in equity."

The tenant in the present case is in a position to fulfil that test, substituting seven years, which is the relevant period under the Act of 1961. So if this is the right approach to the Act of 1961, as we think it is, we are entitled to hold that for the purposes of section 33 (1) there was an agreement for a lease, and therefore a "lease" as defined, for a term which was not less than seven years.

But the landlords have still to get over section 33 (5), the language of which is not very apt to agreements for a lease unless the words "granted" and "grant" are to be read as equivalent to "made." If this is permissible the subsection will still be effective to prevent the mischief at which it was presumably directed, that is, to prevent a landlord granting or agreeing to grant a lease for less than seven years and back-dating the term so as to make it seven years from some anterior date. We do not think that such a construction does undue violence to the language of these sections read as a whole.

If this goes beyond the limits of construction we think the same result follows from the application of section 33 (3), which deals with consecutive leases. The tenant in this case was a person who immediately before the lease was granted—that is, delivered—was the lessee under another lease, i.e. under the agreement for the lease which for the purpose of these provisions is to be regarded as a lease. So he is within section 33 (3) (*a*). The other lease—that is, the agreement for the lease—was not a lease to which section 32 applies because it was for not less than seven years; so section 33 (3) (ii) is satisfied and, accordingly, section 32 does not apply.

In our judgment, therefore, an agreement for a lease for a term of seven years is not caught by section 32, provided that the term begins on or after the date of the agreement, whether or not it is followed by a formal lease. Accordingly we would hold, in agreement with the judge in the court below, that section 32 does not apply to the lease in the present case, and that the liability for internal repairs is governed by the terms of the original lease.

Case 51 *Parker v O'Connor* [1974] 1 WLR 1161 Court of Appeal

A landlord let a dwelling house for a term of 90 years from June 24, 1970, at a rent of £546 a year for the first seven years with increases thereafter in accordance with a schedule. The lease contained full repairing covenants by the tenant who also convenanted to execute all works required by the local authority under any Act of Parliament. The landlord had a right to enter to inspect the state of repair. Clause 16 provided that if, in the event of the death of the landlord, either party should desire to determine the term and within six months of the death should give three months' notice in writing the lease should cease and be void.

In March 1973 the landlord served a notice under section 146 (1) of the Law of Property Act 1925 requiring the tenant to carry out repairs, mainly to the roof and walls, required by the local authority pursuant to a notice served under the Housing Acts 1957–1969. The tenant failed to carry out the work and served a counter-notice claiming the benefit of the Leasehold Property (Repairs) Act 1938. The landlord applied for leave to commence proceedings for re-entry and/or forfeiture and/or damages on the grounds set out in section 1 (5) (*a*), (*b*) and (*d*) of the Act of 1938. The tenant opposed the application and contended that the option to determine in clause 16 brought the lease within section 32 (1) of the Housing Act 1961 and in those circumstances he was not liable for repairs. The county court judge upheld that contention and refused the landlord leave to proceed.

On appeal by the landlord:

Held (1) Allowing the appeal, that though the lease might be determinable under clause 16 in the circumstances there set out, the landlord had no unfettered option thereunder to determine the lease before the expiration of seven years from the commencement of the term and therefore it could not be treated as a lease for less than seven years within the meaning of section 33 (1) of the Housing Act 1961; that accordingly, section 32 (1) of the Act did not apply, the tenant was liable to remedy the state of disrepair under his covenant in the lease, and the landlord was entitled to the leave she sought.

Edmund Davies LJ said (in part)

The question for determination here is whether this 90-year lease is one determinable at the option of the landlord before the expiration of seven years from its commencement, namely, June 24, 1970.

With profound respect to the county court judge, on the face of it I should have thought that the answer to that question was clear: It is not one determinable at the option of the landlord or the personal representatives of her estate before the expiration of seven years from June 24, 1970. On the contrary, no option to determine arises at all save on the death of the landlord, whenever that occurs. How, then, came it about that the experienced county court judge arrived at the opposite conclusion? He was greatly influenced by the decision of this court—in relation to an entirely different statute which employed entirely different language—in *Roberts v Church Commissioners for England* [1972] 1 QB 278. The court was there concerned with the interpretation of a provision in the Leasehold Reform Act 1967, section 3 of which defines a "long tenancy" for the purpose of that Act, which was, as is well known, one to enable tenants of houses held on long leases at low rents to acquire the freehold or an extended term . . .

I do not propose, for the purposes of this judgment, to relate the facts which gave rise to the decision in *Roberts v Church Commissioners for England*, save to say that the provisions in the lease there concerned were materially different from those in this case and that, in holding that the lease there was not granted for a term of years certain exceeding 21 years, Russell LJ said,:

> "In the course of the argument I ventured to suggest a test, which is that to fulfil the definition a tenant must at some point of time be, or have been, in a position to say that, subject to the options to determine, rights of re-entry and so forth, he is entitled to remain tenant for the next 21 years, whether at law or in equity. I remain of the opinion that this is a valid test . . . "

He went on to say that, in the circumstances of that case, the tenant was never in a position to assert his entitlement to remain tenant for the next 21 years.

With profound respect, the only value to be gained from that decision—on wholly different facts and dealing with an entirely different statutory provision—is to illustrate the obvious, namely, that, when the legislature seeks to deal with situations which are either actual or speculative, it experiences no difficulty in finding the necessary words so to do. Thus, section 3 (1), as I have already related, deals with a tenancy which "is (or may become)" terminable before the end of 21 years.

[Counsel] found himself obliged to submit—as he has done—that (turning to the Housing Act 1961) if the tenant is to retain the judgment in his favour that he secured from the county court judge, the opening words of section 33 (2) must be read in this way:

> "For the purposes of this section, a lease shall be treated as a lease for a term of less than seven years if it is, *or may become*, determinable at the option of the lessor before the expiration of seven years from the commencement of the term."

He says that, as the landlord may die before the expiration of seven years from June 1970, the tenant could never say that he was certain to be entitled to possession for that length of time.

Why does [counsel] submit that words of that kind should be added to those actually employed in subsection (2)? He said it was in order "to give business efficacy" to this lease. I do not understand that. The lease seems to me a businesslike document, which gives rise to no kind of ambiguity, and the statute requires no writing-in of further words in order to meet the circumstances of the present case. It is true that the landlord may die. She has survived since the lease was granted in July 1970, but, of course, being (as I gather) a lady of certainly mature years, she may die before the seven years are up. But to my way of thinking, this being a point of first impression, it is wrong to describe this 90 year lease, notwithstanding the proviso for determination in the circumstances contained in clause 16, as one for a term of years of less than seven.

Startling results would follow if the submission made on the tenant's behalf were to prevail. [Counsel] satisfied me, for example, that, in the light of section 149 (6) of the Law of Property Act 1925, every lease expressed to be for life would be a "short" lease within the terms of the Housing Act 1961. Again, the word "determinable" covers, of course, a variety of events—forfeiture for non-payment of rent; forfeiture on bankruptcy; and so on. A number of incidents may cause the premature termination of an otherwise fixed term. But that does not mean that it is a term which is determinable at the unfettered option of the lessor before the expiration of seven years.

Despite the valiant efforts of [counsel] who submitted that we are not here dealing with a common conveyancing situation, it appears to me that there are no remarkable features about this particular lease, and that startling results would follow were section 33 (2) to be construed in the way for which he contends.

For those reasons, I would allow the appeal. It is clear from the judgment of the judge that he was satisfied that the landlord had brought herself within paragraphs (*a*), (*b*) and (*d*) of subsection (5) of section 1 of the Act of 1938; and the proper conclusion is that, had he not construed sections 32 and 33 in the way he did, he would have granted leave because the landlord had established that there was an arguable case for proceeding under section 146.

Note:
(i) In *Department of Transport v Egoroff* [1986] 1 EGLR 89; (1986) 278 EG 1361 it was held that sections 32 and 33 of the Housing Act 1961 did not bind the Crown.

4.3 The interpretation of sections 11–14 of the 1985 Act

There is some doubt as to the meaning of the word "exterior" for the purposes of the implied obligation. In *Douglas-Scott v Scorgie* [Case 7] the roof of a top-floor flat was held to fall within the ambit of the implied obligation. In *Hopwood v Cannock Chase District Council* [Case 8] disrepair of a yard at the rear of the demised premises was held outside the covenant but this decision should be contrasted with that in *Brown v Liverpool Corporation*.

Case 52 Brown v Liverpool Corporation [1969] 3 All ER 1345
Court of Appeal

A small dwelling-house was let by the defendant corporation to the plaintiff and the letting was subject to the provisions of s. 32 of the Housing Act 1961. Access to the house from the road was through a gate, down four shallow steps and across a path comprising three flagstones about seven feet in length. The steps and the path were demised with the house. The steps were in a state of disrepair and the plaintiff fell and suffered injury. In the county court the defendant corporation was ordered to pay damages since the steps and path were held to be part of the structure and exterior of the dwelling-house within the meaning of s. 32 (1) (*a*). On appeal.

Held (1) The county court judge was entitled to find that the steps and path were an integral part of the building to which the covenants to repair implied by s. 32 (1) (*a*) applied.

Dankwerts LJ said (in part)

The question is, simply, whether, for the purposes of s. 32 of the Housing Act 1961, the steps and the short bit of flagstones leading down to the entrance of the house are within the terms "the structure and exterior of the dwelling-house (including drains, gutters and external pipes)".

It is clear to me that this is not part of the structure of the dwelling-house. I think I have a very fair idea of what is meant by the structure of a dwelling-house, and this is not part, of course, of the structure. On the other hand it seems to me equally

clear that the 7 feet of flagstones and the steps up do form part
of the exterior of the dwelling-house. They are attached in that
manner to the house for the purpose of access to this dwelling-
house, and they are part of the dwelling-house which is necessary for the purpose of anybody who wishes to live in the dwelling-house enjoying that privilege. If they have no means of access
of some sort they could not get there, and these are simply the
means of access. The steps are an outside structure, and therefore, it seems to me they are plainly part of the building, and,
therefore, the covenant implied by s. 32 of the Act of 1961 fits
and applies to the obligations of the landlords in this case.

In my view the learned county court judge reached the right
conclusion and I would dismiss the appeal.

Case 53 *Liverpool City Council v Irwin* (1976) 32 P & CR 43
House of Lords

The appellants were the tenants of a council maisonette
in one of three tower blocks built in 1966. The document
by which the maisonette was let to the appellants contained
no covenants on the part of the council. Within 18 months
of their being built the tower blocks had become unfit to
live in by reason of vandalisation of the lifts and staircases,
blockage of the rubbish chutes due to misuse, vandalisation
of the play facilities and drying rooms, overflowing of the
lavatory cisterns and failure on several occasions of the water
supply. The water carried by the overflow pipes of the lavatory cisterns ran on to the balconies of the flats below and
flooded them. The tenants of the flats attempted to stop
the overflowing of the cisterns by bending the arms of the
ball-cocks, but that had the result that the cisterns only half
filled and did not flush properly, resulting in bad sanitation.
The dwellings suffered substantially from damp. By way
of protest, the appellants stopped paying their rent. The
council took proceedings against them for possession, and
they counterclaimed nominal damages (a) for breach of the
landlord's implied covenant for quiet enjoyment, (b) for
breach of the implied covenants to repair. The county court
judge made an order for possession, but found in the appellants' favour on their counterclaim and awarded them nominal damages. The council appealed. On the appeal, the
appellants conceded that there had been no breach of the
landlord's covenant for quiet enjoyment. They submitted
that there was an implied covenant by landlords of multi-

storey buildings to maintain the common parts of such buildings which were in their occupation and intended for the
use of tenants. The Court of Appeal (Lord Denning MR
dissenting in part) allowed the council's appeal.

The tenants appealed by leave of the House of Lords.

Held, Allowing the appeal in part, (1) that there was to
be implied into the contract of letting between the tenants
and the council, in order to complete it and give it a bilateral
character, an easement for the tenants and their licensees
to use the stairs, a right in the nature of an easement to
use the lifts and an easement to use the rubbish chutes;
that there was to be read into the contract such accompany-
ing obligation on the part of the council as the nature of
the contract itself implicity required and no more; that,
whereas in general a servient owner was under no liability
to keep the servient tenement in repair for the benefit of
the dominant owner, where an essential means of access
to units in a building of multi-occupation was retained in
the landlord's occupation there should be an obligation on
the landlord to maintain it unless the obligation was in a
defined manner placed on the tenants, individually or collectively; that the standard of the obligation was to take reasonable care to keep in reasonable repair and usability, taking
into account what a reasonable set of tenants should do
for themselves; that where a passage was constructed and
an easement over it was useless without some artificial light
being provided the obligation included an obligation to
maintain adequate lighting; that, however, in the present
case it had not been shown that there had been any breach
of the council's obligations as defined.

(2) That a water closet cistern which flooded the floor each
time it was used could not be said to be in "proper working
order"; and that, accordingly, the council were in breach
if their implied obligation under section 32 (1) (*b*) (i) of the
Housing Act 1961 and the tenants should recover nominal
obligations damages of £5.

Lord Wilberforce said (in part)

I consider first the tenants' claim is so far as it is based on
contract. The first step must be to ascertain what the contract
is. This may look elementary, even naïve, but it seems to me
to be the essential step and to involve from the start, an approach
different from, if simpler than, that taken by the members of
the Court of Appeal. We look first at documentary material. As

is common with council lettings there is no formal demise, or lease or tenancy agreement. There is a document headed "Liverpool Corporation, Liverpool City Housing Dept." and described as "Conditions of Tenancy." This contains a list of obligations upon the tenant—he shall do this, he shall not do that, or he shall not do that without the corporation's consent. This is an amalgam of obligations added to from time to time, no doubt, to meet complaints, emerging situations, or problems as they appear to the council's officers. In particular there have been added special provisions relating to multi-storey flats which are supposed to make the conditions suitable to such dwellings. We may note under "Further special notes" some obligations not to obstruct staircases and passages, and not to permit children under 10 to operate any lifts. I mention these as a recognition of the existence and relevance of these facilities. At the end there is a form for signature by the tenant stating that he accepts the tenancy. On the landlords' side there is nothing, no signature, no demise, no covenant: the contract takes effect as soon as the tenants sign the form and are let into possession.

We have then a contract which is partly, but not wholly, stated in writing. In order to complete it, in particular to give it a bilateral character, it is necessary to take account of the actions of the parties and the circumstances. As actions of the parties, we must note the granting of possession by the landlords and reservation by them of the "common parts"—stairs, lifts, chutes, etc. As circumstances we must include the nature of the premises, *viz.* a maisonette for family use on the ninth floor of a high block, one which is occupied by a large number of other tenants, all using the common parts and dependent upon them, none of them having any expressed obligation to maintain or repair them.

To say that the construction of a complete contract out of these elements involves a process of "implication" may be correct; it would be so if implication means the supplying of what is not expressed. But there are varieties of implications which the courts think fit to make and they do not necessarily involve the same process. Where there is, on the face of it, a complete, bilateral contract, the courts are sometimes willing to add terms to it, as implied terms: this is very common in mercantile contracts where there is an established usage: in that case the courts are spelling out what both parties know and would, if asked, unhesitatingly agree to be part of the bargain. In other cases, where there is an apparently complete bargain, the courts are willing to add a term on the ground that without it the contract will not work—this is the case, if not of *The Moorcock* (1889) 14

PD 64 itself on its facts, at least of the doctrine of *The Moorcock* as usually applied. This is, as was pointed out by the majority in the Court of Appeal, a strict test—though the degree of strictness seems to vary with the current legal trend—and I think that they were right not to accept it as applicable here. There is a third variety of implication, that which I think Lord Denning MR favours, or at least did favour in this case, and that is the implication of reasonable terms. But though I agree with many of his instances, which in fact fall under one or other of the preceding heads, I cannot go so far as to endorse his principle; indeed, it seems to me, with respect, to extend a long, and undesirable, way beyond sound authority.

The present case, in my opinion, represents a fourth category, or I would rather say a fourth shade on a continuous spectrum. The court here is simply concerned to establish what the contract is, the parties not having themselves fully stated the terms. In this sense the court is searching for what must be implied.

What then should this contract be held to be? There must first be implied a letting, that is, a grant of the right of exclusive possession to the tenants. With this there must, I would suppose, be implied a covenant for quiet enjoyment, as a necessary incident of the letting. The difficulty begins when we consider the common parts. We start with the fact that the demise is useless unless access is obtained by the staircase; we can add that, having regard to the height of the block, and the family nature of the dwellings, the demise would be useless without a lift service; we can continue that, there being rubbish chutes built into the structures and no other means of disposing of light rubbish, there must be a right to use the chutes. The question to be answered—and it is the only question in the case—is what is to be the legal relationship between landlord and tenant as regards these matters.

There can be no doubt that there must be implied (i) an easement for the tenants and their licensees to use the stairs, (ii) a right in the nature of an easement to use the lifts, (iii) an easement to use the rubbish chutes.

But are these easements to be accompanied by any obligation upon the landlord, and what obligation? There seem to be two alternatives. The first, for which the council contends, is for an easement coupled with no legal obligation, except such as may arise under the Occupiers' Liability Act 1957 as regards the safety of those using the facilities and possibly such other liability as might exist under the ordinary law of tort. The alternative is for easements coupled with some obligation on the part of the landlords as regards the maintenance of the subject of them, so that they are available for use.

My Lords, in order to be able to choose between these, it is necessary to define what test is to be applied, and I do not find this difficult. In my opinion such obligation should be read into the contract as the nature of the contract itself implicitly requires, no more, no less: a test, in other words, of necessity. The relationship accepted by the corporation is that of landlord and tenant: the tenant accepts obligations accordingly, in relation *inter alia* to the stairs, the lifts and the chutes. All these are not just facilities, or conveniences provided at discretion: they are essentials of the tenancy without which life in the dwellings, as a tenant, is not possible. To leave the landlord free of contractual obligation as regards these matters, and subject only to administrative or political pressure, is, in my opinion, inconsistent totally with the nature of this relationship. The subject matter of the lease (high rise blocks) and the relationship created by the tenancy demand, of their nature, some contractual obligation on the landlord . . .

. . . I accept, of course, the argument that a mere grant of an easement does not carry with it any obligation on the part of the servient owner to maintain the subject matter. The dominant owner must spend the necessary money, for example in repairing a drive leading to his house. And the same principle may apply when a landlord lets an upper floor with access by a staircase: responsibility for maintenance may well rest on the tenant. But there is a difference between that case and the case where there is an essential means of access, retained in the landlord's occupation, to units in a building of multi-occupation, for unless the obligation to maintain is, in a defined manner, placed upon the tenants, individually or collectively, the nature of the contract, and the circumstances, require that it be placed on the landlord.

It remains to define the standard. My Lords, if, as I think, the test of the existence of the term is necessity the standard must surely not exceed what is necessary having regard to the circumstances. To imply an absolute obligation to repair would go beyond what is a necessary legal incident and would indeed be unreasonable. An obligation to take reasonable care to keep in reasonable repair and usability is what fits the requirements of the case. Such a definition involves—and I think rightly— recognition that the tenants themselves have their responsibilities. What it is reasonable to expect of a landlord has a clear relation to what a reasonable set of tenants should do for themselves.

I add one word as to lighting. In general I would accept that a grant of an easement of passage does not carry with it an obligation on the grantor to light the way. The grantee must take the way accompanied by the primeval separation of darkness from light and if he passes during the former must bring his own illumination. I think that *Huggett v Miers* [1908] 2 KB 278 was decided on this principle and possibly also *Devine v London Housing Society Ltd* [1950] WN 550. But the case may be different when the means of passage are constructed, and when natural light is either absent or insufficient. In such a case, to the extent that the easement is useless without some artificial light being provided, the grant should carry with it an obligation to take reasonable care to maintain adequate lighting—comparable to the obligation as regards the lifts. To impose an absolute obligation would be unreasonable; to impose some might be necessary. We have not sufficient material before us to see whether the present case on its facts meets these conditions.

I would hold therefore that the landlords' obligation is as I have described. And in agreement, I believe, with your Lordships I would hold that it has not been shown in this case that there was any breach of that obligation. On the main point therefore I would hold that the appeal fails.

Case 54 *Campden Hill Towers Ltd v Gardner* (1976) 242 EG 375
Court of Appeal

An underlease of a flat on the third floor of a block provided that the demise should not include any part of the outside walls or roof of the flat. By clause 4 (2) of the underlease the lessee covenanted to pay a service charge in respect of the lessor's obligation under the underlease to keep in repair, *inter alia*, the service installations in and the common parts and the exterior of "the premises," which for the purposes of the underlease were defined as including the whole block of flats and other property including another block of flats. The lessors claimed payment of a service charge in accordance with that covenant, and the lessees refused to pay the whole of it on the ground of the covenant imposed on the lessors by section 32 (1) (*a*) and (*b*) of the Housing Act 1961 to keep in repair the structure and exterior of the dwelling-house and to keep in repair and proper working order the installations in the dwelling-house; they contended that the covenant in the lease was correspondingly of no effect and that the lessors were not entitled to recover the relevant proportion of the service charge. The lessors contended that, save as regarded the matters in parenthesis, section 32 (1) (*a*) imposed an obligation to keep in repair only the structure and exterior of the particular flat demised, and that, for example, the outside walls were expressly excluded from the demise. Under section 32 (1) (*b*) they contended that "the installations in the dwelling-house" were confined to installations actually in the flat demised. The lessees contended that those words applied to anything outside the flat the proper functioning of which was required in order to enable the installation within the flat to function as it was intended to do. The judge gave judgment in favour of the lessees under section 32 (1) (*a*), saying that in the case of a block of flats the intention of the legislature must have been to regard the whole building as the "exterior" of the dwelling-house. The lessors appealed. It was accepted by them for the purposes of the appeal that the underlease was a lease to which section 32 applied.

Held, By consent dismissing the appeal, (1) that the relevant "dwelling-house" for the purposes of section 32 (1) (*a*) of the Act of 1961 was the flat, not the block, and that it was not correct to regard the whole building as the exterior of the dwelling-house; but that anything which, in the ordinary use of words, would be regarded as part of the structure or exterior of the particular dwelling-house, regarded as a separate part of the building, would be within the scope of section 32 (1) (*a*), and that in the present case that paragraph applied to the outside wall or walls of the flat, including that part of the outside wall of the block which constituted a wall of the flat and the outside of inner party walls of the flat, the outer sides of horizontal divisions between the flat and flats above and below it and the structural framework and beams directly supporting the floors, ceilings and walls of the flat.

Quaere, as to the meaning of "premises" in section 32 (1).

(2) That section 32 (1) (*b*) of the Act of 1961 related only to the installations in the physical confines of the flat.

Megaw LJ said (in part)

For the purpose of considering the issue which does arise in the appeal, it is necessary to have in mind the definition of "dwelling-house" for the purpose of section 32, as given in subsection (5) thereof. Subsection (5) reads: ". . . 'lease of a dwelling-house' means a lease whereby a building or part of a building is let wholly or mainly as a private dwelling, and 'the dwelling-house' means that building or part of a building; . . . "

It follows that the relevant "dwelling-house" in this case, for the purposes of section 32(1), is the third floor flat, no. 20, in the building, Gate Hill Court, for that flat is the relevant "part of a building" which is let as a private dwelling. The block of flats is not the "dwelling-house"; the individual flat is the dwelling-house.

Section 32 (1) provides that in the underlease here in question there shall be implied a covenant by the lessors in the terms of paragraphs (*a*) and (*b*), whatever they comprise, and that any covenant inconsistent therewith—that is, purporting to remove from the lessors, or to reduce, the obligations comprised in the paragraphs—shall be ineffective. The subsection does not purport to render ineffective a covenant putting on the lessees any obligation as to repairs outside the scope of paragraphs (*a*) and (*b*).

Section 32 (1) goes, however, further. By the latter part of it, the subsection renders ineffective

"any covenant by the lessee for the repair of the premises (including any covenant . . . to pay money . . . on account of repairs by the lessor) . . . so far as it relates to the matters mentioned in paragraphs (*a*) and (*b*) of this subsection."

The intention and effect of these provisions, particularly as regards covenants to pay money, are, in some respects, obscure. For example, much argument was devoted, before us, to the intended meaning of the words "the premises." What do those words mean? In particular, what do they mean in relation to the facts of the present case, where the "dwelling-house" for the purposes of the subsection is a single flat in a block of flats, and where, further, the relevant covenant in the underlease is concerned with, amongst other things, repairs to two blocks of flats and also other buildings? However, in view of the concluding words of the subsection, we do not think that it matters for the decision in this case how wide or how narrow a meaning ought to be given to "the premises" as used in the subsection, for the concluding words in any event limit the "no effect" of the covenant to the covenant "so far as it relates to the matters mentioned in paragraphs (*a*) and (*b*)" and those paragraphs refer to "the dwelling-house," not "the premises."

There are other aspects also of the provisions of section 32 (1) relating to covenants for the payment of money which we find obscure. It is not necessary for us, however, to try to find light in these dark places, because, as we understand it, it is common ground that the covenant with which we are concerned, clause 4 (2) of the underlease, incorporating the third schedule thereto, is a covenant which in some degree is affected by this provision of section 32 (1). It is accepted that it is a covenant "by the lessee for the repair of the premises." It is a covenant which, in some of its terms, provides for the payment of money "on account of repairs by the lessor." It is a covenant which in some degree "relates to the matters mentioned in paragraphs (*a*) and (*b*) of the subsection." The question is: "in what degree?" This involves examination of the meaning of the paragraphs . . .

. . . We think it right to follow the approach adopted by counsel, and to consider paragraphs (*a*) and (*b*) separately.

Paragraph (*a*): "to keep in repair the structure and exterior of the dwelling-house (including drains, gutters and external pipes)." The lessors contend that one has to look at the demise in the relevant lease and ascertain what is comprised in the demise. Not everything which is a part of the property demised is necessarily within paragraph (*a*) so far as the obligation to keep it in repair is concerned. It relates only to "the structure and exterior." The lessors say, however, that the paragraph cannot apply to anything (with the exception of that in the parenthesis in the paragraph) which is not a part of the property demised. Thus, for example, in the present case "the outside walls" are expressly excluded from the demise.

The lessees contend that the question what is "the structure" and what is "the exterior" of the dwelling-house is a question of fact and degree. It is not limited, or not necessarily limited, to physical objects which are part of the flat itself, whether in the strict terms of the demise, in a conveyancing sense, or more widely as covering what would in ordinary language be regarded as integral parts of the flat. Thus, it could, and probably normally would, extend to include all the exterior walls of the building—of the whole block—or at any rate such of them as, by their disrepair would affect the use of the particular "dwelling-house." Similarly with regard to "the structure." If, for example, a structural member of the building, physically located in a lower floor, would, by its disrepair, affect the safety of flat no. 20 on the third floor, or materially affect its use as a dwelling-house, then that structural member is a part of "the structure . . . of the dwelling-house." Whether, and, if so, how far, on the lessees' contention, "the structure and exterior" could, as a question of fact and degree, be held to include such things as the structure of staircases or lifts or passageways available for use by the lessees, in common with the lessees of other flats, we are not clear. Logically, perhaps, if "the structure of the dwelling-house" includes a structural beam in a lower floor necessary for the support of a third floor flat, it should include also the structure of a necessary or convenient means of access to the flat, including parts of it which are geographically remote from the flat in question. As we understand it, the lessees' contention does not limit the scope of the paragraph to those repairs which are in fact necessary at any given moment to prevent the particular "dwelling-house" from becoming unusable. The paragraph would include all repairs which are in fact carried out to any part of "the structure or exterior of the dwelling-house" as thus interpreted.

We do not accept the contention of either the lessors or the lessees in its entirety, though the true meaning is, we think, nearer to the lessors' contention than to the lessees'.

We do not accept the lessors' contention is so far as it would limit "the structure and exterior of the dwelling-house" to that which, in the conveyancing meaning, is included in the particular terms of the demise in the lease. Anything which, in the ordinary use of words, would be regarded as a part of the structure, or of the exterior, of the particular "dwelling-house," regarded as a separate part of the building, would be within the scope of paragraph (*a*). Thus, the exclusion by the words of clause 2 of the underlease of "any part of the outside walls" would not have the effect to taking outside the operation of paragraph (*a*) that which, in the ordinary use of language, would be regarded as the exterior wall of the flat—an essential integral part of the flat, as a dwelling-house: that part of the outside wall of the block of flats which constitutes a wall of the flat. The paragraph applies to the outside wall or walls of the flat, the outside of inner party walls of the flat, the outer sides of horizontal divisions between flat 20 and flats above and below and the structural framework and beams directly supporting the floors, ceilings and walls of the flat.

We do not accept the lessees' contention so far as it goes further. There may well be obligations on the lessors, whether by their lease or by other statutory provisions, which involve an obligation on them towards the lessees, and towards the lessees of other flats in the block, to keep in repair other parts of the outside walls and other parts of the structure of the block. Paragraph (*a*) of section 32 (1) is not, however, concerned with them as constituting "the structure or exterior of the dwelling-house," for they are not "of the dwelling-house," and the paragraph expressly and deliberately uses the limiting words, as

defined in the section itself, relating the paragraph to "the dwelling-house."

Paragraph (b). The lessors contend that the words "in the dwelling-house" have the effect of limiting the application of the paragraph to "installations" of the prescribed types which are
physically within the dwelling-house. Thus, to take an example
debated in argument, if there is in the flat a hot-water radiator,
the paragraph puts on the lessors the obligation to keep the
radiator "in repair and proper working order." It does not, however, impose any obligation of the lessors in respect of, nor preclude them from making charges in respect of repairs to anything
outside the flat, for example, a boiler in the basement which
heats the water which is supplied to all radiators in all the flats
in the building.

The lessees contend that, despite the words of the paragraph,
"installations *in* the dwelling-house," the paragraph applies to
anything outside the flat the proper functioning of which is
required in order to enable the installation within the flat to function as it is intended to do. If it were not for the words in paragraph (b), "proper working order," it would, we think, be
difficult to find any support for the lessees' contention. The inclusion of those words does, however, provide some possible support. It would, however, produce very odd results if it were
so. First, there is nothing in section 32 which requires a lessor
to provide such installations. Any such obligation would have
to be derived either from non-statutory terms of the lease itself,
which would be a matter of contractual negotiation, or from some
other statute. Secondly, if "proper working order" did include,
for example, the necessity of supply of hot water to a radiator,
or water to a cistern, there would be imposed by statute an absolute obligation, with no qualifications, which in some respects
would be quite outside the 'lessors' control. For example, the
central heating boiler in the basement may be operated by gas.
The gas supply is cut off by the gas board for some reason outside
the control of the lessors, or the water supply is cut off, or limited
to certain times of the day, by the water authority. The hot water
radiator, or the water cistern, while in perfectly good repair and
perfectly good "working order," cannot perform their function.
If the covenant has the meaning suggested by the lessees, the
lessors are liable for breach of the implied covenant.

In our judgment, the meaning of paragraph (b) is as is contended for by the lessors. The installations in the physical confines of the flat must be kept in repair and capable, so far as

their own structural and mechanical condition is concerned, of working properly, but no more than that. The lessors may be under additional obligations, but if so they do not arise from this statute.

We were referred to the judgments of this court and the opinions delivered in the House of Lords in *Liverpool City Council v Irwin* [1976] 2 WLR 562. These would certainly appear to tend to support the lessors' contentions as to the limited scope of paragraph (*b*). As counsel for the lessors himself rightly pointed out to us, however, in *Liverpool City Council v Irwin* a concession was made by counsel for the tenants, in the course of his argument in this court, and the courts thereafter no doubt proceeded on the basis of that concesssion without the necessity for examining it further. The concession, of course, in no way binds the lessees in the present case. It is reported as: "It is accepted that section 32 of the Act of 1961 is limited to the demised premises: ...." Such observations in the judgments as, for example those of Roskill LJ: "... it is to be observed that those statutory obligations are ... very limited in their scope...," must be read subject to the fact of the concession having been made.

4.4 Works held to be outside the implied covenant

It is possible that the works required to remedy the disrepair is outside the implied repairing covenant. This was held to be so both in *Wainwright v Leeds City Council* [Case 55] and *Quick v Taff-Ely Borough Council* [Case 56].

Case 55 *Wainwright v Leeds City Council* (1984) 270 EG 1289
Court of Appeal

The plaintiff was the tenant of the demised house which was owned by the defendant council. It was a back-to-back house in a poor part of Leeds which had been built in the early part of this century and which had no damp-proof course. Ever since he had occupied the premises the plaintiff had been complaining about the state of the premises in various respects including the existence of damp in the cellar and in other parts of the premises. The landlords had carried out a considerable amount of work but had not been able to eradicate the damp. The tenant claimed that under section 32 of the Housing Act 1961 the council-landlord had a duty to provide a damp-course so as to eradicate the damp. The county court judge rejected this submission.

Held (1) The implied covenant did not extend to providing the tenant with a new and different thing, namely, a house with a damp-course in place of a house without one.

(2) The extent of the implied obligation under the Housing Act 1961 was the same for local authority as for private tenancies.

Dunn LJ said (in part)

But the basic submission which was made by [counsel] to the recorder was that the covenant to repair, which was imported into the lease as an obligation under section 32 of the Housing Act 1961, properly construed put upon the landlord the obligation to provide a damp-course so as to eradicate the damp.

The recorder held himself bound by a decision of this court, *Pembery v Lamdin* [1940] 2 All ER 434. That case concerned, as does this case, an old house, 100 years or more in age, built at a time when modern devices for avoiding the consequences of damp were unknown. The covenant in that case was a covenant by the lessor to keep the external part of the premises in good and tenantable repair and condition. The covenant to be implied by the statute is in substantially the same terms. It is a covenant to keep in repair the structure and exterior of the dwelling-house, including drains, gutters and external pipes. In *Pembery v Lamdin* Slesser LJ, with whose judgment Clauson LJ and Luxmoore LJ agreed, dealt with the matter in this way:

> "The first question which arises in this case is what was the nature of the obligation to repair. In order to ascertain that, it is first necessary to consider the nature of the premises which had to be repaired under the covenant. I think that, for the purposes of this case, the principle, which has never been doubted, is to be found stated in a short passage in a judgment of Lord Esher MR in *Lister v Lane & Nesham*. That is a case which has been subsequently followed and approved in *Lurcott v Wakely & Wheeler*. In *Lister v Lane & Nesham*, after reviewing the earlier authorities, Lord Esher MR, who was speaking there of a tenant, says:
>
> > 'Those cases seem to me to show that, if a tenant takes a house which is of such a kind that by its own inherent nature it will in course of time fall into a particular condition, the effects of that result are not within the tenant's covenant to repair. However large the words of the covenant may be, a covenant to repair a house is not a covenant to give a different thing from that which the tenant took when he

entered into the covenant. He has to repair that thing which he took; he is not obliged to make a new and different thing . . .'

Applying that to a landlord, in the same way as it is in that case applied to a tenant, if the counterclaim here made by Mrs Lamdin be correct, she is entitled to receive at the hands of this landlord 'a different thing' from that which she took when she entered into the covenant. She took this old house with a cellar without any waterproof protection, and she is asking the landlord so to repair that house as to give her a cellar which has a waterproof protection and is dry. That is not a right which she can possibly maintain, because the obligation of the landlord is to repair that which is demised, and not to give her something much drier in its nature than that which was demised.

For myself, for the purposes of this case, I do not feel it necessary to go into any further authorities, but I will point out that Sir H H Cozens-Hardy MR in *Lurcott v Wakely & Wheeler* says substantially the same thing,

'Is what has happened of such a nature that it can fairly be said that the character of the subject-matter of the demise, or part of the demise, in question has been changed?'

In the same case, Fletcher Moulton LJ says the same thing,

'Now what is the meaning of keeping old premises in good condition? I can see no difficulty in deciding the meaning of that. It means that, considering that they are old premises, they must be in good condition as such premises.'

If for the words 'old premises' are substituted the words 'not waterproofed', we have here the exact case. They have to be kept in repair in the condition of the house when it was demised, according to the character of the house. Buckley LJ gives judgment to the same effect, approving of what was said in *Lister v Lane & Nesham*."

So, applying the facts of that case to the facts of this case, the tenant in this case took a house without a damp-roof course. What he is asking from the landlord is a house with a damp-proof course, which is a different thing to the house which was the subject of the demise. As Slesser LJ makes clear from the passage of the judgment that I have read, the obligation of the landlord does not go beyond repairing the thing which was the subject of the demise, namely in this case a house without a damp-proof course, so on the facts I find *Pembery v Lamdin* indistinguishable from the facts in this case, and indeed [counsel] realistically accepts that. But, he says, that case and the earlier cases which were cited in the judgment were all cases at common law. They emphasise that the tenant had a choice whether to take an old house, or whether or not to take a house without any method of waterproofing and, having chosen to take the house that he did, he cannot ask the landlord to improve the house so that it is a different house from the house which he originally took. But, says [counsel] a council tenant is in a different situation, because he has no choice in the matter. The council may or may not be under an obligation to house him, but he applies to the council for housing because he has no alternative. He has insufficient means to provide himself with accommodation and, says [counsel] in a situation of that kind the obligation of the council is to provide him with a house which is free from damp. He supports that analogy by reference to section 4 of the Housing Act 1957, which is dealing with houses which are unfit for human habitation. Section 4 provides: "... in determining whether a house is unfit for human habitation, regard shall be had, amongst other things, to whether it is free from damp." [Counsel] says, "take this very case; the plaintiff is in his 50s; he is educationally subnormal, he has been unemployed for years and he has no alternative but to accept the housing that the council give him and, accordingly, the same considerations do not apply to him in the construction of the repairing covenant as would apply to a private tenant who had exercised a choice."

It is worth mentioning that this house is not unfit for human habitation. If it were, the plaintiff would indeed have a remedy under the Housing Act 1957. The only question, as I see it, which arises on this appeal is whether, in construing the statutory covenant contained in section 32 it should be differently construed in the case of a local authority to the way in which it was construed in the case of a private tenant in *Pembery v Lamdin*. I can see no reason why that should be so. I can see no reason why a higher obligation should be put on a local authority than is put on any other landlord by a repairing covenant. With respect to [counsel] most of the arguments which he has adduced in this court and in the written document which he has put in are related to social matters rather than to legal matters.

So far as I am concerned, I find it quite impossible to distinguish this case from *Pembery v Lamdin*.

Case 56 Quick v Taff-Ely Borough Council [1985] 2 EGLR 50; (1985) 276 EG 452 Court of Appeal

The council tenant sought specific performance of the landlord's repairing obligations under section 32 of the

Housing Act 1961. The windows of the demised premises were single glazed with metal frames and there was a central-heating system based on warm air ducts. The house suffered from severe condensation problems and was virtually unusable during the winter. The tenant's furniture and fabrics had become rotten as a result of the condensation problems.

The county court judge held that the landlord was in breach of section 32 of the 1961 Act in respect of the condensation, awarded damages and made a decree of specific performance. In reaching this decision the county court judge accepted a broad principle that anything defective or inherently inefficient for living in or incapable of providing the conditions of ordinary habitation was in disrepair.

Held (1) The principle enunciated by the county court judge went beyond the scope of section 32 of the 1961 Act for which there must be some damage to the structure which had to be made good.

(2) In some cases this could involve curing an inherent defect, thus improving the property to some extent, if that was the only way to make good the damage to the subject matter of the implied covenant.

(3) In the circumstances the repair work to the wooden surrounds and the replacement of plaster did not require in any realistic sense the replacement of the metal windows by wooden-framed windows or windows with PVC frames.

Dillon LJ said (in part)

The case turns on the construction and effect of the repairing covenant in section 32 of the 1961 Act. Before I turn to that, however, I should mention one apparent oddity in the legislation. There is in section 6 of the Housing Act 1957 a provision that, in any contract for the letting of a house for human habitation at an annual rent not exceeding £80 in the case of a house in London and £52 in the case of a house elsewhere, there is to be implied a condition that the house is at the commencement of the tenancy, and an undertaking that the house will be kept by the landlord during the tenancy, fit for human habitation. That section has legislative antecedents, albeit at lower rent levels, in the Housing Act 1936, and before that in the Housing Act 1925 and before that in an Act of 1909. It was amended in 1963 as a result of the creation of the Greater London Council, but without altering the rent levels, It seems that the section as so amended has remained on the statute book ever since, but—for whatever reason—the rent levels have never been increased. Therefore, in view of inflation, the section must now have remarkably little application. It is not available to the plaintiff in the present case because his rent is too high, even though he is an unemployed tenant of a small council house.

The learned judge delivered a careful reserved judgment in which he reviewed many of the more recent authorities on repairing covenants, starting with *Pembery v Lamdin* [1940] 2 All ER 434. His ultimate reasoning seems to me to be on the following lines viz: (1) Recent authorities such as *Ravenseft Properties Ltd v Davstone (Holdings) Ltd* [1980] QB 12 and *Elmcroft Developments Ltd v Tankersley-Sawyer* (1984) 270 EG 140 show that works of repair under a repairing covenant, whether by a landlord or a tenant, may require the remedying of an inherent defect in a building; (2) The authorities also show that it is a question of degree whether works which remedy an inherent defect in a building may not be so extensive as to amount to an improvement or renewal of the whole which is beyond the concept of repair; (3) In the present case the replacement of windows and the provision of insulation for the lintels does not amount to such an improvement or renewal of the whole; (4) Therefore, the replacement of the windows and provision of the insulation to alleviate an inherent defect is a repair which the council is bound to carry out under the repairing covenant.

But, with every respect to the learned judge, this reasoning begs the important question. It assumes that any work to eradicate an inherent defect in a building must be a work of repair, which the relevant party is bound to carry out if, as a matter of degree, it does not amount to a renewal or improvement of the building. In effect, it assumes the broad proposition urged on us by [counsel] for the plaintiff that anything defective or inherently inefficient for living in or ineffective to provide the conditions of ordinary habitation is in disrepair. But that does not follow from the decisions in *Ravenseft* and *Elmcroft* that works of repair *may* require the remedying of an inherent defect.

[Counsel's] proposition has very far-reaching implications indeed. The covenant implied under section 32 is an ordinary repairing covenant. It does not apply only to local authorities as landlords, and this court has held in *Wainwright v Leeds City Council* (1984) 270 EG 1289 that the fact that a landlord is a local authority which is discharging a social purpose in providing housing for people who cannot afford it does not make the burden of the covenant greater on that landlord than it would be on any other landlord. The construction of the covenant must be the same whether it is implied as a local authority's covenant in a tenancy of a council house or is expressly included as a tenant's or landlord's covenant in a private lease which is outside section 32. A tenant under such a lease who had entered into such a repairing covenant would, no doubt, realise, if he suffered from problems of condensation in his house that he could not compel the landlord to do anything about those problems. But I apprehend that the tenant would be startled to be told—as must follow from [the county court judge's] decision—that the landlord has the right to compel him, the tenant, to put in new windows. If the reasoning is valid, where is the process to stop? The evidence of [the expert witness] was that changing the windows and insulating the lintels would "alleviate" the problems, not that it would cure them. If there was evidence that double-glazing would further alleviate the problems, would a landlord, or tenant, under a repairing covenant be obliged to put in double-glazing? [The expert witness] said that a radiator system of heating to all rooms in the place of the warm air system was "necessary"; if the judge's reasoning was correct, it would seem that, if the point had been properly pleaded early enough, the plaintiff might have compelled the council to put in a radiator system of heating.

In my judgment, the key factor in the present case is that disrepair is related to the physical condition of whatever has to be repaired and not to questions of lack of amenity or inefficiency. I find helpful the observations of Atkin LJ in *Anstruther-Gough-Calthorpe v McOscar* [1924] 1 KB 716 at 734 that repair "connotes the idea of making good damage so as to leave the subject so far as possible as though it had not been damaged". Where decorative repair is in question one must look for damage to the decorations, but where, as here, the obligation is merely to keep the structure and exterior of the house in repair, the covenant will come into operation only where there has been damage to the structure and exterior which requires to be made good.

If there is such damage caused by an unsuspected inherent defect, then it may be necessary to cure the defect, and thus to some extent improve without wholly renewing the property as the only practicable way of making good the damage to the subject-matter of the repairing covenant. That, as I read the case, was the basis of the decision in *Ravenseft*. There there was an inherent defect when the building, a relatively new one, was built in that no expansion joints had been included because it had not been realised that the different coefficients of expansion of the stone of the cladding and the concrete of the structure made it necessary to include such joints. There was, however, also physical damage to the subject-matter of the covenant in that, because of the differing coefficients of expansion, the stones of the cladding had become bowed, detached from the structure, loose and in danger of falling. Forbes J in a very valuable judgment rejected the argument that no liability arose under a repairing covenant if it could be shown that the disrepair was due to an inherent defect in the building. He allowed in the damages under the repairing covenant the cost of putting in expansion joints, and in that respect improving the building, because, as he put it, on the evidence "in no realistic sense . . . could it be said that there was any other possible way of reinstating this cladding than by providing the expansion joints which were in fact provided".

The *Elmcroft* case was very similar. There was physical damage from rising damp in the walls of a flat in a fashionable area of London. That was due to an inherent defect in that when the flat had been built in late-Victorian times as a high-class residential flat, the slate damp-proof course had been put in too low and was therefore ineffective. The remedial work necessary to eradicate the rising damp was, on the evidence, the installation of a horizontal damp-proof course by silicone injection and formation of vertical barriers by silicone injection. This was held to be within the landlord's repairing covenant. It was necessary in order to repair the walls and, although it involved improvement over the previous ineffective slate damp-proof course, it was held that, as a matter of degree, having regard to the nature and locality of the property, this did not involve giving the tenant a different thing from that which was demised. The decision of this court in *Smedley v Chumley & Hawke Ltd* (1981) 44 P&CR 50 is to the same effect; the damage to a recently constructed restaurant built on a concrete raft on piles over a river could be cured only by putting in further piles so that the structure of the walls and roof of the restaurant were stable and safe upon foundations made structurally stable.

The only other of the many cases cited to us which I would mention is *Pembery v Lamdin* [1940] 2 All ER 434. There the property demised was a ground-floor shop and basement, built 100 years or more before the demise. The landlord was liable to repair the external part of the premises and there was physical damage to the walls of the basement in that they were permeated with damp because there had never been any damp-proof course. The works required by the tenant to waterproof the basement were very extensive, involving cleaning and asphalting the existing walls, building internal brick walls and laying a concrete floor. This would have involved improvement to such an extent as to give the tenant a different thing from what had been demised and it was therefore outside the repairing covenant. But Slesser LJ appears to recognise at p 438 that repointing of existing basement walls where the mortar had partly perished would have been within the repairing covenant.

In the present case the liability of the council was to keep the structure and exterior of the house in repair—not the decorations. Though there is ample evidence of damage to the decorations and to bedding, clothing and other fabrics, evidence of damage to the subject-matter of the covenant, the structure and exterior of the house, is far to seek. Though the condensation comes about from the effect of the warm atmosphere in the rooms on the cold surfaces of the walls and windows, there is no evidence at all of physical damage to the walls—as opposed to the decorations—or the windows.

There is indeed evidence of physical damage in the way of rot in parts of the wooden surrounds of some of the windows but (a) that can be sufficiently cured by replacing the defective lengths of wood and (b) it was palpably not the rot in the wooden surrounds which caused damage to the bedding, clothes and fabrics in the house, and the rot in the wooden surrounds cannot have contributed very much to the general incovenience of living in the house for which the judge awarded general damages.

There was also, as I have mentioned, evidence of nails sweating in bedroom ceilings, and of some plaster perishing in a bedroom. The judge mentions the sweating nails in his judgment, but I have not found any mention of the perishing of plaster. The judge did not ask himself—since on the overall view he took of the case it was not necessary—whether these two elements of structural disrepair (since the council accepts for the purposes of this case in this court that the plaster was part of the structure of the house) were of themselves enough to require the replacement of the windows etc. They seem, however, to have been very minor elements indeed in the context of the case which the plaintiff was putting forward, and, in my judgment, they do not warrant an order for a new trial or a remission to the judge for further findings, save in respect of the reassessment of damages as mentioned below.

As I have already mentioned, [the expert witness] used the word "alleviate" to describe the effect which the replacement of the windows and the facing of the lintels with insulation materials would have on the problems of condensation. At one point in his judgment the judge refers to "the work propounded by [the expert witness] as necessary to cure the condensation problems". This must be a slip. because alleviation *prima facie* falls short of cure. However, as the extent of alleviation was not probed in the court below, it is inappropriate to make any further comment.

It does appear from [the expert witness'] report that the problems of condensation would have also been alleviated if the plaintiff had kept the central heating on more continuously and at higher temperatures. In that event the walls and windows would have remained warm or warmer and condensation would have been reduced. As to this, the judge appreciated that some people for financial reasons have to be sparing in their use of central heating, and he found that there was no evidence at all to suggest that the life-style of the plaintiff and his family was likely to give rise to condensation problems because it was outside the spectrum of life-styles which a local authority could reasonably expect its tenants to follow. In my judgment, that finding answers the argument that it would be anomalous or unreasonable that this house should be held to be in disrepair because the plaintiff cannot afford to keep the heating on at a high-enough temperature, whereas an identical adjoining house would not be in disrepair because the tenant had a good job and so spent more on his heating. If there is disrepair which the council is by its implied covenant bound to make good, then it is no answer for the council so say that, if the tenant could have afforded to spend more on his central heating, there would have been no disrepair, or less disrepair.

But the crux of the matter is whether there has been disrepair in relation to the structure and exterior of the building and, for the reasons I have endeavoured to explain, in my judgment there has not, quoad the case put forward by the plaintiff on condensation as opposed to the case on water penetration.

The landlord is not obliged to undertake works to remedy a disrepair if the tenant is liable for such works under the duty to use the premises in a tenant-like manner.

Case 57 *Wycombe Area Health Authority v Barnett* (1982) 264 EG 619 Court of Appeal

The tenant of the demised premises left the house to stay with a friend for one night during a period of freezing weather. The tenant in fact stayed for two nights during which the temperature dropped well below freezing. A rising main which passed through the kitchen to the attic and was controlled by a stop-cock, was not lagged and no heating was left on in the house. The mains pipe burst causing substantial damage and the landlords contended that the duty of tenant-like user required the tenant to take precautions when leaving the house in freezing weather having regard to the unlagged mains pipe and the absence of heating. The tenant contended that it was the landlord's duty under s. 32 of the Housing Act 1961 to have the mains pipe lagged. The county court judge held that the tenant acted unreasonably:

Held (1) The landlords' duty under s. 32 was to keep the pipe in good mechanical condition but that an unlagged pipe which, in freezing conditions, became cracked when the water in it turned to ice was not a breach of this condition.

(2) A tenant could not reasonably be expected, under the doctrine of tenant-like user, necessarily to lag an internal water pipe or always to keep the house heated as a precaution against freezing. The extent of such a duty must depend on the circumstances including the length of absence from the house and the severity of the weather. In the present case the tenant had acted reasonably.

Watkins LJ said (in part)

... He [the judge at first instance] was apparently assisted to reach this conclusion by what Lord Denning (as he then was) said in *Warren v Keen* [1953] 2 All ER 1118 at p. 1121 which was as follows:

"The tenant must take proper care of the premises. He must, if he is going away for the winter, turn off the water and empty the boiler; he must clean the chimneys, when necessary, and also the windows; he must mend the electric light when it fuses ... he must do the little jobs about the place which a reasonable tenant would do. In addition, he must not, of course, damage the house wilfully or negligently; and he must see that his family and guests do not damage it—if they do, he must repair it. But, apart from such things, if the house falls into disrepair through fair wear and tear or lapse of time or for any reason not caused by him, the tenant is not liable to repair it."

Pursuant to his grounds of appeal learned counsel for the defendant argues that this basis for finding for the plaintiffs constitutes a failure by the judge properly to confine his consideration of the plaintiffs' claim to an allegation of the damage having been caused by the commission by the defendant of the tort of negligence. Since, however, he conceded that the proceedings in the county court, without objection from either party, were not conducted with strict observance of the pleadings, and that the submissions of both counsel to the judge were in fact concentrated upon the duty of a tenant to act in a tenant-like way in looking after a house, and the duty of the plaintiffs as landlords to carry out the provisions of section 32 of the Housing Act 1961, which undoubtedly applied to the plaintiffs' dwelling-house, this argument clearly cannot assist the defendant in this court. It was but faintly pressed upon us anyway, so it will not I think surprise anyone to learn that this ground must surely fail.

Secondly, it is submitted that the effective cause of the damage was the failure of the plaintiffs, in breach of their duty arising out of the implied covenant under section 32, to lag the pipe or that part of it which is in the attic at the very least because, put more broadly, this duty involves a landlord keeping and maintaining internal water pipes in proper working order at all times and in all circumstances. . . .

I find of assistance in this connection observations made by Megaw LJ in *Campden Hill Towers Ltd v Gardner* [1977] 1 All ER 739. At p. 746 he said:

"In our judgment, the meaning of para (b) is as contended for by the lessors. The installations in the physical confines of the flat must be kept in repair and capable, so far as their own structural and mechanical condition is concerned, of working properly. But no more than that. The lessor may be under additional obligations but, if so, they do not arise from this statute."

I do not think it can rightly be said that an unlagged water pipe is not in a good mechanical condition in this sense merely because it becomes cracked when, in freezing conditions, there is water in it which turns to ice. It will, or may be, otherwise if, for example, a leak develops in a water pipe through its condition becoming out of repair the effects of rust or other process of deterioration. Seeing that there is no suggestion that the water pipe in the plaintiffs' house, before the onset of the frost, was otherwise than in good mechanical condition, they were not in my opinion in breach of the implied covenant created by section

32. This conclusion renders unnecessary any further references to subsection (2) (a) and such slight argument as was addressed to us upon the meaning of the word "works" as used therein.

The third and final submission on behalf of the defendant is to the effect that the learned judge extended the duty of a tenant to act in a tenant-like manner beyond reasonable limits and certainly beyond those contemplated by Lord Denning in *Warren's* case. There is, he said, no obligation upon a tenant to lag water pipes. Lord Denning, in spelling out the obligation of a tenant to perform certain tasks to keep a house in repair, was envisaging, in relation to water pipes and other fittings, circumstances in which it was unoccupied for a fairly long time. It is going much too far to say that a prudent tenant can be expected whenever a cold spell of weather occurs, when contemplating being away from home for a night or two, to turn off the stop-cock and drain the water system. Accordingly, the learned judge was in error in finding that the defendant by omitting to take this precaution had behaved in an untenant-like manner and so was liable for the damage which occurred.

Case 58 London Borough of Newham v Patel [1978] 13 HLR 77
Court of Appeal

In 1974, the tenant was in occupation of a house which was suffering from damp and other defects. The rent paid by the tenant was low, reflecting the condition of the property. The tenant applied for a transfer to alternative accommodation. In 1976, he renewed his application, and then consulted an advice agency, which wrote to the landlord authority stating that the premises were a statutory nuisance and unfit for human habitation. In January 1977, an environmental health officer reported that there was a substantial number of defects in the property, and that it was unfit for human habitation. The authority took the view that it could not be put into good repair by way of temporary repair, and that they would accordingly have to rehouse the tenant, leaving the property empty until it could be demolished.

Accordingly, they resolved to offer alternative accommodation and served notice to quit on the tenant. The tenant rejected one offer of alternative accommodation, and the authority issued proceedings for possession. The tenant defended the action, and counter-claimed for breach of s 32, Housing Act 1961. The county court judge granted the order for possession and dismissed the counterclaim, from which decision the tenant appealed, initially against both grant of order for possession and dismissal of counterclaim. Subsequently, the tenant abandoned the appeal against the grant of an order for possession.

Held (1) Having regard to the prospective life of the property, there was no breach of s. 32, Housing Act 1961; further, there was, having regard to the low rent paid under the tenancy, and the absence of evidence of special damage, no evidence to support an award of damages to the tenant.

Templeman LJ said (in part)

In the pleadings there were various particulars of disrepair, including a large number of damp wall plasters. Some of these particulars I do not think come within the description of structural repair required by s. 32, but undoubtedly there are some, such as damp wall plasters and other items, which do come within that section. However, as I have said, the local authority had taken the view that, in the face of the report from the public health inspector which I have read, the house should be left uninhabitable and uninhabited until it was possible to carry out full redevelopment.

The judge dealt with the counter-claim at p. 20 of the record and he dealt with it in this way:

"The plaintiffs" that is the council "admit in this case that the house is unfit for habitation and agree the defects alleged in the defence and counterclaim but contend that only those set out in para 8 of the reply could amount to breaches of s. 32."

As to the others, it had been submitted by the council that any breaches were technical only. The learned judge continues:

"Mr Patel, the defendant, gave no evidence so there is no evidence of any special pecuniary loss. Mr Stone the principal housing officer for the plaintiffs stated that the rent charged to Mr Patel for 35, Prince of Wales Road is very low (i.e. £2.83 plus £2.65 per week rates). He said 'this is probably as low as you could get for a five bedroomed house' and that the usual rent would be £7.53 per week which is the rent of the alternative accommodation offered at 7, Forty Acre Lane. He also said that the rent of 35, Prince of Wales Road, is as low as it is because the house is scheduled for redevelopment.

Having regard to these facts I find that although the items of disrepair admitted in para 8 of the reply would in normal

circumstances amount to breaches of s. 32 of the Housing Act
1961, by reason of sub-s (3) of that section and in particular
the prospective life of the dwelling house breaches of the term
implied by s. 32 have not been proved.

In any event had breaches been proved I would not have
found, having regard to the low rent charged for 35, Prince
of Wales Road, that the defendant had suffered damage."

In my judgment there was ample evidence on which the
learned judge could take the view that, having regard to the
state of the house which I have outlined and the evidence which
he had heard, the prospective life of the dwelling house affected
the duty of the council under s. 32, and that they were not bound
to carry out repairs which would be wholly useless.

In my judgment, also, the judge was quite right when he took
into account the low rent charged for 35, Prince of Wales Road
and came to the conclusion that the defendant had not suffered
damage. In the pleadings, at p. 12, the damage which is claimed
is damage for:

"the distress and inconvenience of living in a house dilapidated and unfit in the respects pleaded."

In the course of the argument before this court, I think for the
first time (at least it appeared to be for the first time because
counsel seemed to be surprised by the question) the question
was put as to what was the quantum of damages claimed under
the heading of "distress and inconvenience" and counsel airily
said "£300". He said, and said truly, that no one can live in
a damp house without suffering distress and inconvenience. I
accept that and nothing I say in this judgment is intended to
encourage anybody to be left in a house which is damp or in
the condition in which this particular house was. But the council
offered Mr Patel—and Mr Patel accepted—a low rent because
of the condition of the house. Mr Patel cannot have both the
benefit of a low rent and an award of damages for the same
reason—that is why the rent was so low.

The council were, as I have said, heavily criticised in this case
but they were bound to be criticised. If they had spent money
on a house which, having regard to the fact that it is due to
be redeveloped and the state in which it was, meant that money
was wasted in doing those repairs they would be criticised. If
they left the house vacant they would be bound to be criticised
in the present state of the housing demand. Now, because they
let it to Mr Patel at a very low rent, they are being criticised
again.

In any event, those are matters which do not affect the legal problem with which we are faced here. As I have said, it seems to me that, having regard to the damages which were pleaded, the learned judge was quite right in coming to the conclusion that damages had not been set out. In the result, the appeal must be dismissed.

4.5 Damages for breach of the implied covenant under the 1985 Act

Case 59 McGreal v Wake (1984) 269 EG 1254 Court of Appeal

The plaintiff was the tenant of a house let on a short lease. The house suffered from rising damp, wet rot, decayed and open-jointed brickwork and cracked and sagging ceilings in most rooms. The tenant claimed damages against the landlord for breach of the implied covenant under s. 32 of the Housing Act 1961. In the county court the tenant's claim was dismissed on the ground that the tenant had not given notice of the defect to her landlord. The landlord was eventually put on notice of the defects when the local authority, after complaint by the tenant, required the landlord to execute remedial works and when he did not do so the local authority decided to carry out the works at the landlord's expense. In order to facilitate the local authority's operations the tenant moved out and paid for temporary accommodation, including storage charges for her furniture.

Held (1) Where the repairing liability is placed upon the landlord the golden rule is "tell your landlord about the defects".

(2) The tenant had a valid claim for having to live in an unrepaired house for some months after it should have been repaired; that she was entitled to compensation for the work of cleaning the debris and cleaning up after the local authority had completed their operations. She was also entitled to recover reasonable expenditure on redecoration and the costs of storing her furniture and obtaining temporary accommodation.

Sir John Donaldson MR said (in part)

A landlord's covenant to keep in repair involves two different elements—a duty to do the repairs and a duty to do them at a particular time. Late performance may cause loss and damage to the tenant in that he has to live in unrepaired premises whereas, if the duty had been performed timeously, he would have

been living in repaired accommodation. A total or partial failure
to repair will cause expense to the tenant if he does the repairs
himself. In the instant appeal the plaintiff has advanced claims
under both heads.

Delay
    Given that the defendant only had notice of the defects at
the beginning of November, 1979, there was no breach of covenant by him before the expiration of a reasonable time for putting
the house into adequate repair. Basing ourselves upon the local
authority's notice, it seems to us that that time had expired by
January 1, 1980. The local authority completed its work by the
end of June, 1980, but the work of cleaning up kept the plaintiff
out of her house until the end of July. In our judgment, on
these facts, the plaintiff has a valid claim for having to live in
an unrepaired house for some months after it should have been
repaired and, with all respect to the learned judge, we do not
see how this can be described as "negligible".

Failure to repair—cost of repairs
    The defendant landlord failed to do any work pursuant to
his obligation under the covenant, but work was done by the
local authority which *pro tanto* extinguished the landlord's obligation. If this local authority work had been co-extensive with that
which the landlord was obliged to do, the plaintiff might have
had no further claim. That does not, however, seem to have
been the case.
    The facts are not as clear as they might have been because
the learned judge seems to have concentrated upon the claim
based upon the cost of alternative accommodation to the exclusion of other heads of claim. However, it seems to us that consideration had to be given to two different aspects of the cost
of repairs in so far as they fell upon the tenant. The first is the
cost of completing the local authority's work and the second
is the cost of what might be described as co-operating with or
assisting the local authority.

(a) *The cost of completing the local authority's work*
    As we have said, the local authority did no work of decoration,
but we assume that the house was decorated when they moved
in to do the work of repair. Clearly the removal of all or most
of the ceilings would cause extensive damage to decorations and
the other works may also have done so. Although we have been
referred to no authority directly in point, we consider that the

landlord's obligation to effect repairs must carry with it an obligation to make good any consequential damage to decorations. The learned judge has held that the plaintiff's expenditure on redecoration was reasonable and the only possible objection to her recovering the £608.51 which she spent is that it no doubt involved an element of betterment. Betterment was considered by this court in *Harbutt's "Plasticine" Ltd v Wayne Tank and Pump Co Ltd* [1970] 1 QB 447 at pp. 468, 473 and 476, where it was held that a defendant is not entitled to make a deduction to take account of betterment if the plaintiff is unable to make good his loss without betterment. That seems to be this case.

The work of clearing the debris and cleaning up was clearly part of the landlord's obligation, but it was left to the plaintiff to do it. No figure has been put on this work because no one was paid to do it, but we see no reason in principle why the plaintiff should not be compensated for her efforts.

(b) *The cost of co-operation and assistance*

The local authority or their contractors seem to have asked the plaintiff to move out of the house and to take her furniture and carpets with her in order that they might do the work of repair. Very reasonably she agreed and this involved her in the expense of lifting the carpets, removing the furniture, storing, returning the furniture to the house and having the carpets relaid. It also involved her "storing" herself in alternative accommodation.

Green v Eales (1841) 2 QB 225 was regarded by the learned judge as authority for the proposition that a landlord who is under an obligation to repair the house is not also obliged to provide another house for the tenant while the repairs are being effected. The same point was made in *Saner v Bilton* (1878) 7 Ch D 815 by Fry J in the context of repairs to a warehouse. In *Green v Eales* the jury was directed by Rolfe B:

"That the plaintiff was entitled to recover for all his expenses, if they were reasonably incurred, and such as a prudent man would have taken upon him; and he left it to them to say whether, under the circumstances of this case, the entire rebuilding of the wall"

which fell down and ought to have been repaired by the defendant landlord

"and the removal to other premises in the meantime were reasonable expenses . . ."

The jury having awarded all the expenses claimed, the Court of Queen's Bench (Lord Denman CJ) struck out the cost of obtaining alternative accommodation upon the ground that (p. 238):

"We are of opinion that the defendant was not bound to find the plaintiff another residence whilst the repairs went on, any more than he would have been bound to do so if the premises had been consumed by fire."

Griffiths LJ in *Calabar Properties v Stitcher* [1983] 3 All ER 759, 769, referred to this passage from the judgment of Lord Denman and said:

"But I take that passage to do no more than draw attention to the fact that a landlord is not in breach of his covenant to repair until he has been given notice of the want of repair and a reasonable time has elapsed in which the repair could have been carried out. If in this case the landlords had sent workmen round to carry out the repairs promptly on receiving notice of the defect and the defendant for her own convenience had decided to move to a hotel whilst the repairs were carried out, she should not have claimed the cost of the hotel accommodation because the landlords would not have been in breach of the repairing covenant. That Lord Denman CJ meant no more than this is I think apparent from his observation that the tenant might have had a claim on the basis that the time he had to be in alternative accommodation had been lengthened by the delay in carrying out repairs.

For these reasons I do not regard *Green v Eales* as an authority for the proposition that there can be no claim for the costs of alternative accommodation, but if it did purport so to decide, it was in my view wrongly decided."

Case 60 *Taylor v Knowsley Borough Council* [1985] 17 HLR 376
Court of Appeal

The plaintiff was the tenant of the defendant authority in a flat at Halewood, Liverpool. The rent of the flat was £15 per week plus rates. During the winter period in 1982, as a result of a burst pipe, the hot water supply was interrupted. The plaintiff complained of this in January 1982, but the problem was not remedied until June 1982. The plaintiff was therefore without hot water for five months. In addition, the plaintiff was without a central ceiling light in his living room from when the pipe burst, until April 1982, a period to three months. Finally, the plaintiff complained of a leak from the bathroom ceiling, causing dripping and damp, commencing in April 1983, and not repaired until the beginning of 1984, a period of eight months.

The plaintiff was a single man, with relatives in the area. He gave evidence that he used to go to the relatives' homes for a bath, and to the launderette to wash his clothes for a period until, because of the cost, he also did his washing at a relative's home. In the county court, he was awarded £100 damages for the loss of hot water and the absence of a ceiling light, of which £68 could be attributed to launderette costs and sums he paid to relatives for use of facilities. In addition, he was awarded £59 for the dripping in the bathroom. The plaintiff appealed on the grounds that these figures were too low.

Held (1) In the case of a young man with relatives in the area, and in the absence of evidence of severe inconvenience, the damages awarded were not so low as to be obviously wrong.

Fox LJ said (in part)

One has to bear in mind throughout this case that this was a very experienced county court judge who was highly familiar with this sort of case. In fact I do not think that the plaintiff, so far as general inconvenience is concerned, exaggerated or attempted to exaggerate the position at all, because as I read the notes of evidence he did not really suggest that the inconvenience, although it existed, was very great in the circumstances in which he found himself. He did complain of special damage; that I have dealt with.

I therefore reach the conclusion that the judge's figure of £100 for 1982 (about seven weeks' rent) is one which is not so clearly low that this court should interfere with it. The assessment of the evidence was a matter essentially for the judge, and the figure which he reached seems to me to be within the band of possible figures on the evidence.

The other matter was that in 1983 there was dripping due to a burst pipe in the bathroom. That extended over a period of eight months. The figure which the judge awarded as £59. The result was that the total damages slightly exceeded the amount of rent in arrears, leaving the plaintiff with nothing to pay in respect of his arrears of rent.

There is really no evidence of very severe inconvenience at all in relation to the dripping in the bathroom. The plaintiff made an observation, which I think may have been little more than a joke, about having to use an umbrella, and the judge had to assess for himself how far he thought that the plaintiff was in truth inconvenienced by the dripping in the bathroom, which was from a small hole in the ceiling, and which one would have thought could have been very well disposed of by some Polyfiller. He made an assessment of £59, and I see no reason to disagree with that.

The judge made a comment in his judgment about the relevance in assessing damages of the amount of rent which the plaintiff had to pay for the premises, but I did not read that part of the judgment as an attempt to lay down general principles in a case of this sort at all. It was merely part of the background of the particular case with which he was dealing. It seems to me that whatever the approach, the figures which the learned judge arrived at on the evidence which he heard in a very short case are justifiable. For myself therefore I see no reason to interfere with his conclusion, and I would dismiss the appeal.

Case 61 Bradley *v* Chorley Borough Council [1985] 2 EGLR 49; (1985) 275 EG 801 Court of Appeal

The appellant was the tenant of the demised premises and he had moved into the house at a time when it was in a poor state of decoration. In due course the local authority came to the conclusion that the electric wiring required repair which they were under a contractual and statutory obligation to undertake. The landlord contended that it was under no obligation to make good damage to decorations caused by re-wiring. The county court judge referred to the fact that under the tenancy agreement it was the duty of the tenant to maintain the dwelling-house in a clean condition and to be responsible for its internal decoration.

Held (1) Whether or not the tenant's covenant imposed on him a positive duty to decorate (which was by no means clear) this could not override the landlord's duty under section 32 of the Housing Act 1961.

(2) The landlords were under an obligation to make good any consequential damage to the decorations and in some circumstances this may give a tenant the windfall of better decorations than he had before.

Sir John Donaldson MR said (in part)

There is a further difficulty about this part of the learned judge's judgment, and that is this. It is by no means clear that under a covenant by the tenant to maintain the dwelling-house in a clean condition and be responsible for its interior decorations that he is required to redecorate. It may mean—and I would not be minded to decide what it does mean—that he is under an obligation to keep the dwelling-house clean, and whether and to what extent he decorates may be a matter for him. Supposing the learned judge was right and the covenant put upon the tenant a positive obligation to maintain the interior decorations of the dwelling-house, it is quite impossible to rely upon that covenant as putting upon the tenant an obligation to redecorate in order to make good damage done to the decorations in the course of fulfilling a statutory obligation under section 32 of the Housing Act 1961 if the landlord, under that section or an equivalent contractual provision, is under an obligation to do it himself, because in section 33(7) there is a provision that no contrary covenant shall override the landlord's duty.

The learned county court judge also said:

> "If the plaintiff has any right to require the defendants to redecorate he has, in my view, forfeited those rights because of his complete failure to carry out his own obligation to decorate the interior, or even any part thereof."

I know of no doctrine of law or of equity which would produce a forfeiture in that sense. In other circumstances, failures by one party to fulfil his obligations, which are concurrent or related to the obligations of the other party, may well be taken into consideration under a head of damages, but I really do not understand what principle of law the learned judge was applying at that stage.

He went on to hold that there was no implied duty on the borough council to redecorate under the Housing Act—in other words, he was holding that repairs did not include the reinstatement of decorations. At that time a transcript of the decision of this court in *McGreal v Wake* (1984) 269 EG 1254 was not available to the learned judge but it was made available to him between the end of the hearing and the delivery of his judgment, and he appreciated that there was a necessity to distinguish that case. In that case a landlord had wholly failed his obligations. The council had to come in, having served notice, and had done the repair work other than the reinstatement of decorations. They had thereby relieved the landlord of his obligations, albeit at the price of themselves having a claim against the landlord and the tenant was suing the landlord for the cost of consequential redecorations. This court said:

> "Although we have been referred to no authority directly in point, we consider that the landlord's obligations to effect

repairs must carry with it an obligation to make good any consequential damage to the decorations."

The learned county court judge thought that that could be distinguished because he said that I, in giving the judgment of the court in that case, did not intend to say that the implied obligation to decorate applied to a faultless landlord. It is quite correct that we were not considering a faultless landlord in that case, but I am quite unable to see what difference it makes. If the landlord's obligation is as we stated it to be, namely to make good any consequential damage to the decorations, the only difference between a faultless landlord and one who is faultful is that the faultless landlord will do the decorations and there will be no claim from the tenant; the faultful landlord will not, and there will be a claim for the cost of the decorations, as indeed there was in *McGreal's* case, and in addition there may be a claim for the inconvenience of having to live in the house in its undecorated state pending the effecting of the decoration.

In my judgment this case is wholly indistinguishable from the principle stated in *McGreal's* case. *McGreal's* case may be wrongly decided. I say that not as indicating that I think it was, but merely because all things are possible and there has been no appeal to the House of Lords. Subject to that, both we and the learned county court judge are bound to hold that it was the obligation of the Chorley Borough Council to make good any consequential damage to the decorations. In some circumstances that may involve a windfall profit to the tenant because it may be impossible to do that without giving him rather better decorations than he had beforehand. That was also considered in the same case, and we referred to *Harbutt's "Plasticine" Ltd v Wayne, Tank and Pump Co Ltd* [1970] 1 QB 447 as authority for the proposition that if there is no way in which one can put the other party in the same position as he ought to have been without conferring an additional benefit on him, that is the obligation and it is just his good luck.

A good deal of anxiety has been engendered by this case among local authorities, particularly the Chorley Borough Council, that this will involve them in enormous expenditure. If it does involve them in expenditure, that is obviously not a ground for distorting the law. It may be a ground for altering the statute, but that is another matter. But this fear may be exaggerated, because the tenant, who has very torn, damaged wallpaper which is further damaged, may well not be in a position to complain that the landlord has failed to make good consequential damage to the decorations if he is presented with an emulsion-painted wall. It may even be that the existing wallpaper is so damaged anyway that there was no consequential damage to the decorations, looking at the matter in the round, those are decisions which will have to be made on the facts of every case. The law as it exists at the moment is that the landlord's obligation is to make good consequential damage to decorations.

4.6 Implied covenant of tenant-like user

The tenant's use of the demised premises is also subject to the implied covenant to use the premises in a tenant-like manner, which may include the carrying out of day-to-day minor maintenance and usage. This implied covenant is distinct from the repairing obligations in a lease and is effective even where the repairing obligation is imposed on the landlord under the Landlord and Tenant Act 1985, sections 11–14.

Case 62 Warren v Keen [1954] 1 QB 15 Court of Appeal

The subject premises had been let by the plaintiff landlord to the tenant on a weekly tenancy. The landlord was subsequently served with a notice by the local authority to remedy certain defects which rendered the premises unfit for human habitation by reason of their not being wind and water tight. After undertaking the necessary repairs the landlord claimed the cost of the repairs from the tenant contending that it was an implied term of the tenancy that the tenant would use the premises in a tenant-like manner and would keep them wind and watertight. The county court judge held that there was an implied covenant that the tenant would keep the premises in good and tenantable condition.

Held (1) A weekly tenant is not under a general covenant to put and keep the premises in repair. His only duty is to use the premises in a husband-like or tenant-like manner. If the house falls into disrepair through fair wear and tear or lapse of time, or for any reason not caused by him, he is not liable to repair it.

Denning LJ said (in part)

... Apart from express contract, a tenant owes no duty to the landlord to keep the premises in repair. The only duty of the tenant is to use the premises in a husband-like, or what is the same thing, a tenant-like manner. That is how it was put by Sir Vicary Gibbs CJ in *Horsefall v Mather* Holt NP 7 and by

Scrutton LJ and Atkin LJ in *Marsden v Edward Heyes Ltd* [1927] 2 KB 7. But what does "to use the premises in a tenant-like manner" mean? It can, I think, best be shown by some illustrations. The tenant must take proper care of the place. He must, if he is going away for the winter, turn off the water and empty the boiler. He must clean the chimneys, when necessary, and also the windows. He must mend the electric light when it fuses. He must unstop the sink when it is blocked by his waste. In short, he must do the little jobs about the place which a reasonable tenant would do. In addition, he must, of course, not damage the house, wilfully or negligently; and he must see that his family and guests do not damage it: and if they do, he must repair it. But apart from such things, if the house falls into disrepair through fair wear and tear or lapse of time, or for any reason not caused by him, then the tenant is not liable to repair it.

Note:
   (i) The covenant of tenant-like user is implied by law unless expressly stipulated in the lease and should be read in the context of the repairing covenant and the tenant's obligation not to commit waste.
  (ii) In some instances, for example *Wycombe Area Health Authority v Barnett* [Case 57], the circumstance will not be covered by either the landlord's repairing covenant nor the tenant's obligation to use the premises in a tenant-like manner.

4.7 Other implied obligations

A court may imply a term into a lease where it is required to provide "business efficacy" to a lease i.e. so that the lease can be made workable.

Case 63 Duke of Westminster v Guild (1983) 267 EG 762 Court of Appeal

    The plaintiff landlords claimed payment of alleged arrears of rent against the tenant who claimed, by way of defence, damages in respect of loss suffered through failure to repair a drain which, it was claimed, the landlord was bound to repair. The demise included an express grant of a right of way over the landlords' retained property to the public highway. One of the clauses provided for the tenant to pay a "fair proportion" with other lessees of the expenses of making, repairing and scouring walls, drains etc. In 1979 it became apparent that the drain serving the premises was defective and blocked and remedial work involved the tenant in expenditure of the order of £17,000. The tenant argued *inter alia* that the lease imposed an implied contractual obligation to keep in repair and unobstructed the landlords part of the drain. It was further contended that even if the lease imposed no implied obligation the landlords were under a duty of care.

Held (1) The normal test of necessity for the implication of a term in a lease, namely to give business efficacy to the lease, was not satisfied in the present case.

(2) The suggested duty of care based on the landlords' retention of part of the drain subjacent to their own premises could not apply as their was no duty on the landlords' part to repair a drain through which the tenant had an easement to discharge noxious water from his own premises.

Slade LJ said (in part)

When then is the test to be applied in considering whether an obligation is to be implied against the landlords in the present instance? In *Liverpool City Council v Irwin* [1977] AC 239 the House of Lords had to consider the nature and extent of the obligations of landlords of a building in multiple occupation to repair essential means of access. In the Court of Appeal ([1976] QB 319) Lord Denning MR had suggested that the court had power to imply a term if it was reasonable so to do, and held that the landlords were under an implied obligation to repair accordingly. The majority (Roskill and Ormrod LJJ) came to a contrary conclusion. Roskill LJ said (*ibid* at p. 337):

"But I am afraid, with profound respect, I cannot agree with his view that it is open to us in this court at the present day to imply a term because subjectively or objectively we as individual judges think it will be reasonable so to do. It must be *necessary*, in order to make the contract work as well as reasonable so to do, before the court can write into a contract, as a matter of implication, some term which the parties have themselves, assumedly deliberately, omitted to do."

The House of Lords unequivocally rejected the suggestion of Lord Denning MR that the courts have power to introduce terms into contracts merely because they think them reasonable. Nevertheless they supported his ultimate conclusion, by allowing the appeal on rather different grounds. Lord Cross of Chelsea (at pp. 257 and 258) referred to the distinction between two classes of case where the courts are prepared to imply terms in contracts, a distinction pointed out by Lord Simonds and Lord

Tucker in their speeches in *Lister v Romford Ice & Cold Storage Co Ltd* [1957] AC 555 at pp. 579 and 594. The first class of case is where the court lays down a general rule of law that as a legal incident of all contracts of a certain type (sale of goods, master and servant, landlord and tenant and so on) some provision is to be implied. The second class is where there is no question of laying down any *prima facie* rule applicable to all cases of a defined type, but the court is being asked in effect to rectify a particular contract by inserting in it a term which the parties have not expressed. In this second situation, as Lord Cross pointed out, a quite different test is applicable.

In *Liverpool City Council v Irwin* at least the majority of the House of Lords clearly regarded the case as falling within the first class of case referred to by Lord Cross. Lord Wilberforce, with whose speech Lord Fraser of Tullybelton agreed, pointed out (at p. 254 A) that the court was there simply concerned to establish what the contract was, in the absence of a formal tenancy agreement, the parties themselves not having fully stated the terms (see at pp. 253A to C and 254A). He concluded (at p. 254 F-G):

"The relationship accepted by the corporation is that of landlord and tenant: the tenant accepts obligations accordingly, in relation *inter alia* to the stairs, the lifts and the chutes. All these are not just facilities, or conveniences provided at discretion: they are essentials of the tenancy without which life in the dwellings, as a tenant, is not possible. To leave the landlord free of contractual obligation as regards these matters, and subject only to administrative or political pressure, is, in my opinion, inconsistent totally with the nature of this relationship. The subject matter of the lease (high rise blocks) and the relationship created by the tenancy demand, of their nature, some contractual obligation on the landlord."

He regarded it as a "legal incident of this kind of contract" (see at p. 255 A).

Lord Cross likewise thought that the type of case was one which rendered it appropriate for the court to lay down a *prima facie* rule. He pointed out (at p. 259 B) that the general principle is that the law does not impose on a servient owner any liability to keep the servient property in repair for the benefit of the owner of an easement. He said, however (at p. 259 E):

"In such a case I think that the implication should be the other way and that, instead of the landlord being under no obligation to keep the common parts in repair and such facilities as lifts and chutes in working order unless he has expressly contracted to do so, he should—at all events in the case of ordinary commercial lettings—be under some obligation to keep the common parts in repair and the facilities in working order unless he has expressly excluded any such obligation."

The present case is in our judgment distinguishable from the *Liverpool City Council* case in at least two material respects. First there is a formal lease which, on the face of it, represents the apparently complete bargain between the parties. Secondly, this present case is not in our opinion a type of landlord-tenant situation, which gives rise to special considerations, such as the case of a high-rise building in multiple occupation, where the essential means of access to the unit are retained in the landlord's occupation, thus making it appropriate for the court to imply any particular term as a legal incident of the contract.

Accordingly, for the purpose of considering whether the suggested contractual obligation falls to be implied in the present case, we can see no justification for applying a test more favourable to the defendant than the test applicable to the construction of any ordinary commercial lease of unfurnished premises or land which does not fall into a special category such as was referred to by Lord Wilberforce or Lord Cross. While this test is capable of being formulated in many different ways, it is clearly stated by Lord Cross in the *Liverpool City Council* case at p. 258:

"Sometimes, however, there is no question of laying down any *prima facie* rule applicable to all cases of a defined type but what the court is being in effect asked to do is to rectify a particular—often a very detailed—contract by inserting in it a term which the parties have not expressed. Here it is not enough for the court to say that the suggested term is a reasonable one the presence of which would make the contract a better or fairer one; it must be able to say that the insertion of the term is necessary to give—as it is put—'business efficacy' to the contract and that if its absence had been pointed out at the time both parties—assuming them to have been reasonable men—would have agreed without hesitation to its insertion."

This is the test which we consider relevant in the present instance; as Lord Edmund-Davies pointed out in the last-mentioned case (at p. 266 E): "the exercise involved is that of ascertaining the presumed intention of the parties", by which of course he meant *both* parties to the contract.

Case 64   *Wettern Electric Ltd v Welsh Development Agency* [1983] 2 WLR 897. Judge John Newey QC (sitting as a High Court Judge)

The defendants granted the plaintiff manufacturers a lease of a factory, and, when the plaintiffs' business began to expand, they agreed to extend the factory. While the extension was being built, the defendants offered to grant the plaintiffs a licence to occupy a new unit for 12 months on terms set out in a letter of June 21, 1979, similar to those found in a lease. The plaintiffs went into occupation on June 25, but because of inadequate foundations defects appeared in the building and the unit soon became unsuitable for the plaintiffs' use. By December the building had become dangerous and they had to move to other accommodation. A few days earlier, on December 19, the plaintiffs had returned the draft licence to the defendants, duly approved but undated, stating that it was in order. The plaintiffs claimed damages against the defendants for breach of an implied warranty in the licence that the unit was of sound construction and reasonably suitable for the purposes required by the plaintiffs.

On the preliminary issue of liability:

Held, giving judgment for the plaintiffs, (1) That although the plaintiffs had not communicated their acceptance of the licence until December 19, the parties had by their conduct (by the plaintiffs going into occupation and by the defendants permitting it) made a contract for a licence that took effect forthwith, that, although a term that premises were suitable for their purpose was not an implied term of a lease, a term that the premises were fit for the purposes of the licensee could be implied into the terms of a contractual licence if such a term was necessary to give business efficacy to the agreement or to complete an incomplete agreement; that, since the grant of the licence was to enable the plaintiffs to carry on and expand their business while their existing factory was being enlarged, a warranty of soundness and suitability for that purpose was to be included in the terms of the licence and, accordingly, the defendants were in breach of that implied term.

Judge John Newey QC said (in part)

Liverpool City Council v Irwin [1977] AC 239 concerned a 15-storey block consisting of flats let to tenants after they had signed conditions of tenancy prepared by the council. Staircases, lifts and rubbish chutes, which were for use by the tenants, remained in the possession of the council. The document signed by the tenants did not impose any obligations on the council in respect of the means of access to the flats and, in the Court of Appeal [1976] QB 319, Roskill and Ormrod LJJ held that none could be implied. At p. 338 Ormrod LJ commented that since experienced counsel for the tenants had suggested no less than five alternative implied terms, it was not unreasonable to suggest that there could be no certainty what the right implied term (if any) was. Lord Denning MR dissented; he considered that a court should imply a term if it were reasonable to do so.

The House of Lords [1977] AC 239 reversed the Court of Appeal and held that since the conditions of tenancy were incomplete and of a unilateral nature, the court had to complete the contract, that there were to be implied easements for the tenants to use the stairs and rights in the nature of easements to use the lifts and chutes, and that there was to be implied an obligation upon the council to take reasonable care to keep the means of access in reasonable repair and usability. Lord Wilberforce said, at p. 253, that there are varieties of implications which the court think fit to make. One of them, he said, was

> "where there is an apparently complete bargain, the courts are willing to add a term on the ground that without it the contract will not work—that is the case, if not of *The Moorcock*, 14 PD 64 itself on its facts, at least of the doctrine of *The Moorcock* as usually applied. This is . . . a strict test . . ."

Lord Wilberforce did not endorse Lord Denning MR's principle that a court could imply terms because they would be reasonable. He thought that a further category or shade of a continuous spectrum was where the parties had not fully stated the terms of the contract. Lord Cross of Chelsea said, at p. 258:

> "Sometimes . . . what the court is being in effect asked to do is to rectify a particular—often a very detailed—contract by inserting in it a term which the parties have not expressed. Here it is not enough for the court to say that the suggested term is a reasonable one the presence of which would make the contract a better or fairer one; it must be able to say that the insertion of the term is necessary to give—as it is put— 'business efficacy' to the contract and that if its absence had been pointed out at the time both parties—assuming them to have been reasonable men—would have agreed without hesitation to its insertion."

In the present case the licence granted by the defendants to the plaintiffs bore a resemblance to a lease in that it related to land, it was for a fixed period and because many of the terms contained in the letter of June 21, 1979, resembled covenants usually to be found in leases. The licence differed from a lease in all the important respects in which licences differ from leases and to which I have referred previously. A reason for the defendants having offered the plaintiffs a licence rather than a lease was to prevent the plaintiffs from becoming entitled to the protection of the Landlord and Tenant Act 1954.

If the defendants had granted a lease to the plaintiffs, it is clear from *Sutton v Temple*, 12 M & W 52 and subsequent cases that a term as to suitability could not have been implied. Since, however, the plaintiffs were granted a licence, there is no reason why the prohibition of such a term in leases should be applied. *Francis v Cockrell*, LR 5 QB 501 and *Maclenan v Segar* [1917] 2 KB 325 show that terms as to suitability may be implied in licences. They were, however, cases involving personal injuries whereas, fortunately, in the present case no one suffered physical injury.

My view is that it is possible for terms as to fitness for purpose to be implied in licences, but that, except perhaps in relation to safety, there are none which the courts imply *prima facie* in the way that such terms are implied in sale of goods, hire and the like. If any term as to suitability was to be implied in the contractual licence in this case it must, I think, be on the application of the test propounded in *The Moorcock*, 14 PD 64 as clarified by *Reigate v Union Manufacturing Co (Ramsbottom) Ltd* [1918] 1 KB 592 and by *Liverpool City Council v Irwin* [1977] AC 239 or because it is necessary to complete an incomplete contract as in *Irwin*, or both.

The issue asks whether a warranty was to be implied and not a mere obligation to take reasonable care. The warranty proposed in (a) is two-fold: namely, that unit 7 should be of "sound construction" and that it should be "reasonably suitable for the purposes required by the plaintiffs." The warranty proposed in (b) is the same as in (a) except that it excludes liability for defects not discoverable by reasonable means. The plaintiffs' reason for putting forward (b) as an alternative to (a) is because the term implied by McCardie J in *Maclenan v Segar* [1917] 2 KB 325 was in that qualified form.

In *The Moorcock*, 14 PD 64 and in *Liverpool City Council v Irwin* [1977] AC 239 the terms implied required only that the body held liable should have taken reasonable care, but in the former the river bed was not owned or controlled by the wharfingers and, in the latter, vandals were likely to undo the work of the council at any time. In contrast, unit 7 was owned by the defendants, had been built on their instructions, and had only just been completed when the plaintiffs were allowed into occupation. In *Maclenan v Segar* [1917] 2 KB 325 the hotel was an old one and might conceivably have concealed or developed defects which were not discoverable by exercise of reasonable care and skill. The position in the present case was quite different. Unit 7 was completely new and the defendants did or could have employed engineers and architects capable of discovering any defects.

Asking, as *The Moorcock*, 14 PD 64 test requires, whether it was necessary in order to give efficacy to the licence agreement that the defendant should have warranted as set out in (a) of the issue that unit 7 was of sound construction or reasonably fit for the purposes required by the plaintiffs, namely, the manufacture of plastics and composite materials, I think that the answer must be "yes." The sole purpose of the licence was to enable the plaintiffs to have accommodation in which to carry on and expand their business while their existing factory was being enlarged. If anyone had said to the plaintiffs and the defendants' directors and executives at the time when the licence was being granted: "Will the premises be sound and suitable for the plaintiffs' purposes?" they would assuredly have replied: "Of course; there would be no point in the licence if that were not so." The term was required to make the contract workable.

The defendants' letter of June 21, 1979, which the plaintiffs were required to approve was not unlike the conditions of tenancy which the tenants in *Liverpool City Council v Irwin* [1977] AC 239 were required to sign. In each case the terms provided were one-sided. If I had not thought that a warranty of soundness and suitability for the plaintiffs' purposes was to be implied on the application of *The Moorcock* test, I would have thought that an identical term would have had to be implied in order to complete the contract as the parties must clearly have intended.

5 DAMAGES FOR DISREPAIR

5.1 Damages for breach of tenant's repairing covenant at common law

An action for damages for non-repair may be brought by the landlord at any time during the term and after its expiry. The measure of damages at common law are usually as follows:

(i) Where proceedings are taken during the term, the measure is the amount by which the value of the reversion is diminished by reason of the breach.

(ii) Where proceedings are taken at the end of the term, the measure is the cost to the landlord of effecting the repairs plus any loss of rent thereby sustained.

Case 65 Mills v Guardians of the Poor of the East London Union (1872) LR 8 CP 79 Keating J

On June 15, 1859, the plaintiff granted a lease to the defendants for twenty-one years, determinable at the option of either party at the expiration of the first seven or fourteen years. In February, 1866 (the first seven years of the term having elapsed), the lessees received notice from a railway company to treat for the purchase of their interest in the premises, under the Lands Clauses Consolidation Act, 1845 and the compensation payable to them by the company was assessed by an arbitrator on April 16, 1867; on July 29, 1870, judgment was signed for the amount, and an assignment was executed by the lessees, and the company took possession of the premises on November 21, 1870.

On June 19, 1868, the company gave the lessor notice to treat in respect of his interest, and he sent in a claim on the 29th; but nothing further was done—the proposed line being abandoned.

In 1871, the lessor brought an action against the lessees for breaches of their general covenant to repair accruing as well before as since the assignment by the latter to the company.

Upon a case stated by an arbitrator for the opinion of the court as to the principle upon which the damages were to be assessed:

Held (1) That there was nothing to prevent the lessor from recovering substantial damages in respect of breaches committed after the notice to treat, but before the assignment by the lessees to the railway company; and that the proper measure of damages was the amount by which the plaintiff's reversion had become deteriorated at the date when the company took possession under the assignment, viz., November 21, 1870.

Keating J said (in part)

Then as to the principle on which the damages are to be assessed, I think they are not limited to nominal damages. I think the rule laid down in the more recent cases, viz. that the true measure of damages is the extent to which the lessor's reversion is damnified by the want of repair, is the sounder rule, notwithstanding the other rule has the sanction of the high authority of Lord Holt. The arbitrator will practically have no difficulty in assessing the damages upon this principle.

Case 66 *Joyner v Weeks* [1891] 2 QB 31 Court of Appeal

On May 20, 1887, the plaintiff, together with several other persons beneficially interested in the reversion, executed a lease of the house No. 10, to Samuel Lewis, who was the tenant of Nos. 9 and 11, which were subject to the same trusts as No. 10; this lease was for a term of twenty-one years, to commence on March 25, 1889, when the defendant's lease of No. 10 would expire. The rent was £300 and Lewis covenanted to lay out £200 in making alterations to No. 10 and the adjoining houses Nos. 9 and 11, for the purpose of establishing communication between them. He also covenanted to keep the premises in repair. The defendant had carried on a millinery business at No. 10, and Lewis a draper's business at Nos. 9 and 11, and the object was to throw the three ground floors into one shop for Lewis's business. Immediately after the expiration of the defendant's lease Lewis made the alterations, and in the course of them demolished some parts of No. 10, which were out of repair; other parts of No. 10 were also out of repair, and the cost of putting them into repair would have been £45. Lewis had made no claim to be reimbursed the cost to which he was put in repairing, and on the terms of his lease it was clear that he had no right to make any such claim. The plaintiff brought an action against the lessee for damages for breach of a covenant to surrender at the expiration of his lease (which was dated November 10, 1868, and expired March 25, 1889), well and sufficiently repaired in accordance with the terms of the lease. The cost of making good the dilapidations was proved before me to be £70; the plaintiff's counsel claimed as damages for the breach of covenant the whole amount of this cost. The defendant, without admitting liability, had paid into court £45, but his counsel contended that under the circumstances only nominal damages should be awarded.

Held (1) The general rule with regard to the measure of damages in an action for breach of a covenant by a lessee to deliver up the demised premises in repair is that such damages are the cost of putting the premises into the state of repair required by the covenant.

(2) Such measure of damages is not affected by the fact that, by reason of the terms of a lease granted by the lessor to another lessee from the expiration of the defendant's term, the lessor is at the time of action brought no worse off than he would have been if the defendant's covenant had been performed.

Lord Esher MR said (in part)

A great many cases have been cited, of which one only was directly in point, though another was as nearly as possible in point; and a series of dicta of learned judges have been referred to, which seem to me to show that for a very long time there has been a constant practice as to the measure of damages in such cases. Such an inveterate practice amounts, in my opinion, to a rule of law. That rule is that, when there is a lease with a covenant to leave the premises in repair at the end of the term, and such covenant is broken, the lessee must pay what the lessor proves to be a reasonable and proper amount for putting the premises into the state of repair in which they ought to have been left. It is not necessary in this case to say that that is an absolute rule applicable under all circumstances; but I confess that I strongly incline to think that it is so. It is a highly convenient rule. It avoids all the subtle refinements with which we have been indulged to-day, and the extensive and costly inquiries which they would involve. It appears to me to be a simple and businesslike rule; and, if I were obliged to decide that point, I am very much inclined to think that I should come to the conclusion that it is an absolute rule. But it is not necessary to determine that point in the present case. The rule that the measure of damages in such cases is the cost of repair, is, I think, at all events, the ordinary rule, which must apply, unless there be something which affects the condition of the property in such a manner as to affect the relation between the lessor and the lessee in respect to it. The question is whether there is any such circumstance in the present case. I think that there clearly is not. The circumstances relied upon by the defendant did not affect the property as regards the relation between the lessor and the lessee in respect to it. They arose from a relation, the result of a contract between the plaintiff and a third person, to which the defendant was no party, and with which he had nothing to do. It was said that this contract passed an estate in the premises to such third person. If it had done so, I think it would have made no difference; but it did not; it only gave an interesse termini during the continuance of the defendant's term, and could not take effect to give an estate as between the plaintiff and the third person until the relation between the plaintiff and the defendant was at an end. At the moment of the determination of the lease between the plaintiff and the defendant, the premises were out of repair. And, if we cannot look at the contract between the plaintiff and the third person, or anything that took place under it, there was nothing but the ordinary case of the breach of a covenant to leave the premises in repair. In my opinion the contract between the plaintiff and the third person cannot be taken into account; it is something to which the defendant is a stranger. So, also, anything that may happen between the plaintiff and the third person under that contract after the breach of covenant is equally matter with which the defendant has nothing to do, and which cannot be taken into account. These are matters which might or might not have happened, and, so far as the defendant is concerned, are mere accidents. The result is that there is nothing to prevent the application of the ordinary rule as to the measure of damages in such a case. There is no decision to the contrary of what we are now deciding. In all the period of time during which leases containing such covenants have been common, there is no case in which such a contention as that of the defendant has been allowed to prevail. There are cases in which arguments as nearly as possible analogous to that of the defendant have not been assented to; for example, the case where the plaintiff had entered into a verbal agreement with a third person for the pulling down of the premises at the expiration of the term. The case of *Morgan v Hardy* 17 QBD 770 appears to be in point. In that case Denman, J, gave an elaborate considered judgment to the effect that the measure of damages in an action upon a covenant to leave in

repair was the amount that it would cost to put the premises
into such repair as was contemplated by the covenant, and that
the existence of such a contract as there is here with a third
person, and suchlike circumstances, could not be considered.
That case is, of course, not an authority binding upon us; but
it is one to which we should pay regard in deciding this case.
Besides that, there is the case of *Inderwick v Leech* 1 TLR 95.
Though that case is not exactly in point, all the reasoning of
the judgment of Lopes, LJ, which was affirmed in the Divisional
Court by Lord Coleridge, CJ, and Cave, J, and afterwards on
appeal by this court upon the authority of *Rawlings v Morgan*
18 CB (NS) 776 points in the direction of the conclusion at which
we are arriving, viz., that, if anything could prevent the application of the ordinary rule that the measure of damages is the
cost of such repairs as were contemplated by the covenant, it
could only be something in the condition of the premises which
affected the relation between the lessor and lessee in respect
of them, and that contracts made between the lessor and a third
person must be disregarded. The rule I have mentioned is a
good working rule, and I believe it to be the legal rule.

Note:
   (i) The decision in *Joyner v Weeks* should be read subject to
       para 5.2.

5.2 The operation of the Landlord and Tenant Act 1927

Under section 18 (1) of the Landlord and Tenant Act 1927 a ceiling
is placed on the amount of damages which can be recovered
from a tenant for non-repair. Whether the landlord's action is
brought during or on the termination of the lease the landlord
cannot recover more than the amount (if any) by which the value
of the reversion is diminished by the breach.

Statute 3: Landlord and Tenant Act 1927. Section 18
Provisions as to covenants to repair
18.—(1) Damages for a breach of a covenant or agreement to
keep or put premises in repair during the currency of a lease,
or to leave or put premises in repair at the termination of a lease,
whether such covenant or agreement is expressed or implied,
and whether general or specific, shall in no case exceed the
amount (if any) by which the value of the reversion (whether
immediate or not) in the premises is diminished owing to the
breach of such covenant or agreement as aforesaid; and in particular no damage shall be recovered for a breach of any such

covenant or agreement to leave or put premises in repair at the termination of a lease, if it is shown that the premises, in whatever state of repair they might be, would at or shortly after the termination of the tenancy have been or be pulled down, or such structural alterations made therein as would render valueless the repairs covered by the covenant or agreement.

(2) A right of re-entry or forfeiture for a breach of any such covenant or agreement as aforesaid shall not be enforceable, by action or otherwise, unless the lessor proves that the fact that such a notice as is required by section one hundred and forty-six of the Law of Property Act 1925, had been served on the lessee was known either:

(a) to the lessee; or

(b) to an under-lessee holding under an under-lease which reserved a nominal reversion only to the lessee; or

(c) to the person who last paid the rent due under the lease either on his own behalf or as agent for the lessee or under-lessee;

and that a time reasonably sufficient to enable the repairs to be excuted had elapsed since the time when the fact of the service of the notice came to the knowledge of any such person.

Where a notice has been sent by registered post addressed to a person at his last known place of abode in the United Kingdom, then for the purposes of this subsection, that person shall be deemed, unless the contrary is proved, to have had knowledge of the fact that the notice had been served as from the time at which the letter would have been delivered in the ordinary course of post.

This subsection shall be construed as one with section one hundred and forty-six of the Law of Property Act 1925.

(3) This section applies whether the lease was created before or after the commencement of this Act.

Case 67 *Smiley v Townshend* [1950] 2 KB 311 Court of Appeal

The assignee of a long lease of premises, containing full covenants to repair, which was assigned to him two years before the date of the termination of the lease, when the premises were already requisitioned, was sued by his landlord on the termination of the lease for breaches of the covenants to repair. The premises at the date of the termination of the lease were still requisitioned, and the date of the termination of the requisition was undetermined. It was contended for the defendant that, although, following *Joyner v Weeks* [1891] 2 QB 31, before March 25, 1928, the damages would have been assessed as at the end of the lease, the effect of s. 18, (1) of the Landlord and Tenant Act, 1927, was that they must be assessed by reference to the time when the possession of the premises actually reverted into the possession of the landlord; that accordingly the court must look into the future to see what the condition of the premises then might be; and that the requisitioning authority still might make good some or all of the dilapidations. It was also contended that there would be no damage to the landlord from any want of decorative repair during the period of the requisition, since the landlord could not benefit from the doing of decorative repair or suffer by its omission: he could not benefit from the doing of the decorative repair because, by the time the requisition was terminated, the benefit of it to the premises would have worn off; and he could not suffer from its omission, because, by virtue of s. 10 of the Requisitioned Land and War Works Act, 1948, he received compensation for all dilapidations which befell during the period of requisitioning. Accordingly, by reason of either argument, the damages in the action could not be more than nominal.

Held, (1) The damages must be assessed not by reference to the time when the land reverted into the possession of the landlord at the termination of the requisition, but as at the date of the termination of the lease, although the defendant, the assignee of the lease, could never have had the right to go into possession to do the repairs.

(2) The proper measure of damages was the difference in the value of the reversion at the termination of the lease, between the premises in their then state of disrepair and in the state in which they would have been if the covenants had been fulfilled. The question, therefore, here was: how much was the market value of the landlord's interest diminished at the end of the lease by the disrepair.

(3) Future events, after the termination of the lease, could not in themselves reduce or extinguish the damages, but they might be taken into account in so far as they threw light on the value of the reversion as at the date of the end of the lease.

(4) In cases where it was plain that the repairs were not going to be done by the landlord, the cost of them was little or no guide to the diminution in value of the reversion, which might be nominal. But where the repairs had been or were going to be done by the landlord, the cost might

be a very real guide to that value. Where it was open to question whether the repairs would be done by the landlord, the cost might afford a starting figure, but it should be scaled down, according to the circumstances, remembering that the real question was: what was the injury to the reversion?

Denning LJ said (in part)

The question is what is the proper measure of damages for that breach? It was strongly urged before us that the damages should be nominal. Mr Shelley [counsel for the defendant] put his argument in this way: he said that before March 25, 1928, the damages would have had to be assessed as at the end of the lease: see *Joyner v Weeks* [1891] 2 QB 31; but that the effect of the Landlord and Tenant Act 1927 is that they must be assessed by reference to the time when the land actually reverts in possession to the landlord; and that, if that time has not yet arrived, as it has not done here, the court must look into the future to see what the condition of the premises will be. It may be in this case that the corporation will make good all the dilapidations. Mr Shelley points out that they have already done the outside painting. They may do more. They may do all. If they do so, the landlord will get his premises back fully repaired, so why should he get damages as well? He cannot, therefore, show that he will suffer any damage.

Mr Blundell [also for the defendant] put the argument rather differently. He said that there could be no damage to the landlord from any want of decorative repair during the time of this assignee, because the landlord could not benefit from the doing of decorative repairs, or suffer by the omission of them. On the one hand, the landlord would not benefit, for, if the defendant had in fact done all the decorative repairs during his time (that is in 1945, 1946 or 1947), the landlord would not have benefited at all, because, by the time the requisition comes to an end, whenever that may be, the benefit of them would have worn off. Indeed, the plaintiff's valuer, in the course of what, if I may say so, was a very skilful cross-examination by Mr Blundell, admitted that the value of the decorative work would have been exhausted in the course of a long requisition and the value would have quite worn off.

. . . But the answer to them both is that the damages must be assessed not by reference to the time when the land reverts in possession, but as at the end of the lease. I take it from authorities which this court is not at liberty to disregard that the proper measure of damage is the difference in value of the reversion at the end of the lease between the premises in their then state of unrepair and in the state in which they would have been if the covenants had been fulfilled. That test was laid down by this court in *Hanson v Newman* [1934] Ch 298. What has to be considered is the diminution in value of the reversion at the end of the lease; and I take the word "reversion" to mean the landlord's then interest in the premises. If he is the owner and the premises are requisitioned, then the reversion is his freehold, subject to the existing requisition, because that is the landlord's then interest in the premises. The question is, therefore: how much was the market value of the landlord's interest diminished at the end of the lease by reason of the disrepair for which the then assignee was responsible?

The cost of executing the repairs may sometimes be accepted as the measure of damages.

Case 68 *Jones v Herxheimer* [1950] 2 KB 107 Court of Appeal

By a tenancy agreement of March 25, 1943, premises consisting of four rooms on the first floor and one on the ground floor of a house were let to the defendant for one year from that date. The tenant covenanted to keep, and at the determination of the tenancy to deliver up, the interior of the premises in good and tenantable repair. When the tenant gave up possession in 1949, the landlord found the rooms in a bad state of decorative repair, had them redecorated throughout, and relet them. The landlord claimed the cost of those redecorations. The county court judge having given judgment for the landlord, the tenant contended that there was no evidence of damage to the reversion and, accordingly that the landlord should, having regard to s. 18 (2) of the Landlord and Tenant Act, 1927, not have been awarded more than nominal damages.

Held (1) Where a tenant fails to repair demised premises in accordance with the covenants in his lease, the lack of repair may itself be evidence of damage to the reversion and the cost of effecting the necessary repairs may be evidence of the extent of that damage. It is not an invariable rule of law that in all cases in estimating the damage resulting from a breach of a covenant to repair it is necessary, having regard to s. 18 (1) of the Landlord and Tenant Act, 1927, to place a value upon the reversion repaired and upon the reversion unrepaired and to treat the difference as the diminution in the value of the reversion. Such a method of calculation, while the right criterion to apply in most cases, is not appropriate in a simple case where the tenancy is of a few rooms in a house and where there can be no question of the sale of the rooms apart from the house. In such a case, if there is evidence that the repairs which the landlord has done (being repairs within the covenant) were no more than were reasonably necessary to make the rooms fit for reoccupation or reletting, the proper cost of the repairs may be regarded *prima facie* as representing a diminution in the value of the reversion due to the tenant's breach of covenant.

(2) There was evidence on which the judge could hold that the cost of executing the repairs was the measure of the damage to the reversion.

Jenkins LJ said (in part)

In *Hanson v Newman* [1934] Ch 298 an action had been brought in 1932 for possession of the premises, comprised in a lease for a term expiring in 1938, for breach of the repairing covenants therein contained. The plaintiff had recovered judgment in default of defence for possession and damages to be assessed by a master. The proceeding before the court was an appeal by the defendant from the master's assessment of the damages, and the question in issue was whether the master, who had assessed the damages in accordance with the terms of s. 18 (1) of the Landlord and Tenant Act, 1927, at the sum found by him to represent the amount by which the reversion in possession at the date of the forfeiture of the lease (i.e., the date of the writ) had been diminished by the defendant's breaches of covenant, ought to have allowed a claim by the defendant to set off against the amount so assessed the difference between the value of the reversion in possession at the date of the forfeiture and its value at the same date as a reversion expectant upon the expiration of the term in 1938.

Luxmoore J and the Court of Appeal held that there could be no such set-off. Luxmoore J in the course of his judgment said:

"Under the law before the Landlord and Tenant Act, 1927, was passed, a landlord could recover by way of damage at the termination of his term the actual cost of executing the repairs required to fulfil the covenant. The Landlord and Tenant Act, 1927, has not changed the law in that respect;

all that it has done is to impose a limit on the amount of those damages. The material section to be considered is s. 18 of the Landlord and Tenant Act, 1927.''

Luxmoore J read s. 18 (1), and went on to discuss what was meant in the section by the phrase "reversion immediate or not," concluding that the word "reversion" was used "as referring, in the case where the lease has terminated, to the land which has reverted." Then he said this on the effect of the section on the amount of damages recoverable: ·

> "What the section provides for is that the damages for breach of covenant on the termination of a lease are not to exceed the amount by which the value of the reversion, whether immediate or not, in the premises is diminished owing to the breach of such covenant or agreement; that is, you take the value of the reversion as it is with the breach—the value of the property which has reverted as it is subject to the breach—and you take it as it would be if there were no breach, and you provide that the amount of damage shall not exceed the amount by which the value of the property repaired exceeds the value of the property unrepaired."

In the Court of Appeal Lawrence LJ and Romer LJ both expressed full approval of Luxmoore J's judgment, and Lawrence LJ, in particular, adopted the passage to which we have just referred, quoting it at length and saying that he "could not express it better."

In *Salisbury (Marquess) v Gilmore* [1942] 2 KB 38, premises in New Bond Street had been let to the defendant for a term of fourteen years from September 29, 1925. The tenant had asked for a new lease in 1937 but was then informed that the plaintiff landlords intended to pull the premises down (which intention would have been an answer to any claim by the tenant for a new lease under s. 5 of the Landlord and Tenant Act, 1927, and *prima facie* a defence under s. 18 (1), to any claim against the tenant for damages for non-repair at the termination of the lease). In 1939 the tenant vacated the premises and left them out of repair, being still under the impression that they were to be pulled down. Thereafter, the plaintiffs, having, as they said, abandoned their intention to pull down the premises, claimed damages for breach of the covenants to repair. The evidence showed that the plaintiffs had not abandoned their intention to pull down the premises until a date after the termination of the tenancy.

The actual question in the case was not concerned with the quantum of damages recoverable under s. 18 (1), but was simply whether, in the circumstances which we have stated, the defendants were not precluded by the latter part of the sub-section from recovering any damages at all, and the Court of Appeal (reversing Hilbery J) held that they were so precluded. But MacKinnon LJ in the course of his judgment did in fact deal with the necessity of proof of damage to the reversion under s. 18 (1), and expressed the view that there was no evidence at the trial of any diminution in the value of the reversion by reason of any breach of covenant to repair or yield up in repair.

[Counsel] relied on the following passage in MacKinnon LJ's judgment:

"The only evidence as to breach was under (b) the covenant to deliver up in repair, upon a survey and schedule of dilapidations made after such delivery up. As to the effect of this breach on the value of the reversion the first surveyor could only say that the depreciation was 'the cost of doing the repairs,' but on cross-examination said 'I am not in a position to answer' (as to the depreciation) 'because it is a question of the value of the premises and as a surveyor assessing dilapidations I was only concerned with the cost of making the repairs.' The other surveyor, on being asked what was the depreciation, answered: 'I think the cost of the work is the only possible criterion.' But he also said, in cross-examination, that the only real value of the premises was the site value, and 'you would get as much for the site as for the site with the building on it.' On this I am clear that the learned judge was wrong in that passage of his judgment in which he says: 'I accept the evidence of the plaintiffs' witnesses. ... I am satisfied that the cost of making good the want of repair is as nearly as it can be assessed the same as the diminution in the value of the reversion resulting from the breaches of covenant to yield up in repair.' There was no evidence of any diminution of value in the reversion, and the judgment, if given for the plaintiffs, should have been for nominal damages only." ...

... Lastly, in *Landeau v Marchbank* [1949] 2 All ER 172, a case in which on the determination of a lease the premises had been sold at an admittedly good price for conversion into two flats and two maisonettes, Lynskey J rejected a calculation of damages based on the cost of effecting repairs in accordance with the covenants less the cost of those rendered valueless by the contemplated conversion, and held that there was no evidence of any diminution in the value of the reversion, and that the plaintiff was entitled to nominal damages only.

[Counsel] relied in particular on a passage in which the judge expressed the view that "the fact that repairs are necessary is not in itself even *prima facie* evidence of damage to the value of the reversion." With the passage just quoted, as a general proposition, we are unable to agree. We find nothing in the earlier authorities to justify the conclusion, as a matter of law, that in no case and in no circumstances can the fact that repairs are necessary, and the cost of those repairs, be taken as at least *prima facie* evidence of damage to the value of the reversion and of the extent of such damage. There must be many cases in which it is in fact quite obvious that the value of the reversion has, by reason of a tenant's failure to do some necessary repair, been damaged precisely to the extent of the proper cost of effecting the repair in question. Nor do we understand the Lords Justices in *Hanson v Newman* (*supra*) as purporting to lay down an invariable rule of law to the effect that in all case and in all circumstances the procedure of placing values on the reversion repaired and the reversion unrepaired, and ascertaining the difference, must necessarily be gone through in order to ascertain the diminution in the value of the reversion attributable to the want of repair. Nor do we regard MacKinnon LJ in *Salisbury* (*Marquess*) *v Gilmore* (*supra*) as intending to do anything more than to hold that, on the evidence tendered by the plaintiffs in that particular case, the cost of effecting the repairs could not be regarded as any index of the diminution (if any) in the value of the reversion which the want of repair had occasioned.

In the present case the "reversion" for the purposes of s. 18 (1) consists simply of the four first-floor rooms and one ground-floor room formerly comprised in the defendant's tenancy, i.e., not a whole house but merely a set of rooms in a house: *Hanson v Newman* (*supra*). The matter is thus uncomplicated by any question of site value such as materially affected the evidence regarding the New Bond Street premises in *Salisbury* (*Marquess*) *v Gilmore* (*supra*). Nor is there here any question of change of user (as in *Portman v Latta* [1942] WN 97) or of sale and physical alteration (as in *Landeau v Marchbank* (*supra*)).

In the present case, the landlord having resumed possession of five rooms in his house which had been let for residential purposes, and intending to use or re-let them for residential purposes, found that, through the tenant's breach of covenant, it was necessary for him to do certain repairs to the rooms in order to put them in what he considered a fit state for occupation or re-letting for residential purposes. Accordingly, he spent money on effecting those repairs which he would not have had to spend if the covenant had been duly performed.

In such a case, if there is evidence that the repairs done, being repairs within the covenant, were no more than was reasonably necessary to make the rooms fit for occupation or re-letting for residential purposes, we fail to see why the proper cost of those repairs should not be regarded *prima facie* as representing a diminution in the value of the reversion due to the tenant's breach of covenant, being money which the landlord, acting as an ordinary prudent owner, had to spend on the property owing to the breach and would not have had to spend but for the breach. . . .

. . . The surveyor's intention presumably was to show that there was no diminution in the value of the reversion according to the calculation prescribed in *Hanson v Newman* (*supra*). That calculation is no doubt the right criterion to apply in many if not most cases, and we do not for a moment intend to cast any doubt on its validity as a measure of the damages recoverable under s. 18 (1), in cases to which it is appropriate. But we certainly deprecate its introduction as a *sine qua non* into all cases, including a small and simple case like the present concerned with a letting of some of the rooms in a house, where it becomes a purely hypothetical calculation wholly removed from the practical realities of the matter.

Case 69 *Drummond v S & U Stores Ltd* (1981) 258 EG 1293
Glidewell J

> The plaintiff was the freehold owner of shop premises let to the defendant tenants. The lease contained covenants by the tenants to repair and decorate the premises, the general repair covenant stipulating
>
> > "from time to time and at all times during the said term well and substantially to repair, cleanse and put and keep in good and substantial repair and condition, the premises"
>
> A further stipulation required the tenants to pay to the landlord all costs, charges and expenses [including solicitors', counsel's and surveyors' costs, charges and fees] incurred by the lessor in, or in contemplation of, any proceedings in respect of the lease under sections 146 and 147 of the Law of Property Act 1925. The landlord alleged, *inter alia*, that the tenants had failed to put and keep the premises

in good and substantial repair and had not painted or decorated them is accordance with the covenants and claimed, *inter alia*, damages for the diminution of the value of the reversion.

Held (1) The proper measure of damages was the diminution in the value of the reversion but in the absence of direct evidence the cost of the repairs may be a useful guide.

(2) The amount of damages was to include value added tax where the landlord was not registered for such tax.

(3) A landlord's arrangements with a new tenant were *res inter alios acta* as regards the old tenant against whom damages were being claimed.

Glidewell J said (in part)

In my judgment, the proper measure of damages for breach of a covenant to repair is in the first place based upon the amount by which the reversion is depreciated. Authority for that proposition, which is well established, is to be found in the decision of the Court of Appeal in *Smiley v Townshend* [1950] 2 KB 311, in which, in the course of his judgment, Denning LJ (as he then was) said:

> "I take it from authorities which this court is not at liberty to disregard that the proper measure of damage is the difference in value of the reversion at the end of the lease between the premises in their then state of unrepair and in the state in which they would have been if the covenants had been fulfilled. That test was laid down by this court in *Hanson v Newman*. What has to be considered is the diminution in value of the reversion at the end of the lease; and I take the word 'reversion' to mean the landlord's then interest in the premises."

He then went on to deal with a matter which was germane to that case, but which is totally irrelevant in the present case, and he then said:

> "The question is, therefore: how much was the market value of the landlord's interest diminished at the end of the lease by reason of the disrepair for which the then assignee was responsible?"

That then is the first principle. But it is apparent that evidence of the value of the premises in their state of disrepair may be difficult to come by, because of course, since most leases, particularly of commercial premises, envisage the premises being let in repair, or at any rate subject to the liability of a previous tenant to repair, the majority of comparable evidence relates to lettings of property in repair rather than in disrepair. Thus it may be very difficult indeed to obtain and put forward evidence of a comparable property in disrepair. Certainly no such evidence has been called before me. Thus it follows that evidence of the cost of putting the property into the state of repair required by the lease is relevant evidence and will very often be *prima facie* evidence, or at any rate the starting point, from which the amount of the diminution in the value of the reversion may be deduced. In *Smiley v Townshend*, Denning LJ dealt with that matter at the bottom of p 322 where he said this:

> "In cases where it is plain that the repairs are not going to be done by the landlord, the cost of them is little or no guide to the diminution in value of the reversion, which may be nominal: see *Espir v Basil Street Hotel Ltd* and *James v Hutton*. But in cases where the repairs have been, or are going to be, done by the landlord, the cost may be a very real guide. That is shown by the recent case of *Jones v Herxheimer* to which we were referred. In cases where it is open to question whether the repairs will be done by the landlord, as in the present case"

which I should say was a case where the premises were under requisition, so contained facts peculiar to its own situation

> "then the cost may afford a starting figure; but it should be scaled down according to the circumstances, remembering that the real question is: what is the injury to the reversion? That is what the judge did here, as I read his judgment; he used the cost merely as an aid in assessing the diminution in value of the reversion."

Singleton LJ . . . in the same decision, said this:

> "In the course of his judgment in *Landeau v Marchbank* the judge appears to have said: 'It seems to me that, having regard to those decisions, the fact that repairs are necessary is not in itself even *prima facie* evidence of damage to the value of the reversion. In certain circumstances, it may be an important factor, but of itself the fact that a certain amount of repair needs to be done does not, in my view, necessarily mean that there is damage to the reversion.' If I may respectfully say so, I agree with the judgment in that case except that I would substitute the word 'conclusive' for the words 'even *prima facie*'. Evidence of lack of repair is not conclusive evidence

of damage to the value of the reversion; but it may well be, and is generally held to be, *prima facie* evidence of it."

I note in passing that where Denning LJ spoke of the situation where repairs had been or are going to be done by the landlord, nobody in the circumstances of that case was considering a situation where it might in fact be a future tenant who actually arranged for the repairs to be done in agreement with the landlord, some financial satisfaction for his doing so being arranged between them. No doubt, if that matter had been in issue there, his Lordship would have considered that if the future tenant actually does the repairs, but receives some satisfaction from the landlord for doing them, either by direct payment or by reduction in the rent which he has to pay, then that is equivalent to the landlord doing the repairs. Certainly that is my view.

The third matter of which I remind myself is that superimposed on the common law, as I have sought to set it out, is section 18(1) of the Landlord and Tenant Act 1927, which provides:

'Damages for a breach of a covenant or agreement to keep or put premises in repair during the currency of a lease, or to leave or put premises in repair at the termination of a lease, ... shall in no case exceed the amount (if any) by which the value of the reversion ... in the premises is diminished owing to the breach of such covenant or agreement as aforesaid.'...

In other words, even in a case where it is right to treat the cost of doing repairs as a starting point or as *prima facie* evidence, nevertheless, if it is shown by other evidence clearly that the loss to the reversion is some lesser sum, then the damages cannot exceed that lesser sum. ...

The only evidence that I have as to the cost of carrying out such works [to the interior of the premises] is the evidence of [the surveyor] on behalf of the landlord, because the tenants, taking the view on advice that this is not the proper measure at all, just have not sought to advance evidence as to what would be the proper figure, if that were the standard to adopt. The only figures I have on behalf of the tenants are figures which would suffice to bring the premises up to some lesser standard. So I can only accept, and I do accept, the evidence on behalf of the landlord as to the cost of bringing the interior of the premises up to the standard required by the lease with the exception of those items to which I have already specifically referred and with which I have dealt, that is to say, the electrical installation, the small items for clearing rubbish, the firescreen, and the defective floorboards.

Those figures do not take into account value added tax, and it is the landlord's case that since the tenants have not done the work, the landlord may well wish to put the premises into the condition required by the lease, and if she were going to do so, she would incur value added tax. She would have to pay value added tax, and since she is not registered for value added tax, she would not be able to reclaim it. On the other hand, the tenants say that what the landlord is most probably going to do, on the evidence, is to relet these premises to somebody else. Any tenant, they say, is almost bound to be registered for value added tax and thus if the landlord arranges for the new tenant actually to do the work, whether there is a financial arrangement between them matters not for this purpose, value added tax will not enter into it because the new tenant will be able to claim back the value added tax which the landlord would not be able to claim back. Thus, says [counsel] the landlord being under an obligation to mitigate her damages, is under an obligation to adopt that method of carrying out the work in order to save the tenant from being responsible for payment of value added tax as part of the damages. (If this is the proper method of approach at all!)

My mind has fluctuated about that question, but I have come to the conclusion in the end that the argument on behalf of the landlord is correct in relation to this matter. There are two reasons for that conclusion: the first is, as I suggested in argument, that if [counsel's] argument is correct it means that, albeit the landlord may very well in fact relet the premises, nevertheless the effect of depriving her of value added tax on the damages, or as part of the damages, would effectively be to close her other options, that is to say, if she changed her mind and decided that she would like to sell the premises and put the money to some other use but that she wanted to sell them in lease condition, then she would have to incur value added tax and she would not have recovered it as part of the damages.

I was reminded by [counsel] that a decision to which he had referred me during the course of his opening, that in *Haviland v Long* [1952] 2 QB 80, another decision of the Court of Appeal, while not exactly on all fours with this, was helpful. That was a case in which the tenants were in breach of a covenant to repair and the landlords entered into a fresh new lease with other tenants who agreed to carry out the repairs. The landlords agreed to reimburse them out of the sum they recovered from the old tenants by way of payment for the dilapidations. The old tenants said, "Well, you are going to get the new tenants to do the repairs. They only get anything from you if we pay you anything, so that there is no need for us to pay you anything. Thus, no obligation on you will arise to pay the new tenants anything." But the court held that that was a matter which was *res inter alios acta*. In other words, it was nothing to do with the respective obligations or rights as between the landlord and the old tenant, and that really this was merely a mechanism by which the work of repair was to be done. That authority does seem to me to establish the principle for which [counsel] is contending, and I have come to the conclusion that the damages, if properly assessable on the basis of the cost of repair, should properly include also value added tax, or rather, should include an item equal to the amount of value added tax which the landlord would suffer on such costs.

As I have said, that is dealing with the matter on the basis of the landlord's approach; but the tenants' approach was quite different. The evidence of [a surveyor] called on behalf of the tenants, was effectively this: that while he conceded that there was a general need for redecoration, internally and externally, and some need for repairs, he believed that most potential purchasers would anticipate, and a tenant of the lease for 14 years or longer would be prepared to accept, the state of disrepair and would discount the cost of decoration. His final conclusion was that the proper rental value of the property was some £2,500 per annum. He capitalised that to give a capital value of £25,000 in a good state of repair, and he deducted from it what he described as a spot figure of £2,500, which he believes was the kind of sum which a purchaser would seek to deduct for initial essential repairs. He then came back to the question of rental value and said that although a purchaser would, he thought, deduct his spot figure of £2,500, he did not think a prospective tenant would deduct anything at all. I must confess I fail to understand the logic of that distinction, but nevertheless, that was his evidence.

What in effect was being said to me in this respect by [the surveyor] was that I should really completely disregard all the detailed evidence about the cost of repairs; that, albeit the premises did require repair and a good deal of decoration, except for possibly some element of structural repairs, a new tenant (and it was firmly argued that the probability is that these premises will be let) would want to put in a scheme of decoration and install fixtures and fittings which would suit his own business. Thus, if the landlord carried out the decorations before hand, it might well be that a great deal of what the landlord did would be totally wasted because the new tenant would simply scrap it and put in something different, or carry out a different scheme of decorative repair.

That argument was particularly advanced because there was evidence from [a surveyor] that he was, and is, and has for some time been, in negotiation with a bus company to lease these premises to them. I should say that the premises are situated on a street corner, and it looks very much as though they were purpose built as a corner shop, with living accommodation alongside and above, at some time in the middle or later half of the 19th century, and they stand some little distance from the centre of Bury St Edmunds in a position that has been described as a secondary shopping position, but they are immediately across the crossroads on which they stand from a bus station. Thus it would no doubt be extremely convenient to the bus company to locate themselves in the premises, and if they do take a lease of the premises they apparently intend to use them for the purposes of a ticket office and a travel agency generally. I am not sure whether that includes international as well as national travel, but that is perhaps irrelevant.

In town and country planning terms, that does not involve of itself a material change in the use of the premises because a shop is defined in the relevant order as including a ticket office or agency, but it is, in ordinary terms of course, a somewhat different type of institution from a retail shop selling clothing or any other article. There is obviously a difference between the way in which a building is used if, on the one hand, the occupier is a retail trader with a shop and all the accoutrements of a sales shop and storage accommodation above, and the way in which the premises will be used if the front part were a ticket office and a travel agency and the remainder were used partly for storage of documents and the like, but very largely as office accommodation. What is urged upon me is, particularly if the bus company go there, they will want, to a large extent, the property to be fitted out and decorated to meet their own needs.

[The surveyor] on the other hand, while I think conceding that to a modest extent a tenant, particularly the bus company, might have special needs, said that of course the bus company was not the only potential tenant and if they were not satisfied he envisaged that the tenant might well be a small shopkeeper. Small shopkeepers are notoriously short of capital and, in his view, it would be quite common for a small shopkeeper to welcome the fact that the landlord had had the premises redecorated, and simply to enter them, accepting the landlord's decorations virtually as they stood, and immediately start trading. So [the surveyor's] evidence was that of course all, or certainly most, of the expenditure required to put the premises into the condition required by the lease would be to the advantage of a new tenant and would not be wasted.

Faced with these two conflicting views of gentlemen equally eminent in their own professions, I can only base myself, to an extent, on my own experience, such as it is on these matters, and obviously it is somewhat limited. I have come to the conclusion that [the surveyor's] point is only partially right. I do think that it is probably right in relation to the shoproom in particular, and possibly in relation to the second room on the ground floor, that any tenant would want to put in fittings and fixtures to suit his own trade, and would want his own decorative scheme. He probably would want his own shopfront on the exterior, though the ability to install anything very much in this particular situation must be limited.

On the other hand, I cannot see why, if the upper floors and the ancillary rooms on the ground floor were cleaned up and redecorated, they should not be equally useful for the purpose to which the bus company would put them, as they would be for storage purposes. It may be that the tenant may not like the exact shade that the landlord chooses, but he will get newly decorated premises. I do not accept that if he got them undecorated he would expect to pay the same rent. I think that any tenant coming into these premises, if asked to go into them in their present situation, would say, "Well, yes, but look at the state of repair and decoration. I am going to have to spend quite a lot of money". While I accept that he might not necessarily do the sort of detailed calculation that [the surveyor] has done, I do think that he would expect in some way or another to be compensated for taking the premises in their present state of repair and decoration.

While I have said that the proper approach is to see whether in the first place there is evidence from which one can go straight to the diminution in the value of the reversion, that demands having clear valuation evidence, both of the value of the premises in a proper state of repair (that required by the lease) and in the present state of repair. As to the first, the value is disagreed to a very considerable extent, although I have got clear evidence from them about it. As to the second, I really have no clear evidence at all. All I have got is [the surveyor's] deduction of what he calls a spot figure of £2,500 which, with the greatest respect to him, he did not seek to base upon anything more

than his experience, which is a very generalised way of saying,
"Well, that seems about right". That is not sufficient, in my view,
for me to enable myself to say that is the diminution in the value
of the reversion, and it is not sufficient to displace the evidence
of the cost of repairs as being a useful way, or at any rate a
starting point, for deciding the diminution in the value of the
reversion.

So I go back to what I have already said about the cost of
the repairs. The exterior, as I have said, has already been agreed
at £1,976.50. The rubbish has been agreed at £30—for clearing
the rubbish. The electrical works I have already assessed at
£1,000, and the firescreen at £150. The balance in the Scott Schedule is some £3,584. My arithmetic can be checked, but it is
certainly a figure in that order, after disregarding deducting the
exterior and the other items to which I have just referred. From
that, as I have said, some discount should properly be made
because of my view that the tenant would not require or want
a complete redecoration of the ground floor but would only want
cleaning up and some partial preparation towards redecoration,
and also because, as I have already said, I am not satisfied by
the landlord's evidence about the floorboards.

All in all I have come to the conclusion that the repairs figure,
which I should adopt as being a reasonable one, is a sum of
£6,250. I have already indicated that it is my view that value
added tax should be added to that. Subject to what counsel say,
I have calculated that at £937.50.

There remains the question of anything over and above that.
[The surveyor] said that his total claim for the diminution in
the value of the reversion was originally £10,000, of which some
£8,500 was the cost of repairs. By definition, when he reduced
the exterior repairs by about £1,000, the total figure must have
come down by about £1,000, so that reduced it to £9,000, of
which £7,500 was the cost of repairs. The other £1,500 broadly
was made up as follows: that in [the surveyor's] view the landlord
is entitled to be compensated for the fact that whoever does
the repairs, time will elapse before they can be completed, and
thus the landlord will be receiving no rent during that time.
Moreover, [the surveyor] suggested that there should be added
to that a further period of time to enable the landlord to enter
into a new lease with the tenant. All in all, said [the surveyor],
what the landlord should have is compensation for something
like six months' loss of rent which, though he had given evidence
that in his view the proper rent was £4,000, he said, "Well, let
us put that at £1,500". I hope I have followed his thought process

correctly. I have really summarised a series of propositions which he put forward.

The evidence, as it emerged, about the time that would be necessary to enable the work to be carried out, eventually was very near agreement. The respective experts take the view that from the time when the tenants are first under notice to carry out works to the time (I am now talking about notice on the old tenant) when the works could have been completed would be something between 13 and 16 weeks. I think it right to accede to [the surveyor's] suggestion that there should be a quarter's rent, or compensation to the landlord for loss of a quarter's rent during that period of time.

On the other hand, I see no reason why there should be any more than that. After all it has been absolutely apparent to this landlord for a very long time that this tenant was not going to carry out the repairs. It must have been apparent to the landlord that the tenant was not going to reoccupy. The tenant, as I see it, had no rights to a new lease under the Landlord and Tenant Act 1954 and none has been suggested. I can see no reason why the landlord, had she wished to do so, should not have negotiated with a new tenant before the expiry of the old lease, and thus been ready the moment the old lease expired either to get a new tenant to do the repairs or to do them herself if she had sufficient funds to enable her to do so. The fact that she did not is a matter for her and her advisers. I suspect that it was because of these negotiations with the bus company that were likely to produce a more attractive proposition than any other tenant was able to offer, but that is perhaps an irrelevance. That, however, is my reason for not giving more than compensation for one quarter's loss of rent.

That, added to the matters to which I have already referred, adding £6,250; value added tax at 15 per cent on that sum, £937.50; and a quarter's rent, which is half of [the surveyor's] figure of £1,500, that is to say £750, brings me to a total of £7,937.50. Subject to my arithmetic being checked, I give judgment to the plaintiff for that amount.

There remains the question of the costs, that is to say, whether the landlord is entitled to anything by way of costs under paragraph 18 in the schedule to the lease. The argument here, on behalf of the tenants, is that the action was started unreasonably soon after the section 146 notice had been served. If this action had been heard immediately the writ was issued, there would have been an absolute answer to the claim for forfeiture in that not sufficient time had been given to enable the works to be done. On the evidence before me that submission is entirely justified on the facts because, as I have already said, it is agreed that at least 13 weeks would have been required, and the writ was issued substantially less than 13 weeks after the service of the section 146 notice. Thus, submits [counsel], since that, in effect, invalidates the notice, or at any rate renders the proceedings in respect of forfeiture abortive at the time when they were served, the landlord should not be entitled to recover any of the costs of that section 146 notice or associated with it. On the other hand, it is in my view clear that this clause is intended to ensure that if the landlord, in order to get the repairs done, or t get damages for paying to have them done, as well as obtaining possession of the premises, does have to serve a section 146 notice, that the landlord should not have to bear any part of the cost occasioned by the service of that notice. I have come to the conclusion that if any part of that cost is not claimable as costs in these proceedings (a matter which happily I do not have to decide —it is a matter for argument on taxation) then the landlord is entitled to recover such additional or earlier costs and expenses.

Since the paragraph in the lease reads: "All costs, charges and expenses incurred by the lessor in or in contemplation of any proceedings in respect of this lease", . . . I have concluded that such costs should be on a solicitor and client basis rather than on a party and party basis.

Note:
   (1) In *Elite Investments* (Case 118) the court held that where the landlord was not registered for VAT and it was not a realistic option for the landlord to do the works then VAT should not be added to the damages.

The "reversion" in section 18 (1) is the reversion expectant on the existing lease.

Case 70 *Terroni v Corsini* [1931] 1 Ch 515 Maugham J

The plaintiffs and the defendant were partners. One of the partnership assets was the lease of the premises on which the business was carried on, expiring on March 25, 1930. On October 7, 1929, the landlord granted to the three partners a reversionary lease for fourteen years from March 25, 1930, at an increased rent. On October 29, 1929, by an agreement made between the parties for dissolution of the partnership, it was provided that the partnership assets should be sold to the highest bidder of the three partners and proceeds divided, the defendant's share being one-half; also, that the date for completion should be November 18, 1929, and that the defendant should out of his share make certain payments, and should pay the rent under the lease, all rates, taxes and outgoings in respect of the premises, and "all trade debts and other liabilities whatsoever in respect of the said premises and business" down to the date fixed for completion, making these payments out of his share of the proceeds of sale. The agreement came before the court for construction, and it was declared that the phrase, "other liabilities whatsoever in respect of the said premises," included the liability in respect of damages which the landlord could, on November 18, 1929, have recovered for breach of the repairing covenants in the lease. On an application for a decision whether at that date the damages recoverable by him in respect of non-repair were to be estimated on the basis of the depreciation in market value of the reversion expectant on the determination of the lease, or of that expectant on the determination of the reversionary lease:

Held (1) That the "reversion" was the immediate reversion expectant on the lease, and that the fact that a reversionary lease had been granted, to take effect at a date after the date for the assessment of damages, was immaterial.

Maugham J said (in part)

I would observe that the question of the measure of damage for breach of covenant to repair has been the subject of many decisions, some of which before the date of the coming into force of the Landlord and Tenant Act, 1927, had led to an unjust state of affairs, because landlords were entitled to receive large sums from tenants at the expiration of the leases in respect of worthless properties which they immediately pulled down. It is true that the question of the damages in the case where the action is brought during the term was well settled by decisions: the amount being, not that required to put the premises in repair, but that by which the reversion was depreciated in value. Accordingly, it may be said that, in regard to an action brought during the term for damages for breach of covenants to repair, s. 18 (1) of the Act of 1927 does very little, if anything, to limit the damages recoverable, while, on the other hand, the damages recoverable if the action is brought at the expiration of the term may no doubt be diminished by reason of the provision of the sub-section, the latter part of which has a most material effect on the damages which a landlord may recover. The question here is whether the word "reversion" refers to the reversion on the lease irrespective of the reversionary lease granted before the date of the assessment of damages, or whether, as the doctrine of *interesse termini* has been abolished, and the reversionary lease created a term of years effective in law and equity as from March 25, 1930, I ought to regard the word "reversion" as meaning reversion expectant on the determination of the reversionary lease.

The point is not easy to determine, but in my judgment, the "reversion" is the reversion immediately expectant on the lease irrespective of that expectant on the reversionary lease. The former, I think, is the "reversion" indicated in s. 18 (1) of the Landlord and Tenant Act, 1927, and I do not think that the fact that a term of years has been created to take effect from March 25, 1930 (a future event at the date when damages must be assessed), affects the question.

I come to that conclusion with some reliance on *Joyner v Weeks* [1891] 2 QB 31. In that case the plaintiff as lessor was suing upon a covenant contained in a lease by which the defendant as lessee covenanted to leave the demised premises in repair. While the term was running, the plaintiff made a demise of the premises to a third person to take effect from the termination of the lease to the defendant, and that demise contained a covenant to pull down and alter the premises. The official referee to whom the matter was referred found that the plaintiff in the circumstances had suffered no loss, and gave judgment for the plaintiff for one farthing. The Court of Appeal, however, took a different view, and held that the correct measure of damages was the cost of putting the premises into the state of repair required by the covenant, and that this was not affected by the grant of a subsequent lease to another lessee from the expiration of the defendant's term. The value of that decision is less than it was, because the doctrine of *interesse termini* has been abolished: but the decision of the Court of Appeal is based, not only upon that doctrine as then extant, but also upon the ground that the covenants contained in the subsequent lease in force at the date when the plaintiff's right of action arose, but unperformed at that date, could not be held to take away or modify that right.

5.3 Section 18 and the relevance of reletting

Case 71 *Haviland v Long* [1952] 2 QB 81 Court of Appeal

The defendant tenants being in breach of their covenant to keep and leave the premises in repair, the plaintiff landlords, shortly before the lease terminated, entered into a fresh lease with other tenants, who, while paying what was a full economic rent for premises in repair, agreed to carry out the repairs, the landlords undertaking to reimburse them out of any sum recovered from the old tenants by way of dilapidations. It was contended for the defendants that having regard to the terms of the new lease the value of the reversion had not been diminished, that the landlords had therefore suffered no loss, and had lost their right to recover damages.

Held (1) That at the time when the new lease was entered into the landlords had a contingent right to recover damages should the original tenants eventually be in breach of their covenants, and did not lose that right by reason of the bargain made with the new tenants. It was the fact that the repairs required to be done and not the circumstances in which the landlords and their new tenants agreed upon the manner of meeting the charge which was the governing consideration.

(2) (*Per Denning LJ*) The fact that the landlord has an undertaking from a new tenant to do the repairs does not go in diminution of damages. It is *res inter alios acta*.

Somervell LJ said (in part)

What is plain is that, as the facts show, this is not the type of case for the purpose of which the law was altered, as it was altered by section 18 (1) of the Act of 1927. This is a case where the building is still required in substantially the same form and where the repairs which the tenant failed to do have to be done in order to put the building into a state which will enable it to be used in the manner in which it is required at present to be used; whereas the Act was passed to meet primarily a case where the building was going to be pulled down or turned to some different purpose, so that the repairs were not required and the sum which the landlords recovered under the covenant would not be expended in whole or in part on the repairs covered by the covenant.

But that does not end the matter, because the Act may have produced a result which on the face of it had not been intended. The judge decided that the defendants were liable on their covenant for £1,170, and it is from that decision that they appeal. The argument is this. [Counsel] says—I hope I shall do justice to his argument, for I still do not find it altogether easy to follow— that if you look at the matter as on March 25, 1949, when the lease had come to an end, by that time it mattered not financially to the landlords whether the repairs were done or were not done. It was the new tenant who had to do them, and though the landlords had undertaken to recover or to take all practical steps to recover from the old tenants damages for breach of covenant to repair, [counsel] said—he faced up to it, but he was forced really to say this—that by this particular method of dealing with their rights, which existed contingently or conditionally on January 14, 1949, when the new agreement was made, the landlords had lost those rights; that the cost of repairs would fall, therefore, not on the old tenant but on the new tenant, and the new tenant would be unable to derive any advantage from subclause (5a) because the landlords, having suffered no diminution in the value of the reversion, had lost their right to recover.

As I have said, I find that argument very difficult to follow. The landlords, when they entered into the new lease, had certain rights against the tenants under the old lease, and these included the then contingent right of recovering damages from those tenants if they failed to put the premises into repair. If they should perform the covenant, *cadit quaestio*: the premises for which the new tenants would be paying the stipulated rent of £1,900 would then be, as was intended, premises which were in a good state of repair, and they would not have had to expend any money on repairing them. But if the premises were not left in a good state of repair, the landlords plainly would have the right to recover damages from the old tenants. The damage to the reversion would be measured by the cost of the repairs, because it was everybody's intention to go on using the building as it was before, and it was economic to do so. I cannot see why that right should be lost because it is made a term in a bargain. It is obvious that if the landlords had not had this right, because, for example, there was no repairing covenant, or because for some reason they had abandoned their right to enforce it, the new lease would have been in different terms. The new tenants would never have agreed to pay what was the economic rent for a repaired building and do the repairs, unless they had been satisfied, quoad those repairs which were covered by the old lease, that they would get, through the landlords, the sum, however it was quantified, which the old tenants were liable to pay as damages for the breach of their covenant. I cannot myself understand how it can be said that because a man has bargained with a right he loses it.

In my opinion, that is much better put than I have put it, or could put it, in a paragraph in the judge's judgment, in which he says: "In my judgment it is the fact that they"—i.e., the repairs—"require to be done and not the circumstances in which the landlord and his new tenant agree upon the manner of meeting the charge, which is the governing consideration."

Denning LJ said (in part)

The measure of damage is the extent by which the market value of the reversion at the end of the lease was diminished by the want of repair. That depends on whether the repairs are going to be done or not. In cases where they have been or are going to be done the cost of repair is usually the measure of damage. The fact that the landlord has an undertaking from a new tenant to do the repairs does not go in diminution of damages. It is *res inter alios acta*.

Case 72 *Jaquin v Holland* [1960] 1 WLR 259 Court of Appeal

On the termination of a tenancy containing a covenant to keep and yield up the demised premises "in good and tenantable repair," the landlord spent £19 10s. in putting the premises into a lettable condition and the premises were immediately relet at the same rent as in the earlier tenancy. The premises were situated in an area where there was a high demand for houses to let. In an action by the landlord for damages for breach of the repairing covenant, the diminution in value of the reversion under section 18 (1) of the Landlord and Tenant Act, 1927, was found to be £50, this sum being based upon the estimated reduction in selling value of the premises. It would have cost about £100 to put the premises in good and tenantable repair. It was contended for the tenant that in the circumstances the sum of £19 10s. represented the true measure of damage since the premises were immediately relet at the same rent subject to the payment of that sum or, alternatively, because the lettable value of the freehold should be taken into consideration:

Held (1) The test for assessing the measure of damages for breach of a repairing covenant at common law was the amount that was necessary to put the house into a proper condition for letting in accordance with the terms of the covenant, so that it would be taken by a reasonable man wanting a house in reasonable condition, having regard to the nature and type of house involved.

(2) That the damages so assessed would have been over £50, and, applying section 18 (1) of the Act of 1927, £50—the

amount by which the value of the reversion was diminished—was the sum to which the landlord was entitled.
Even if one lease immediately succeeded another, there
must always be a notional moment of time when the unin-
cumbered freehold estate was vested in the landlord and
the value of the reversion was therefore the value of the
freehold as it had come back into the hands of the landlord
before he let it again.

Devlin LJ said (in part)

Having ascertained the amount of work that it is necessary
to do in accordance with *Proudfoot v Hart*, 25 QBD 42 and having
put a figure on it, that does not necessarily conclude the matter,
because section 18 of the Landlord and Tenant Act, 1927, provides that the damages are not to exceed the amount, if any,
by which the value of the reversion in the premises is diminished.
So that one has to go on to inquire to what extent the value
of the reversion has been diminished. That inquiry the registrar
made, and he came to the conclusion that the reduction in the
selling price amounted to £50, that is to say, he appears to have
held that, notwithstanding that it would cost at least £91 13s.
6d. in his view to put the premises into good and tenantable
repair, the damage to the reversion did not amount to more
than £50. He arrived at that conclusion because of the shortage
of houses in Sevenoaks and the desirability of them from the
point of view of buyers. Thus he was saying that a buyer who
was making a bid for this house, if it were put on the market,
would say to himself: "I will put up with £41 odd of damage
to the house, which I shall have to spend on repairs, because
houses are short and it is very desirable to get one." I am not
at all sure—and I should like to guard myself against deciding
it and reserve the point for consideration when it arises—
whether that was the right thing to do. I can imagine, for example, a house that is worth £5,000, which is let, let us say, at
a rental of £250 per annum, where at the end of the tenancy
£50 worth of damage had been done, and £50 would have to
be spent on it in order to put it into good and tenantable repair.
That is an appreciable sum, if you look at it from the point of
view of the rent the landlord is getting. It is 20 per cent. of
the rent. On the other hand, if you look at it from the point
of view of the capital value of the house, it may not matter very
much. Even if there were no particular shortage or particular
desirability of houses to be taken into consideration, I can still
imagine that an auctioneer might be found who would say:

"Well, where the damage is so small a figure as £50, a prospective buyer, in making his bid, is likely to disregard it altogether." I do not think that it necessarily follows from that that it is the intention of this Act that it should be disregarded altogether, or that a landlord will just have to put up with what is in effect a real loss. As I say, I would desire to reserve my opinion on that question. It does not arise here, and it does not arise because [counsel], for the landlord, is not asking for the higher figure of £91. He is content, very sensibly, with the figure of £50 which has been found by the registrar as the reduction in the selling price. I say "very sensibly" because these are small figures, and there has been a good deal of litigation about them already. Although he contended before the county court judge that £91 was the right figure, the county court judge rejected it, but gave him still something more than the registrar gave him, that is to say, the sum of £50, and he has taken that sum of £50. So the question does not arise here . . .

. . . There must always be a notional moment of time, even if one lease immediately succeeds the other, in which the estate finds its way back into the hands of the landlord, and the value of the reversion is therefore the value of the freehold as it has come back into the hands of the landlord before he lets it out again. That that is what is intended by the meaning of "reversion" in this section of the Act is, I think, made clear by the judgment of Lawrence LJ in *Hanson v Newman* [1934] Ch 298. He referred to the words of the Act—"shall in no case exceed the amount (if any) by which the value of the reversion (whether immediate or not) in the premises is diminished"—and he said:

> "The expression 'whether immediate or not' in the above passage, is I think explained by reference to the case of *Joyner v Weeks* [1891] 2 QB 31, to which our attention has been called. . . . A reversion may not be a reversion in possession (i.e., it may not be immediate) by reason of the freeholder having granted a reversionary lease, and in that case the reversionary lease is to be disregarded in assessing the damages."

That is dealing with the position in which the landlord has already got a reversionary lease before the termination of the one which is being considered for the purpose of dilapidations. But, in my judgment, the position must be exactly the same whether the second lease is granted before the completion of the first lease or after it. It still has to be disregarded, and what has to be ascertained as the value of the reversion is the value of the freehold.

Case 73 Family Management v Gray (1979) 253 EG 369 Court of Appeal

The headlessee, G., held long leases of two buildings which were occupied as a dry cleaning shop and delicatessen respectively with accommodation above. When the long leases expired in 1974 the sub-lessees negotiated new twenty-year terms from G. containing covenants by them to put and keep the premises in repair. In 1976, the reversioners sued G. for damages for breach of his repairing covenant, thus attracting the operation of section 18 (1) of the Landlord and Tenant Act 1927. The Official Referee heard evidence on the level of rents obtained from the sub-lessees and determined a loss of £100 per annum in each shop at eight years' purchase to the landlords in respect of the damage to the reversion.

Held (1) The damage to the reversion under section 18 (1) of the Landlord and Tenant Act 1927 was either nil or *de minimis* as the sub-lessees, in negotiating their new rents in 1974 were prevented by the operation of section 34 of the 1954 Act form alleging their own default under the repairing covenants to reduce the rent.

(2) As the sub-lessees were under full repairing obligations to the headlessee, the rent on renewal could not have been reduced by reason of the dilapidations.

Megaw LJ said (in part)

In the course of the argument complicated and difficult problems were suggested. I need refer only to one of the many authorities cited, namely *Smiley v Townshend* [1950] 2 KB 311.

The headnote reads:

"The assignee of a long lease of premises, containing full covenants to repair, which was assigned to him two years before the date of the termination of the lease, when the premises were already requisitioned, was sued by the landlord on the termination of the lease for breaches of the covenants to repair. The premises at the date of termination of the lease were still requisitioned, and the date of the termination of the requisition was undetermined."

It was contended that one had to have regard to the fact that the premises being requisitioned at the date when the reversion fell in, the loss to the landlord must be assessed by reference to the time when they actually physically reverted to his possession.

The relevant holdings set out in the headnote are first, "The damages must be assessed not by reference to the time when the land reverted into the possession of the landlord at the termination of the requisition, but as at the date of the termination of the lease." Next is holding number (5) which reads: "Future events, after the termination of the lease, could not in themselves reduce or extinguish the damages, but they might be taken into account in so far as they threw light on the value of the reversion as at the date of the end of the lease." At first reading that appears not only cryptic but possibly self-contradictory. However, when one comes to look at the relevant passage in the judgment of Denning LJ at p 320, the principle becomes clear.

"What has to be considered is the diminution in value of the reversion at the end of the lease; and I take the word 'reversion' to mean the landlord's then interest in the premises. If he is the owner and the premises are requisitioned, then the reversion is his freehold, subject to the existing requisition, because that is the landlord's then interest in the premises. The question is, therefore: how much was the market value of the landlord's interest diminished at the end of the lease by reason of the disrepair for which the then assignee was responsible?

Any other view would give rise to great difficulty. For instance, if the future cost of repair to the landlord were the measure, the court would be asked to deduct the estimated amount of repairs which will be done by the corporation after the lease comes to an end."

Denning LJ continues

"[Counsel] took another instance which is not within the last half of section 18 (1). He took the example of a house let on a long lease which was, by reason of its large size and great number of rooms, not suitable for occupation as a dwelling-house at the present day, but only for use as a warehouse, for which decorative repairs would be valueless. If the decorations were not in fact done, he said, the court would take that fact into account, even though it did not fall within section 18. I agree that the court would do so, but the reason would be because in such a case the damage to the reversion would be nil. At the end of the lease the premises would be of as much value as a warehouse as a highly decorated dwelling-house. These illustrations show that, although future events do not in themselves reduce or extinguish the damages, nevertheless they may properly be regarded in so far as they throw light on the value of the reversion at the end of the lease."

So events which follow upon the determination of the lease but which are independent of any fact or consideration which was either operative or potential at the date when the lease expired cannot affect the determination of the loss to the value of the reversion. As I read the judgment cited it decides that factors which existed, either as operative or potential factors but which had substance and reality at the date when the reversion fell in, were to be considered as having a bearing on the valuation of the loss or damage to the reversion by the failure on the part of a lessee to comply with his covenants under a lease.

Upon that basis it was requisite in this case for the learned judge to address his mind to a factor which had become a reality by the date of the hearing, but which existed potentially at the date when the reversion fell in in December 1974, namely the right of the respective tenants of the two shop premises to look for a fresh lease under section 34 of the Landlord and Tenant Act of 1954. Such leases were, indeed, negotiated between the plaintiffs and the respective sublessees (as they had hitherto been) and those leases themselves incorporated full repairing leases putting the respective lessees under an obligation to put and keep the premises in good and substantial repair. That in my view is a factor which must be taken into account at the time the court is asked to determine the proper figure for compensation for the damage to the reversion. It may produce the result that the reversioner has sustained no damage at all.

[Counsel] in his able argument to this court, has contended that this begs the question. He relied on the necessity to look at the position as if, in a free market, there were in prospect a sale with vacant possession to a willing tenant. Thus although there may be some force in the suggestion that the prospect of the court's granting a lease to a prospective purchaser if there was no lease negotiated might have its impact, in the circumstances of a case such as this that ought to be disregarded. What should be looked at was the actuality of the case in relation to the condition of the premises at the end of 1974. It was thus relevant to look at comparable premises in that area to find what were comparable rents in order to determine whether or not the landlords might have done better with the bargain that they had made if, in fact, the premises had been kept in the state of repair which was required by the leases and which had been held by the defendant.

That as I see it does not fall within the principle enunciated by Denning LJ in *Smiley v Townshend*. Moreover, it denies recognition of what were the realities of the situation. The fact that 20-year leases were granted perhaps does not in itself matter, and to that extent I would accept the argument put forward by [counsel], but that there were leases in prospect and that there was a right on the part of the sublessees to look for new leases, and that the chances were that they would arise by negotiation or be granted by the court was a reality which ought and had to be recognised. From my reading of the learned judge's judgment, that was not given its due weight.

He accepted the proposition put forward that one had to look at the situation as though this was a case where vacant possession could be given in an open market to a willing prospective tenant, and upon that basis he said that the decrease in the annual rental value was £100 in respect of each shop, and so on. If he had taken into account, as was called for, the full impact of section 34 of the Landlord and Tenant Act 1954 in the history of this matter, he would have been led to the conclusion that when the reversion fell in at the end of 1974 the damage to the reversion had been reduced either to nothing or something so close to it as to be *de minimis* and not to require or call for judicial assessment . . .

. . . the proper figure was really zero or minimal. There had been no damage to the reversion which was capable of real assessment save as a minute figure.

5.4 Date of assessment of damages

Case 74 Hanson v Newman [1934] 1 Ch 298 Court of Appeal and Luxmoore J

A lessee having neglected to carry out the covenants in the lease as to painting and repairing the demised premises, was sued by the landlords for possession and damages for the breaches of covenant. No defence having been put in it was adjudged that the landlords had judgment for possession, and mesne profits and damages, to be assessed and certified by a Master. The Master assessed the damages at the amount by which the reversion in possession at the date of the forfeiture of the lease (namely, the date of the issue of the writ) was diminished by non-repair. The tenant, having claimed that he was entitled to set off the amount found by the Master to be the difference between the value of the reversion in possession at the date of the forfeiture and the

value of the reversion expectant on the expiration of the
term if the lease had not been forfeited, the Master refused
the claim and decided that the tenant was not entitled to
any set-off by reason of the acceleration of the reversion
consequent upon the forfeiture. The tenant, relying on s.
18 of the Landlord and Tenant Act, 1927, appealed to the
judge:

Held (1) (by Luxmoore J and the Court of Appeal) That
there could be no set-off, and that in assessing damages
under the section in the circumstances of the case the court
had to ascertain the actual value of the property in its unrepaired state at the date of re-entry and the value which the
property would then have had if there had been no breach
of covenant, and the amount of damage sustained by the
landlords was the difference between the value of the property as it stood and the value it would have had if the
tenant had carried out his obligation under the covenants
in the lease.

Luxmoore J said (in part)

The question which has to be determined on this summons
is what is the measure of damage for breach of covenant to repair
in a case where the lease has been forfeited by re-entry? Is the
fact that the forfeiture has accelerated the termination of the
leasehold term to be taken into account or not?

Under the law before the Landlord and Tenant Act, 1927, was
passed, a landlord could recover by way of damage at the termination of his term the actual cost of executing the repairs required
to fulfil the covenant. The Landlord and Tenant Act, 1927, has
not changed the law in that respect; all that it has done is to
impose a limit on the amount of those damages.

Lawrence LJ said (in part)

The expression "whether immediate or not" in the above passage, is I think explained by reference to the case of *Joyner v
Weeks* [1891] 2 QB 31, to which our attention has been called
by [counsel]. A reversion may not be a reversion in possession
(i.e., it may not be immediate) by reason of the freeholder having
granted a reversionary lease, and in that case the reversionary
lease is to be disregarded in assessing the damages. In my judgment what the court has to do in assessing damages under the
section in the circumstances of this case is to ascertain the actual
value of the property at the date of re-entry and the value which
the property would then have had if there had been no breach

of covenant; and the difference between these two values is the amount of the damages sustained by the landlord (that is to say) the difference between the value of the property as it stands and the value which it would have had in case the tenant had fulfilled his obligations under the covenants in the lease. I cannot express it better than the learned judge has expressed it in his judgment in the present case, when he says:

> "What the section provides is that the damages for breach of covenant on the termination of a lease are not to exceed the amount by which the value of the reversion, whether immediate or not, in the premises is diminished owing to the breach of such covenant or agreement; that is, you take the value of the reversion as it is with the breach—the value of the property which has reverted as it is subject to the breach— and you take it as it would be if there were no breach, and you provide that the amount of damage shall not exceed the amount by which the value of the property repaired exceeds the value of the property unrepaired."

[Counsel] has addressed an ingenious argument to the court. He contended that the right procedure to adopt in assessing damages under the section is to ascertain the value of the reversion before the breach (that is to say, when the lease has a certain number of years still to run), and then ascertain the actual value of the property after the breach has been committed, and the landlord has re-entered under the proviso for re-entry; and then set-off the value of the reversion before the breach was committed, against the actual value of the property upon which the lessor has re-entered. How that method could be applied to the case of a continuing breach such as the present [counsel] did not explain, but be that as it may I think that this contention is ill-founded. It is plain that the reversion referred to in the section means the freehold or leasehold estate of the landlord subject to the lease or sub-lease, and that it would not be right to adopt any such procedure as [counsel] has contended for.

Romer LJ said (in part)

Here there was a continuing breach of a covenant to repair. The landlords, after taking the proper steps to end the tenancy, issued their writ on August 9, 1932, for the purpose of recovering possession and damages for breach of the covenant to repair. By issuing that writ they elected finally to determine the tenancy, as they had power to do under the proviso for re-entry contained in the lease. That was a proviso, of course, for which the landlords had stipulated at the time the lease was granted. The section says in those circumstances the value of the reversion has to be ascertained. The value of the freehold therefore has to be ascertained subject to so much, if any, of the term of the lease as remains unexpired, and, inasmuch as on August 9 they elected to determine and did determine the lease, no part of the term is unexpired. The value of the unencumbered freehold has to be ascertained.

Note:
   (i) Where the lease has not been forfeited etc. the term date is the date for the assessment of terminal dilapidations.
   (ii) In *Associated Deliveries Ltd v Harrison* [Case 92] the Court of Appeal held that the service of a writ operated as a decisive election to forfeit, put an end to the covenants and fixed the date for the assessment of the damages.

5.5 Covenants outside the scope of section 18 (1)

Case 75 *Moss Empires Ltd v Olympia (Liverpool) Ltd* [1939] 3 All ER 460 House of Lords

Certain premises were leased by the plaintiffs to the defendant company's assignors. The lessees covenanted to expend £500 per annum on repairs and decoration or to pay the lessors the difference between £500 and the amount actually expended. It was found as a fact that from 1933 to 1935 the lessees did not spend the stipulated sum. This action was brought by the lessors claiming damages for breach of covenant, or, alternatively, for money due on the covenant:

Held (1) The covenant was legal, as the amount payable thereunder was not payable as "damages for breach of a covenant to repair" within the meaning of the Landlord and Tenant Act, 1927, s. 18 (1), but was payable as debt, being in respect of each year the difference between £500 and the amount in fact expended in performing the repairing covenants.

(2) As the covenant ran with the land, this was not a bare obligation to pay money which did not touch the thing demised, but was binding upon the assignees.

(3) As the sum was payable whether or not there were breaches of the covenant, it was not a penalty.

Lord Atkin said (in part)

My Lords, I think that the answer is that the defendants are not being sued for damages for breach of covenant to repair. They are being sued in debt on covenant to pay a fixed sum of money. The covenants must no doubt be read together. So read, they form part of a carefully devised and co-ordinated arrangement by which in substance the liability of the tenant for repairs during the term is limited to £500 per annum, which sum he has to pay whether or not repairs are necessary.

There were years during the term in which the covenants to paint—namely, subcll. (v) and (vi)—would not be operative at all. In any year, the general covenant to keep in repair might not require the expenditure of £500. Subcl. (vii), therefore, could not be construed to impose an obligation to spend £500 on repairs and decoration in the performance of the covenants to repair where the covenants to repair did not themselves require the expenditure of such a sum. In other words, the covenant in subcl. (vii) must be construed as a covenant to spend during each year up to £500 in the performance of the repairing covenants. The balance of £500 nevertheless had to be paid to the lessors, and quite plainly, therefore, as it seems to me, that balance is not payable as "damages for breach of a covenant to repair" within the meaning of the Landlord and Tenant Act, 1927. One may suppose three possible conditions in any given year. 1. No repairs at all required by the repairing covenants to be executed on the premises. 2. £300 only required by the repairing covenants to be expended on repairs, and duly expended. 3. £700 required by the covenants to be expended on repairs, and nothing expended. In conditions 1 and 2, neither £500 nor £200 has any relation to damages for non-repair. In the last case, there would be a breach of the repairing covenant, but £500 would be payable, not as damages for breach of the covenants, but as a sum agreed to be paid as a means of satisfying the obligation to repair. I think, therefore, that the sums claimed in this action are not damages, but debt. The amount to be paid is not determined by the amount of damages for breach of repairing covenants, but by the amount in fact expended in performing the repairing covenants. The Landlord and Tenant Act, 1927, has no application, and, if it does not apply in its ordinary and natural construction, I do not understand how there can be said to exist any principle of law which would avoid an agreement not in terms avoided by the statute sought to be applied. The defence of the statute fails.

Case 76 *Eyre v Rea* [1947] 1 All ER 415 Atkinson J

The defendant, the assignee of a lease, granted sub-leases of parts of the premises to five sub-tenants who, by arrangement with him, converted the premises into five separate

flats. The defendant thereby was guilty of breaches of covenants in the lease not to alter the internal planning of the
premises, not to permit the premises to be used otherwise
than as a private dwelling-house in one occupation, and
not to underlet or part with the possession of any part of
the premises. In an action by the landlord for forfeiture for
breach of covenant the judge refused a claim by the defendant for relief against forfeiture under s. 146 (2) of the Law
of Property Act, 1925, and granted a decree of forfeiture
and an order for possession. On a claim by the landlord
for damages for the breaches of covenant.

Held (1) The measure of damages prescribed in the Landlord and Tenant Act, 1927, s. 18, for breach of covenant
to keep and put premises in repair should not be extended
to a breach of this nature, and, notwithstanding the fact
that the premises, as converted, were, from a financial point
of view, more valuable, the plaintiffs were entitled to the
cost of restoring them to the state of an unconverted single
dwelling-house, plus the loss of rent during the period of
conversion.

Atkinson J said (in part)

On the question of damages, we have had an interesting argument. The plaintiffs say: "The damages we are entitled to are
what it will cost us to put the house back into the condition
in which it was. This action is merely based on the conversion,
and we are entitled to have the house given back to us in the
state in which it was, that is, single occupation. We are entitled
to the cost of the re-converting. Only in that way can justice
be done to us. That was the house that we let, that was the
house which the defendant assured us he was going to maintain
in that condition, that was the house which the covenants provided we should get back at the end of the lease, and we are
entitled to have that re-converted." The plaintiffs also say: "Apart
from what we want and what we are entitled to in that way,
we are under a moral obligation to other owners of leases of
houses in that road to perform the covenants which we have
made them undertake. We may not be legally bound to, but
we would regard it as a great breach of faith to tolerate one
of these houses being maintained as a block of flats when we
have made everybody else covenant that he will not do any such
thing. That is what we say our right is."

Counsel for the defendant for a time created a doubt in my
mind, because he did not draw the distinction between the

breach of a covenant of this kind and the breach of a covenant to keep and put premises in repair. He referred to s. 18 of the Landlord and Tenant Act, 1927, . . . He says that the only measure of damages under that breach of covenant to repair is: What would have been the value of the premises if they had been delivered up in a proper state of repair, and what is the value of the premises in the state in which they have been delivered up? There may be cases in which no one would dream of repairing, in which a house was almost certainly going to be pulled down at an early date, and in a case of that kind quite a small sum might be found to be due, or, at any rate, the cost of repairs would not be the measure of damages. That has been emphasised in *Hanson v Newman* [1934] Ch 298, but, again, that is a case dealing only with repairs. There a lessee objected to carrying out the covenants of the lease as to painting and repair. It was held that, in assessing damages under s. 18 of the Landlord and Tenant Act, 1927 the court had to ascertain the actual value of the property in its unrepaired state at the date of re-entry and the value which the property would then have had if there had been no breach of covenant, and the amount of damage sustained by the landlord is the difference between the two values.

On the strength of that, counsel argues that the plaintiffs have now got something which, from the financial point of view, is more valuable than the house would have been if it had been in single occupation. They can let it for a higher rent, he says, and, therefore, they have suffered no damage. I cannot assent to that argument. Section 18 is limited to damages for a breach of a covenant to repair. The cases cited to me also dealt merely with covenants to repair. It seems to me that I cannot extend that principle to a breach of a covenant of this sort and say to the plaintiffs: "Despite that covenant and although you let and are entitled to receive back an unconverted house, that is, a house suitable for single occupation, because you have got something which you may be able to let at a higher rent than the house which are you entitled to have back, you have suffered no damage."

The plaintiffs have their rights, and I have to measure their rights so far as they are not modified by some provision in an Act of Parliament. I think that what they are entitled to is the cost of restoring this house to the condition in which they were entitled to have it returned to them, that is, an unconverted house. The cost of that is £896 12s. The evidence is that it will take two to two and a half months to do the work, during which no rent can be earned, and the damage for that will be another £50. Therefore, the order will be that there will be forfeiture of the lease, a declaration that the plaintiffs are entitled to possession, and judgment in their favour for £140 rent, the sum of £194 16s. for mesne profits, and for £946 12s. damages for breach of the covenants set out in the statement of claim, and costs.

5.6 Other heads of damage

A landlord may be able to claim under other heads of damage provided there is a causal relationship between the loss and the disrepair. A landlord may be entitled to compensation for loss of rent during the period in which the repairs are being undertaken. Other considerations may apply if he does not intend to carry out the works.

Case 77 *Birch v Clifford* (1891) 8 TLR 103 Wright J

This was an action for £535 11s. 7d. damages for breach of covenants to repair and deliver up in repair. The lease, which was granted in 1869, expired at Michaelmas, 1890, and provided that the tenant should deliver up the premises on a fixed day in good repair—the day being the last day of the tenancy. At the expiration of the tenancy the landlord brought the present action for damages (the premises not being delivered up in repair), and claimed the amount necessary to put them in repair, and an additional sum for the time when the premises would be useless owing to the repairs not having been done. At the trial before Mr Justice Wright on July 22, 1891, the defendant failed to sustain a defence which he had put upon the record, and his Lordship referred the question of the amount of damages to which the plaintiff was entitled to an arbitrator. The arbitrator reported that the damages to which the plaintiff was entitled amounted to £425 5s., and further reported that such sum did not include any compensation (as claimed by the surveyor for the plaintiff) for the loss of rent since Michaelmas, 1890, or for the non-user of the said messuage and premises by the plaintiff during the repair thereof.

Held (1) The landlord was entitled to a compensation for non-user of the premises during the time which would be occupied in putting them in the state of repair in which the tenant should have left them.

Wright J said (in part)

I think the plaintiff is entitled to the compensation which he claims. It probably would not be assessed at the full amount of the rent for the time taken in doing the repairs, the parties having claimed £75 compensation and agreed to take £50 . . .

Note:
(i) In *Woods v Pope* (1835) 6 Car & P 1461 the court held that if a tenant, who is bound to repair, leave, and at the end of the tenancy the premises be out of repair, the jury may give the landlord, in an action against the tenant, not only the amount of the actual expense of the repairs, but also a compensation for the loss of the use of the premises while they were undergoing repair.

If a landlord consults a surveyor or solicitor for the preparation of a schedule of dilapidations or any requisite notice the costs cannot be claimed as part of the landlord's damages.

Case 78 Lloyds Bank Ltd v Lake [1961] 1 WLR 884 Sir Brett Cloutman QC

A lessor leased a seventeenth-century cottage and premises, the lessee covenanting to keep the interior in good and tenantable repair, while the lessor covenanted to maintain the roof, outside walls and boundary walls. The lessee sub-let the premises to the sub-lessee, the defendant, who undertook to repair and maintain the premises and boundary walls and to deliver up the premises in good and tenantable repair. As provided by the head-lease and the sub-lease, both leases terminated on the death of the lessee, which occurred in 1957. The lessor having died, his executors served a schedule of dilapidations on the lessee's executors, the plaintiffs, for breaches of repairing covenants in the head-lease, claiming £1,000. The schedule included items for external and roof repairs for which the lessee was not liable; it also included treatment and repairs for woodworm. That claim was settled for £715. The plaintiffs served their own schedule of dilapidations on the defendant in respect of breaches of his repairing covenants with estimates amounting to £1,397 13s. (£907 13s. for cost of repairs and decorating work including exterior and roof repairs; £430 for treatment for woodworm, also including work to the roof and exterior; and £60 for work to the garden). The plaintiffs brought an action against the defendant claiming damages for breaches of repairing covenants but limiting their claim for dilapidations to the £715 which they had agreed to pay to the lessor's executors. The plaintiffs also claimed by way of damages, solicitors' and surveyors' fees which they had incurred in settling the lessor's claim against them and in preparing the schedule of dilapidations and claim against the defendant. The official referee found as a fact that a fair and reasonable estimate of the damage caused to the plaintiffs by the defendant's breaches of his repairing covenants was £715. On the plaintiffs' claim:

Held (1) That as the lessor had covenanted to repair the roof, exterior and boundary walls, the plaintiffs could not include those items as part of the damage suffered from the breaches of the defendant's covenants, but they could include the cost of disinfestation from woodworm because although some woodworm was to be expected in an old cottage, it was so serious that constructional work was necessary (i.e., the removal and replacement of floorboards) to make the premises acceptable to a future tenant.

(2) That although the plaintiffs' reversionary interest in the property was momentary and notional since the plaintiffs' lease determined at the same time as the defendant's lease, that did not prevent the reversionary interest from being valued.

(3) That on the facts the defendant did not have notice that his lease was an underlease and in the circumstances the damages for breach of repairing covenants in the defendant's sub-lease had to be assessed independently from those in the head-lease; quite apart from the agreement regarding the breaches in the head-lease, a fair and reasonable estimate of the damage to the plaintiffs' reversion was £715 which the plaintiffs were therefore entitled to recover.

(4) That the plaintiffs could not recover from the defendant the solicitors' costs and surveyors' fees which they had incurred in settling the lessor's executors' claim against them because the defendant had no notice of the head-lease and therefore that part of the plaintiffs' loss did not flow naturally from the defendant's breach.

(5) That the plaintiffs, in the absence of any express provision in the sub-lease could not recover from the defendant the solicitors' costs and surveyors' fees which they incurred in respect of their claim against the defendant.

H H Sir Brett Cloutman QC said (in part)

But I am quite satisfied that with property having what one witness called "charm value" the great anxiety of a purchaser is, or should be, the presence of worm, or, say, dry rot, or death-watch beetle, or defective drains; and once the property is in really sound repair, the additional value on a sale may well be more, and even much more, than the cost of repairs. I am satisfied that the damages the plaintiffs claim do not exceed the diminution in the value of the reversion due to the defendant's breaches: see section 18, Landlord and Tenant Act, 1927.

But then [counsel] says that in the circumstances of this case the plaintiffs' reversion is not to be confused with the head-lessor's reversion. The plaintiffs' reversionary interest in the expiry of the defendant's lease is momentary and notional, since at the same time the plaintiffs yielded up their interest to the freeholder. The saleable value of the plaintiff's reversion is, therefore, nil, and it is still nil if the property is not in repair. And if it be said that the plaintiffs are liable to the freeholder because of the defendant's breaches, then on the authority of *Ebbetts v Conquest* [1895] 2 Ch 377 this is not to be taken into consideration in the absence of notice to the defendant of the plaintiffs' own head-lease. And if the plaintiffs' liability is not to be taken into account, there is only nominal damage to a nominal reversion (see *Espir v Basil Street Hotel Ltd* [1936] 3 All ER 91).

I am greatly indebted to [counsel's] careful arguments and industry in the defence of this claim, and I will add that this reasoning is ingenious and almost attractive; but I have no doubt at all that it is wrong. As a matter of simple logic it will not do to say that because the value of property in repair is nil, therefore, the value is still nil if it is out of repair due to the breaches of the outgoing tenant. Not at all. The value is minus £X, which is what the tenant must pay someone to take over, first the fag-end of the lease, and later the last moment of the lease. Certainly, the reversion is only momentary and notional (see *per* Devlin LJ in *Jacquin v Holland*, [1960] 1 WLR 258) but this need not prevent it from being valued. In *Espir v Basil Street Hotel Ltd*, (*supra*) the sub-tenant had acquired the head landlord's reversion of the lease of the mesne tenant. In those circumstances, any diminution in the value of the mesne tenant's reversion of 15 days of the lease of the sub-tenant was only nominal, and I do not think that case helps at all.

Then, as to the argument on the plaintiffs' side that the defendant is liable for the sum that the sub-lessee had to pay the freeholder, because he had notice of the fact that Vera Flood-Page was herself a tenant, and the defendant's denial of any such notice, both parties rely on *Ebbetts v Conquest (supra)*. The plaintiffs say that the defendant had such notice from the date his sub-lease was expressed to determine on Vera Flood-Page's death. The defendant says that his lease is not expressed to be an underlease, and that it by no means follows, merely because it is determinable on the sub-lessor's death, that it is an underlease. In the course of argument I put the case of a landlord who wished to ensure that on his death his estate would be quickly wound up, and suggested that he might limit his grant to his own life. I still think it is not an unreasonable possibility.

In the circumstances, the plaintiffs have not satisfied me that the defendant had notice that his was an underlease. It follows that the damages for breach of repairing covenants on the defendant's lease must be assessed independently from those on the Flood-Page lease.

Up to this point the argument seems academic, since for the reasons I have given I assess the damage to the reversion on the defendant's lease at the figure of £715, which is the same as the sum agreed on the head-lease. But the matter does not end here. In the first place, the plaintiffs seek to add to their claim their own solicitors' costs of £73, of which it was agreed that £40 10s. was attributable to the claim against the defendant, and £32 10s. to negotiating the settlement of the claim by Coussmaker's exeuctors against the plaintiffs. In addition they claim £73 10s., their own surveyor's fee on the schedule of dilapidations on the defendant's lease, and a further £42 10s., their surveyor's fee for settling the Coussmaker claim on the head-lease.

In so far as these further claims relate to the head-lease and depend upon the question of notice of the head-lease, and this must cover the £32 10s. law costs and the £42 10s. surveyor's fee, they must fail in the absence of notice. It would be otherwise if there were notice of the head-lease and a covenant by the sub-lessee to indemnify his lessor against the head landlord's claims (see *Clare v Dobson* [1911] 1 KB 35).

Furthermore, the defendant's covenants are not by any means the same as the head-lease covenants, even though I accept that the damages due to the breach of the former are justly limited to the amount for which the claim on the latter was settled. In spite of this, the measure of damages was necessarily different, and the costs incurred by the plaintiffs *vis-à-vis* Coussmaker's executors are not the necessary consequences of the defendant's breaches of his own covenants (see *Penley v Watts* (1841) 7 M & W 601). However, the basic ground upon which I reject this part of the claim is that the plaintiffs have not satisfied me that the defendant had notice in any shape or form of the head-lease, and this part of their loss does not flow naturally from the defendant's breach.

There remains now the final question whether the plaintiffs can recover their own solicitors' costs before action against the defendant, £40 10s., and £73 10s. their surveyor's fee in respect of the schedule for breaches of the defendant's lease. In *Maud v Sandars* [1943] WN 246 Lewis J did not think the surveyor's fee in such a case was recoverable as damages. No doubt in a case of relief for forfeiture the court may require a defendant to pay solicitors' and surveyors' charges as a condition of relief; but that is not this case (see *Skinners Co. v Knight* [1891] 2 QB 542) . . .

. . . Of course, in a strictly drawn lease there is often found a specific provision making the lessee liable for such expenses, and in such a case the amount is included in the damages. But I think that is precisely because the law and the practice are as Lewis J stated.

In this state of the authorities and of the practice as I know it, I think I must follow the decision in *Maud v Sandars*, (*supra*) and if a different practice is to be laid down, this must be by the Court of Appeal.

Note:

 (i) Most leases should contain a covenant by the tenant to pay the landlord's costs of a terminal schedule of dilapidations and notices in or in contemplation of any proceedings under sections 146 or 147 of the Law of Property Act 1925. It may be appropriate to include a covenant by the tenant to pay the costs of all reasonable supervisory work and reinspections after the service of a section 146 notice.

 (ii) Under section 146 (3) of the 1925 Act "A lessor shall be entitled to recover as a debt due to him from a lessee, and in addition to damages (if any), all reasonable costs and expenses properly incurred by the lessor in the employment of a solicitor and surveyor or valuer, or otherwise, in reference to any breach giving rise to a right of re-entry or forfeiture which, at the request of the lessee, is waived by the lessor, or from which the lessee is relieved, under the provisions of this Act." Note the limitation on this under section 2 of the Leasehold Property (Repairs) Act 1938.

(iii) In *Drummond v S & U Stores Ltd* [Case 69] Glidewell J held that the covenant to pay all costs, charges and expenses incurred by the landlord in, or in contemplation of, any proceedings in respect of this lease involved an obligation to pay costs on a solicitor–client basis (now in effect replaced by the indemnity basis).

5.7 Damages and subtenancies

Some of the factors to which regard must be had were considered in *Lloyds Bank Ltd v Lake* [Case 78]. If a sub-lessee is in breach of his repairing covenant the measure of damages is the diminution in the value of the sub-lessor's reversion. If the sub-lessee has notice of a superior landlord the sub-lessor's liability to the superior landlord should be taken into account.

Case 79 Ebbetts v Conquest [1895] 2 Ch 377 Court of Appeal

By indenture of lease dated May 8, 1840, certain hereditaments forming part of the estate of St Botolph Without, Bishopsgate, were demised by the trustees of St Botolph to Thomas Rouse for sixty-one years from Michaelmas Day, 1837. The lease contained a covenant by the lessee during the term to keep the premises in good and sufficient repair and condition, and a covenant to yield them up at the end of the term in good repair, reasonable use and wear and damage by fire excepted.

By underlease dated March 24, 1851, Rouse sub-let a part of the property to Benjamin Oliver for forty-seven and a half years from Lady Day, 1851, less ten days. The underlease contained covenants substantially identical with the covenants above referred to in the lease. This underlease showed, on the face of it, that it was an underlease and not a lease by a freeholder, the rent being reserved to Rouse, his executors, administrators, and assigns, and there being several references to "the superior landlord."

The plaintiffs were trustees of the will of Rouse, and his interest in the premises comprised in the lease was vested in them.

On August 9, 1882, the premises comprised in the underlease were assigned to William Booth for the residue of the term thereby created, which would expire, it will be observed, ten days before Michaelmas, 1898.

Booth having failed to keep the premises in repair, the plaintiffs commenced this action in 1894 against Conquest (the executor of Oliver) and Booth, to recover damages under the covenant in the underlease to keep the premises in repair, and, so far as necessary, to have the estate of Oliver administered by the court.

That there had been a breach of covenant was not denied; and by an order dated December 5, 1894, it was referred to the official referee to inquire and report what damages had accrued to the plaintiffs by reason of all breaches committed or allowed since August 10, 1882, of any of the covenants to repair contained in the underlease of March 24, 1851.

The defendants contended before the official referee, that when an action was brought during the continuance of a tenancy for breach of a covenant to keep the property in repair, the proper measure of damages was the extent of injury done to the marketable value of the reversion. Evidence was given to show that at the end of the term the site would have to be cleared to be of any value, the only profitable way of dealing with it being to treat it as building ground, the buildings being worth nothing but to be pulled down. The evidence went to show that if they were put into repair they would be worth £200 more to pull down and carry away than if not put into repair. The defendants contended, therefore, that at most the value of the plaintiffs' reversion had only been diminished to the extent of £200 by the want of repair. The official referee did not adopt this view, but held that as the plaintiffs, at the expiration of their term, would have to pay the full expenses of putting the buildings into repair, that expense must be taken into account in assessing the damage they had sustained. He considered that on the evidence the expense of putting the buildings into repair would be about £1,500 and, allowing for the time to elapse before that sum would become payable, he assessed the damages at £1,305.

Held (1) The measure of damages for breach of a covenant to keep demised property in repair is not the same in the case of an underlease as in that of a direct lease with a freehold reversion.

(2) Where the underlessee has notice that there is a superior landlord, the immediate lessor's liability over to that landlord must be taken into account; and the cost of putting the property into repair at the end of the term may properly be considered for that purpose.

Lindley LJ said (in part)

Now, the underlease itself shows plainly, and the underlessee must have known perfectly well, that his lessor was himself a lessee, and that he himself was taking an underlease; for not only is the rent reserved to the immediate lessor, his executors, administrators, and assigns—not his heirs and assigns—but we see in the underlease constant references to the superior landlord; for example, liberty is reserved to the agents of the superior landlord to come in and do repairs, and there is a covenant not to do anything which will annoy the immediate lessor's landlord or the tenants of the superior landlord.

The covenants which are contained in the underlease, and with which alone we have to deal, are covenants to repair, namely, covenants to put the demised premises into repair, to keep them in repair, and to deliver them up at the end of the term in good repair.

There is not in this underlease any covenant to indemnify the immediate lessor against his liability to his superior landlord in respect of repairs, and under these covenants the immediate lessor cannot get nearly so much in the shape of damages as he might if he were suing upon a covenant for indemnity—for instance, he could not recover the costs of proceedings brought against him by the superior landlord. The property demised by the underlease is out of repair. The plaintiffs are reversioners, having a reversion only of ten days; but they are liable on the expiration of their lease to deliver up this property to their landlord in proper repair. That is not disputed, and that circumstance is all-important in investigating what is the amount of damages to which they are entitled for breach of the covenant on which they sue. The underlease itself has not yet run out. When this action was commenced there were from four to four and a half years to run, and there are now about three and a half years. The action is not brought for a breach of the covenant to leave in repair, because the time for suing on that covenant has not arrived; it is brought for a breach of the covenant to keep in repair.

Now, what is the rule as to ascertaining the damages for a breach of such a covenant? The breach is not in controversy. It appears to me that this is an ordinary action for a breach of contract, and that the general principle applicable to it is that laid down in *Hadley v Baxendale* 9 Ex 341. Alderson B, in delivering the considered judgment of the court, says:

"We think the proper rule in such a case as the present is this: Where two parties have made a contract which one of them has broken, the damages which the other party ought to receive in respect of such breach of contract should be such

as may fairly and reasonably be considered either arising naturally, i.e. according to the usual course of things, from such
breach of contract itself, or such as may reasonably be supposed to have been in the contemplation of both parties, at
the time they made the contract, as the probable result of the
breach of it. Now, if the special circumstances under which
the contract was actually made were communicated by the
plaintiffs to the defendants, and thus known to both parties,
the damages resulting from the breach of such a contract,
which they would reasonably contemplate, would be the
amount of injury which would ordinarily follow from a breach
of contract under these special circumstances so known and
communicated."

In applying that rule to this case, it is important to notice
that the underlessee knew the position of his immediate lessor,
for the underlease disclosed the fact that it was an underlease.
It appears to me that, in ascertaining the damages which the
plaintiffs have sustained by reason of the breach by the defendants of their contract, the plaintiffs liability over to their lessor
must be taken into account, for it was one of the circumstances,
special if you like, but known to and reasonably within the contemplation of the underlessee. To put the matter in another form,
there are certain rules for ascertaining damages on a breach of
covenant, and in the case of a breach of covenant to repair there
are certain subsidiary rules for ascertaining the amount of those
damages. The cases establish that, in an action brought before
the term has expired for a breach of covenant to keep in repair,
you must look at the value of the plaintiff's reversion. Now,
upon the principle of *Hadley v Baxendale* (*supra*), the damage for
which the defendants are liable is the difference in value between
the reversion with the covenant performed as it ought to be,
and the value of that reversion with the covenant unperformed,
which it ought not to be. The learned official referee has taken
that view, and he has assessed the damages upon that principle.
He says: "The principle I go upon is this: the term is very nearly
at an end—it has got three and a half to four years to run. The
value of this ten days of reversion if the property was in repair
is so much, if the property is out of repair it is so much, and
the difference is £1,300." He gets at it in this way. He says:
"It will cost £1,500 to put it in repair, and I will discount that
and make it £1,305." [Counsel] says that is wrong in principle,
because that is really giving the plaintiffs an indemnity when
there is no covenant for it. My answer to that is, it may be in

this particular case an indemnity; but if the plaintiffs were suing upon a covenant of indemnity, they might get a great deal more. [Counsel] says you must treat this as an ordinary case of landlord and tenant where the landlord is the reversioner. If we were dealing with a reversion in the fee, I think that very likely £1,305 would not be the measure of damages; but you cannot leave out the cardinal point in this case, on which the whole case turns, namely, the tenant's liability over. It seems to me, therefore, that the principle which the learned referee has adopted is right, and the question whether his figures are right has not been brought before us. I think, therefore, that the appeal ought to be dismissed, and dismissed with costs.

The position where the sub-lessor's reversion is nominal and where there is no obligation to repair carried over to the superior landlord was considered in *Espir v Basil Street Hotel*.

Case 80 *Espir v Basil Street Hotel Ltd* [1936] 3 All ER 91 Court of Appeal

E. was the tenant of part of certain premises under a lease for a term of 98 years, and he sublet that part to B. for the unexpired residue of that term less the last 15 days. E.'s superior landlord then let to B., for a term of 999 years, the whole of the premises, subject to E.'s interest in the part. B., in breach of a covenant in his sub-lease, made considerable structural alterations to the whole of the premises, which B. used for the purpose of running an hotel. E. brought an action against B. for breach of the conditions in the sub-lease. The county court judge awarded E. £60 damages, which he assessed on the basis of the restoration work which would have to be done to that part of the premises in which E. had an interest, before E. could let that part to some other person. B. appealed:

Held (1) The proper measure of damages was the diminution in the value of E.'s reversion due to B.'s breach of covenant, and not the cost of restoring the premises.

(2) As B. was entitled to possession of the whole of the premises for 999 years, apart from E.'s reversion of part for 15 days, and B. had acquired possession of the whole of the premises for the unitary purpose of running an hotel, there was no evidence of diminution in the value of E.'s reversion and E. was entitled only to nominal damages.

Slesser LJ said (in part)

... the right principle appears to me that which has been enunciated in the case of *Whitham v Kershaw* (1886) 16 QB D 613. That was an action for waste brought by the reversioner against the tenant upon a covenant by the tenant not to commit waste on the demised property, and the question arose as to what was the proper measure of damage. It is pointed out by Lord Esher, MR, that:

> "It would be wrong to say that the reversionary value had necessarily been diminished by the cost of restoring the property to its original condition."

He seemed to think, as I understand him in that case, that:

> "The value of the reversion might be diminished, but the question of how much injured would be a question of value, and the proper way to ascertain the damages, would be to ask skilled valuers to say how much the property has been diminished in value;"

and therefore he does not take the view that the test is the measure as to how much would have to be spent to restore the property to the same condition as that in which the tenant originally received it, but he says that the right measure is to ask how much the property, that is the value of the reversion, has been diminished in value. Now, I agree with [counsel] when he says that in considering how much the reversion has been diminished in value, you are not limited to the consideration of the duration of that reversion. It is, I think, an element to be taken seriously into consideration, that the particular reversion in this case could only exist for 15 days if the covenants in the lease between the plaintiffs and the defendants were duly performed. [Counsel] says that there always is a possibility that in one way or another the lease will fall in before that time: there may be a bankruptcy and a disclaimer; there may be a failure in the payment of rent; there may be breaches of covenant putting an end to the lease, or the like; we need not speculate on what may happen. He says there is a possibility, great or small, that in fact this reversion will be for more than 15 days, and he says that is a matter which ought properly to be taken into account. I think he is entitled to make that submission, because, as was pointed out in an early case dealing with repairs, the case of *Davies v Underwood* (1857) 2 H & N 570, by Watson, B, the great object of a covenant of this sort is not to put money into the pockets of a lessor, but to enforce the performance of the acts stipulated for; and that is not necessarily limited to that one consideration, but nevertheless, one has to have regard to the probabilities of the case. In this case, as I see it, there is this important circumstance which cannot be disregarded, namely, that the defendants themselves have, by agreement with the head landlords, acquired possession of the remainder of the premises; they are therefore, apart from these 15 days, and apart from these breaches of covenant, really entitled in substance to the possession of the whole of the premises throughout the whole of the period, because, of course, the 15 days is merely a draughtsman's method of producing the necessary legal result that there shall not be a complete merger; but they cannot, in themselves, contemplate, if there be only 15 days, that for those 15 days the plaintiffs will be able to let these premises. There is specific power given in the lease between the London Electric Railway Company and the defendants to use these premises as an hotel, and they always have been so used by them as I understand. All these matters must be taken into consideration. Having regard to the fact, first of all, that there are only these 15 days, having regard to the fact that the defendants have really acquired possession of the whole of the premises for one unitary purpose, that of running an hotel, I find it very difficult, as a practical man, to make that notional severance of these premises which [counsel] asks us to make. What [counsel] says, as I understand his argument, is this: eliminate the blue part, imagine the plaintiffs once more coming into possession of their part and imagine that they have regained possession for one reason or another for a substantial period during which they might let it (that is something considerably more, I think, than 15 days): they are entitled to say: "We are now entitled to let these two floors which are ours, in the condition which they would have been in if there had been no breach of a covenant, and we are entitled, therefore, to ask that these premises be substantially put back, or if that is too rigorous a claim, we are entitled to say that the reversion has been injured to the extent that these holes have been made in the floors, and the premises are not self-contained, and these windows overlap into other premises, so that there may be disputes about them." That is the argument which is addressed to us, and I see nothing in law to say that those matters, considered in a proper case, might not be a reason for saying that a reversion had been injured in value; but in my view when the realities of this particular case are looked at, I find it impossible to say that this reversion has been so diminished in value. As I say, the fact that the whole thing has become one hotel, one unit, the fact that clearly the defendants have now become possessed either by lease from the plaintiffs or by lease from the London Electric Railway Company of the whole of these premises to run as one hotel, brings me to the conclusion that in reality, the only interest which can practically be considered in this case of the plaintiffs', is the interest for 15 days in the upper part of this building. I cannot believe, therefore, that in putting in this staircase which, without putting it too favourably, is admittedly an improvement of the whole premises and not a detriment from anybody's point of view—I cannot believe that it can properly be said that there has been any essential damage to this reversion, and I think the learned judge was wrong when he assessed these damages at £60. This is not an action for waste, it is an action on the covenant, and there is nothing to prevent the plaintiffs, as I understand the law, from recovering nominal damages. It might be otherwise if it were an action in case, but it is an action in contract; therefore I think that if the plaintiffs here are awarded 40s. in place of the £60 which the learned judge has given to them, they will have recovered all that they can show the reversion has suffered through the facts which I have recited.

5.8 No damages because of demolition or alteration

No damages are recoverable for failure to put or leave premises in repair at the termination of the lease if it is shown that the premises would at or shortly after termination either be pulled down or be so altered structurally as to render such repairs valueless.

Case 81 Salisbury (Marquess) v Gilmore [1942] 2 KB 38 Court of Appeal

> In 1926 the first plaintiff demised to the first defendant, G., premises for a term of fourteen years from September 29, 1925, by a lease which contained a tenant's covenant to leave the premises in repair at the expiration of the term. The second defendant, M., was the assignee of the term. In 1937 M. asked for a renewal of the lease but was informed that the plaintiffs (who had become the landlords in 1936) intended to pull down the premises at the expiration of the lease. On September 29, 1939, M. vacated the premises and left them out of repair, being still under the impression that the premises were being pulled down. It was not till he received a letter dated December 5, 1939, from the plaintiffs'

agents claiming damages for breach of covenant that he became aware that the scheme for forthwith pulling down and rebuilding the premises had been abandoned.

Held (1) That no restriction on building came into operation at the outbreak of the war or until October 7, 1940, and that the evidence showed that the plaintiffs had not abandoned their intention to pull down the premises until a date after the termination of the tenancy.

(2) That the material part of s. 18 (1) of the Act of 1927, was capable of construction without transposing any of the words, and as M. could show that at the moment when the covenant to leave the premises in repair fell to be performed the building was going to be pulled down at or shortly after the termination of the tenancy, he was entitled to the relief given by the sub-section.

(3) *Per MacKinnon LJ* (a) There was no evidence that the value of the reversion on the lease was diminished by the failure to deliver up in repair and on this ground alone only nominal damages would be recoverable by the plaintiffs. (b) Even nominal damages were not recoverable because no claim for breach of covenant lay having regard to ss. 5 and 18 of the Act of 1927, to the refusal to grant a renewal of the lease in 1937 on the ground that the premises were being pulled down at the termination of the lease and to the failure to communicate any change of intention to M. until over two months after the termination of the lease. As by the intimation that the premises were to be pulled down at the termination of the lease M. had been deprived of the right to obtain from the court a renewal of the lease under s. 5, sub-s. 3 (*b*) (ii), of the Act, the principle enunciated by Lord Bowen in *Birmingham and District Land Co. v London and North Western Ry. Co.* (1888) 40 Ch. D. 268 applied and afforded M. a defence to the claim for damages.

Lord Greene MR said (in part)

It must now be considered whether in the circumstances stated the second branch of s. 18 (1) of the Landlord and Tenant Act, 1927, frees the defendant from liability to pay damages for breach of the covenant to deliver up in repair. That branch is worded in a way which at first sight appears crabbed and ungrammatical. Hilbery J took the view that no coherent meaning could be given to it without transposing certain of the words. I do not share his difficulty. I find no necessity and accordingly no justification for rewriting the relevant words in the way in which he has rewritten them. But in order to make the matter clear, I must examine the actual language of the relevant part of the section. Its broad purpose is not open to doubt. Before it was enacted, a lessor could recover damages from his tenant for breach of a covenant to deliver up in repair notwithstanding that the buildings were going to be pulled down or structurally altered in such a way as to make it useless to perform the covenant. The enforcement of the covenant in such circumstances was regarded as an unjust enrichment of the lessor and the legislature in s. 18 (1) set itself to remove the injustice.

. . . The words which Hilbery J found incapable of construction as they stand are the words "if it is shown that the premises . . . would at or shortly after the termination of the tenancy have been or be pulled down." It may be asked why the words "would have been or be" were used rather than words referring to the intention of the lessor. The answer is that a building might be destined for demolition for some reason other than the intention of the lessor, for example—under a demolition order or a compulsory purchase under a street widening scheme. It was therefore necessary to use words of general import expressing the future fate of the building whatever the cause of that fate might be. The draftsman might have used the expression "were going to be pulled down at or shortly after the termination of the tenancy," but he preferred to express futurity in a different but grammatically legitimate way. Two more points must be borne in mind in considering the structure of the sentence. The first is that the point of time in relation to which the fate of the building is to be considered is that at which the covenant to deliver up falls to be performed, namely, the termination of the lease. The other is that the date at which the tenant is to prove the intended fate of the building is the date at which the action claiming damages for breach of the covenant is heard which is necessarily subsequent to the termination of the lease. These considerations appear to me to explain the construction of the sentence. The words "would have been" are, I think, grammatically correct to express in a statement in *oratio obliqua* ("if it is shown that") made at a subsequent date (the date of trial) in relation to what at an earlier date (the termination of the lease) was a future event which at that date was in contemplation. The moment before the termination of the tenancy it would be correct for the tenant to say "I say that this house will be pulled down at the termination of the tenancy." If at a date later than the termination of the tenancy he wishes to describe the future fate of the house regarded from the same moment of time he would say, if he spoke grammatically, "I say that this house would have been pulled down at the termination of the tenancy." What else as a matter of English could he say? He could not say "I say that the house will be pulled down at the termination of the tenancy" since the termination of the tenancy has already taken place, nor could he say "I say that this house would be pulled down at the termination of the tenancy." He might have said, if the sub-section had been so framed, "I say that this house was going to be pulled down at the termination of the tenancy" and this seems to me to be an accurate paraphrase of the language used. It is, I think, incorrect to say that the words "would have" make it necessary to imply a conditional sentence such as "if it had not been for the landlord's action in claiming damages" or "if it had not been for some extraneous cause." No such implication is in my view necessary. The remaining words "be pulled down" must, I think, be linked up to the words "would" and "shortly after the termination of the tenancy" so that this limb of the sub-section will run "if it is shown that the premises would shortly after the termination of the tenancy be pulled down." Here the draftsman has, I think, to some extent sacrificed grammar to conciseness. But his difficulty was a real one as he had to deal with an event, namely, pulling down shortly after the termination of the tenancy which at the relevant time, namely, the hearing of the action might be past or future and he has apparently used the words "would be" to meet this difficulty. However this may be, I am of opinion that if the tenant can show at the trial that at the moment when the covenant fell to be performed the building was one which was going to be pulled down at or shortly after the termination of the tenancy he is entitled to the relief which the sub-section gives.

The question then arises, what is the test by which the fate of the building as at the relevant date—namely, the date at which the covenant ought to be performed—is to be ascertained? I have already pointed out that a building may be destined for demolition either because the landlord has so determined or because some extraneous authority has decided to exercise its powers in that behalf. I have also pointed out that the crucial date is the date of the termination of the lease. Once that date has passed, the tenant is no longer in a position to fulfil his covenant: and if it is shown that before that date arrives the landlord has decided to pull down the building and that this intention is still existing at that date, the requirements of the sub-section are in my opinion satisfied. Hilbery J took a different view of the meaning of the sub-section. My grounds for differing from him sufficiently appear and it is no disrespect on my part if I do not examine his reasons in detail. [Counsel] on behalf of the plaintiffs felt himself unable to argue in favour of a construction different from that which I have set out above. He admitted that if the intention of the plaintiffs to pull down the building still prevailed at the termination of the lease, the sub-section would apply and that a change of intention at a later date would not assist him. His point was that the intention must on the facts be treated as having been abandoned at the outbreak of the war or, at any rate, before September 29. I have given my reasons for rejecting this view.

Case 82 *Keats v Graham* [1959] 3 All ER 919 Court of Appeal

The plaintiff was the present landlord of certain premises which were let to the defendants by the plaintiff's predecessor in title under a lease dated August 25, 1952, for a term of three years from that date. After the three years the defendants held over on the terms of the lease, which contained, among other covenants on the part of the lessees, (a) a covenant to yield up the premises in good repair, and (b) a covenant to use the premises for no other business than that of "stove enamelling and spraying and metal finishing". Permission to erect the premises and to use them for storage purposes for a period of seven years ending on April 1, 1956, had been given to the then landlord by the local authority on March 23, 1949, under the Town and Country Planning Act, 1947, subject to the condition that the premises were removed at the end of the seven years and the permitted use was to be discontinued unless permission to retain them and to continue the use for a further period were granted. In June, 1953, the defendants were granted permission by the local authority to use the premises for stove enamelling until April 1, 1956. On February 15, 1954, an application by the plaintiff for permission to retain the premises after April 1, 1956, and to continue to use it, after that date, for stove enamelling or any industrial use, was refused by the local authority. By a letter dated October 17, 1956, the defendants were informed of the failure of an application which they had made to the Minister of Housing and Local Government for permission to continue the use of the premises for the purposes of their business. On December 12, 1956, the local authority sent to the defendants a letter which may have been really intended for the plaintiff, but the plaintiff never saw it. In this letter the local authority referred to the letter of February 15, 1954 (which was sent to the plaintiff's representative), and to the Minister's letter of October 17, 1956, to the defendants, upholding the decision of the local authority, and requested a written assurance within the next fourteen days that the premises would be removed without delay. On January 31, 1957, the defendants wrote to the plaintiff saying that they would be leaving the premises in about four to six weeks' time, and they terminated the tenancy on March 28, 1957. No further steps had been taken by the local authority in regard to the removal of the premises. In May, 1957, the plaintiff let the premises to another tenant, and in November, 1957, he received permission from the local authority to retain the premises until December 1, 1962, and to use them for storage and light industrial purposes. In an action by the plaintiff against the defendants for damages for breach of the covenant to yield up the premises in good repair, the defendants relied on s. 18 (1) of the Landlord and Tenant Act, 1927.

Held (1) By virtue of s. 18 (1) of the Landlord and Tenant Act, 1927, damages were not recoverable for breach of the covenant to yield up the premises in good repair for the following reasons:

(a) the date at which it had to be shown for the purposes of s. 18 (1) whether the premises would "at or shortly after the termination of the tenancy have been or be pulled down" was the date of the termination of the tenancy, viz., March 28, 1957.

(b) on the evidence (including therein the letter of December 12, 1956) the defendants had discharged the burden of proof that at March 28, 1957, the premises would shortly thereafter he pulled down.

Lord Evershed MR said (in part)

I turn now to s. 18 (1) of the Landlord and Tenant Act, 1927 . . .

The language which I have read was subjected to some critical consideration in this court in *Salisbury v Gilmore* [1942] 1 All ER 457. Lord Greene, MR, for example, dealt with the criticism of the language which had led the learned judge at first instance to come to the conclusion that the words, as they stood, could not be given any effective meaning. I need not take time by reading what Lord Greene, MR, said, because what it came to was that the formula that the premises "would at or shortly after the termination of the tenancy have been or be pulled down" meant (at any rate for the purposes of this case) that the premises were going at that date to be pulled down, then or shortly thereafter. Having referred to *Salisbury v Gilmore*, I add this which is relevant about it: it was a case in which no one but the landlords (the plaintiffs) and the tenants were concerned, that is to say, it was a case in which no local authority had taken any part; but the landlords had indubitably intended, and made plans accordingly for, the pulling down and reconstruction of the premises. The lease terminated on September 29, 1939, which was a little more than three weeks after the outbreak of the war, and the point arose because, war having broken out and certain regulations later having come into force, the landlords had had to abandon their intention; therefore they sought to say that, whatever might have been their intention prior to the outbreak of war, at the date of the action the fact was that they no longer intended to pull the premises down, because they could not have done so, however much they wanted to. The court, however, held that for determining the question raised by the formula in s. 18 (1) of the Act of 1927 one had to look at the date September 29, 1939, when the tenants went out and the lease determined, and at that date the proper inference was that the original intention of the landlords still subsisted.

One other matter of a little importance is also dealt with in the judgment of Lord Greene, MR. The formula which I have read could not be simply expressed by such a formula as "if it is shown that the landlords intended to pull down the premises", or some similar form of words, because, as Lord Greene, MR, observed, the formula had to cover the case where the pending destruction or pulling down depended, not on any intention of the landlords, but on the effect of some local authority activity such as a demolition order, or a compulsory purchase order under a town planning scheme.

I now turn to the present case. I venture to put the problem posed by the preliminary issue and s. 18 (1) of the Act of 1927 in this form: What, at the termination of the tenancy, as a matter of fact, is the answer to the question, Were the premises then going to be shortly pulled down? That question can only be answered by forming a view on all the material that was then available.

Case 83 *Cunliffe v Goodman* [1950] 2 KB 237 Court of Appeal

A tenancy was granted in 1943 "for the duration of the war" on terms that the tenant would deliver up the property on termination of the tenancy in a good and tenantable state of repair. On termination of the tenancy, C. sued G. for breach of the covenant. Although G. admitted the breach of covenant, in his defence he relied on section 18 of the Landlord and Tenant Act 1927. In order to escape liability, the tenant was required to prove that C. had formed the intention to pull down the premises. To determine the matter involved construing correspondence between C. and her professional advisors and the facts that the London County Council, as town planning authority, had not approved C.'s proposal to redevelop the property, nor had the Hammersmith Borough Council granted a building licence at the date when the tenancy was terminated.

Held (1) That a firm intention—a decision—on the part of the landlord, at the relevant date, must be proved by the tenant. It must be shown that the landlord had made up his mind and that his project had moved out of the zone of contemplation—the sphere of the tentative, the provisional and the exploratory—and had moved into the valley of decision.

(2) *Per Asquith LJ.* It must be shown that the landlord had decided, in so far as in him lay, to bring about the demolition of the premises and that he had a reasonable prospect of being able to bring about that demolition by his own act of volition. A man could not be said to "intend" a particular result if its occurrence, though it might not be wholly uninfluenced by his will, were dependent on so many other influences, accidents and cross-currents of circumstance that, not merely was it quite likely not to be achieved at all, but, if it were achieved, his volition would have been no more than a minor agency, collaborating with, or not thwarted by, the factors which predominantly determined its occurrence. If there were a sufficiently formidable succession of fences to be surmounted before the result at which he aimed could be achieved, it might well be unmeaning to say that he intended that result.

Not only was proof of "intention" unsatisfied if the person said to "intend" had too many hurdles to overcome or too little control of events: the term was equally inappropriate, if, at the material date, that person was in effect not deciding to proceed, but was feeling his way and reserving his decision until he should be in possession of financial data sufficient to enable him to determine whether the project would be commercially worth while.

Asquith LJ said (in part)

The question to be answered is whether the defendant (on whom the onus lies) has proved that the plaintiff, on November 30, 1945 "intended" to pull down the premises on this site. This question is in my view one of fact. If the plaintiff did no more than entertain the idea of this demolition, if she got no further than to contemplate it as a (perhaps attractive) possibility, then one would have to say (and it matters not which way it is put) either that there was *no* evidence of a positive "intention," or that the word "intention" was incapable as a matter of construction of applying to anything so tentative, and so indefinite. An "intention" to my mind connotes a state of affairs which the party "intending"—I will call him X—does more than merely contemplate: it connotes a state of affairs which, on the contrary, he decides, so far as in him lies, to bring about, and which, in point of possibility, he has a reasonable prospect of being able to bring about, by his own act of volition.

X cannot, with any due regard to the English language, be said to "intend" a result which is wholly beyond the control of his will. He cannot "intend" that it shall be a fine day tomorrow: at most he can hope or desire or pray that it will. Nor, short of this, can X be said to "intend" a particular result if its occurrence, though it may be not wholly uninfluenced by X's will, is dependent on so many other influences, accidents and cross-currents of circumstance that, not merely is it quite likely not to be achieved at all, but, if it is achieved, X's volition will have been no more than a minor agency collaborating with, or not thwarted by, the factors which predominantly determine its occurrence. If there is a sufficiently formidable succession of fences to be surmounted before the result at which X aims can be achieved, it may well be unmeaning to say that X "intended" that result.

Here there were a number of such fences. The approval of the London County Council, as the town-planning authority for London, had to be obtained, and was refused in respect of the first rebuilding plan. A building licence had to be obtained from Hammersmith Borough Council. The first plan never reached the stage at which such a licence could usefully be applied for. As to either plan, a licence, if forthcoming, might have been granted on terms, and those terms might have deprived the project of all commercial attraction—deprived it of the character of a "business proposition." Such licences are often granted conditionally on a maximum selling price for the structure as rebuilt, or—if it be not sold, but let—conditionally on a maximum rent:

and in respect of the second scheme a maximum rent of an unattractive level was in fact proposed by the local authority.

This leads me to the second point bearing on the existence in this case of "intention" as opposed to mere contemplation. Not merely is the term "intention" unsatisfied if the person professing it has too many hurdles to overcome, or too little control of events: it is equally inappropriate if at the material date that person is in effect not deciding to proceed but feeling his way and reserving his decision until he shall be in possession of financial data sufficient to enable him to determine whether the project will be commercially worth while.

A purpose so qualified and suspended does not in my view amount to an "intention" or "decision" within the principle. It is mere contemplation until the materials necessary to a decision on the commercial merits are available and have resulted in such a decision. In the present case it seems to me that (assuming that the plaintiff was, both before and after November 30, 1945, disposed to demolish and rebuild if she could do so on remunerative terms) she never reached, in respect of the first scheme, a stage at which she could decide on its commercial merits; nor, in respect of the second scheme, the stage of actually deciding that that scheme was commercially eligible—unless indeed she must be taken not merely to have repudiated her architect's authority but to have decided that it was commercially ineligible. In the case of neither scheme did she form a settled intention to proceed. Neither project moved out of the zone of contemplation—out of the sphere of the tentative, the provisional and the exploratory—into the valley of decision.

Case 84 *Hibernian Property Co Ltd v Liverpool Corporation* [1973] 1 WLR 751 Caulfield J

The plaintiffs were freehold reversioners of a house and land held by a municipal corporation first under a lease and then by holding over and paying rent. The corporation, who covenanted to keep and leave the house in good and tenantable repair and condition, were in breach of the repairing covenants. The house was designated as unfit for human habitation and was included in a clearance area under section 42 (1) of the Housing Act 1957. Thereupon the corporation made a compulsory purchase order in respect of the house and served a notice to treat and a notice of entry. If the corporation had complied with the repairing covenants the house would either have been excluded from the clearance area or would have had an enhanced value because it would have been habitable and in good repair. In an action against the corporation for breach of covenant to repair the plaintiffs claimed damages as representing the difference between the compensation they would receive for the agreed market value of the house in covenanted repair and condition and the compensation payable to them as the agreed site value with the house designated as unfit for human habitation. The corporation relied on section 18 (1) of the Landlord and Tenant Act 1927, pleaded that only site value was payable to the plaintiffs, and called no evidence.

On the claim:

Held, Giving judgment for the plaintiffs, (1) that the proper test was to define the extent to which the value of the reversion had been diminished.

(2) That section 18 (1) of the Act of 1927 was inapplicable on the facts, for it had not been shown that the house would at or shortly after the termination of the tenancy have been or be pulled down; and that, accordingly, there was damage to the reversion and the plaintiffs were entitled to recover the agreed amount of damages, assessed at the date of the notice of entry.

(3) Section 18 (1) of the Act of 1927 contemplates the decision to pull down the house being that of the lessor only and the section cannot be construed as enabling a municipal corporation to contend that they are given relief on a claim against them for damages for their own failure to comply with covenants to repair so that the house has to be demolished.

Caulfield J said (in part)

I think that the proper test is to define the extent to which the value of the lessor's reversion has been diminished. If the lessor intends to demolish the premises, there is no damage to the reversion. The most common example is that of the landlord who intends to demolish at the expiration of a lease and then to re-erect. The second part of section 18 beginning with the words "in particular" is not expressed to apply to breaches of a repairing covenant during the currency of the lease. In any event, on my findings of fact, I do not think that the second part of section 18 is applicable to the facts of this case. My first reason is that, on the facts, it has not been shown that these premises would at or shortly after the termination of the tenancy have been or be pulled down. Secondly, the last part of section

18 certainly, I think, contemplates the lessor making a decision to pull down or so structurally alter the premises that any repairs that would be shown to be necessary to achieve compliance with the covenants in the lease would be rendered nugatory. I do not, however, think that the section is even capable of being construed as enabling a municipal corporation, by its own failure to comply with covenants to repair so that the house has to be demolished, to contend that the second part gives it relief in a claim for damages for breach of covenant.

This is my view, whether the plaintiffs' claim is deemed to be made during the currency of the lease or at its termination. If I am wrong, it would, I think, mean that whenever a corporation was a lessee of property with an obligation to keep the property in repair, it could well find it more profitable to fail to comply with its contractual obligations than to discharge them. This, to my mind, does not make sense and I do not think that it is the law. I am fortified in this view because, if the corporation is satisfied that a certain area should be classified as a clearance area under section 42, it has a statutory duty to exclude from that area any building which is not unfit for human habitation. Obviously, in such a case the compensation to the owner of the property is much greater than site value.

Can it be the law that a local authority can allow property of which it is the lessee to fall into disrepair in breach of its own covenant, then, having gone through the formalities of compulsory purchase, pay only site value? I do not think that it can be. As I see it, the corporation would be rewarding itself for its breach of its own obligation. I therefore conclude that there was damage to the reversion in this case and that the plaintiffs are entitled to recover damages.

The final question is to determine the date in reference to which the damages fall to be assessed. Certain figures have been agreed for two different dates. If the correct date is the date of the notice to treat—namely, January 8, 1970—the figure is £1,600 less the site value of £135. If the date is the date of trial, it is £2,100 less £135. On this question, I was referred to *West Midland Baptist (Trust) Association (Inc.) v Birmingham Corporation* [1970] AC 874. The plaintiffs argue that nothing happened after the notices to treat and to enter were served. As far as I can see, that is right. Nothing did happen except that the defendants continued to pay rent.

[Counsel] emphasised that the plaintiffs averred in the statement of claim that the defendants' tenancy terminated with the making of the compulsory purchase order. The defendants in their defence so admitted. [Counsel] argued that the proper date was the date of the notice of entry. It is conceded by the plaintiffs that all the formalities that should follow the making of a compulsory purchase order have been properly followed by the defendants. The procedure is that, after the making of a compulsory purchase order, the Minister has to confirm that order. Thereafter, the notice to treat is served.

In my judgment, the notice to treat does not alter the relationship of the parties, but the notice of entry does. I think that the date upon which damages should be assessed is the date of the notice of entry. It so happens that the notice of entry accompanied the notice to treat. The date of the notice of entry is January 9, 1970. Accordingly, on the agreed figures, the plaintiffs are entitled to recover the sum of £1,465 and there will be judgment accordingly.

5.9 Leasehold Property (Repairs) Act 1938

Statute 4: Leasehold Property (Repairs) Act 1938. Section 1

Restriction on enforcement of repairing covenants in long leases of small houses

1.—(1) Where a lessor serves on a lessee under sub-section (1) of section one hundred and forty-six of the Law of Property Act 1925, a notice that relates to a breach of a covenant or agreement to keep or put in repair during the currency of the lease all or any of the property comprised in the lease, and at the date of the service of the notice three years or more of the term of the lease remain unexpired, the lessee may within twenty-eight days from that date serve on the lessor a counter-notice to the effect that he claims the benefit of this Act.

(2) A right to damages for a breach of such a covenant as aforesaid shall not be enforceable by action commenced at any time at which three years or more of the term of the lease remain unexpired unless the lessor has served on the lessee not less than one month before the commencement of the action such a notice as is specified in subsection (1) of section one hundred and forty-six of the Law of Property Act 1925, and where a notice is served under this subsection, the lessee may, within twenty-eight days from the date of the service thereof, serve on the lessor a counter-notice to the effect that he claims the benefit of this Act.

(3) Where a counter-notice is served by a lessee under this section, then, notwithstanding anything in any enactment or

rule of law, no proceedings, by action or otherwise, shall be taken by the lessor for the enforcement of any right of re-entry or forfeiture under any proviso or stipulation in the lease for breach of the covenant or agreement in question, or for damages for breach thereof, otherwise than with the leave of the court.

(4) A notice served under sub-section (1) of section one hundred and forty-six of the Law of Property Act 1925, in the circumstances specified in subsection (1) of this section, and a notice served under subsection (2) of this section shall not be valid unless it contains a statement, in characters not less conspicuous than those used in any other part of the notice, to the effect that the lessee is entitled under this Act to serve on the lessor a counter-notice claiming the benefit of this Act, and a statement in the like characters specifying the time within which, and the manner in which, under this Act a counter-notice may be served and specifying the name and address for service of the lessor.

(5) Leave for the purposes of this section shall not be given unless the lessor proves:

(a) that the immediate remedying of the breach in question is requisite for preventing substantial diminution in the value of his reversion, or that the value thereof has been substantially diminished by the breach;

(b) that the immediate remedying of the breach is required for giving effect in relation to the premises to the purposes of any enactment, or of any byelaw or other provision having effect under an enactment, or for giving effect to any order of a court or requirement of any authority under any enactment or any such byelaw or other provision as aforesaid;

(c) in a case in which the lessee is not in occupation of the whole of the premises as respects which the covenant or agreement is proposed to be enforced, that the immediate remedying of the breach is required in the interests of the occupier of those premises or of part thereof;

(d) that the breach can be immediately remedied at an expense that is relatively small in comparison with the much greater expense that would probably be occasioned by postponement of the necessary work; or

(e) special circumstances which in the opinion of the court, render it just and equitable that leave should be given.

(6) The court may, in granting or in refusing leave for the purposes of this section impose such terms and conditions on the lessor or on the lessee as it may think fit.

Note:
(i) See Chapter 6 for the relevant cases on the operation of the 1938 Act.

5.10 Damages for breach of landlord's repairing covenant

Section 18 of the Landlord and Tenant Act 1927 does not apply to a tenant's claim for damages for breach of a landlord's repairing obligation.

Case 85 *Hewitt v Rowlands* [1924] All ER 344 Court of Appeal

By an agreement in writing, dated March 8, 1875, the plaintiff became the tenant of a dwelling-house for a term of five years at an annual rent of £60. It was agreed that the landlord should "keep the cottage dry and the outside in repair." On the termination of the five years' tenancy the tenant remained in occupation as a yearly tenant. The present landlord purchased the property in 1920. In 1921 the tenant received from the landlord a notice to quit the premises on October 1, 1921, but, as the premises were within the operation of the Increase of Rent and Mortgage Interest (Restrictions) Act, 1920, he remained in possession after the expiry of the notice as a statutory tenant. During 1921 the tenant complained to the landlord of the house being damp, and on November 25, 1921, a written notice was given to the landlord's solicitors that the premises were "very damp," the landlord being requested "to take immediate steps to make the premises damp proof." The landlord having failed to execute the repairs in accordance with the notice, the tenant commenced an action to recover damages for breach of the agreement. The tenant had not incurred any expenditure in connection with the repairs.

Held (1) In assessing the damages the tenant was not entitled to complain of any damage suffered before the notice of want of repair was given, but, the breach being a continuing breach, the damages should be assessed down to the date of assessment.

(2) The measure of damages was the difference between the value to the tenant of the premises from the date of the notice to repair down to the date of the assessment of damages in their present condition and their value if the landlord on receipt of the notice to repair had fulfilled the obligations of the covenant to repair; but so much of the damages as were due to defects which the landlord was

not bound to remedy must be excluded from the assessment.
(3) The fact that the tenant was a statutory tenant in no way affected the landlord's liability under his covenant.

Bankes LJ said (in part)

I will endeavour to explain the grounds on which I think he ought to proceed in assessing the damages to which the tenant is entitled. First of all, the tenant is not entitled to complain until he has given his landlord notice to do the repairs, and that notice was given in November, 1921. Next, the breach here complained of being a breach of the continuing covenant, the damages will have to be assessed down to the date of assessment, so that the period which the registrar will have to consider is the period between the date when the notice to repair was given and the date when he in fact assesses the damage. *Prima facie* the measure of damages for breach of the obligation to repair is the difference in value to the tenant during that period between the house in its then condition, and its value if the landlord on receipt of the tenant's notice had fulfilled the obligation to repair. But, in considering that value, it is necessary to consider what the extent of the landlord's obligation to repair was, and in reference to this matter a difficult question arises which is a matter for the registrar to decide on the facts. He must consider whether, having regard to the age and structure of this house, the damage complained of is the result of a failure on the part of the landlord to do anything which he was under an obligation to do. It appears, according to his statement, that the main cause of the dampness is the saturation of the stone which composes part of the house owing to the absence of a damp course, and he must consider whether, on the facts, the case falls within the class of cases of which *Lister v Lane and Nesham* [1893] 2 QB 212 is one, and there are others to the same effect. *Lister v Lane and Nesham* was explained by Fletcher Moulton, LJ, in *Lurcott v Wakeley and Wheeler* [1911] 1 KB 905 and to the extent to which the registrar may find, after directing himself properly with reference to those decisions, that the dampness is caused by a state of things which the landlord is under no obligation to remedy under this covenant, he will, of course, exclude that from his consideration in assessing the damages.

I hope I have expressed sufficiently clearly the view which the registrar must take in assessing the damages. Perhaps I could express it shortly in this way: that the measure of damages is the difference in value to the tenant of the premises from the date of the notice to repair down to the date of the assessment of damages, between the premises in their present condition and their value if the landlord on receipt of the tenant's notice to repair had fulfilled the obligations of the covenant.

As I say I regret that there has been all this litigation about this comparatively small matter, and I should still hope that the parties might see their way to come to some final settlement of it. We can only deal with it on the facts as they come before us, and our decision is that the matter must go back to the registrar for his reconsideration and for an assessment of such damages as he thinks proper after this direction to award. We think the tenant must have the costs because the landlord's contention has been really from the first that, under the circumstances, all that the tenant was entitled to was nominal damages. I think, having regard to the amount which the registrar has now said he has given as general damages, that that is really the argument he accepted and on which he based his decision.

The tenant claiming damages against the landlord for breach of a repairing covenant may claim under several heads of damage.

Case 86 *Calabar Properties Ltd v Stitcher* [1984] 3 All ER 759
Court of Appeal

In October, 1975 the tenant acquired the lease of a flat in a block of flats with the intention of living there permanently with her husband. The lease contained a repairing covenant by the landlords requiring them to maintain the external parts of the block in good repair. In January, 1976 the tenant complained to the landlords that rainwater was penetrating into the flat and causing damage to the decorative work. Despite further complaints by the tenant the landlords took the view that the dampness and damage were not their responsibility and consequently failed to carry out any external repairs to the flat. The tenant and her husband remained in the flat for five years, even though the dampness caused the husband to suffer ill-health, until January, 1981 when the flat became uninhabitable and the tenant and her husband were forced to rent alternative accommodation. When the landlords sued the tenant for charges due from her under the lease she counterclaimed for damages for breach of the landlords' covenant to repair but did not plead any particular head of damage, such as the cost of the alternative accommodation. The tenant also sought an order requiring the landlords to repair the flat. The action was tried in December, 1982. The judge found that the dampness and damage to the flat were caused by the landlords' breach of the repairing covenant and held that the measure of damages for breach of a landlord's covenant to repair was the diminution in the market value of the premises during the period between the first request to carry out repairs and the date when damages were assessed. The judge accordingly ordered the landlords to repair the flat and awarded the tenant (i) special damages of £4,606.44 for diminution in the market value of the flat between January, 1976 and December, 1982 based, in the absence of other evidence of value, on the cost of repairs and redecoration carried out by the tenant, less a reduction of one-third of the cost to take into account the betterment resulting from the redecoration, and (ii) general damages of £3,000 for the discomfort, loss of enjoyment and ill-health suffered by herself and her husband during the period they occupied the deteriorating flat. However, the judge refused to award the tenant damages either (i) for the outgoings on the flat during the period when it was uninhabitable and she and her husband had to live elsewhere, on the ground that such damages would be comparable to an award for the cost of alternative accommodation while the flat was being repaired and such an award was an irrecoverable head of damage, or (ii), assuming the flat to be a marketable asset, for loss of rental value arising out of the notional loss of rent during the period it was uninhabitable, on the ground that such damage was too remote. The tenant appealed against the judge's refusal to award damages under those two heads. The landlords contended, *inter alia*, that no award should be made under those heads because they had not been pleaded in the counterclaim.

Held (1) The fundamental principle in measuring damages payable to a tenant for breach of a repairing covenant by the landlord was that the object of the damages was to restore the tenant to the position he would have been in if there had been no breach. Thus, the diminution in the value of the premises was not necessarily the measure of the damages for breach of a landlord's repairing covenant, while, on the other hand, the cost of alternative accommodation could be recoverable. Accordingly, where the tenant had acquired premises for his personal occupation and intended to occupy them after the landlord had effected the necessary repairs, the tenant was entitled to damages to compensate him for (a) the cost of alternative accommodation if he had been forced by the lack of repair to move out temporarily, (b) the cost of any repairs paid for by the tenant and (c) the unpleasantness of living in deteriorating premises until they became uninhabitable. A tenant was not entitled to damages based on the diminution in the market value of the premises unless to the knowledge of the landlord he had acquired the premises with the intention of reselling or subletting them or unless he was driven out of occupation by the breach and forced to sell the premises.

(2) Applying those principles, it followed that because the tenant had acquired the flat as a home rather than as an investment the proper measure of her damages was the reasonable cost of alternative accommodation while the flat was being repaired, the cost of any repairs and redecoration done by her (without any reduction for betterment) and compensation for the discomfort, loss of enjoyment and ill-health endured while the flat was deteriorating. However, since the tenant had not pleaded the cost of alternative accommodation as an item of special damage and had not contested the judge's reduction of damages for betterment, the judge's award of damages would not be disturbed in respect of those items. The tenant's claim for reimbursement of the outgoings on her flat for the period it was uninhabitable failed because such outgoings were a necessary consequence of retaining the lease of the flat and would have been offset by the outgoings included in the award for alternative accommodation if that had been claimed. The tenant's claim for notional loss of rent also failed because that was merely another aspect of a claim for diminution in value of the flat as a marketable asset and such a claim was not open to the tenant because she had bought the flat as a home rather than as a marketable asset. In all the circumstances therefore the tenant's appeal would be dismissed.

Stephenson LJ said (in part)
"In measuring and assessing any tenant's damages for breach of a landlord's repairing covenant the court must, I think, always start with the fundamental principle that they are so far as is possible by means of a monetary award, to place the plaintiff in the position which he would have occupied if he had not suffered the wrong complained of, be that wrong a tort or a breach of contract". I take that statement from the judgment of

Donaldson LJ in *Dodd Properties (Kent) Ltd v Canterbury City Council* [1980] 1 All ER 928 at 938, [1980] 1 WLR 433 at 456, a case in which this court applied that principle by awarding the owners as damages for negligence and/or nuisance the cost of repairing a building damaged by the defendants' operations, and the lessees of the building their loss of profits through dislocation of their business. The diminution in the building's value in the open market was not considered as a basis for assessing the damage of either of the plaintiffs. That basis was, however, considered appropriate to the assessment of damages for the negligence of a surveyor at the suit of a purchaser of the surveyed property in *Perry v Sidney Phillips & Son (a firm)* [1982] 3 All ER 705, [1982] 1 WLR 1297, where the court awarded the plaintiff the difference in price between what he paid for the property and its market value as it should have been described at the time of purchase with interest and damages for distress and discomfort, vexation and inconvenience, since his conduct in the circumstances had been reasonable. So the true measure of damages for persons owning or occupying land, whether in tort or contract, depends on the position of the plaintiffs and all the circumstances in which they have suffered loss and damage, in the light of the fundamental principle to which I have referred.

Griffiths LJ said (in part)

In this case on the findings of the judge the landlords after notice of the defect neglected their obligation to repair for such a length of time that the flat eventually became uninhabitable. It was also clear that, unless ordered to do so by an order of the court, the landlords had no intention of carrying out the repairs. In these circumstances the tenant had two options that were reasonably open to her: either of selling the flat and moving elsewhere or alternatively of moving into temporary accommodation and bringing an action against the landlords to force them to carry out the repairs and then returning to the flat after the repairs were done.

If a tenant chooses the first option then the measure of damages would indeed be the difference in the price he received for the flat in its damaged condition and that which it would have fetched in the open market if the landlord had observed his repairing covenant. If, however, the tenant does not wish to sell the flat but to continue to live in it after the landlord has carried out the necessary structural repairs it is wholly artificial to award him damages on the basis of loss in market value, because once the landlord has carried out the repairs and any consequential redecoration of the interior is completed there will be no loss in market value. The tenant should be awarded the cost to which he was put in taking alternative accommodation, the cost of redecorating, and some award for all the unpleasantness of living in the flat as it deteriorated until it became uninhabitable. These three heads of damage will, so far as money can, compensate the tenant for the landlord's breach.

But it was said that the court cannot award the cost of the alternative accommodation because of the decision in *Green v Eales* (1841) 2 QB 225, 114 ER 88 and in particular the passage in the judgment of Lord Denman CJ in which he said (2 QB 225 at 238, 114 ER 88 at 93):

> "We are of opinion that the defendant was not bound to find the plaintiff another residence whilst the repairs went on, any more than he would have been bound to do so if the premises had been consumed by fire."

But I take that passage to do no more than draw attention to the fact that a landlord is not in breach of his covenant to repair until he has been given notice of the want of repair and a reasonable time has elapsed in which the repair could have been carried out. If in this case the landlords had sent workmen round to carry out the repairs promptly on receiving notice of the defect and the tenant for her own convenience had decided to move to a hotel whilst the repairs were carried out she could not have claimed the cost of the hotel accommodation because the landlords would not have been in breach of the repairing covenant. That Lord Denman CJ meant no more than this is I think apparent from his observation that the tenant might have had a claim on the basis that the time he had to be in alternative accommodation had been lengthened by the delay in carrying out repairs.

For these reasons I do not regard *Green v Eales* as an authority for the proposition that there can be no claim for the costs of alternative accommodation, but if it did purport so to decide, it was in my view wrongly decided.

If the tenant in this case had claimed for the cost of alternative accommodation it would in principle have been an allowable head of damage. It would naturally have been closely investigated on the evidence: was her (and her husband's) true reason for leaving the flat that they found the conditions intolerable, or were there other reasons for going to live in the Isle of Man?, was the cost of the alternative accommodation reasonable? and so forth. However, the claim was not made and I agree that it is now too late to put it forward.

Case 87 *McCoy & Co v Clark* [1982] 13 HLR 87 Court of Appeal

The defendant was the tenant of a flat on the second floor of a house. From 1977 he was complaining to the plaintiff landlords of dampness in his flat, resulting from water ingress through the roof. The roof was not repaired until 1981. The plaintiff took action for rent arrears, and the defendant counterclaimed for damages, for the diminution in value of the premises, for damage to property, for damage to health which resulted in pain, his admission to hospital with pneumonia for nine days, and feeling ill for a period of five or six weeks thereafter, and on account of the landlord's behaviour which he alleged amounted to a nuisance.

The judge held that there was dampness, caused by a leaky roof, and that the defendant had complained about it. He noted that the flat was not important to the defendant, but that it was just used as a place to sleep, and awarded damages amounting to 10% of the rent for the first two years of disrepair, and amounting to 20% for the second two years. He awarded £10 for damage to property.

The judge found that the defendant's illness had been caused in part by his own conduct, and that he had had a comfortable time in hospital, and awarded a sum of £100 reduced by 50%. He concluded that although there had been a nuisance, which was not *de minimis*, it was too trivial a matter for damages to be awarded. The tenant appealed against all the awards, save that for the property.

Held (1) The leaky roof had been the main cause of the dampness; it was not correct to award damages at a lower rate because the flat was not important to the tenant, as the damages ought to be proportional to the reduction in the comfort for which the tenant was paying; the award was too low and would be doubled.

(2) It was not right to take into account the fact that the tenant had a comfortable time in hospital, and £100 was not sufficient compensation for his suffering; it, too, would be doubled (although also reduced by 50%).

(3) As the judge had found that a tort had been committed in relation to the nuisance, which went beyond *de minimis*, £5 ought to be awarded.

Sir David Cairns said (in part)

... I am satisfied, not only that the judge did find, but that it is the right finding, that the main cause of this dampness and the main cause of the flat being worth less to the defendant than it otherwise would have been was the plaintiffs' breach in relation to the roof.

On that basis, was the compensation that was awarded to the defendant for it adequate? In my view it was not. It is all very well to say that the defendant was not spending a great deal of the day in the flat and that he was using it mainly as a sleeping place. If he had the flat as a sleeping place and was willing to pay £9 a week for the flat for that purpose, then he is entitled to a flat which is comfortable for that purpose, and if it is substantially reduced in the degree of comfort, then I think what he ought to recover is something proportional to that reduction. It is obviously not easy to reason out a particular figure. In so far as there is a certain suggestion in the learned judge's judgment that he took the figures which had been put before him by counsel on the two sides and had arrived at something in between the two, I would not seriously attributute that to him as a course of reasoning; obviously, if he did arrive at the figure in that way, it would not have been the right way. However, he did arrive at a figure, and I can only say that I am satisfied that it is much too low. I would double the figures of the learned judge, and award 20% in respect of the first 113 weeks and 40% in respect of the last 68 weeks.

Now we come to the pneumonia. So far as that is concerned, as I have said, the judge said that he would have awarded £100 if he had thought it was entirely the plaintiffs' fault, but he thought that the defendant was 50% to blame for it and therefore he reduced his award for that to £50. There is no appeal on either side as to that proportion. It is accepted that the defendant had not behaved sensibly in regard to keeping himself warm, and perhaps in other ways, and to that extent he rightly had his damages reduced. But the question is whether £100 would be a sufficient compensation for what he suffered ...

That is the position. What we have is pneumonia, which is admittedly due to the plaintiffs' breach of the implied duty under the tenancy agreement. Would £100 be adequate compensation to a man for the pain which he suffered, about nine days in hospital and five or six weeks afterwards, feeling rather ill?

Well, pain of that character—pain which sends him off to hospital to be looked after there, nine days in hospital and five or six weeks feeling rather ill afterwards—and that evidence as

to the five or six weeks was accepted by the judge, who makes
a finding to that effect. I cannot think that in these days £100
would be sufficient compensation for that. The judge took into
account that the defendant had a comfortable time in hospital.
I daresay he did; I daresay his hospital bed was more comfortable
than that at his flat, No 2 Everington Street, but I do not think
that that is a matter which can be taken into account. That he
did have the hospital treatment and that that brought about substantial recovery within nine or ten days and complete recovery
within five or six weeks thereafter, is of course something which
makes the damages less than they would have been if he had
not had that treatment, but in my view this again is a figure
which is too low, and again I am of the opinion that the appropriate figure would be double that assessed by the judge, bringing the £50 up to £100.

Where the tenant is one of many tenants in a block of flats the
amount of damages may be based on the repair cost for the
whole block.

**Case 88 *Marenco v Jacramel Co Ltd* [1964] EGD 349 Court of
Appeal**

The tenant (Mrs Marenco) bought an underlease of flat
10, Chasewood Court, Mill Hill, dated May 29, 1962, for
a term of 90 years, less 10 days, from December 25, 1955,
at a cost of £2,450, and held simply on a ground rent of
£18 a year. The landlords covenanted to "keep and maintain
the exterior of the flat and the building of which it forms
part ... entrances, passageways, staircases, roads, ways,
paths ... gardens, structures and fences ... in good repair
and condition and properly maintained and ... to paint all
outside woodwork and ironwork..." For her part, Mrs Marenco agreed to pay by way of further rent a proportion of
the costs of insuring the building and a fair proportion of
the cost of keeping clean and lighting the entrance hall and
staircase, and to contribute a rateable or due proportion of
the expense of making, repairing, maintaining, rebuilding
and cleansing and lighting the exterior of the flat and the
building of which it formed part, including fences, etc.
By notice in writing of October 2, 1963, Mrs Marenco
required the landlords within 21 days to repair or restore

the light in the entrance hall and staircase; maintain the fences bordering the building in good repair; render and repair the concrete drive, and clear the beds of the gardens of nettles and weeds and otherwise maintain the same in a neat and tidy condition. By a letter of October 23, 1963, the landlords said that they were not prepared to carry out the works until the other underlessees had contributed to the cost of previous works and given security for future contributions. Mrs Marenco was ready, willing and able to pay a fair proportion of the cost of the works and asked the landlords what was her share, but the landlords failed or neglected to tell her. There were eleven other underlessees in the blocks of flats.

Held (1) The amount of damages was to be based on the cost of repair for the whole block of flats and it was wrong to divide the amount of damages by the number of tenants. The landlords may be liable in the same sum to all the tenants.

Danckwerts LJ said (in part)

At the trial, the landlords called no evidence and submitted no case. The trial judge had correctly found that the landlords were in breach of their covenant, and that the sum of £384 odd estimated by Mrs Marenco based on estimates obtained, was a reasonable cost of carrying out the work. However, the trial judge had gone on to say that if this were a single house and Mrs Marenco the only tenant, then she would be entitled to claim the full cost of the repairs; she would have established that the property had diminished in value, and the cost of repairs would be an indication of the diminution; but that as she was only one of 12 tenants in two blocks of flats and the amenities were enjoyed by the other 11 tenants, the whole of the £384 could not be attributable to her flat. All the flats were equally affected by the breaches, and a fair assessment of the diminution was one-twelfth of £384, which was £32. And as in addition to the landlords' covenant the underlease contained corresponding obligations on the tenant to pay a proportion of the cost of carrying out the services and repairs, which, in Mrs Marenco's case, was one-twelfth, or £32, she had lost nothing. Therefore, concluded the trial judge, she had not established any damage and the action failed, and the landlords must have their costs.

That approach was wrong. Mrs Marenco had an interest in the whole covenant and was not really interested in what happened to the other tenants. Her covenant was for the landlords to repair. Her contribution could occur only after the landlords had repaired the premises. The measure of diminution was what had been the effect of the failure of the landlords to carry out repairs upon the value of Mrs Marenco's flat, and not upon the value of any other flat. It was simply her flat in which she was specifically interested. The repairs had not yet been done. The appeal should be allowed and judgment entered for £384 3s., less the amount of her contribution towards the repairs, which meant that she would succeed as to £352 2s. 9d.

Willmer LJ said (in part)
... where the trial judge went wrong was in taking the view that the diminution of value was to be divided by 12 because Mrs Marenco was a tenant of only one of the 12 flats. The landlords had covenanted with Mrs Marenco, and no doubt with the other tenants equally, although the court did not know, to keep the whole of the exterior, garden and roadways and not one-twelfth of them. Mrs Marenco's property had been diminished in value by the whole cost of the repair, and not by one-twelfth of it. Any other view would mean that the landlords would be able to break their covenant with complete impunity. On the basis of the trial judge's judgment, no tenant would have any right to enforce the covenants into which the landlords had entered. That could not be right, but it was the conclusion to which one was driven by the erroneous process of dividing by 12 the damage Mrs Marenco had sustained. It was quite right that the landlords might be equally liable to the other 11 tenants. Be it so, if that was right, he (Wilmer, LJ) did not shrink from it. It might be that the other 11 tenants had suffered damage to the same extent. The court did not know the terms of their leases, but in any case, if the landlords were fearful that that might be the result, they could put it right at any time by executing the necessary repairs to comply with their covenant. In those circumstances Mrs Marenco was entitled to the full amount claimed, subject to the agreement to pay one-twelfth of the sum as her proper contribution.

6 REMEDIES FOR DISREPAIR

6.1 Other remedies for disrepair

In the event of a failure by a party to the lease to comply with his express or implied repairing obligations it is generally agreed that the following remedies are available to the landlord:

(a) Damages for breach of covenant.
(b) Forfeiture of the lease.
(c) Entry and repair.

The following remedies are available to the tenant.

(a) Damages for breach of covenant.
(b) Set-off against rent.
(c) Specific performance.
(d) Appointment of receiver.

6.2 Landlord's remedy: Forfeiture and the section 146 notice

For a landlord to be able to forfeit a lease a right of re-entry must be reserved in the lease. An essential prerequisite to the forfeiture of the lease in these circumstances is the service of a notice under section 146 of the Law of Property Act 1925.

Statute 5: Law of Property Act 1925. Section 146

Restrictions on and relief against forfeiture of leases and underleases
146.—(1) A right of re-entry or forfeiture under any proviso or stipulation in a lease for a breach of any covenant or condition in the lease shall not be enforceable, by action or otherwise, unless and until the lessor serves on the lessee a notice:

(a) specifying the particular breach complained of; and
(b) if the breach is capable of remedy, requiring the lessee to remedy the breach; and
(c) in any case, requiring the lessee to make compensation in money for the breach;

and the lessee fails, within a reasonable time thereafter, to remedy the breach, if it is capable of remedy, and to make reasonable compensation in money, to the satisfaction of the lessor, for the breach.

265

(2) Where a lessor is proceeding, by action or otherwise, to enforce such a right of re-entry or forfeiture, the lessee may, in the lessor's action, if any, or in any action brought by himself, apply to the court for relief; and the court may grant or refuse relief, as the court, having regard to the proceedings and conduct of the parties under the foregoing provisions of this section, and to all the other circumstances, thinks fit; and in case of relief may grant it on such terms, if any, as to costs, expenses, damages, compensation, penalty, or otherwise, including the granting of an injunction to restrain any like breach in the future, as the court, in the circumstances of each case, thinks fit.

(3) A lessor shall be entitled to recover as a debt due to him from a lessee, and in addition to damages (if any), all reasonable costs and expenses properly incurred by the lessor in the employment of a solicitor and surveyor or valuer, or otherwise, in reference to any breach giving rise to a right of re-entry or forfeiture which, at the request of the lessee, is waived by the lessor, or from which the lessee is relieved, under the provisions of this Act.

(4) Where a lessor is proceeding by action or otherwise to enforce a right of re-entry or forfeiture under any covenant, proviso, or stipulation in a lease, or for non-payment of rent, the court may, on application by any person claiming as under-lessee any estate or interest in the property comprised in the lease or any part thereof, either in the lessor's action (if any) or in any action brought by such person for that purpose, make an order vesting, for the whole term of the lease or any less term, the property comprised in the lease or any part thereof in any person entitled as under-lessee to any estate or interest in such property upon such conditions as to execution of any deed or other document, payment of rent, costs, expenses, damages, compensation, giving security, or otherwise, as the court in the circumstances of each case may think fit, but in no case shall any such under-lessee be entitled to require a lease to be granted to him for any longer term than he had under his original sub-lease.

(5) For the purposes of this section:

(a) "Lease" includes an original or derivative under-lease; also an agreement for a lease where the lessee has become entitled to have his lease granted; also a grant at a fee farm rent, or securing a rent by condition;

(b) "Lessee" includes an original or derivative under-lessee, and the persons deriving title under a lessee; also a grantee under any such grant as aforesaid and the persons deriving title under him;

(c) "Lessor" includes an original or derivative under-lessor, and the persons deriving title under a lessor; also a person making such grant as aforesaid and the persons deriving title under him;

(d) "Under-lease" includes an agreement for an underlease where the underlessee has become entitled to have his underlease granted;

(e) "Underlessee" includes any person deriving title under an underlessee.

(6) This section applies although the proviso or stipulation under which the right of re-entry or forfeiture accrues is inserted in the lease in pursuance of the directions of any Act of Parliament.

(7) For the purposes of this section a lease limited to continue as long only as the lessee abstains from committing a breach of covenant shall be and take effect as a lease to continue for any longer term for which it could subsist, but determinable by a proviso for re-entry on such a breach.

(8) This section does not extend:

(i) To a covenant or condition against assigning, underletting, parting with the possession, or disposing of the land leased where the breach occurred before the commencement of this Act; or

(ii) In the case of a mining lease, to a covenant or condition for allowing the lessor to have access to or inspect books, accounts, records, weighing machines or other things, or to enter or inspect the mine or the workings thereof.

(9) This section does not apply to a condition for forfeiture on the bankruptcy of the lessee or on taking in execution of the lessee's interest if contained in a lease of:

(a) Agricultural or pastoral land;

(b) Mines or minerals;

(c) A house used or intended to be used as a public-house or beershop;

(d) A house let as a dwelling-house, with the use of any furniture, books, works of art, or other chattels not being in the nature of fixtures;

(e) Any property with respect to which the personal qualifications of the tenant are of importance for the preservation of the value or character of the property, or on the ground of neighbourhood to the lessor, or to any person holding under him.

(10) Where a condition of forfeiture on the bankruptcy of the lessee or on taking in execution of the lessee's interest is contained in any lease, other than a lease of any of the classes mentioned in the last subsection, then:

(a) if the lessee's interest is sold within one year from the bankruptcy or taking in execution, this section applies to the forfeiture condition aforesaid;

(b) if the lessee's interest is not sold before the expiration of that year, this section only applies to the forfeiture condition aforesaid during the first year from the date of the bankruptcy or taking in execution.

(11) This section does not, save as otherwise mentioned, affect the law relating to re-entry or forfeiture or relief in case of nonpayment of rent.

(12) This section has effect notwithstanding any stipulation to the contrary.

The person on whom the section 146 notice should be served was considered in *Old Grovebury Manor Farm Ltd v W Seymour Plant Sales Ltd* (No. 2).

Case 89 *Old Grovebury Manor Farm Ltd v W Seymour Plant Sales Ltd (No. 2)* (1979) 38 P & CR 374 Walton J

By clause 2 (10) of a lease dated January 3, 1975, whereby certain property was demised to the second defendant by the plaintiff landlords, the second defendant convenanted, as tenant, not to assign, underlet or part with the possession of the demised premises without the written consent of the landlords. The lease contained a proviso for forfeiture on a breach of covenant. On September 23, 1976, the second defendant purported to assign the residue of the lease to the first defendant without first obtaining the landlords' consent. The landlords served a notice on the second defendant under section 146 of the Law of Property Act 1925 requiring the breach to be rectified, and later they brought an action to forfeit the lease.

On a preliminary issue as to whether the section 146 notice had to be served by the landlords on the assignor or the assignee:

Held (1) That the notice under section 146 of the Law of Property Act 1925 had to be served on the assignee and not on the assignor because the assignee was the person in whom the term was properly vested and because the object of the section was to give the persons who were affected by the proposed forfeiture of the lease an opportunity of considering their position.

Walton J said (in part)
The question is when one has had an assignment as one has had here, which is in flagrant breach of the provisions of the lease, whether the section 146 notice which must nevertheless undoubtedly be served has to be served by the landlord upon the assignor or the assignee. Section 146 (1) says that it must be served upon the lessee. [Counsel for the landlords] has basically argued that the assignment purported to be made by the orginal lessee is one which—and he has used a variety of epithets concerning it—is *quoad* the landlords invalid or is unlawful, or the legitimacy of the assignee's title to the lease is disputed by the landlords.

He says that under those circumstances the landlord naturally serves the person with whom he was in contractual relationship and not the person with whom he says he has no such relationship, being entitled to forfeit the lease as a consequence of what has taken place by way of the assignment in breach of covenant.

I think if one stands back and looks at the object of the section, one becomes immediately highly suspicious of that approach. The object of the section is to give the person who is affected by the proposed forfeiture of the lease by the landlord an opportunity of considering his position. It may not, of course, be an opportunity which will enable him to put everything to rights. There are a large number of breaches of covenant, and the present is a very good example of their number, which are breaches which are of their very nature irremediable. Under those circumstances, it is not possible for the person to whom the notice is addressed, in any event, to remedy the breach. It has been well established by a series of cases that nevertheless the section 146 notice must go, but of course in those cases, as the section itself says, if the breach is not capable of remedy the lessor does not in the terms of the notice have to require the lessee to remedy it.

But the whole purpose of the notice is to give the person to whom it is addressed reasonable time, depending on the circumstances of the case, for him to consider his position. If authority for that is required, it is to be found in the speech of Lord Russell of Killowen CJ in *Horsey Estate Ltd v Steiger* [1899] 2 QB 79.

It follows from that that the notice would not be of much use unless it is addressed to a person who can make some use of it. The most obvious use that can be made of it in the case of irremediable breach, a breach which cannot be remedied, is that the person to whom it is addressed will put himself in a position to apply for relief from forfeiture, as is provided by section 146 (2). What in any particular circumstances he ought to do to put himself in the best position to persuade the court to grant him relief from forfeiture of course depends very much upon the facts of each particular case.

But unless the notice is addressed to the person who is in a proper position and to whose advantage it will be to make such application, the notice would be totally useless. In a case such as the present, where there has been an assignment in breach of covenant, it would be utterly and completely useless— at any rate in the vast majority of cases—to address the notice to the assignor. The assignor has by now parted with all his interest in the property. Whatever the situation may be as between the assignee and the landlord—which I shall examine in a moment—as between the assignor and the assignee the assignor has parted with all interest in the property, doubtless at a price, and although it is conceivable that there might be some contractual comeback between the two, the chances are that there will be none.

In any event the landlord serving the section 146 notice cannot know that there would be any such comeback. So if the notice is addressed to the assignor tenant it is probably addressed to the wrong person, and therefore as a purely practical matter one would not expect it to have to be addressed to him.

The effect of the service of the writ claiming forfeiture was considered in *Associated Deliveries Ltd v Harrison*.

Case 90 *Associated Deliveries Ltd v Harrison* (1984) 272 EG 321
Court of Appeal

The plaintiff was an underlessee of premises and after six years of the twenty one year lease a subunderlease was granted to A and thereafter assigned to B. In October 1979 a writ was served on A and B claiming forfeiture of the lease, but the premises were not repossessed until November 1980. The importance of the date lay in the fact that between those dates extensive deterioration has occurred to the premises due in large part to vandalism.

Held (1) The service of the writ operated as a decisive election to forfeit, put an end to the covenants and fixed the date for the assessment of damages.

Dillon LJ said (in part)
The rule that service of a writ operates as a decisive election to forfeit and puts an end to the term of the lease in question and so has the result that the quandam lessee is a trespasser thereafter, has been laid down in the clearest terms by decisions which are binding on this court today. I refer in particular to the decision in *Jones v Carter* (1846) 15 M & W 718 and the decision of this court in *Canas Property Co Ltd v KL Television Services Ltd* [1970] 2 QB 433. The latter case decided conclusively that the relevant moment when the determination of the lease and notional re-entry into the premises took place was the date of the service, rather than the issue, of the writ. Consequently it follows that from the date of service a landlord is entitled to recover payments for the occupation of the land from the ex-lessee as trespasser as mesne profits, or damages for trespass, and not as rent under the lease. He may well find this advantageous to him, in that mesne profits may be higher than the rent. If not, however, he must abide by his election.

None the less, [counsel] sought to argue that liability under the covenant to deliver up continues. As one way of putting the argument he referred to the decision of the House of Lords in *Photo Productions Ltd v Securicor Transport Ltd* [1980] AC 827, and particularly to the distinction which Lord Diplock in his speech in that case drew between primary obligations and secondary obligations. Lord Diplock said this:

"When there has been a fundamental breach or breach of condition, the coming to an end of the primary obligations of both parties to the contract at the election of the party not in default, is often referred to as the 'determination' or 'rescission' of the contract or, as in the Sale of Goods Act 1893 'treating the contract as repudiated'."

He then referred to certain cases where:

"the bringing to an end of all primary obligations under the contract may also leave the parties in a relationship, typically that of bailor and bailee, in which they owe to one another by operation of law fresh primary obligations of which the contract is the source."

He went on also to consider the secondary obligations which would arise at the end of the primary obligations and in particular the secondary obligation to pay damages arising on breach of the primary obligations, which might none the less be, and was in that particular case, tempered by the continuance of a provision in the contract, namely a liability exclusion clause.

[Counsel] submits that the obligation to deliver up is a secondary obligation of the sort Lord Diplock was referring to, which therefore survived the breach of the primary obligations and the determination of the contract. Alternatively, the obligation to deliver up was itself a primary obligation, which survived.

I cannot accept those submissions. The obligation to repair and the obligation to deliver up in good repair are both, as I see it, primary obligations, and the obligation to deliver up is an obligation to deliver up at the expiration or sooner determination of the term; that is, in the events which happened, the service of the proceedings in October 1979. I see no basis in the *Photo Productions* case for holding that that obligation to deliver up continued to apply as at a much later date. The former lessee in all these cases where the lease has been forfeited for breach of covenant is evicted as a trespasser in an action for ejectment and not on the covenant to deliver up.

[Counsel] also relied strongly on some observations of Roskill LJ in this court in the case of *Industrial Properties (Barton Hill) Ltd v Associated Electrical Industries Ltd* [1977] QB 580, particularly at p 610, where the learned Lord Justice made comments to the effect that a landlord could sue on the covenant in a lease even though his estate in the land or the estate granted by the lease was gone. That case, however, was concerned with a wholly different state of affairs. It was concerned with the question whether the tenant could deny his landlord's title after the term of the lease had expired and so avoid liability on his covenant on the ground that in truth the landlord had had no title to grant to the tenant the term the tenant had enjoyed. It was not a case concerned with forfeiture by the landlord of the tenant's interest at all; it was not a case concerned with intervention by a third party claiming by title paramount either. What it established was that the tenant was estopped from denying his landlord's title and so could be sued on the covenant, despite the expiration of the term and despite any defects in that title. In the present context of forfeiture proceedings the estoppel is the other way, as was pointed out by Parke B in *Jones v Carter*, in that the landlord having elected to forfeit the lease by the unequivocal act of serving proceedings for possession, is estopped from treating the term of the lease and the covenants in the lease as still on foot for the purpose, in *Jones v Carter*, of suing the tenant for rent. I do not therefore find in Roskill LJ's observations anything that assists [counsel] in the context of the present case.

He puts his submission more attractively on the ground that the defendants' attitudes, and not least the defence served by Mr Harrison [original first defendant], precluded that plaintiff from getting possession except by order of the court. Mr Pritchard [second defendant] was in possession and Mr Harrison, by his pleading, was asserting that the lease continued in force and so the defendants, having relied on the lease, should not now be heard to say that the covenants in it no longer subsisted. It is not put so much on estoppel as the allied principle that a party cannot blow hot and cold in that if he takes the benefit under a document he must take the burden of it also; or, as it is sometimes put, if he is holding under the lease or under colour of the lease he must accept the restrictions of the lease also.

In support of this submission [counsel] referred to a number of well-known authorities which are concerned with relief against forfeiture. One is *Dendy v Evans* [1910] 1 KB 263, a decision of this court. That held that where relief against forfeiture is granted, then the granting of the relief restored the lessee to his position as if the lease had never been forfeited and so entitled him to recover interim rent from an underlessee. Nobody doubts the correctness of that decision, but it is a long way from the present case in that in the present case relief against forfeiture was neither sought nor ever granted.

[Counsel] referred also to two decisions which were concerned with what might happen during the twilight period until it was known whether relief against forfeiture, which had been claimed, was going to be granted or not. One of those was the decision of the Vice-Chancellor in *Meadows v Clerical, Medical & General Life Assurance Society* [1981] Ch 70, where it was held that, during the period while an application for relief against forfeiture was pending, the lessee had a sufficient standing to apply under the Landlord and Tenant Act 1954 for the grant of a new tenancy. No doubt whether he got the new tenancy would depend upon whether he got relief against forfeiture in the end.

The other decision on the same lines was a decision of this court in *Driscoll v Church Commissioners for England* [1957] 1 QB 330, where during the period while an application for relief against forfeiture was pending the tenant made an application to the Lands Tribunal for the variation of the covenants in the lease, and it was held that he had a sufficient interest in the property to support that application. The only direct relevance of the case is that in his judgment Denning LJ recognised a parallel between the case where forfeiture was claimed and the case where the right to forfeit was disputed. He said, at p 340:

"... although a writ is an unequivocal election, nevertheless, until the action is finally determined in favour of the landlord, the covenant does not cease to be potentially good. For instance, the forfeiture may not be established; or relief may be granted in which case the lease is re-established as from the beginning."

There is, therefore, this twilight period during which it is not clear whether a forfeiture is going to be effective, if, for instance, the allegations of breach of covenant are denied, or if for any reason it is said that the procedural requirements of modern statutes have not been complied with, or relief against forfeiture may be granted, which will restore the original lease *ab initio*. Problems can arise in that period; we were referred to a decision of this court in *Peninsular Maritime Ltd v Padseal Ltd* (1981) 259 EG 860, in which, on a cross-undertaking in damages from the lessee whose lease was alleged to have been forfeited, a landlord was ordered by way of interim injunction to restore and repair, as far as he could, the lift service to the upper floors demised by the lease of a particular building. That, as it seems to me, is the sort of state of affairs which may well arise and would have to be dealt with, as it was in the *Peninsular Maritime* case, on the accepted principles applicable to the grant of interlocutory relief. It is not a decision which binds this court to conclude that the landlords' covenants, let alone the tenants' covenants, continue to subsist and be enforceable during the twilight period; it is a practical decision, essentially on balance of convenience, to deal with a problem that has arisen until such time as the court can decide whether the covenants subsist or not. I do not therefore find it of great assistance in this case, except in that it was the occasion for drawing the attention of the court to the decision of Younger J in *Wheeler v Keeble Ltd* (1914) [1920] 1 Ch 57.

In *Wheeler v Keeble* the plaintiffs had issued a writ to forfeit a lease, claiming possession of the premises and damages for breaches of covenant contained in the lease. They moved for an interlocutory injunction to restrain the defendant from erecting, or permitting to remain erected, certain lettering on the front of the premises in breach of the covenants contained in the lease. In point of fact the notice was removed and the case was argued mainly on the question of costs and on the right of the plaintiffs to apply to enforce the covenant in the lease after the service of their writ claiming possession and thus forfeiting the lease.

The case was argued at considerable length, not least by Mr Clauson, as he then was, for the plaintiffs, and Younger J delivered a careful and thorough judgment. He cited first the case of *Jones v Carter* and he read the important passage in the judgment of Parke B. He then referred to earlier authority to the same effect in the judgment of Ashurst J in the case of *Birch v Wright*, decided in (1786) 1 TR 378, and at the foot of p 63 he said this:

> "It seems to me that no change has been made by subsequent procedure in the principles which are laid down in these two cases, and that accordingly it is not permissible for the plaintiffs in this action—based as it is on the determination of the lease— either in the writ itself or in any proceedings subsequent to the writ to claim relief on the footing that the lease is a subsisting lease, the terms of which continue to be binding on the defendants. In my opinion therefore the plaintiffs are not entitled to obtain the injunction which they ask by simply referring to the terms of the lease. If they are entitled to an injunction at all it must be apart from the terms of the lease and solely in respect of their own interest in the premises and of some irreparable injury which may be sustained by them through the acts of the defendants on the plaintiffs' own property in case those acts are likely to continue."

By that he plainly meant an injunction founded on a cause of action in tort.

He went on to refer to various arguments that had been submitted, including an argument that the breach of covenant relied on was a continuing breach. In respect of that he said:

> "If it was a continuing breach, it ceased to be a breach by the destruction of the covenant."

By that I understand him to mean the destruction of the covenant by the re-entry of the landlord by the service of the writ claiming possession.

He then carefully examined a decision of Stirling J in the case of *Read v Wotton* [1893] 2 Ch 171 and he held that he was entitled not to follow that decision because it was not consistent with earlier authorities and had apparently been decided without full argument. In particular Younger J rejected the view, which Stirling J had expressed in his judgment, that he was entitled to award damages for breach of a covenant in the lease down to the date of the assessment of the damages at the trial.

The rejection of that view of Stirling J is, in my judgment, supported by a passage in the judgment of Denning LJ in *Smiley v Townshend* [1950] 2 KB 311, at p 319, when he was referring to an argument that what might happen, in a case where at the determination of the lease the premises were in the hands of a requisitioning authority, was that the requisitioning authority might thereafter do the repairs which were the subject of a claim for damages, so that the landlord would suffer no damage. Denning LJ said:

> "I appreciate the force of both those arguments; and, if the correct measure of damage were such a sum as represents the damage which the landlord will sustain when he gets the premises back, that would have great weight. But the answer to them both is that the damages must be assessed not by reference to the time when the land reverts in possession, but as at the end of the lease. I take it from authorities which this court is not at liberty to disregard that the proper measure of damage is the difference in value of the reversion at the end of the lease between the premises in their then state of unrepair and in the state in which they would have been if the covenants had been fulfilled."

Therefore, as it seems to me, Younger J's decision in *Wheeler v Keeble* is correct in principle and should be applied. [Counsel] cannot succeed in this appeal without our holding that Younger J's decision was wrong, and for my part I am not prepared to hold that.

6.3. Contents and service of the section 146 Notice

The contents of the section 146 notice is stipulated in section 146 (1), namely it must

   (i) specify the breach complained of, and
  (ii) require the breach to be remedied, if it is capable of remedy, and
 (iii) require compensation in money.

In addition, if the Leasehold Property (Repairs) Act 1938 applies the notice must contain a statement that the tenant can serve a counternotice claiming the provisions of that Act. For a section

146 notice to comply with the 1938 Act it must be served before the breach is remedied.

Case 91 SEDAC Investments Ltd v Tanner (1982) 44 P & CR 319.
Mr Michael Wheeler QC (sitting as a deputy High Court judge)

Clause 2 (2) of a lease for 14 years from August 24, 1974, contained a general repairing covenant by the lessees. Clause 2 (4) gave the lessors a right to call on the lessees to remedy a breach and, if they failed to do so, the lessors could themselves remedy it. On April 25, 1980, the lessees, without appreciating their obligation to repair, became aware that stonework on the front wall of the premises was so loose that fragments at first floor level were falling on the pavement below. They informed the lessors so as to make sure that the lessors' insurance covered them against any possible claims for injuries to passers-by. The lessors made immediate arrangements for a chartered engineer to inspect the premises. His opinion was that repair work should be carried out as a matter of urgency. Following the engineer's advice the work was started on May 1 and was completed by May 9 at a cost of about £3,000. On January 5, 1981, the lessors' solicitors served a notice under section 146 (1) of the Law of Property Act 1925 pointing out that the lessees were in breach of the covenant in clause 2 (2) of the lease and that the lessors had remedied the breach. The notice required compensation of £3,000 to be made to the lessors. It further stated that if the lessees failed to comply with the notice, the lessors intended to claim damages against them. The lessees' solicitors served a counter-notice claiming the benefit of the Leasehold Property (Repairs) Act 1938. In their covering letter they made it clear that the counter-notice was without prejudice to the lessees' claim that the lessors' section 146 notice was void.

On the lessors' summons for leave under section 1 (2) of the 1938 Act to commence proceedings against the lessees for damages for breach of the repairing covenant:

Held, Dismissing the summons, (1) that on its true construction section 146 (1) of the 1925 Act related to a breach of any covenant and not merely to a breach of a repairing covenant, that it was primarily concerned with claims for, and relief against, forfeiture and that the notice given under it must contain the information mentioned in paragraphs (a), (b) and (c), i.e. the breach complained of, requiring the lessee to remedy the breach, if possible, and requiring the

lessee to make compensation in money for the breach; that
reading those provisions with section 1 (2) of the 1938 Act,
the section 146 notice required to be served clearly contemplated a situation where the breach had not been remedied
at the date of the service of the notice; and that, accordingly,
the lessors' notice under section 146 was ineffective since
the breach had been remedied by the lessors and the notice
could not give the lessees the information referred to in section 146 (1) (a), (b) and (c) and thus the lessors were no
longer in a position to give a valid section 146 notice.

(2) That the scheme of section 1 of the 1938 Act contemplated a process beginning with a lessor giving a valid section 146 notice and if such a notice, to be effective, must
be served before the breach was remedied the service of
the notice would be invalid where, as here, the lessor remedied the breach before attempting to serve the notice; that
without a valid section 146 notice the lessees were deprived
of their right to serve a valid counter notice; and that, accordingly, the court had no jurisdiction to give the lessor leave
to commence proceedings for damages because that jurisdiction arose only when the lessee served a counter-notice.

Mr Michael Wheeler QC said (in part)
That being the position under section 146 (1) itself, what is
meant by the reference in section 1 (2) of the 1938 Act and section
18 (2) of the Landlord and Tenant Act 1927 to "such a notice
as is specified in section 146 (1) of the Law of Property Act 1925?"
In my judgment it means—and means only—a notice which contains the information required by section 146 (1) (a), (b) and (c).
As I have already stated, the natural meaning of those paragraphs is that they relate to a breach which, at the date of the
service of the notice, has not yet been remedied: and if that
is the correct construction of section 146 (1) it is difficult to avoid
the conclusion that the section 146 notice which the lessor has
to serve under section 1 (2) of the 1938 Act as a prerequisite
to enforcing a right to damages for breach of a repairing covenant
is similarly a notice which relates to a breach which at the date
of service has not yet been remedied.

If this be so, it would seem to follow that a lessor is no longer
in a position to give a valid section 146 notice if the breach in
respect of which he desires to claim damages has already been
remedied.

In construing section 1 of the 1938 Act the following points
appear to me to be relevant:

(i) under section 1 (2) the lessee's right to give a counter-notice claiming the benefit of the Act does not arise unless and until the lessor has duly served a section 146 notice on the lessee.

(ii) Under section 1 (3), once the lessee has given the counter-notice the lessor can only take proceedings for forfeiture or damages for breach of the repairing covenant in question with the leave of the court.

(iii) The importance which the Act attaches to the lessee's right to give a counter-notice is underlined by section 1 (4) which requires the lessor's section 146 notice to contain a conspicuous statement of the lessee's right to give a counter-notice and relevant details of the manner and time of service: and a notice which does not give that information is a bad notice.

(iv) Under section 1 (5), leave of the court is not to be given unless the lessor brings himself within one or more of five separate heads: of these, the last (set out in section 1 (5) (*e*)) is that the lessor proves "special circumstances which in the opinion of the court, render it just and equitable that leave should be given." It was under this head that the district registrar would have been prepared to act in the present case.

(v) Each of the first four of the separate heads in section 1 (5) imposes on a lessor who seeks leave of the court to commence proceedings the need to prove that the immediate remedying of the breach *is* required (my emphasis) for the purpose there stated. Thus in section (5) also, the draftsman appears to be contemplating that the breach will not yet have been remedied at the time when the lessor seeks the leave of the court.

In the light of the foregoing, it seems to me that the scheme of section 1 of the 1938 Act as a whole contemplates a series of consecutive steps which must be taken before the court can give leave to a lessor to enforce a claim for damages for breach of a repairing covenant, namely:

(1) The lessor must have served a section 146 notice which complied with section 1 (2) and section 1 (4) of the 1938 Act.

(2) The lessee must then have served a counter-notice which also complied with section 1 (2).

(3) The lessor must then have brought himself within one or more of the heads set out in section 1 (5).

If this be so, the power of the court to give a lessor leave to commence proceedings as contemplated by section 1 (3) of the 1938 Act arises (and arises only) where the lessor has duly served a section 146 notice and the lessee has then duly served

a counter-notice. The whole scheme of section 1 appears to commence with—and to hinge upon—the service of a valid lessor's
section 146 notice: and if, therefore, I am right in holding that
a section 146 notice, to be effective, must be served *before* the
breach is remedied, I am forced to the conclusion that in a case
such as the present, where the lessor remedied the breach before
attempting to serve a notice under section 146 (1) of the Law
of Property Act 1925, he has thereby put it out of his power
to serve a valid section 146 notice at all, with the result that
he has deprived the lessee of his right to serve a counter-notice:
and the consequence of this seems inevitably to be that the court
has no jurisdiction to give the lessor leave to commence proceedings for damages because that jurisdiction arises, as I have
already indicated, only when (and because) the lessee has served
a valid counter-notice.

I frankly confess that I have reached this conclusion with surprise and regret. Surprise, because the scheme of section 146
(1) of the 1925 Act itself (and more particularly as applied by
section 18 of the Landlord and Tenant Act 1927 and section 1
of the 1938 Act) appears to make no provision whatsoever for
the situation where the consequences of the breach of the repairing covenant require (or might reasonably be thought to require)
urgent attention and where, for example, the lessor takes immediate remedial action either of his own volition or, perhaps,
because the lessee is unable or unwilling to take the necessary
action sufficiently promptly. Regret, because I can see no reason
why, in such circumstances, the lessor should (as I have felt
bound to hold) be unable to apply to the court for leave to commence proceedings for damages merely because of his failure
to serve a notice which, on the facts of the present case, would
be unlikely to have had any effect other than, perhaps, to produce
a request by the lessees that the lessors should put in hand the
necessary repairs and that they should sort out the question
of the quantum of damages once that had been done. I see no
merit in the argument that by remedying the breach themselves
the lessors have thereby prevented the lessees from doing so,
possibly at less cost. That is a point which might well be argued
in the action for damages itself if the lessors got leave to commence such an action: so, too, could the more difficult question
as to whether the lessors could establish a claim for damages
having regard to the limitation on damages imposed by section
18 (1) of the 1927 Act. But I see no reason in principle why the
court should be unable to give leave to commence proceedings
for damages in any circumstances whatsoever (and even, it

would seem, in a "special circumstances" case which might otherwise come within section 1 (5) (*e*) of the 1938 Act) merely because a valid section 146 notice had not been served before the breach complained of had been remedied.

It is true that although under section 1 (2) a claim for damages for breach of a repairing covenant cannot be enforced by an action commenced prior to the last three years of the lease except with leave of the court, the lessor ceases to be under this restriction once the three year period has been reached *provided* (and that will be the position in the case before me) the claim for damages will not by then have become statute-barred. But I am bound to say that this possible impact (or lack of impact) of statutory limitation on the circumstances of any particular case seems to be undesirably and unsatisfactorily fortuitous.

It is also true, as was pointed out in argument, that in the present case, the lessors might have protected their position in other ways. For example, (1) they might have invoked clause 2 (4) of the lease and called upon the lessees to remedy the breach; and they could have reinforced this by seeking, or threatening to seek, a mandatory injunction on the lessees to undertake the necessary remedial work: alternatively, (2) they might have served a notice under section 146 (1) of the 1925 Act (however general and imprecise the terms of that notice might, in the circumstances, have had to be) and might have also stated that in view of the urgency they regarded it as essential (and, *ex hypothesi*, as reasonable) that the lessees should at least commence to remedy the breach within, say, 48 hours.

Note:

   (i) See the criticism of this decision in *Hamilton v Martell Securities* [Case 104].

In the normal course of events a reasonable time must be allowed in which to execute the repairs.

Case 92 *Myers v Oldschool* [1928] EGD 167 Divisional Court

In 1924 the defendant acquired the lessee's interest in the houses, which were divided into upper and lower floors, as separate rateable hereditaments, and were let to separate sets of weekly tenants of a very poor class. On December 3, 1926, the plaintiff wrote to the defendant representing that the plaintiff was the owner of the ground interest and complaining of the condition of the houses. The plaintiff was the ground landlord. On January 10, 1927, the plaintiff served his notice of forfeiture under section 146 of the Law of Property Act, 1925, for breach of covenant. It was a three months' notice, and was in respect of all the premises, and contained schedules of dilapidations in respect of each of the houses. There were about two thousand items on the schedules, which involved, among other things, the taking off and replacement of the roofs of houses on one side of a street in the months of January, February, March and a part of April. All the houses were occupied by tenants who could not be disturbed under the Rent Restrictions Act. The action was brought on the expiration of the three months given by the notice, and judgment was given for the plaintiff, but relief was granted to the defendants on the terms that the repairs must be done to the satisfaction of a surveyor, and that all the costs of the action and mesne profits, as well as two guineas damages, should be paid by the defendant.

Held (1) In considering whether a reasonable time had elapsed regard must be had to all the circumstances.

Slater J said (in part)
The position was that they were concerned in that case with seventeen separate leases for seventeen houses. The substantial question for decision was whether between the service of the notice and the issue of the writ a reasonable time had elapsed to enable the defendant to remedy the repairs. The houses were let in floors or rooms to poor people. They were occupied from the roof to the cellar by a great number of poor people—men, women and children. In considering the question whether a reasonable time had elapsed regard must be had to all the circumstances. The period allowed was three months and three days. The nature of the case, the admitted facts and the expert evidence showed conclusively that the plaintiff had not allowed a reasonable time to elapse before action.

Case 93 Scala House and District Property Co Ltd v Forbes [1974] 1 QB 573 Court of Appeal

By a lease dated February 8, 1968, the lessees covenanted not to assign underlet or part with the possession of the demised premises without the landlord's consent. The lease was assigned to the first defendant with the landlord's consent and he used the premises as a restaurant. He intended to enter into an agreement with the second and third defendants to manage the restaurant but the written agreement, in fact, created a subtenancy and, therefore, he was in breach of covenant. The plaintiff, who had acquired the reversion of the lease, served on the defendants a notice under section 146 of the Law of Property Act 1925 requiring them to remedy the breach and, after 14 days, issued a writ for possession of the premises. Nield J held that the breach was capable of remedy and, since 14 days between the notice and the issue of the writ was too short a time for the defendants to remedy the breach, he dismissed the action.

On appeal by the plaintiff:

Held (1) Allowing the appeal but granting relief from forfeiture, that a breach of covenant not to assign underlet or part with possession was not a breach capable of remedy within the meaning of section 146 (1) of the Law of Property Act 1925 and, therefore, 14 days was a sufficient time to elapse between the service of the notice under the section and the date of the writ.

Russell LJ said (in part)

So the first question is whether a breach of covenant such as is involved in the present case is capable of remedy. If it is capable of remedy, and is remedied in reasonable time, the lessor is unable to prove that a condition precedent to his ability to seek to forfeit by action or otherwise has been fufilled. Here at once is a problem. An unlawful subletting is a breach once and for all. The subterm has been created. . . .

In *Hoffmann v Fineberg* [1949] Ch 245 (Harman J), the lessee, in breach of user covenants, allowed the premises to be used for illegal gambling, for which there were convictions. The section 146 notice did not call for the breach to be remedied. It is not clear whether the illegal user continued at the date of the notice. Again the decision was based on the "stigma" aspect as making the breach incapable of remedy within a reasonable time. Harman J said, at p. 257: ". . . on the facts of this case this is a breach where mere cesser is no remedy." The judgment referred to another immoral user case of *Egerton v Esplanade Hotels, London Ltd* [1947] 2 All ER 88 (Morris J), in which the notice did not call for the breach to be remedied: it was decided on the stigma point, on the facts of that case, that the breach was not capable of remedy within a reasonable time. Morris J said at p. 91:

"Merely desisting from the wrongful user or not continuing to commit further breaches is not, . . . on the facts of this case, a way of remedying the breach."

Neither case was considered on the possible shorter ground that a user covenant breach when the user had ceased before the section 146 notice was incapable of remedy for that very reason.

Glass v Kencakes Ltd [1966] 1 QB 611, a decision of Paull J, was of this nature. The lease forbade the use of the upper part of the premises otherwise than for residential purposes. The lessee sublet that part to D, who caused and permitted their use for the business of prostitution unknown to the lessee. The sublease contained a similar covenant. The section 146 notice was simply based upon the fact of business use. It asserted that the breach was incapable of remedy. The judge held that the breach of the sublease by D was incapable of remedy by him: apparently he considered that the person who caused or permitted such a use could not, by the cesser of such use, remedy the breach, because the stigma on the premises could not be blotted out within a reasonable time so long as the man responsible remained sub-tenant. He therefore could not remedy his breach. Paull J pointed out that in the *Rugby School* case [1934] 1 KB 695, in *Egerton v Esplanade Hotels, London Ltd* [1947] 2 All ER 88 (both cases of immoral user) and in *Hoffmann v Fineberg* [1949] Ch 245 (the illegal gambling case) it was in each case the tenant under the lease sought to be forfeited who was directly responsible for the breach: and that in the *Borthwick-Norton* case [1950] 1 All ER 798 the lessee had in breach suffered and permitted the immoral user by a subtenant. Paull J decided, however, that, where the breach alleged was merely of a user by a subtenant for which the lessee whose lease was sought to be forfeited could not be said to have permitted or suffered or to be in any way responsible for, the breach was not incapable of remedy by the lessee, the remedy required being not only the cesser of the user in breach but also the ending of the subterm with all expedition by forfeit-ure. Paull J was much impressed by the argument that where there was a lease for a large block of flats, one of which without any fault of the lessee, was used for a short time in breach of the user covenant in the lease by a subtenant, he should not be put in the situation that he was not capable of remedying the breach and must therefore be put to the expense of seeking relief from forfeiture. He held in that case that the notice was bad since it asserted that the breach was not capable of remedy.

Two points are to be noticed in that case. First: Paull J did not address his mind, particularly in the case of the large block of flats mentioned, to the possible situation of the lessee if the subletting in question, and therefore the unlawful user, had come to an end before discovery by the head lessor, when no remedial step would have been available to the lessee, and whether in such case the lessee could only have sought relief. Second: the decision in terms says nothing of a case (other than "stigma" cases) where the lessee is directly responsible for the breach by a business user contrary to covenant. . . .

After this review of the cases I come to the conclusion that breach by an unlawful subletting is not capable of remedy at all. In my judgment the introduction of such breaches into the relevant section for the first time by section 146 of the Act of 1925 operates only to confer a statutory ability to relieve the lessee from forfeiture on that ground. The subterm has been effectively created subject only to risks of forfeiture: it is a complete breach once for all: it is not in any sense a continuing breach. If the law were otherwise a lessee, when a subtenancy is current at the time of the section 146 notice, would have a chance of remedying the situation without having to apply for relief. But if the unlawful subletting had determined before the notice, the lessee could only seek relief from forfeiture. The only escape from that wholly unsatisfactory difference would be to hold that in the second example by some analogy the lessor was disabled from issuing a writ for possession. But I can find nothing in the section to justify that limitation on the common law right of re-entry, bearing especially in mind that a lessor might discover a whole series of past expired unlawful sublettings which might well justify a refusal to grant relief in forfeiture proceedings.

I stress again that where there has been an unlawful subletting which has determined (and which has not been waived) there has been a breach which at common law entitles the lessor to re-enter; nothing can be done to remedy that breach; the expiry of the subterm has not annulled or remedied the breach; in such case the lessor plainly need not, in his section 146 notice, call upon the lessee to remedy the breach which is not capable of remedy, and is free to issue his writ for possession, the possibility of relief remaining. Can it possibly be that, while this is the situation in such case, it is otherwise if the lessee has failed to get rid of the subterm until after a notice is served? Is the lessee

then in a stronger position and the lessor in a weaker position?
In my judgment not so.

Case 94 Expert Clothing Service & Sales Ltd v Hillgate House Ltd
[1985] 2 EGLR 85; (1985) 275 EG 1011 Court of Appeal

The least of 1978 provided that the defendant tenant was
to have "full licence and permission to demolish and reconstruct the interior and roof of the demised premises" subject
to the proviso that "the tenant shall commence the said
works of demolition and reconstruction within a period of
three years from the commencement date". A subsequent
county court consent order provided that the reconstruction
was to be "substantially completed and ready for occupation
by or before the 28th day of September 1982 and fully completed as soon as reasonably possible thereafter". When no
works had been commenced by that date the plaintiffs' solicitors served on the defendants a section 146 notice which
stipulated that the breaches complained of were incapable
of remedy. The defendants claimed relief from forfeiture.

Held (1) The breach of covenant to reconstruct was capable
of remedy within section 146 (1).

(2) If the section 146 notice had required the defendant
to remedy the breach and if the plaintiffs had allowed a
reasonable time to comply with the covenant, the dependant
might have undertaken the reconstruction. Such reconstruction [together with appropriate monetary compensation]
would have remedied the breach. The section 146 notice
was, therefore, invalid.

(3) In all the circumstances the plaintiffs had not waived
their right to forfeit.

Slade LJ said (in part)

. . . in considering whether or not remedy within a reasonable
time is possible, a crucial distinction (which I infer from the judgment did not feature prominently in argument before the learned
judge) falls to be drawn between breaches of negative user covenants, such as those under consideration in the *Rugby School*
and the *Esplanade Hotels* cases, and breaches of positive covenants. In the two last-mentioned cases, where the relevant
breaches consisted of allowing premises to be used as a brothel,
even full compliance with the covenant within a reasonable time
and for a reasonable time would not have remedied the breach.
As Maugham LJ pointed out in the *Rugby School* case (at p 94);
"Merely ceasing for a reasonable time, perhaps a few weeks

or a month, to use the premises for an immoral purpose would be no remedy for the breach of covenant which had been committed over a long period." On the facts of cases such as those, mere cesser by the tenant of the offending use within a reasonable period and for a reasonable period of time could not have remedied the breaches because it would not have removed the stigma which they had caused to attach to the premises. The harm had been irretrievably done. In such cases, as Harman J pointed out in *Hoffman v Fineberg* [1949] Ch 245 at p 257, mere cesser will not enable the tenant to "make his record clean, as he could by complying, though out of time, with a failure to lay on the prescribed number of coats of paint".

In contrast with breaches of negative user covenants, the breach of a positive covenant to do something (such as to decorate or build) can ordinarily, for practical purposes, be remedied by the thing being actually done if a reasonable time for its performance (running from the service of the section 146 notice) is duly allowed by the landlord following such service and the tenant duly does it within such time.

In the present case there is no question of the breach of the covenant to reconstruct having given rise to any "stigma" against the lessors or the premises. Significantly, the lease in 1982 still had 20 years to run. [Counsel] has, I think, been able to suggest no convincing reasons why the plaintiffs would still have suffered irremediable damage if (i) the section 146 notice had required the lessee to remedy the breach and (ii) the lessors had then allowed a reasonable time to elapse sufficient to enable the lessee to comply with the relevant covenant, and (iii) the lessee had complied with the covenant in such reasonable time and had paid any appropriate monetary compensation. Though he has submitted that a requirement, directed to the defendants, to remedy the breach would have been purposeless, on the grounds that they had neither the financial means nor the will to do the necessary work, these are matters which, in my opinion, a landlord is not entitled to prejudge in drafting his notice. An important purpose of the section 146 procedure is to give even tenants who have hitherto lacked the will or the means to comply with their obligations one last chance to summon up that will or find the necessary means before the landlord re-enters. In considering what "reasonable time" to allow the defendants, the plaintiffs, in serving their section 146 notice, would, in my opinion, have been entitled to take into account the fact that the defendants had already enjoyed 15 months in which to fulfil their contractual obligations to reconstruct and to subject the defendants to a cor-

respondingly tight timetable running from the date of service
of the notice, though, at the same time, always bearing in mind
that the contractual obligation to reconstruct did not even arise
until June 29 1981, and that as at October 8 1982 the defendants
had been in actual breach of it for only some 10 days. However,
I think they were not entitled to say, in effect: "We are not going
to allow you any time at all to remedy the breach, because you
have had so long to do the work already."

In my judgment, on the remediability issue, the ultimate question for the court was this: If the section 146 notice had required
the lessee to remedy the breach and the lessors had then allowed
a reasonable time to elapse to enable the lessee fully to comply
with the relevant covenant, would such compliance, coupled
with the payment of any appropriate monetary compensation,
have effectively remedied the harm which the lessors had suffered or were likely to suffer from the breach? If, but only if,
the answer to this question was "no", would the failure of the
section 146 notice to require remedy of the breach have been
justifiable? In the *Rugby School, Esplanade* and *Hoffman* cases, the
answer to this question plainly would have been "no". In the
present case, however, for the reasons already stated, I think
the answer to it must have been "yes".

My conclusion, therefore, is that the breach of the covenant
to reconstruct, no less than the breach of the covenant to give
notice of charges, was "capable of remedy". In reaching this
conclusion, I find it reassuring that no reported case has been
brought to our attention in which the breach of a positive covenant has been held incapable of remedy, though I do not suggest
that cases of this nature, albeit perhaps rarely, could not arise.

The service of the section 146 notice is governed by section 196
of the Law of Property Act 1925.

Statute 6: Law of Property Act 1925. Section 196

Regulations respecting notices
196.—(1) Any notice required or authorised to be served or given
by this Act shall be in writing.

(2) Any notice required or authorised by this Act to be served
on a lessee or mortgagor shall be sufficient, although only
addressed to the lessee or mortgagor by that designation, without his name or generally to the persons interested, without
any name, and notwithstanding that any person to be affected by
the notice is absent, under disability, unborn, or unascertained.

(3) Any notice required or authorised by this Act to be served shall be sufficiently served if it is left at the last-known place of abode or business in the United Kingdom of the lessee, lessor, mortgagee, mortgagor, or other person to be served, or, in case of a notice required or authorised to be served on a lessee or mortgagor, is affixed or left for him on the land or any house or building comprised in the lease or mortgage, or, in case of a mining lease, is left for the lessee at the office or counting-house of the mine.

(4) Any notice required or authorised by this Act to be served shall also be sufficiently served, if it is sent by post in a registered letter addressed to the lessee, lessor, mortgagee, mortgagor, or other person to be served, by name, at the aforesaid place of abode or business, office, or counting-house, and if that letter is not returned through the post-office undelivered; and that service shall be deemed to be made at the time at which the registered letter would in the ordinary course be delivered.

(5) The provisions of this section shall extend to notices required to be served by any instrument affecting property executed or coming into operation after the commencement of this Act unless a contrary intention appears.

(6) This section does not apply to notices served in proceedings in the court.

Note:

(i) As a result of the Recorded Delivery Service Act 1962 the recorded delivery service can be used as an alternative to the registered service.

A person is deemed to have knowledge of the service of a section 146 notice if the provisions of section 18 (2) of the Landlord and Tenant Act 1927 are applicable.

Statute 7: Landlord and Tenant Act 1927. Section 18 (2)

18.—(2) A right of re-entry or forfeiture for a breach of any such covenant or agreement as aforesaid shall not be enforceable, by action or otherwise, unless the lessor proves that the fact that such a notice as is required by section one hundred and forty-six of the Law of Property Act 1925, had been served on the lessee was known either:

(a) to the lessee; or
(b) to an under-lessee holding under an under-lease which reserved a nominal reversion only to the lessee; or

(c) to the person who last paid the rent due under the lease either on his own behalf or as agent for the lessee or under-lessee;

and that a time reasonably sufficient to enable the repairs to be executed had elapsed since the time when the fact of the service of the notice came to the knowledge of any such person.

Where a notice has been sent by registered post addressed to a person at his last known place of abode in the United Kingdom, then, for the purposes of this subsection, that person shall be deemed, unless the contrary is proved, to have had knowledge of the fact that the notice had been served as from the time at which the letter would have been delivered in the ordinary course of post.

6.4 Landlord's remedy: Relief for the tenant or waiver

If the landlord's claim for forfeiture is successful it will result in the obtaining of possession of the demised premises. The tenant may, however, be able to successfully sustain a claim that the landlord has waived his right to forfeit the lease or the tenant may be able to obtain relief from forfeiture.

Case 95 *Farimani v Gates* (1984) 271 EG 887 Court of Appeal

The tenant held the long lease of a building which became severely damaged by fire and there was a delay in reaching a settlement with the insurers. The appellant-tenant had covenanted to insure and keep insured the demised premises and in the event of damage or destruction by fire to lay out the insurance moneys in rebuilding or repairing the premises. Having served the section 146 notice the land-lord made a peaceable re-entry and forfeited the lease. In the county court the tenant's claim for relief from forfeiture was dismissed but it had been tried in that court on the basis that the breach complained of was not the breach speci-fied in the section 146 notice.

Held (1) That the breach of the obligation to lay out the insurance moneys was not a breach of a repairing covenant and therefore the landlord's section 146 (1) notice was not rendered invalid by a failure to include the statements required by the Leasehold Property (Repairs) Act 1938;

(2) That the breach was a breach of a single obligation, not a continuing one;

(3) That the tenant's obligation to lay out the insurance moneys was subject to an implied obligation to do so within

a reasonable time and was broken when that time had passed;

(4) That the acceptance of rent by the landlord after that breach constituted a waiver of the right to forfeit, so that his subsequent entry into possession was unlawful.

Griffiths LJ said (in part)

It is submitted that the section 146 notice was invalid because it did not comply with section 1 (1) and (4) of the Leasehold Property (Repairs) Act 1938 which provides:

"1 (1) Where a lessor serves on a lessee under subsection (1) of section one hundred and forty-six of the Law of Property Act, 1925, a notice that relates to a breach of a covenant or agreement to keep or put in repair during the currency of the lease a house of a rateable value of one hundred pounds or less, and at the date of the service of the notice five years or more of the term of the lease remain unexpired, the lessee may within twenty-eight days from that date serve on the lessor a counter-notice to the effect that he claims the benefit of this Act.

(4) A notice served under subsection (1) of section one hundred and forty-six of the Law of Property Act, 1925, in the circumstances specified in subsection (1) of this section, and a notice served under subsection (2) of this section shall not be valid unless it contains a statement, in characters not less conspicuous than those used in any other part of the notice, to the effect that the lessee is entitled under this Act to serve on the lessor a counter-notice claiming the benefit of this Act, and a statement in the like characters specifying the time within which, and the manner in which, under this Act a counter-notice may be served and specifying the name and address for service of the lessor."

It is conceded that the section 146 did not contain the statement set out in subsection (4). Whether or not it should have done so depends upon whether the covenant upon which the landlord relied was a covenant to keep or put in repair within the meaning of section 1 (1). The tenant points to the concluding words of the covenant "And if such money shall not be sufficient for such purpose they the lessees will at their own cost complete the rebuilding and repairing of such premises respectively and make them fit for habitation" and says, as a matter of plain English, that is a covenant to put in repair within the meaning of subsection (1), and he relies upon the obiter view expressed by Buckley

J as to the nature of such an obligation in *Re King decd* [1962] 1 WLR 632 at p. 645:

"... in the present case the covenant to reinstate the premises does, in my judgment, constitute a covenant to repair in accordance with the ordinary sense of that word in the English language; and if, as has been held, a covenant to repair in a lease is apt to impose upon the tenant an obligation to reinstate the premises if they are burnt down, it seems to me difficult to say that a covenant to reinstate the premises if they are burnt down is not a covenant to repair."

There would, I think, be considerable force in that argument if the landlord's complaint in the section 146 notice was of a failure to reinstate. But, despite the wording of the notice, as I have pointed out the parties chose to treat the notice and to litigate upon the basis that the complaint in the notice was of a failure to lay out the insurance moneys. The covenant, or that part of the covenant upon which the landlord relied, was a breach of the obligation to use the insurance moneys for rebuilding, which is a quite distinct obligation from the obligation to reinstate which has to be fulfilled whether or not the tenant obtains any insurance moneys. But it is, of course, of prime importance to a landlord to be able to ensure that insurance moneys are used to rebuild and such clauses are to be found in almost every lease. Such a covenant is not, in my view, a repairing covenant within the meaning of section 1 (1) of the Leasehold Property (Repairs) Act 1938, and accordingly the notice was not invalid because it did not comply with section 1 (4).

... If an obligation is to perform an act by a given time, once that time has elapsed and the act has not been performed, there is a breach of a single obligation and not of a continuing one. The fact that it still lies within the power of the lessee to perform the act cannot affect the nature of his obligation. In this field of law a reference to a continuing breach is a way of referring to breaches of a continuing obligation and does not refer to the ability to remedy a single breach.

In my view the tenant's construction of the covenant to lay out the insurance moneys is correct. In order to give the clause business efficacy, there must be implied a term that the tenant will lay out the moneys within a reasonable time. Without such an implied term the tenant might be able to delay for years after a fire, which cannot have been the intention of the parties. There is no difference between an obligation to perform an act by a given date and an obligation to perform an act within a reasonable time. If the tenant fails to perform the act within a reasonable time he has broken his obligation, which is a single and not a continuing obligation: see *Re King* [1963] 1 Ch 459, in which Lord Denning MR said at p. 478:

"Let me next take the covenant to reinstate. Suppose the premises are damaged by fire. The lessee does not reinstate within a reasonable time. The breach is over once and for all, but its effect continues."

Therefore, on the assistant recorder's finding, the tenant was in breach of his obligation to lay out the insurance moneys by the date of the section 146 notice. That breach, it is conceded, was waived by acceptance of rent. The breach was a once-and-for-all breach of a single obligation and, as it had been waived, it could not thereafter be relied upon as a ground for forfeiture. Therefore I conclude, albeit by a very different route from that which I should have followed had I been free to do so, that the landlord was not entitled to forfeit the lease by way of re-entry and that the appeal should be allowed and an order for possession made in favour of the tenant.

Note:
 (i) In *Official Custodian of Charities v Parway Estates Developments Ltd* (1984) 270 EG 1077 the Court of Appeal rejected the tenant's claim that the right to forfeit had been waived because (i) of a letter written by the landlords to receivers appointed to receive income under the Law of Property Act 1925 and (ii) that publication in the *London Gazette* of information as to a winding up imputed knowledge to the landlords.
 (ii) See also DW Williams "Relief and Waiver in Forfeiture". Law Society's Gazette [1986] 12 March 767.

It may be that the tenant or subtenant may be able to successfully apply for relief from forfeiture.

Case 96 *Central Estates (Belgravia) Ltd v Woolgar (No 2)* [1972] 1 WLR 1048 Court of Appeal

In 1957 the tenant, then aged about 60, took an assignment of a long lease of a house in Pimlico. He supported himself by letting furnished rooms in the house. The lease contained a covenant against nuisance on the premises with a proviso for re-entry in case of breach. On June 23, 1970, the tenant was convinced of unlawfully keeping a brothel at the house.

He was discharged conditionally for 12 months. On July 23, 1970, the landlords served notice under section 146 (1) of the Law of Property Act 1925 on the tenant complaining that he had been unlawfully keeping a brothel at the premises and had been convicted of that offence.

The landlords' agents, knowing of the tenant's conviction, made internal office arrangements that no further rent should be demanded or accepted. By a clerical error in September 1970 a demand for £10, the quarter's rent due on September 29, was sent out. On September 22 the tenant paid the £10 and was given a receipt.

In December, 1970 the plaintiffs claimed possession of the house. Judge Stockdale held that since the tenant, when he paid the September rent, knew that it was the landlords' intention to forfeit the lease there had been no waiver of the forfeiture. The judge allowed the tenant's counterclaim for relief under section 146 (2) of the Act of 1925 in view of circumstances which in combination he held to be wholly exceptional, including the tenant's age and health, the fact that there was no evidence that the landlords' good name or the value of their estate had suffered from the breach and that they stood to gain and the tenant to lose about £9,000 from a forfeiture.

On appeal by the landlords and cross-appeal by the tenant:

Held (1) Allowing the cross-appeal, that the landlords' demand for and acceptance of rent through their agents with knowledge of the breach of covenant effected a waiver of the forfeiture.

(2) Dismissing the appeal (Buckley LJ *dubitante*), that in view of the many mitigating factors in favour of the tenant and the wholly exceptional circumstances, the judge's exercise of this discretion under section 146 (2) of the Act of 1925 would, if it were necessary, be affirmed.

Lord Denning MR said (in part)

The cases on waiver are collected in the notes to *Dumpor's Case* (1603) 4 Co Ref 119b in *Smith's Leading Cases*, 13th ed. (1929), pp. 39–44. Those notes show that the demand and acceptance of rent has a very different effect according to how the question arises. If it is sought to say there is *a new tenancy* by acceptance of rent; for instance, after a notice to quit has expired, the question always is, as Lord Mansfield said: '*Quo animo* the rent was received and what the real intention of both parties was'': see

Doe d. Cheny v Batten (1775) 1 Cowp 243, 245; and *Clarke v Grant*
[1950] 1 KB 104. But, if it is sought to say that an existing lease
continues in existence by waiver of forfeiture, then the intention
of the parties does not matter. It is sufficient if there is an unequivocal act done by the landlord which recognises the existence
of the lease after having knowledge of the ground of forfeiture.
The law was well stated by Parker J in *Matthews v Smallwood*
[1910] 1 Ch 777, 786, which was accepted by this court in *Oak
Property Co Ltd v Chapman* [1947] KB 886, 898:

> "It is also, I think, reasonably clear upon the cases that whether
> the act, coupled with the knowledge, constitutes a waiver is
> a question which the law decides, and therefore it is not open
> to a lessor who has knowledge of the breach to say 'I will
> treat the tenancy as existing, and I will receive the rent, or
> I will take advantage of my power as landlord to distrain; but
> I tell you that all I shall do will be without prejudice to my
> right to reenter, which I intend to reserve'. That is a position
> which he is not entitled to take up. If, knowing of the breach,
> he does distrain, or does receive the rent, then by law he
> waives the breach, and nothing which he can say by way of
> protest against the law will avail him anything."

I know that Harman J in *Creery v Summersell and Flowerdew &
Co Ltd* [1949] Ch 751, 761, said that in waiver of forfeiture "the
question remains *quo animo* was the act done". But that statement
was explained by Megaw J in *Windmill Investments (London) Ltd
v Milano Restaurant Ltd* [1962] 2 QB 373. He said, at p. 376, that
it meant only that

> "it is a question of fact whether the money tendered is ten-
> dered as, and accepted as, rent, ... Once it is decided as a
> fact that the money was tendered and accepted as rent, the
> question of its consquences as a waiver is a matter of law."

Similarly Sachs J in *Segal Securities Ltd v Thoseby* [1963] 1 QB 887
said, at p. 898:

> "It is thus a matter of law that once rent is accepted a waiver
> results. The question of *quo animo* it is accepted in forfeiture
> cases is irrelevant in relation to such acceptance."

So we have simply to ask: Was this rent demanded and accepted by the landlords' agents with knowledge of the breach?
It does not matter that they did not intend to waive. The very
fact that they accepted the rent with the knowledge constitutes
the waiver. The position here is quite plain. The agents, who

had full authority to manage these properties on behalf of the
landlords, did demand and accept the rent with full knowledge.
It may be that the instructions did not get down the chain of
command from the partner to the subordinate clerk who issued
the demands and gave the receipts for rent. That cannot affect,
to my mind, the legal position. It comes within the general rule
that the knowledge of the agent—and of his clerks—is the knowledge of the principal. A principal cannot escape the doctrine
of waiver by saying that one clerk had the knowledge and the
other received the rent. They must be regarded as one for this
purpose. The landlords' agents knew the position and they accepted the rent with knowledge. That is a waiver.

I know that the judge found that the agents had no intention
to waive, and finds also that the tenant knew they had no intention to waive. That seems to me to make no difference. The
law says that if the agents stated in terms: "We do not intend
to waive," it would not have availed them. If an express statement does not avail a landlord, nor does an implied one. So
it does not avail the landlords here.

For these reasons I hold that the forfeiture was waived by
the demand and acceptance of rent.

In case I am wrong on this point, I go on to consider the
next point about relief from forfeiture. It is settled law that, when
a tenant keeps a brothel in breach of covenant, that breach is
one which is not capable of remedy. So, if a landlord gives a
notice under section 146, he need not require it to be remedied
(see *Rugby Schools (Governors) v Tannahill* [1935] 1 KB 87 and *Egerton v Esplanade Hotels, London, Ltd* [1947] 2 All ER 88) and the
same has been applied to a gaming case *Hoffman v Fineberg* [1949]
Ch 245. It has also been said that relief is not to be exercised
in favour of persons who suffer premises to be used as a brothel:
see *Borthwick-Norton v Romney Warwick Estates Ltd* [1950] 1 All
ER 362, *per* Hilbery J, affirmed by this court in [1950] 1 All ER
798. But I think that is going too far. In a somewhat parallel
case under the Rent Acts, a county court judge allowed a tenant
to remain in possession, and this court affirmed his decision:
see *Yates v Morris* [1951] 1 KB 77. It seems to me that in a proper
case—I emphasise "in a proper case"—the court can grant relief
from forfeiture even for a breach of covenant against immoral
user. After all, the statute does give a discretion to the court.
It would not be right for the court to take away that discretion
by applying a fixed rule of law that relief could never be given
where a tenant has been convicted of keeping a brothel. It is
true, as I said when this case was previously before us: "forfeiture

was the almot inevitable consequence: relief is rarely given for such a breach". But it may sometimes be given. Suppose there was a breach by a tenant four or five years ago—a conviction of immoral user—but never any breach since. The landlord did not know of it at the time. Then, after four or five years, he discovers it and he seeks to forfeit. I should say it was plain in such case as that it would be open to the court to grant relief. The present case is not nearly so strong a case, but the judge, who saw the witnesses and considered the whole case, thought it was a case for relief. It is to be noticed that the past user has not affected the value of the premises. The stigma has not diminished the value of the landlords' estate. And there are many mitigating factors in favour of the tenant. . . .

Note:

(i) In *Smith v Metropolitan City Properties Ltd* [1986] 1 EGLR 52 (1986) 277 EG 753 the former tenant (against whom forfeiture proceedings had been completed and the landlord had re-entered) attempted to reopen the question of relief against forfeiture by invoking the ancient equitable jurisdiction of the court. Walton J rejected this argument.

(ii) In *Cremin v Barjack Properties Ltd* (1984) 273 EG 299. The defendant-tenants had been guilt of dilatory completion of works of repair and of a series of procedural failures. In the High Court McNeill J dismissed an appeal from a master's order on the ground that the tenants had had enough tolerance shown to them and their conduct did not justify the granting of relief. The Court of Appeal noted that even though the tenants' conduct was unsatisfactory, the High Court judge had not apparently taken into account the fact that the defects in the property had been remedied. The Court of Appeal granted relief from forfeiture.

6.5 Leasehold Property (Repairs) Act 1938

The 1938 Act applies to all proceedings (damages and forfeiture) where the lease was granted for seven years or more and three years or more are unexpired at the date of the section 146 notice or the commencement of the action as the case may be. Where the Act applies the landlord cannot proceed without first serving a notice in the form specified by section 146 which must also inform the tenant of his right to serve a counter-notice. If the tenant serves a counter-notice within 28 days no further proceedings can be taken without leave of the court.

Statute 8: Leasehold Property (Repairs) Act 1938

Restriction on enforcement of repairing covenants in long leases of small houses

1.—(1) Where a lessor serves on a lessee under sub-section (1) of section one hundred and forty-six of the Law of Property Act 1925, a notice that relates to a breach of a covenant or agreement to keep or put in repair during the currency of the lease all or any of the property comprised in the lease, and at the date of the service of the notice three years or more of the term of the lease remain unexpired, the lessee may within twenty-eight days from that date serve on the lessor a counter-notice to the effect that he claims the benefit of this Act.

(2) A right to damages for a breach of such a covenant as aforesaid shall not be enforceable by action commenced at any time at which three years or more of the term of the lease remain unexpired unless the lessor has served on the lessee not less than one month before the commencement of the action such a notice as is specified in subsection (1) of section one hundred and forty-six of the Law of Property Act 1925, and where a notice is served under this subsection, the lessee may, within twenty-eight days from the date of the service thereof, serve on the lessor a counter-notice to the effect that he claims the benefit of this Act.

(3) Where a counter-notice is served by a lessee under this section, then, notwithstanding anything in any enactment or rule of law, no proceedings, by action or otherwise, shall be taken by the lessor for the enforcement of any right of re-entry or forfeiture under any proviso or stipulation in the lease for breach of the covenant or agreement in question, or for damages for breach thereof, otherwise than with the leave of the court.

(4) A notice served under subsection (1) of section one hundred and forty-six of the Law of Property Act 1925, in the circumstances specified in subsection (1) of this section, and a notice served under subsection (2) of this section shall not be valid unless it contains a statement, in characters not less conspicuous than those used in any other part of the notice, to the effect that the lessee is entitled under this Act to serve on the lessor a counter-notice claiming the benefit of this Act, and a statement in the like characters specifying the time within which, and the manner in which, under this Act a counter-notice may be served and specifying the name and address for service of the lessor.

(5) Leave for the purposes of this section shall not be given unless the lessor proves:

(a) that the immediate remedying of the breach in question is requisite for preventing substantial diminution in the value of his reversion, or that the value thereof has been substantially diminished by the breach;

(b) that the immediate remedying of the breach is required for giving effect in relation to the premises to the purposes of any enactment, or of any byelaw or other provision having effect under an enactment, or for giving effect to any order of a court or requirement of any authority under any enactment or any such byelaw or other provision as aforesaid;

(c) in a case in which the lessee is not in occupation of the whole of the premises as respects which the covenant or agreement is proposed to be enforced, that the immediate remedying of the breach is required in the interests of the occupier of those premises or of part thereof;

(d) that the breach can be immediately remedied at an expense that is relatively small in comparison with the much greater expense that would probably be occasioned by postponement of the necessary work; or

(e) special circumstances which in the opinion of the court, render it just and equitable that leave should be given.

(6) The court may, in granting or in refusing leave for the purposes of this section impose such terms and conditions on the lessor or on the lessee as it may think fit.

Restriction on right to recover expenses of survey, etc
2.—A lessor on whom a counter-notice is served under the preceding section shall not be entitled to the benefit of subsection (3) of section one hundred and forty-six of the Law of Property Act 1925, (which relates to costs and expenses incurred by a lessor in reference to breaches of covenant), so far as regards any costs or expenses incurred in reference to the breach in question, unless he makes an application for leave for the purposes of the preceding section, and on such an application the court shall have power to direct whether and to what extent the lessor is to be entitled to the benefit thereof.

Saving for obligation to repair on taking possession
3.—This Act shall not apply to a breach of a covenant or agreement in so far as it imposes on the lessee an obligation to put

premises in repair that is to be performed upon the lessee taking possession of the premises or within a reasonable time thereafter.

Application to past breaches

5.—This Act applies to leases created, and to breaches occurring, before or after the commencement of this Act.

Court having jurisdiction under this Act

6.—(1) In this Act the expression "the court" means the county court, except in a case which any proceedings by action for which leave may be given would have to be taken in a court other than the county court, and means in the said excepted case that other court.

Application of certain provisions of 15 and 16 Geo 5 c 20

7.—(1) In this Act the expressions "lessor", "lessee" and "lease" have the meanings assigned to them respectively by sections one hundred and forty-six and one hundred and fifty-four of the Law of Property Act 1925, except that they do not include any reference to such a grant as is mentioned in the said section one hundred and forty-six, or to the person making, or to the grantee under such a grant, or to persons deriving title under such a person; and "lease" means a lease for a term of seven years or more, not being a lease of an agricultural holding within the meaning of the Agricultural Holdings Act 1948.

(2) The provisions of section one hundred and ninety-six of the said Act (which relate to the service of notices) shall extend to notices and counter-notices required or authorised by this Act.

The application of the 1938 Act to a particular covenant was considered in *Starrokate Ltd v Burry*.

Case 97 Starrokate Ltd v Burry (1982) 265 EG 871 Court of Appeal

The respondents were the tenants of business premises and held under a lease of seven years. Under the lease the tenants covenanted:

"At all times during the said term well and substantially to repair decorate cleanse maintain amend and keep the interior of the demised premises and the windows thereof and all additions made thereto and the fixtures and fittings therein and the interior walls and appurtenances thereof

and the sewers drains and services serving only the
demised premises with all necessary reparations cleansings and amendments whatsoever (damage by fire only
excepted)."

When the premises fell into alleged disrepair the landlords
served a section 146 notice on the tenants requiring them
to remedy certain breaches of covenant which was complied
with by the tenants. Within six months a further section
146 notice was served on the tenants which alleged thirteen
breaches of covenant, one of which was the unhygienic condition of a toilet contrary to the requirements of the public
health authority. The principal complaint of the landlords
was that the premises, instead of being used as a restaurant
in accordance with the user covenant, was being used for
the operation of amusement machines to the annoyance of
adjoining occupiers.

Held (1) The breaches alleged in the landlords' notice were
not breaches of a "covenant or agreement to keep or put
in repair" within section 1 (1) of the 1938 Act.

(2) The notice was not invalid under section 1 (4) of the
1938 Act.

Dunn LJ said (in part)
... [counsel] submits that the object of the Act is to protect
tenants from oppressive notices. He submits that this notice is
an oppressive notice, because it alleges a number of breaches,
some of them trivial. He accepts that the landlord could have
relied for his forfeiture possibly just on the breach of a covenant
not to commit a nuisance. As he says, the landlord having chosen
not to do that, and having, in colloquial language, thrown the
book at the tenants, the landlord must take the consequences.
He relies in particular on the words in subsection (4) of section
1 of the Leasehold Property (Repairs) Act 1938 and submits that
in as much as this notice relates to a breach of a covenant or
agreement to put or keep in repair, then the notice is not valid.

The short answer to those submissions which has been given
by [counsel] is that the breach alleged in paragraph (10) of the
notice is not a breach of a covenant or agreement to keep or
put the premises in repair. The breaches alleged in the paragraph
are that the lavatory is in a dirty and unhygienic condition and
does not comply with the requirements of the local authority.
He submits that the second of those breaches is plainly a breach
of the covenant to comply with the requirements of the local

authority. And so far as the breach of the agreement or covenant to cleanse the property is concerned, he submits that, although it appears in what is loosely called the repairing covenant, it is in fact not an obligation to repair or keep in repair; it is an obligation to cleanse, and he points to the terms of that covenant which contain obligations other than a strict obligation to repair and keep in repair. Accordingly [counsel] submits that this notice is not caught by the provisions of the Leasehold Property (Repairs) Act.

He referred us to two decisions of this Court, *Sidnell v Wilson* [1966] 2 QB 67 and *Middlegate Properties Ltd v Messimeris* [1973] 1 WLR 168, where it was said that the mischief which the 1938 Act was designed to overcome was where an unscrupulous land-lord bought premises in a dilapidated condition knowing that it was dilapidated, and then endeavoured to obtain possession of the premises from the tenant even though sufficient time remained under the lease for the tenant to be able to comply with the requirement.

[Counsel] submitted that, bearing in mind that that is the mis-chief which this Act was designed to prevent, then notices of this kind should not be construed strictly, but that a liberal and commonsense construction should be put upon them.

Speaking for myself I do not find it necessary to approach the case in that way, because in my judgment [counsel] is right when he says that the breaches set out in the notice, and in particular in paragraph 3 (10) of the notice, are not breaches of a covenant or agreement to keep or put in repair. The fact that a particular obligation is contained in the same clause of a lease as an obligation to repair, and that that clause may be compendiously described as "the repairing covenant" does not mean that every obligation contained in the clause constitutes an agreement "to keep or put in repair" within the meaning of section 1 (1) of the Leasehold Property (Repairs) Act. Each obligation in the clause must be given its natural and ordinary meaning. An obligation to cleanse is not an obligation to repair. On that short ground I would allow the appeal. The case must be remitted to the county court for a fresh trial.

May LJ said (in part)
I understand from the argument in this case that it is the prac-tice, where it is alleged that there are breaches of a covenant or agreement to keep or put in repair within section 1 (1) of the 1938 Act, as well as alleged breaches of other covenants under the same lease or tenancy agreement, to serve two notices: the

first specifying the breaches of the repairing covenants with the additional appropriate notice under the 1938 Act, the other specifying the remaining breaches without any such notice.

Now I think that the mischief against which section 1 in particular of the 1938 Act was directed was not, as [counsel] submitted, oppressive landlords, but that of tenants having to face claims based upon alleged breaches of repairing covenants when there remained in existence a sufficient residue of the term of the demise during which appropriate repairs could be carried out.

In these circumstances, notwithstanding the provisions of section 1 (4) of the 1938 Act, and although counsel for the appellant in this particular appeal was not prepared to argue that a notice specifying breaches of a covenant or agreement to keep or put in repair together with breaches of other covenants could be held to be good in part and bad in part, I am not satisfied that in an appropriate case a court could not sever such a notice and allow proceedings on the alleged breaches of covenants other than those to keep premises in repair. However, it is not necessary for the decision of this appeal for me to express any final view upon this point.

Case 98 Baker v Sims [1959] 1 QB 115 Court of Appeal

The plaintiffs were the landlords of premises let for a term of 99 years less seven days expiring on December 18, 1959. In 1953 the landlords served on the defendant, in whom the lease was then vested, a notice under section 146 of the Law of Property Act, 1925, alleging breaches of the repairing covenants in the lease. The defendant served a counter-notice pursuant to the Leasehold Property (Repairs) Act, 1938, claiming the benefit of that Act. In 1954 the defendant assigned the lease to a company and it was subsequently surrendered. These proceedings were started in 1957 by the landlords against the defendant for damages for breaches of the repairing covenants of the lease. The preliminary point was taken that the action was incompetent because the leave of the court under section 1 (3) of the Act of 1938 was a prerequisite to the jurisdiction of the court:

Held, (1) That effect could not be given to the purpose of section 1 of the Leasehold Property (Repairs) Act, 1938, unless a limitation was read into subsection (3) to make it consistent with subsections (1) and (2), and that in subsection (3) the provision that "no proceedings shall be taken" by the lessor for breach of covenant or for damages for breach thereof must be read as "no proceedings contemplated in the preceding subsections shall be taken" and, accordingly, that the leave of the court was only required where more than five years of the term remained unexpired.

Lord Evershed MR said (in part)

I have come to the conclusion here that you cannot give effect to what I regard as the manifest purpose of this Act, dealing with a particular mischief, unless you do read into subsection (3) the requisite limitation to make it consistent with subsections (1) and (2). [Counsel] forcefully said: "It is all very well, but what are the words you are going to read in?"; and that argument must be met. I think the answer is that the words "no proceedings," in the context, and following, as they do, the reference to a "counter-notice served under this section," must be treated as meaning "no relevant proceedings," or "no such proceedings"; or, put in another way, that "no proceedings . . . shall be taken" ought to be read as meaning "the proceedings contemplated in the preceding subsections of this section shall not be taken." I do not shrink from the fact that my conclusion involves no doubt an appreciable and substantial gloss upon the strict terms of the subsection. But it is only by so interpreting them that I can achieve the consistency in the subsection which a reading of the whole section seems to me inevitably to demand. And I am comforted to this extent: such a reading of the section cannot be condemned as wholly irrational. In the case, which came before this court, of *Kanda v Church Commissioners for England* [1958] 1 QB 332. Morris LJ used this language in reference to this section:

> "There might, however, be circumstances under which an assignee who had gone into possession had proceeded at once to remedy all disrepair and to bring it about that the premises were in a condition that satisfactorily complied with the covenants of a lease. It might be, therefore (and it is to be remembered that the provisions now under consideration only apply where more than three years of the term of a lease remain unexpired), that a court would not necessarily be disposed to give leave to take proceedings against an assignee."

That was a case in which the question was raised whether a judgment should be set aside because leave had not been given as against a particular party. It is, however, true to say that the particular point with which we are concerned was never debated. My brother Pearce, who was then sitting with Morris

LJ, has told us quite plainly that the matter never was in their minds at all. I only, therefore, refer to that passage in support of what I have said—that you cannot condemn as irrational, or on the face of it wrong, a reading of subsection (3) in the sense in which I would interpret it, which happens to be the way in which Morris LJ read the whole section. . . .

. . . Before I leave the case I ought to refer to *Cusack-Smith v Gold* [1958] 1 WLR 611. That was an action before Pilcher J of a somewhat complicated kind. The substance of it was an action for damages for breach of a repairing covenant; and the plaintiff had got before the court no less than 10 defendants. The tenth defendant was one who had a limited interest as a sublessee at the time when a notice on the landlord's part under section 146 and pursuant to subsection (2) of section 1 of the Act of 1938 was served. The tenth defendant was not directly served, but the notice was apparently pinned to the premises, and the judge held that that operated as service upon the tenth defendant. He (the tenth defendant) did not himself serve a counter-notice; but the ninth defendant—a limited company on whom the landlord's notice was directly served—had served a counter-notice. By the time that the action was commenced the tenth defendant's interest had wholly terminated; but he was joined as a defendant and sued in respect of his responsibility for the alleged breaches of covenant. He took the point that the action was not competent, at any rate against him, because no leave had been obtained to serve him, the tenth defendant. The judge rejected that view, and he interpreted the word "lessee" in the relevant parts of the Act of 1938, as amended, as excluding the tenth defendant, who, when the action started, had no interest in the premises at all. The case was, therefore, somewhat relied upon by [counsel] because, of course, when this action was started the lease was surrendered and there was, therefore, no lessee. On the other hand, the point here was different, because beyond question the defendant here had served a counter-notice, which the tenth defendant in *Cusack-Smith* had not. Therefore this case was not of itself sufficient to carry him home. I would, for my part, prefer to express no view on the particular ground upon which Pilcher J decided the *Cusack-Smith* case: it is not necessary for the decision of this case and, therefore, I say no more about it, and I must not thereby be taken either as approving or as disapproving the particular construction of the word "lessee" which there commended itself to Pilcher J. That matter can await a further occasion on which such a point must directly be decided.

Note: (i) The five year period is now three years.

If the tenant does not serve a counter-notice no leave of the court is required.

Case 99 *Church Commissioners for England v Ve-Ri-Best Manufacturing Co Ltd* [1957] 1 QB 238 Lord Goddard CJ

In November, 1946, the defendants, the tenants of premises demised by a lease made in 1898 for a term of 78½ years from March 25, 1898, mortgaged the premises by way of legal charge to secure an advance. In June, 1955, the landlords served on the tenants and on the mortgagees a notice pursuant to section 146 of the Law of Property Act, 1925, alleging breach by the tenants of certain repairing covenants in the lease and requiring the same to be remedied within six months. In accordance with the provisions of section 1 (4) of the Leasehold Property (Repairs) Act, 1938, the notice contained a statement to the effect that a counter-notice claiming the benefit of that Act might be served. On July 20, 1955, the mortgagees served on the landlords a counter-notice claiming the benefit of the Act of 1938. No counter-notice was served by the tenants and on March 1, 1956, the landlords, without first obtaining the leave of the court, issued a writ against the tenants claiming damages for breach of covenant and possession. The tenants objected to the proceedings as being improperly constituted and invalid on the ground that the mortgagees were "a lessee" for the purposes of section 1 (3) of the Leasehold Property (Repairs) Act, 1938, and the counter-notice served by the mortgagees precluded the landlords from bringing the proceedings without the leave of the court:

Held (1) That a mortgagee by legal charge was to be regarded as included in the term "lessee" for the purposes of both section 146 of the Law of Property Act, 1925, and section 1 of the Leasehold Property (Repairs) Act, 1938, but that there was no obligation to serve a notice of breach of covenant on a mortgagee and that, therefore, since the landlords had served notice upon the tenants who were "the lessee" in possession, the tenants, who had chosen not to serve a counter-notice, could not, in an action against them by the landlords, take advantage of the fact that the mortgagees, who were not and had no right to be a party to the action, and who had no right to receive a notice, had also been served and had served a counter-notice; accordingly, there was no need for the landlords to obtain the leave of the court under section 1 (3) of the Act of 1938 before bringing the proceedings.

Lord Goddard CJ said (in part)

Under section 146 of the Act of 1925 there is a necessity to serve *the* lessee. A lessee, at any rate, was served here and that was the lessee in possession. There was no obligation on the landlords to serve the mortgagee, nor was there any right in the mortgagee to say that he ought to have been served; that would seem to follow from *Egerton v Jones* [1939] 2 KB 702 for, as I have said, I do not see any distinction between who is a lessee for the purpose of being served with a notice under section 146, and who is a lessee for the present purpose. It is clear that the mortgagee could be described as "a lessee," but the action here is brought against the defendants as "the lessee" in the sense of the lessee in possession. The defendants have executed a legal charge of the lease, but they are "the lessee," and as "the lessee" have had the notice served upon them. They have not chosen to take any advantage of the Act of 1938 by serving a counter-notice, and I cannot see, therefore, with all respect to [counsel's] argument, why the landlords have not got a right to bring this action. Nor do I see why the defendants, not having served a counter-notice, can take advantage of the fact that the building society, who have no right to receive a notice and on whom there was no obligation to serve a notice, did purport to enter, or did enter, a counter-notice. The building society are not a party to this action and they have not a right to be made a party to the action, except in the sense that they are, as mortgagees, entitled to take advantage of the right, given by subsection (4) of section 146 of the Act of 1925, of coming to the court and asking for an order vesting the lease in them, and the court may then vest the lease in them, subject to such terms as the court may think fit to impose. I think that it would be a very novel ground of interference if I held that, because somebody else, on whom it was not obligatory to serve a notice, had been served with a notice—whether for the purpose of information, courtesy, or by mistake, or for whatever reason—a defendant in the position of these defendants, who could have taken advantage of the Act by serving a counter-notice, was entitled to say:

> "I am not going to serve a counter-notice: I have no desire to take advantage of the Act, but I say that somebody who is not a party to this action and who had no right to receive notice, did serve a counter-notice."

For these reasons I think that the point of law raised on the pleadings, namely, whether this action can be commenced without the leave of the court, must be decided in favour of the plaintiffs, and I so decide.

Where the landlord seeks the leave of the court regard must be had to the standard of proof required.

Case 100 Land Securities PLC v Receiver for the Metropolitan Police District [1983] 1 WLR 439 Sir Robert Megarry V-C

The tenant occupied a building under a lease for 99 years from November 5, 1965. The lease contained a full repairing covenant. In about 1977 the granite panel cladding on the building was found to be in an unsatisfactory condition. A dispute arose between the landlord and the tenant about the extent of the repairs that were necessary and the materials and methods to be used. In November 1979 the tenant began proceedings by writ in the Queen's Bench Division against the landlord and others claiming damages for negligence in the erection of the building; those proceedings were still pending. In July 1982 the tenant began proceedings by originating summons in the Chancery Division against the landlord claiming, *inter alia*, declarations that a proposed replacement of the granite cladding by stainless steel cladding would be an improvement within section 3 of the Landlord and Tenant Act 1927, that the landlord had unreasonably withheld consent to the work, and that the tenant was entitled to carry out the work without the landlord's consent. In October 1982, after service on the tenant of a notice under section 146 of the Law of Property Act 1925 specifying breach of the covenant to repair and service by the tenant of a counter-notice claiming the benefit of the Leasehold Property (Repairs) Act 1938, the landlord issued a summons seeking leave under section 1 of the Act to bring an action for forfeiture of the lease and damages. On December 21, 1982, Master Chamberlain gave the landlord leave to proceed up to the close of pleadings and until the proceedings under the Landlord and Tenant Act 1927 had been set down and a date fixed for hearing.

On the tenant's appeal to the judge:

Held (1) That on an application for leave under section 1 of the Leasehold Property (Repairs) Act 1938 the landlord had to make out a *prima facie* or arguable case that at least

one of the paragraphs of section 1 (5) of the Act was satisfied,
for which purpose he had only to make out his case without
the need for the court to evaluate evidence by the tenant
in rebuttal; that, on the facts and the evidence, in view of
the low standard of proof required, paragraphs (a) and (d)
of the subsection had been satisfied, and there was no prohibition on the granting of leave to the landlord; but that,
in view of the desirability of having all disputed matters
resolved at the same time, and since what the landlord
wanted could be resolved more conveniently and economi-
cally in the proceedings begun by the tenant under the Landlord and Tenant Act 1927, the court in its discretion would
refuse the landlord leave to proceed with a claim for forfeiture and damages.

Sir Robert Megarry V-C said (in part)
... there was considerable argument about what was decided
in *Sidnell v Wilson* [1966] 2 QB 67. [Counsel] adopted the approach
appearing in the headnote. On an application for leave under
the Act of 1938, a landlord did not have to "satisfy" the court
that there had been a breach of the repairing covenant; for the
application was merely of an interlocutory nature, and as the
question whether or not there had been such a breach would
have to be determined at the trial, it would be wrong to determine
it on the interlocutory application, and so try it twice over.
Instead, the landlord merely had to establish that there was a
"prima facie case" that there had been a breach. That was the
view of Lord Denning MR and Harman LJ. Diplock LJ, on the
other hand, held that the landlord merely had to establish an
"arguable case" that one or more of the conditions in section
1 (5) had been satisfied.

[Counsel's] contention was that the difference in these two
views was not merely whatever difference there might be
between a *"prima facie"* case and an "arguable" case, but that
there was in some way a difference between the process of establishing a breach of covenant and the process of establishing that
one of the paragraphs of section 1 (5) had been satisfied. On
the first process, the requirement was only that there should
be a *prima facie* case. But this did not apply to the second, since
the question whether one of the heads of section 1 (5) was satisfied would have to be determined once and for all on the application for leave to bring the proceedings, and so, unlike the
question whether there was any breach of covenant, would not
arise for a second time at the trial. I pressed [counsel] to discover
what had to be shown in establishing that one of the paragraphs

of section 1 (5) had been satisfied, but although he readily prof-
fered a collection of the matters that had to be taken into consideration, he put forward no clear standard in place of the *"prima
facie"* or "arguable" case that had to be shown on establishing
a breach of covenant. The standard was different, he said, but
the difference was not explained, beyond being one that was
more exacting than was indicated by the words *"prima facie"*
and "arguable."

I do not think that this contention is right. One must begin
with the words of section 1 (5). There is no separate requirement
of establishing a breach of covenant; instead, the existence of
a breach is clearly assumed under each head in section 1 (5)
except the last. Thus under pargraph (a), what the lessor must
prove is that "the immediate remedying of the breach in question
is requisite for preventing substantial diminution in the value
of his reversion," and so on. The word "proves" governs a compound requirement which includes the immediate remedying
of the breach, and this being requisite to prevent substantial
diminution in the value of the reversion. I do not see how the
existence of the breach can be segregated out of this compound
requirement and given a different standard of proof from the
rest of it. Instead, all that I think that Lord Denning MR and
Harman LJ were doing was to say that as the existence of the
breach would have to be determined at the trial, at this interlocutory stage only a *prima facie* case for the existence of such a breach
need be shown, with the result that this must be the standard
required for the whole of each paragraph of section 1 (5) in which
a breach of covenant lay embedded. It is plain from *Sidnell v
Wilson* [1966] 2 QB 67, 77, that Lord Denning MR was considering
not merely whether there was a breach of covenant but whether
the landlord had brought himself within section 1 (5) (a), which
must mean the whole of section 1 (5) (a); and on the facts of
that case Lord Denning MR was holding that the landlord had
done this, provided he had sufficiently established a breach.
Accordingly the thrust of the judgment was on this latter point
rather than on the whole of paragraph (a); but that does not
mean that the rest of paragraph (a) was being ignored.

[Counsel] contended that this view was wrong. He said that
section 1 of the Act nowhere in terms refers to proving that
a breach of a repairing covenant has been committed; and that
indeed is the case. Section 1 (1) refers to the service under the
Law of Property Act 1925 of "a notice that relates" to a breach
of a repairing covenant; section 1 (2) refers to a "right to damages
for a breach of such a covenant" and a notice served under section

146 (1) of the Law of Property Act 1925, and a counter-notice; section 1 (3) refers to proceedings for forfeiture or damages "for breach of the covenant or agreement in question"; and section 1 (4) refers back to notices served under subsections (1) and (2). Thus when section 1 (5) (a) refers to the immediate remedying of "the breach in question," it appears to be assuming that there is a breach. Yet obviously the court should give no leave to bring proceedings within the section if there has in fact been no breach of covenant, even though not until section 1 (5) is reached does there seem to be anything to raise the question whether a breach has in fact been committed. [Counsel] however, contended that this issue arose under section 1 (3), and that in deciding in *Sidnell v Wilson* [1966] 2 QB 67 what standard of proof should be applied in determining whether or not there had been a breach of covenant, the Court of Appeal was really construing section 1 (3) and not section 1 (5). He had to accept, however, that there was not a word in any of the judgments about section 1 (3), although all the members of the court considered section 1 (5) (a); and I do not see how the decision could possibly be treated as a decision on the meaning and effect of a subsection that the judgments do not even mention. If any emphasis is needed, it is supplied by the terms of section 1 (3); for as I have indicated, this is expressed in terms of imposing a prohibition or taking proceedings for forfeiture under a proviso or stipulation in the lease, or for damages, for breach of the covenant or agreement, and not in terms of whether or not there has in fact been such a breach.

In the end, I think that all that a landlord has to do on an application for leave is to make out a *prima facie* case (or perhaps a *bona fide* arguable case) that at least one of the paragraphs of section 1 (5) is satisfied; and this includes making out such a case for there being a breach of the repairing covenant. I think that this includes paragraph (e), even though it does not mention any breach of covenant; for I do not see how a landlord could establish that there are special circumstances making it just and equitable for leave to be given unless he has established a *prima facie*, or arguable, case that there has been a breach of covenant. *Sidnell v Wilson* [1966] 2 QB 67 is a decision on the word "proves" in section 1 (5), and the standard of proof that it lays down applies to the whole of the contents of paragraphs (a) to (e). If the term "*prima facie* case" is used, I think that this is to be understood in the sense of a case made out by the landlord, without the need to evaluate any rebutting evidence put forward by the tenant. That is why Diplock LJ, at p. 80, used the term *"bona fide* arguable case"; and the unanimous view of the court that the point ought not to be tried twice over seems to point strongly to the phrase *"prima facie* case" bearing the meaning that I have indicated . . .

. . . In reaching this conclusion, I do not overlook *In re Metropolitan Film Studios Ltd's Application* [1962] 1 WLR 1315. In that case Ungoed-Thomas J said, at p. 1324, that the discretion under the Act of 1938:

> "is of an interlocutory nature, not to be exercised to exclude the lessor from his rights subject to the wide discretion given to the court under section 146 [of the Law of Property Act 1925], unless the court is clearly convinced that, despite compliance with the requirements specified in the paragraphs of subsection (5), the application should be refused."

In so far as this suggests that, once subsection (5) is satisfied and the discretion of the court is opened, leave should always be given unless the court is "clearly convinced" that it should not, I would have some difficulty in agreeing with it. Proceedings for forfeiture and damages are burdensome on tenants, even though relief from forfeiture may be granted, and the Act of 1938 was plainly passed so as to prevent oppression from the threat of such proceedings. With all respect, I would have thought that the discretion of the court was much less fettered than is suggested by subjecting it to the words "clearly convinced." The fact that one of the paragraphs of subsection (5) must have been satisfied before the discretion is opened does of course of itself point towards the landlord being given leave to bring the proceedings; but there may be many other factors present which ought to be considered in deciding whether or not to grant leave, including the fact that only *prima facie* evidence is required under subsection (5), and I do not see why in balancing all the relevant matters nothing save a clear conviction that leave should be refused should suffice for refusing leave.

The effect of the 1938 Act on a landlord's claim for costs and expenses incurred in, or in contemplation of any proceedings under sections 146 or 147 was considered in *Middlegate Properties Ltd v Gidlow-Jackson.*

Case 101 *Middlegate Properties Ltd v Gidlow-Jackson* (1977) 34 P & CR 4 Court of Appeal

The appellant tenant was the assignee of a lease of a house which at all material times had three years or more to run.

The lease contained covenants by the tenant to repair and (by clause 7 of the schedule) to pay and discharge legal costs and surveyor's fees of and incidental to the preparation of, *inter alia*, any statutory notice relating to breach of covenant. The landlords served a notice on the tenant under section 146 of the Law of Property Act 1925 relating to breaches of covenant to repair, setting out the legal costs and surveyor's fees which they had incurred in relation to the notice. The tenant served a counter-notice under section 1 of the Leasehold Property (Repairs) Act 1938. Subsequently, the tenant carried out the repairs. On a claim by the landlords in the county court to recover the legal costs and surveyor's fees of the section 146 notice, the judge held that they were entitled to recover the sum claimed and gave judgment in their favour accordingly. The tenant appealed, and the question was whether sections 1 (3) or 2 of the Act of 1938 applied to prevent the landlords recovering the sum claimed, it being admitted that they had not obtained the leave of the court in accordance with those provisions.

Held, Dismissing the appeal, (1) that section 2 of the Act of 1938 was inapplicable since it applied only where the lessor was claiming to be entitled to the benefit of section 146 (3) of the Law of Property Act 1925 and in the present case the landlords were not relying on that subsection but claiming only under clause 7 of the schedule to the lease.

(2) That section 1 (3) of the Act of 1938 applied only in relation to a claim for damages and in the present case the landlords' claim was not for damages for a breach of contract but for a debt due under the lease.

Megaw LJ said (in part)

... The clause in question, clause 7 of the schedule to the lease, so far as it is relevant, is in these terms:

"That the lessee will permit the estate trustees and the agent and the surveyor with or without workmen and others at all reasonable times in the daytime to enter upon the demised premises and take particulars of additions improvements fixtures and fittings thereto or therein and to view and examine the state and condition of the demised premises or any part thereof and the reparation of the same and of all defects decays and wants of reparation found in breach of the covenants herein contained to make and give or leave notice in writing at or upon the demised premises to or for the lessee who will with all proper despatch and in any case within three months then next following well and sufficiently repair and amend the premises accordingly. And will pay and discharge on demand all costs charges and expenses (including legal costs and any fees payable to a surveyor) incurred by the estate trustees of and incident to the preparation and service of such notice or of any statutory notice relating to any breach of covenant."

. . . there are two particular matters in this subsection to which I should call attention as being relevant to the issue in this appeal. First, in the opening words, ". . . reasonable costs and expenses properly incurred by the lessor in the employment of a solicitor and surveyor or valuer, . . ." are expressly, and I have no doubt deliberately, described in the statute as being "a debt": "A lessor shall be entitled to recover *as a debt* due to him from a lessee, and in addition, to damages (if any), . . ." So that there, apart from any question of any express covenant in the lease, the legislature has described the expenses of the preparation of a notice which the landlord has reasonably to incur in employing a solicitor and surveyor or valuer as being "a debt due" to the landlord from the lessee.

The second matter to which it is necessary to call attention is that the subsection, as I think, quite clearly on its terms, in relation to giving the lessor the entitlement to recover those sums, is confined to two cases: (i) where the lessee has requested the landlord to waive the right of re-entry or forfeiture for the breach of covenant and the landlord has agreed, and (ii) where, under the provisions of subsection (2) of section 146, the court has decided that the lessee should be relieved. It has no application to a case where neither of these events has occurred. In the present case, as I have said, neither of these events occurred because, on the notice being given, the repairs were duly carried out and therefore nothing arose in relation to any question of waiver, or relief given by the court.

So much for the Act of 1925.

The other relevant statute is the Leasehold Property (Repairs) Act 1938. The general purpose of that Act was to make provision that if a period which by the date with which we are here concerned had become a period of three years or more remained of a lease before it was due to expire and the landlord wished to seek to exercise his right of re-entry or to take proceedings in respect of a breach of covenant in the lease he had to obtain the consent of the court before such proceedings could be carried to fruition. . . .

... What is, to my mind, a less simple question is whether the plaintiffs are entitled to recover having regard to the provisions of section 1 (3) of the Act of 1938. I have already read it; I will not read it again. It is fairly conceded by [counsel] on behalf of the plaintiff-respondents that if the claim in this case is properly to be regarded as a claim for damages for breach of a term of the lease then by virtue of section 1 (3) of the Act the plaintiffs could not seek to enforce that claim without first having obtained the leave of the court, which has not been asked for and has not been given.

The question is a short one, whether it is simple or not. In that subsection, do damages for breach of the convenant or agreement in question, properly interpreted, cover this claim, which is a claim for moneys which are said to be due by virtue of the express provisions of clause 7 of the schedule to the lease?

One possible view, I suppose, would be that, because those moneys have been demanded by virtue of the agreement and have not been paid, therefore it can be described as being a claim for damages for failure to comply with the lease by non-payment, rather than as a claim for debt.

This self-same matter was considered by Roskill J in *Bader Properties Ltd v Linley Property Investments Ltd* (1967) 19 P & CR 621. In that case, as a second and relatively minor point on the issues before him, Roskill J held that where there was an express provision (in terms identical with the provisions in the present case) giving the landlord the right to recover the legal and survey expenses in respect of the preparation of a section 146 notice the landlords did not require the consent of the court under any of the provisions of the Act of 1938, including, as I understand it, the provisions of section 1 (3). The basis of that decision, as I understand it, was that the claim was not to be treated as being a claim for damages for breach of contract but was to be treated as being a claim for debt—money due under the contract. That decision was binding on the judge in the court below, and, as Mr Gidlow-Jackson has rightly pointed out to this court, the judge in the court below was bound to follow it, but we are not bound to follow it; we are entitled to overrule it. To that extent we are in a different position from that of the judge. If I thought that the decision of Roskill J was wrong, I should have no hesitation in so holding and giving effect to that view. In my judgment, however, there is no reason to regard that decision of Roskill J as being wrong. On the contrary, I think that it obtains strong support from the wording of the provision of section 146 (3) of the Law of Property Act 1925, to which I called special attention when I read that subsection. In that subsection there is no doubt that the legislature has deliberately treated the expenses incurred in the employment of a solicitor and surveyor in the preparation of a section of 146 notice as properly being described as a debt due from a lessee, by contradistinction from damages for breach of contract. It is perfectly true that that subsection is not dealing with a case where there is an express covenant in the agreement, but I see no reason why the wording expressly used by the statute in relation to a case dealing with statutory provisions should be given a materially different meaning in relation to the words used in an express covenant such as the words used here.

6.6 Relief in respect of internal decorative repairs

A special form of relief is available in respect of internal decorative repairs under section 147 of the Law of Property Act 1925.

Statute 9: Law of Property Act 1925. Section 147

Relief against notice to effect decorative repairs
147.—(1) After a notice is served on a lessee relating to the internal decorative repairs to a house or other building, he may apply to the court for relief, and if, having regard to all the circumstances of the case (including in particular the length of the lessee's term or interest remaining unexpired), the court is satisfied that the notice is unreasonable, it may, by order, wholly or partially relieve the lessee from liability for such repairs.
  (2) This section does not apply:

  (i) where the liability arises under an express covenant or agreement to put the property in a decorative state of repair and the covenant or agreement has never been performed;
  (ii) to any matter necessary or proper
    (a) for putting or keeping the property in a sanitary condition, or
    (b) for the maintenance or preservation of the structure;
  (iii) to any statutory liability to keep a house in all respects reasonably fit for human habitation;
  (iv) to any covenant or stipulation to yield up the house or other building in a specified state of repair at the end of the term.

(3) In this section "lease" includes an underlease and an agreement for a lease, and "lessee" has a corresponding meaning and includes any person liable to effect the repairs.

(4) This section applies whether the notice is served before or after the commencement of this Act, and has effect notwithstanding any stipulation to the contrary.

6.7 Landlord's self-help

If the tenant is in breach of his repairing obligations and there is no provision in the lease allowing the landlord to enter and undertake the repairs, the tenant may be able to obtain an injunction to stop the landlord from entering to repair.

Case 102 Regional Properties Ltd v City of London Real Property Co Ltd (1979) 257 EG 64 Oliver J

> The premises consisted of a basement, lower ground floor, ground floor and seven upper floors of which the top floor was surmounted by a mansard roof rising from a flat roof. The two tenants of the office building brought two interlocutory motions for injunctions in interrelated actions. The tenants of the premises covenanted, *inter alia,*
>
>> "The Lessee will at its own cost and charges from time to time and at all times during the said term well and substantially repair and maintain whiten colour paper pave cleanse amend and renew and keep so repaired maintained whitened coloured papered paved cleansed amended and renewed in every respect the said building and the Lessors' fixtures therein and the foundations and the roof thereof including the structure and the main walls and timbers thereof and the drain thereof and all buildings now or hereafter to be erected on the said piece or parcel of land and to cause the lift of the said building to be inspected and maintained at regular intervals by maintenance contractors."
>
> When the roof began to leak the freeholders obtained a judgment for damages against the first tenants who were the tenants of parts of the office block (including the roof). The first tenants then brought an action for an injunction to restrain the freeholders from entering to repair the roof. Although the tenants were in breach of their repairing covenant the freeholders had no right of entry to repair the

roof. In the second action the tenants of the other parts of the block sought an injunction against the tenants whose demise included the roof. The tenants of these other parts, who were not themselves in occupation, wished to protect their subtenants against damage caused by the penetration of water from the leaking roof and, hence, wished to carry out repairs themselves to the roof and sought an injunction to prevent the "tenants of the roof" from obstructing access for this purpose.

Held (1) On the first motion, that the tenants of the roof were entitled to an injunction but, that in view of mutual undertakings, an injunction was not necessary.

(2) The unusual relief sought in the second motion would be refused taking into account, *inter alia*, the undertaking given by the tenants of the roof which satisfied the freeholders in the first action.

Oliver J said (in part)
On the first motion
[Counsel] says that their claim is a very simple one for an injunction in aid of a legal right. His clients, he says, are tenants of the roof. The landlord has reserved no right of entry to do repairs and if (for reasons of its own) it is unwilling to forfeit the lease, it has already recovered damages which are in the course of being assessed and the landlord has no right whatever to go on to the plaintiffs' property for any purpose other than the limited purposes which are specified in the lease. He submits that they cannot, on the one hand, claim to keep the lease on foot for the purposes of enforcing the covenant and receiving rent and, at the same time, ignore the exclusive possession which the lease confers upon the lessees. In aid of his submissions [counsel] relies upon a series of authorities going back to *Barker v Barker* [1829] 3 C & P 557, *Doe v Rowlands* 9 C & P 734, and a decision of the Court of Appeal in *Stocker v Planet Building Society* [1879] 27 WR 877 where James LJ says this:

"Where a reversioner has granted a lease with no power of reentry reserved on breach of a covenant to repair, can he give himself the right to enter and do the repairs? It is a plain invasion of the rights of property. He has no more right than any stranger has. There is no suit in point of law for what has been done. As a matter of law according to the present legal rights in this country there is no right in a reversioner to go in and do necessary repairs."

and Brett LJ was of the same opinion. He said he thought it was one of the clearest cases he had ever heard, and there was a wrongful act for which an action in trespass would lie; Cotton LJ also in fact concurred. In the light of that decision, [counsel] submits that there is no remotely arguable defence against a formal injunction and accordingly no question of any balance of convenience arises on this motion, for the court is not entitled, as he would submit, just because it may be convenient, in effect to authorise an entry on to somebody else's property in the absence of even a colour of a right to do so.

Against this, [counsel] would argue, first of all as a matter of construction of the lease, that his client reserves a right of entry. That argument—which he accepts is his weakest argument—rests upon effectively rewriting what is erroneously described in the lease as a reservation but is in fact clearly a grant. I need not, I think, rehearse the argument in detail because it does not really appear to me to be a tenable one. Then [counsel] argues that in any event the injunction should not be granted for a number of reasons. First of all, he says the plaintiffs do not come to the court with clean hands. The basis of that submission is that, although a plaintiff may if he wishes exert his legal rights so as to compel a defendant to provide him with some financial advantage, he ought not to receive the aid of the court in supporting his legal right if that is done to enable him—or if in fact it does enable him—to continue to be in breach of covenant. But, although it is accepted that the plaintiffs are in breach of covenant, in respect of which, of course, the defendant has elected to rely upon its remedy in damages, it is not accepted and I do not think that I can infer it in the light of the disputed evidence that there is, or will necessarily be, a breach of covenant beyond those covenants for which damages are already being assessed in the Queen's Bench Division and which will not be remedied. I find the case substantially indistinguishable from the *Stocker* case to which I have referred and, despite a note in *Woodfall* to the effect that the result of that case might be different today, I am not at all sure that I see why. No reason is given, and the mere fact that a hundred years has passed and that property rights are perhaps less carefully protected by the law than heretofore, does not, I think, justify me in declining to follow a decision of a strong and unanimous Court of Appeal. Secondly, it is submitted that damages are an adequate remedy, but, in saying that, it is also asserted that the damages are going to be nominal only. I do not think there is anything in this point and it seems to me that the case of *Shelfer v City of London Electric*

Lighting Co [1895] 2 Ch 388, to which I have been referred, and particularly the judgment of AL Smith LJ, is really a clear authority which runs directly counter to the proposition that Lord Cairns' Act authorises the courts, as it were, to grant a compulsory licence to execute threatened trespasses.

Finally, it is said that, although it has not yet been claimed, the defendants are entitled to, and will, claim specific performance of the covenant to repair. In the first place there is, as I see it, grave doubt whether such a covenant in the case of a tenant's covenant is capable of specific performance. That is based on a case of *Hill v Barclay* (1810) 16 Ves 402, and, although that case may logically be much weakened as an authority, if indeed it ever was more than a mere dictum, by the decision of Vice-Chancellor Pennycuick in *Jeune v Queens Cross Properties* [1974] ·Ch 97, the textbooks are unanimous in rejecting such a remedy. But allowing that the doubt might be resolved in the defendants' favour I really cannot see how it helps them on this motion. In the first place, this is a case where the defendants could quite easily do the repairs themselves if they were prepared to forfeit the lease. They declined to do that. They distinctly admitted the claim and they had actually got judgment for damages, and the whole basis of the way their case has been put in the Scott Schedule submitted to the Official Referee runs entirely counter to the notion that the covenant was to be performed by the plaintiffs. But, leaving that little difficulty aside, the concept of a decree of specific performance seems to me to be in direct antithesis of the relief which is claimed on this motion. A decree of specific performance would require Regional to carry out the work. What the defendants seek on the motion is to resist an injunction which would prevent them carrying out the work for themselves, and that is not specific performance.

I think here that the real key lies, as [counsel] suggests, in the question: "Are the defendants, City, themselves entitled to an injunction in order to enable them to enter?" None has been actually sought. I am wholly unable to see how one could be sought in these circumstances. If, then, the injunction claimed by Regional is refused, the court is, in effect, giving its blessing to a position in which, in order to protect its own property in exercising its legal rights, the plaintiffs would have to resort to self-protection; while the defendants, if they seek to carry out their threat, can only do so not only by a deliberate trespass but possibly, and indeed probably, by violence to the property and even to persons. I do not think that this court can permit that. I am far from saying that the attitude taken by Regional is either reasonable or commendable, but it is, I think, one which the law permits them to take and for which they are entitled to seek the law's protection. So far, therefore, as the motion in the first action is concerned, the plaintiffs clearly would, I think, succeed were it not for a circumstance to which I will come in a moment, and I would have been prepared to grant an injunction in accordance with the terms of the notice of motion, and, of course, against the usual cross-undertaking in damages.

What in fact has now occurred is that, in connection with the second motion, the hearing of which has not yet been concluded, some evidence has been filed by [counsel] indicating the sort of work which his clients say is necessary to put the roof into, at any rate, temporary shape, and he has stated in open court that his clients were proposing to carry that work out. [Counsel] then indicated that, if that could be framed in the form of an undertaking, he, indeed, would be prepared to give an undertaking in the terms of the notice of motion, and, since [counsel] is, as I understand it, prepared to offer an undertaking to the court, the terms of which I think have now been settled (and I will hear counsel about those) it seems that there is really nothing left in this motion except the question of costs.

On the second motion

So I am prepared to approach the motion on the basis that there is an arguable point here and that brings me to the question of the balance of convenience. Much has been said here about the necessity for making the premises wind and water-tight over the coming winter. [Counsel] has pointed out that if he is allowed to go in with his workmen and do all such work as is necessary any damage which may be sustained by [counsel's] clients is minimal and indeed [counsel's] clients may in fact get a windfall out of it; therefore he says the convenience lies all on one side. I am bound to say that I regard this motion as a most unusual one. It was of course envisaged in the *American Cyanamid* case [*American Cyanamid Co v Ethicon Ltd* [1975] AC 396] that there might be situations of a very unusual nature where the general principles which were applied in that case might require some modification. But in this case it seems to me that [counsel] is right in saying that in the ultimate analysis the question between his clients and [counsel's] clients is one of damages and [counsel's] clients have no interest in these premises except a financial one and if they suffer damage as a result of continued lack of repair then damages will be an adequate remedy for them.

[Counsel] says the damages will be difficult to assess. I am bound to say I think that is greatly exaggerated. I do not see any real difficulty in assessing the damages if, as [counsel's] clients fear, there is some adverse consequence as a result of disrepair on the rent reviews which are due to take place. Secondly, of course, this is a case which I think I must approach with a good deal of caution in view of the fact that what is really sought on this motion is to pre-empt the trial. That is not a fatal objection, of course, to relief on motion, but I think it is a circumstance which the court has to take into account in assessing whether it is right at this stage to grant all the relief which the plaintiff is claiming and that particularly is so where an undertaking is offered which, at least on one view of the facts, would be sufficient to preserve the position pending the hearing of the action. [Counsel] also suggests that to concede the unusual relief which is claimed in this case would, or might, expose his clients to yet an additional claim for damages in that [counsel's] clients, in addition to the damages which of course are being assessed between [counsel's] clients and [counsel's] clients, in the Queen's Bench Division, might seek to withhold any sums which they expend on repairs from the rent and thus expose clients to yet a further claim at the hands of clients.

In all the circumstances I do not think this is a case where it would be right that I should grant to the plaintiffs the very unusual and stringent relief that they claim. Had [counsel] failed to offer any sort of undertakings which might remotely appear to be satisfactory I might have taken a different view. But in the light of the undertaking, which was sufficient at any rate to satisfy [counsel's] landlords, who are the persons with whom he has a direct contractual relationship, I think that I, too, should be satisfied with that undertaking.

Where the landlord has a right, on the tenant's default, to enter and undertake the repairs and claim the cost from the tenant there is a difference of opinion as to whether the Leasehold Property (Repairs) Act 1938 applies.

Case 103 *Swallow Securities Ltd v Brand* (1981) 260 EG 63 McNeill J

By a lease, the tenant covenanted to keep the demised premises in repair. By clause 3 (6), she covenanted that, if she should make default in the performance of her repairing obligations, she would permit the landlords to enter to carry out the necessary repairs "and to repay to the lessors on demand the cost of such repair, decoration, maintenance or reinstatement, including any solicitor's, counsel's and surveyor's costs and fees reasonably incurred by the lessors in respect thereof such costs to be recoverable by the lessors as if the same were rent in arrear." Subsequently, the landlords brought proceedings against the tenant, by their statement of claim alleging that, in breach of covenant, she had failed to keep the demised premises in repair and that they had carried out the necessary works at a cost of £3,272.45 and claiming that sum. The master struck out the statement of claim on the ground that the proceedings were void for failure to comply with section 1 (3) of the Leasehold Property (Repairs) Act 1938. The plaintiffs appealed. It was common ground that none of the relevant notices provided for by section 1 of the Act of 1938 had been served and that the leave of the court had not been sought to bring the proceedings purusant to section 1 (3). The question for the court was whether the sum claimed was damages or, as the landlords contended, a debt.

Held, (1) Dismissing the appeal, that clause 3 (6) of the lease was wholly inconsistent with the purposes of section 1 of the Act of 1938; that a sum that had not been ascertainable at the date of the lease and that was ascertainable only as the cost of repairs carried out on the failure of the tenant to do those repairs in breach of covenant and, further, being a sum fixed at the whim of the landlords in agreement with contractors of their choice, could not be treated as a debt; that clause 3 (6) removed from the tenant the choice given to her by the lease to carry out the works of repair at her own expense with contractors of her choice; that it not only removed from her the protection of the notice to do the repairs provided for by clause 3 (4) of the lease but also deprived her of the option of having the work done by a contractor of her choice at a price agreed by her; that, in any event, the provision that the amount to be charged or added as arrears of rent was to include solicitor's, counsel's and surveyor's reasonable fees offended against the basic principles of debt unless there were to be imported some provision such as that such fee should be taxed or be subject to such adjudication as to reasonableness as should be laid down by some taxing or professional authority; that no such provision need be imported for the efficacy of the lease; and that, accordingly, the sum claimed was not a debt but a claim for damages for breach of covenant and thus offended against section 1 (3) of the Act of 1938.

McNeill J said (in part)

I have already referred, and the modern law as set out, for example, by the House of Lords in *White and Carter (Councils) Ltd v McGregor* [1962] AC 413 where the distinction is put by Lord Keith of Avonholm, dealing with an argument advanced for the appellants, as follows

"In the former case there is a plain breach of contract making the repudiating party liable in damages, unless where a claim for specific implement is available. In the latter case, according to the submission made, he is liable contractually for a debt at least where the consideration for performance by the other party is expressed in money."

There is, as I see it, no doubt that the distinction between debt and damages still remains in our modern law. It has been recognised in some of the hire-purchase cases. I need refer only to one, *Re Apex Supply Co. Ltd* [1942] CL 108 where Simonds J said in relation to the contract there under consideration: ". . . this is a contract for the payment of a certain sum in a certain event and, that event having happened, that sum is payable." Accordingly, as he said, no question there arose as to whether the sum was a penalty or liquidated damages.

So far as authority to support his proposition that what is claimed here is claimed in debt and not in damages was concerned, [counsel] conceded that there was no authority directly in point, but he invited my attention to two cases where disputes between landlord and tenant had been involved. In *Moss Empires Ltd v Olympia (Liverpool) Ltd* [1939] AC 544 the lease contained the following covenant by the tenants (I read from the headnote): "to expend during each year of the said term on . . . repairs and decoration a sum of £500 and at the end of each year of the said term to produce to the lessors evidence of such expenditure or to pay to them at the end of each such year a sum equal to the difference between the amount so expended and £500. . . ." That covenant was held to create a debt and was not a covenant to pay damages for breach of a covenant to repair within section 18 (1) of the Landlord and Tenant Act 1927. If it had been within that subsection, the damages would have been limited to the amount, if any, by which the value of the reversion had been diminished owing to the breach of covenant (see *per* Lord Atkin: "I think, therefore, that the sums claimed in this action are not damages but debt"). It is worth noting that that case was plainly put by the late Lord Radcliffe (then Cyril Radcliffe KC) for the landlords in this way: "The action is not based on any allegation of failure to repair the premises, but on the allegation that the respondents undertook to pay a specified sum of money in a certain event, which they did not pay on the event happening."

In *Plummer v Ramsey* (1934) 78 SJ 175 Branson J held that the relevant clause in the lease there gave the landlord the power to elect whether he would accept a specified sum of money in lieu of the tenant's obligation to repair. If the landlord elected to accept the money that sum was not, as the tenant contended, liquidated damages for breach of the covenant to repair or a penalty but a specific sum payable on the exercise of the election.

It will be immediately apparent that neither of those cases resembles the present case on the facts. There is here no fixed sum payable on a certain event unrelated to the cost of repairs. On the contrary, the sum claimed is precisely that which it cost the landlord to do the repairs—repairs that in breach of covenant the tenant had not done. It would, I think, be absurd to treat this as no more than a fortuitous coincidence.

There are, I think, two features of those cases that distinguish them from the present case: (1) the sum in question was predetermined without reference to the cost or expense of the event on which it was payable; (2) it became payable, or fell to be taken into account, whether or not a breach of agreement in the true sense was established. Thus, the £500 in *White and Carter (Councils) Ltd v McGregor* (supra) was payable whether or not repairs were required, still less whether a breach of covenant was established. Like, in *Re Apex Supply Co Ltd* (supra) the *ratio decidendi* seems to me to have been, or to have depended on, the fact that a sum certain was payable on a certain event. Accepting, therefore, historically and as a matter of the present law that a real and significant difference exists between a claim in debt and a claim in damages, I turn to consider the present case.

Section 1 of the Act of 1938 was intended to have, and did have, a specific purpose, that is to say, to prevent forfeiture of a lease covered by the Act for breach of covenant unless three things happened: (i) a notice pursuant to the Act; (ii) the opportunity for a counter-notice; and (iii) leave. These provisions do not apply to forfeiture of a lease or a claim for possession of rented property for non-payment of rent, but in the ordinary way the purpose of the statute is to prevent, unless those formalities are carried out, forfeiture of a lease for breach of, *inter alia*, a repairing covenant. I need not repeat the relevant subsections that I set out at the commencement of this judgment. The effect, and, to my mind, the landlord's intended purpose, of clause 3 (6) of this lease was to circumvent those provisions by claiming that the landlord might, without the notice to the tenant required in the event of a breach of the covenant to repair pursuant to clause 3 (4) of the lease, enter and do works and charge the tenant with the cost thereof. Further, by stating in clause 3 (6) that such cost was recoverable as arrears of rent the landlord could put himself in the position, by relying on arrears of rent, of relieving himself, contrary to the purpose and intention of the Act, of the material obligations, whereas in truth here the forfeiture or claim for possession is founded on a breach of the covenant to repair—a covenant for breach of which, if forfeiture were sought, the procedure under sections 1 and 146 of the Act of 1925 would be necessary. In *Moss Empires Ltd v Olympia (Liverpool) Ltd* (supra) Lord Macmillan pointed out that the lease there antedated the Act of 1927 by some three years and observed that it could not be said that the covenants in that lease had been entered into with any idea of defeating or evading section 18. In my view, in the present lease clause 3 (6) did have that purpose and intent.

Accordingly, I consider, first, that clause 3 (6) is wholly inconsistent with the purposes of section 1 of the Act of 1938 and section 18 (1) of the Act of 1927; secondly, that I cannot and do not treat as a debt a sum not ascertainable at the time of the contract and ascertainable only as the cost of repairs carried out on the failure of the tenant to do those repairs in breach of covenant and, further, being fixed at the whim of the landlord in agreement with contractors of his choice; thirdly, that the clause removes from the tenant the choice given to her by the lease to carry out the works of repair at her own expense with contractors of her choice; fourthly, that the clause not only removes from the tenant the protection of the notice to do the repairs provided for by clause 3 (4) but also deprives her of the option of having the work done by a contractor of her choice at a price agreed by her; and, finally, that in any event the provision that the amount to be charged or added as arrears of rent is to include solicitor's, counsel's and surveyor's reasonable fees offends against the basic principles of debt as recognised over the centuries unless there is to be imported, as I do not think must necessarily be imported for the efficacy of this lease, some provision such as that such fee should be taxed or be subject to such adjudication as to reasonableness as is laid down by some taxing or professional authority. In my view, therefore, the sum claimed is at best thinly described as debt but in truth the claim is a claim for damages for breach of covenant and so offends against section 1 (3) of the Act of 1938.

Case 104 Hamilton v Martell Securities Ltd [1984] 1 All ER 665 Vinelott J

Certain property including land and buildings was demised by the plaintiff under a lease dated May 21, 1963, amended by a deed dated April 7, 1971, to the defendant lessee. A right of way over certain roads for the purpose of access was reserved. The lessee's covenants included covenants to pay the lessor all costs, charges and expenses (including the legal costs and fees payable to a surveyor) which might be incurred by the lessor in respect of any proceedings under sections 146 and 147 of the Law of Property Act 1925; to repair and maintain the demised property; to allow the lessor on reasonable notice to enter the property to view its condition and to give notice in writing to the lessee of all defects and repairs required to be remedied within three months of the date of notice or sooner if necessary; and in default of the lessee carrying out such repairs to allow the lessor to enter the property and make repairs at the lessee's expense repayable by the lessee to the lessor on demand. One of the roads fell into serious disrepair. The lessor complained to the lessee and asked for repairs to be carried out forthwith. On January 25, 1982, the lessor informed the lessee that his letter should be treated as a notice under the lease to carry out repairs. It was further stated that since the lessee had not carried out repairs the lessor was enclosing an estimate of cost prepared by his surveyors. The letter gave the lessee an opportunity to consider it and to make alternative proposals. Nothing happened. On April 2, 1982, the lessor informed the lessee that the repairs were being put in hand without delay and that costs of the work must be borne by the lessee. No reply was received. The lessor tried to reach arrangements with the lessee without success. Since the condition of the road was deteriorating the work was started by the lessor on October 12, 1982, and later completed. The lessor's summons for leave under section 1 (3) of the Leasehold Property (Repairs) Act 1938 to take proceedings for damages for breach of covenant to repair was dismissed by Master Barratt.

Held (1) Where a tenant fails to comply with a repairing covenant in a lease which expressly confers on the landlord the right to enter on the demised premises, carry out the repairs and recover the cost from the tenant, an action by the landlord to recover the cost of the repairs is, having regard to the express terms of the covenant, a claim for a debt due under the lease rather than a claim for damages for breach of the covenant within s 1 (1) and (2) of the Leasehold Property (Repairs) Act 1938, and accordingly the landlord does not require leave under s 1 (3) to bring the action against the tenant.

Vinelott J said (in part)

The difficulty which confronts the lessor is that McNeill J decided in *Swallow Securities Ltd v Brand* (1981) 260 EG 63 that a provision giving a lessor the right, in the event of the failure of the lessee to carry out repairs in accordance with a repairing covenant, himself to remedy the want of repair and to recover the cost from the lessee, is a right to damages within s 1 (2) of the 1938 Act, and that the lessor cannot therefore enforce his claim to recover the cost without the leave of the court. If *SEDAC Investments* (1982) 44 P & CR 319 was rightly decided, the court has no jurisdiction to give leave after the want of repair has been remedied. If both these decisions are correct, a provision in a lease giving the lessor the right in the event of failure of the lessee to carry out repairs in compliance with the repairing covenant himself to remedy the want of repair and to recover the cost of so doing, is of no practical utility. Indeed, a provision of this kind is worse than useless; it is a trap. For under s 4(1) of the Defective Premises Act 1972, a lessor who, under the lease, undertakes an obligation to repair, owes to persons who might reasonably be expected to be affected by defects in the premises, [a duty] to see that they are reasonably safe. That duty is extended by sub-s (4) to the case where, under the lease, the lessor is given the right, expressly or impliedly, to enter the demised premises and carry out repairs. He is under the same duty as a lessor within sub-s (1) as from the time when he first is, or by notice or otherwise, can put himself in a position to exercise the right. A lessor who reserves the right, in the event of the failure of the lessee to carry out repairs under a repairing covenant, to enter and carry out the repairs himself, falls prima facie within sub-s (4), at least after he has given, or is in a position to give, any notice which, under the terms, express or implied in the lease, he is required to give before he exercises that right.

Thus the effect of including such a provision is to expose the lessor to a potential liability to third parites without giving him any effective remedy against his lessee.

If, to protect himself from liability, he enters and does the necessary works of repair, he cannot enforce his claim to recover the cost without the leave of the court and, the want of repair having been remedied, the court has no jurisdiction to grant him leave. Further, it must be at least doubtful whether the court would have jurisdiction to give him leave to commence proceedings to recover the cost of works which he proposes to carry out but has not yet carried out. In any event, the danger to third parties might be so pressing that he could not delay the necessary repairs while he made an application for leave, which might possibly be opposed or taken to appeal. . . .

However, there is a more fundamental objection to the decision of McNeill J. He was not referred to two important decisions, one of Roskill J and the other of the Court of Appeal. The latter was, of course, binding on him.

In *Bader Properties Ltd v Linley Property Investments Ltd* (1968) 19 P & CR 620 the lessor sought to forfeit a lease for breach of a covenant not to underlet. The action for forfeiture was preceded by the service of notice under s 146, which alleged breaches of the covenant not to underlet and of the lessee's covenant to repair. The main issues were whether the lessor had given a licence to underlet and, if it had, whether it had waived the breach. The lessee succeeded on both these points, but there was a further claim.

The lease contained a covenant by the lessee to pay all expenses, including solicitors' costs and surveyors' fees incurred by the lessor incidental to the preparation and service of a notice under s 146 of the Law of Property Act 1925. The lessor had incurred solicitors' and surveyors' charges in connection with the service of the s 146 notice. Roskill J, after referring to s 14 of the 1881 Act, to s 146 (3) of the 1925 Act, and to s 2 of the 1938 Act, said (at 642–643):

"Pausing there, such a counter-notice as contemplated by section 2 of the Act of 1938 was served, and no leave was obtained from the court. The plaintiffs here, however, do not seek to recover by virtue of any statutory provision; they seek to recover by virtue of the express covenant in the lease, and that covenant requires the defendants to pay all expenses incurred by the lessor incidental to the preparation and service of the notice. [Counsel for the defendants] sought to argue that that covenant was affected by the legislation to which I have just referred, and that so long as that legislation operated (as it would until nearly the end of the lease, unless, of course, it were meanwhile repealed), it was ineffective. If, however, a statutory provision is to be relied upon as restricting otherwise plain contractual rights, one would expect to find clear provision to that effect in the statute. [Counsel] was unable to point to any such provision. Moreover, having regard to what Fry LJ said in *Skinners' Company v Knight* ([1891] 2 QB 542 at 545)—that the expenses there in question were not compensation for breach of the covenant—I take the view that, where the parties have expressly covenanted for expenses of this kind to be paid by one to the other, there is nothing in the various statutory provisions to prevent effect being given to that covenant."

That decision, as it seems to me, is inconsistent with the last of the reasons given by McNeill J for his conclusion that the claim by the lessor in the *Swallow Securities* case was a claim for damages and not a claim to recover a debt due from the lessee, namely that a provision that such an amount be added as arrears of rent offends against the basic principle of debt as recognised over the centuries, unless there is imported some provision for review of the amount claimed. Moreover the decision of Roskill J in *Bader Properties* that the claim to recover the costs and expenses incidental to the s 146 notice was not affected by the 1938 Act, must I think apply a fortiori to the claim in *Swallow Securities* and the claim in the instant case, to recover moneys actually expended by the lessor in making good a want of repair arising by reason of a breach by the lessee of a repairing covenant.

The decision of Roskill J was affirmed by the Court of Appeal in *Middlegate Properties Ltd v Gidlow-Jackson* (1977) 34 P & CR 4. In that case, the lease contained a similar covenant by the lessee to pay the lessors' legal costs and surveyors' fees of and incidental to the service of a s 146 notice.

Megaw LJ, having pointed out that under s 146 (3) the lessor was entitled to recover such costs and expenses as a debt due to him from a lessee, referred to the decision of Roskill J in *Bader Properties* and said (at 10):

"The basis of that decision, as I understand it, was that the claim was not to be treated as being a claim for damages for breach of contract but was to be treated as being a claim for

debt—money due under the contract. That decision was binding on the judge in the court below, and, as Mr Gidlow-Jackson
has rightly pointed out to this court, the judge in the court
below was bound to follow it but we are not bound to follow
it; we are entitled to overrule it. To that extent we are in a
different position from that of the judge. If I thought that the
decision of Roskill J was wrong, I should have no hesitation
in so holding and giving effect to that view. In my judgment,
however, there is no reason to regard that decision of Roskill
J as being wrong. On the contrary, I think that it obtained
strong support from the wording of the provision of section
146 (3) of the Law of Property Act 1925, to which I called
special attention when I read that subsection. In that subsection there is no doubt that the legislature has deliberately
treated the expenses incurred in the employment of a solicitor
and surveyor in the preparation of a section 146 notice as properly being described as a debt due from a lessee, by contradistinction from damages for breach of contract. It is perfectly
true that that subsection is not dealing with a case where there
is an express covenant in the agreement, but I see no reason
why the wording expressly used by the statute in relation to
a case dealing with statutory provisions should be given a
materially different meaning in relation to the words used in
an express covenant such as the words used here." ...

... That decision is, of course, binding on me and, in my
judgment, compels the conclusion in the instant case that the
lessor's right to recover the cost of repairs to the brown road
is not a right to damages for breach of a covenant to repair,
within s 1 (1) and (2) of the 1938 Act. As I have said, these
decisions, and the decision of the Court of Appeal in *Sidnell
v Wilson*, were not cited to McNeill J. His attention was also
not drawn to the difficulties which later emerged in *SEDAC
Investments Ltd v Tanner* [1982] 3 All ER 646, [1982] 1 WLR 1342
in applying s 1 (5) to a case where a want of repair has actually
been remedied by the lessor, nor to the difficulties which, it
seems to me, would equally confront a lessor who sought leave
to bring proceedings to recover the cost of carrying out repairs
before he had actually carried them out.

Counsel for the lessor submitted that the decision of Michael
Wheeler QC in *SEDAC Investments* was also wrong ...

The situation which arose in *SEDAC Investments* was, in fact,
very unusual and may well not have been contemplated by the
legislature. It is difficult to imagine circumstances in which a

lessor who reserves a right to enter and remedy a state of disrepair arising from the lessee's breach, would not also have the right, expressly or by necessary implication, to recover the cost. In so far as he has the right to recover the cost, the right is wholly outside the ambit of the 1938 Act. Equally a lessor who does not reserve the right to enter and remedy a want of repair arising from a breach of the lessee's covenants, and who none the less does so is, in law, a trespasser, and it is not obvious that he would be entitled to recover the moneys he has spent as damages for breach of covenant, or that he could rely on the lessee's breach of covenant in allowing the want of repair to arise as founding a claim for damages or for forfeiture, once he has himself remedied the state of disrepair. However, the point does not arise for decision and I express no concluded opinion on it.

Note:
  (i) This decision was followed in *Colchester Estates (Cardiff) v Carlton Industries plc* [1984] 2 All ER 601 and *Elite Investments Ltd v T I Bainbridge Silencers Ltd* [Case 118].

6.8 Tenant's remedy: Set-off against rent

Set-off is an appropriate remedy where a disrepair has occurred which the landlord has not remedied after notice; in such a case the tenant may be able to carry out the repair work himself and set-off the cost of such repair against the rent payable to the landlord.

Case 105 *Lee-Parker v Izzet* [1971] 1 WLR 1688 Goff J

  In an action for the enforcement of a registered charge on several separate properties the mortgagees claimed, *inter alia*, that contracts made by the mortgagor with the various occupiers for the purchase of the properties were not binding on them (the mortgagees) and for delivery up to them of the relevant properties. The court ruled, on the particular facts, that the occupiers' contracts with the mortgagor were not now enforceable against the mortgagees but that the occupiers were entitled to liens on the properties for deposit money and interest thereon.

  On the question whether occupiers having a tenancy had a right of set off or a lien for the cost of repairs which the morgagor, in breach of his covenant as landlord, had failed to carry out or whether they had a lien based on their relationship with the mortgagor as vendor, for the value of any permanent improvement effected by the repairs:

Held (1) That irrespective of the rules of set off, the occupiers had a right at common law to recoup themselves out of future rents for the cost of the repairs in so far as those repairs fell within the express or implied covenants of the landlord, provided he was in breach and after due notice given to him.

(2) That as against the mortgagees there could be no set off for repairs falling outside the landlord's covenants.

(3) That the occupiers had no claim to a lien on the property based either on the landlord and tenant or vendor and purchaser relationship since they did the repairs to remedy the mortgagor's breach of a purely collateral agreement and, further, they were primarily in possession as tenants and enjoying the benefit of the work they had done.

Goff J said (in part)

... the third and fourth defendants further claim a lien for the cost of the repairs or alternatively for the value of any permanent improvement effected thereby, and they also claim a set off against rent in their capacity as tenants.

First, they say that in so far as the first defendant was, as landlord, liable to do the repairs by the express or implied terms of the tenancy agreement, including the covenants imported by section 32 (1) of the Housing Act 1961, they, having done them themselves, are entitled to treat the expenditure as a payment of rent, for which reliance is placed on *Taylor v Beal* (1591) Cro Eliz 222. That is dicta only and the actual decision must have been the other way, because one of the majority in opinion thought the point was not open on the pleadings ...

... *Taylor v Beal* (1591) Cro Eliz 222 is not cited in *Halsbury* at all. *Surplice v Farnsworth* (1844) 7 Man. & G 576, 584 does not help on this issue since the only question there was whether the performance by the landlord of his repairing covenant was a condition the breach of which entitled the tenant to quit, and discharge him from any further liability during the breach, for the payment of rent; and it was held that it was not. Similarly *Hart v Rogers* [1916] 1 KB 646, where the tenant had not done the repairs, does not help on this point. *Waters v Weigall* (1795) 2 Anst 575 which is cited in the footnote to *Surplice v Farnsworth*, 7 Man & G 576, 586 does, however, support *Taylor v Beal*. In *Waters v Weigall*, 2 Anst 575 it was a case of sudden emergency due to a tempest but Macdonald CB laid down a quite general proposition as follows, at p. 576:

> "I do not see how you entitle yourself to the interposition of this court. If the landlord is bound in law or equity to repair in consequence of the accident that has happened, and you were right in expending this sum in repairs for him, it is money paid to his use, and may be set off against the demand for rent. If you fail in making these points, your ground of relief is destroyed in equity, as well as at law."

In *Taylor v Webb* [1937] 2 KB 283 the question which went to the Court of Appeal was the extent of the liability under a covenant to repair, fair wear and tear excepted, but du Parcq J had held the covenants to repair and to pay rent being independent, the tenant could maintain his cross-claim for damages although he had not paid the rent. Conversely, the landlord can sue for rent although he has not repaired. But again that does not touch the point in *Taylor v Beal*, Cro Eliz 222.

I do not think this is bound up with technical rules of set off. It is an ancient common law right. I therefore declare that so far as the repairs are within the express or implied covenants of the landlord, the third and fourth defendants are entitled to recoup themselves out of future rents and defend any action for payment thereof. It does not follow however that the full amount expended by the third and fourth defendants on such repairs can properly be treated as payment of rent. It is a question of fact in every case whether and to what extent the expenditure was proper.

For the sake of avoiding misunderstanding I must add that of course the *Taylor v Beal* right can only be exercised when and so far as the landlord is in breach and any necessary notice must have been given to him.

In so far as the repairs fall outside the landlord's covenants there can in my judgment be no set off against the plaintiffs.

Case 106 British Anzani (Felixstowe) Ltd v International Marine Management (UK) Ltd [1979] 2 All ER 1063 Forbes J

The plaintiffs developed a block of reclaimed land by building and then leasing warehouses on it. By an agreement dated June 7, 1973 the plaintiffs agreed to construct a warehouse and lease it to the defendants. The agreement contained a provision that the plaintiffs would make good at their own expense any defects in the floor of the warehouse occurring within two years of completion caused by inadequate design or faulty materials or workmanship, and provided that, notwithstanding the completion of the lease, the agreement was to continue in force between the parties. On April 24, 1974 the parties signed a lease of the warehouse for a term of 21 years. The lease contained no covenant by the landlord to repair. A similar arrangement was later made in respect of a second warehouse. By actions commenced in 1975 and 1978 the defendants alleged that serious defects had appeared in the floors of both warehouses making them unusable, and claimed damages of more than £1 million from the plaintiffs. They also refused to pay any further rent. In 1977 the plaintiffs issued a writ claiming possession, and unpaid rent and mesne profits amounting to over £570,000. The defendants admitted owing some £540,000 but claimed that the amount owing was subject to a set-off in respect of their counter-claim. It was ordered that a preliminary issue be tried whether the defendants were entitled in law or in equity to deduct or set-off against their admitted liability for rent and mesne profits the damages claimed against the plaintiffs for breach of the agreement of June 7, 1973 and the lease. It was contended on behalf of the plaintiffs that the defendants were not entitled to a set-off because (i) an unliquidated or unquantifiable demand could not be used as a set-off in equity, (ii) in the very nature of rent there could be no set-off against it, and (iii) the counterclaim did not arise out of the lease or the relationship of landlord and tenant on which the demand for rent was based and was therefore not sufficiently closely connected with the plaintiffs' claim for rent to support an equitable set-off.

Held (1) An unliquidated demand could give rise to an equitable set-off against a claim for a debt, and, since unliquidated damages by their nature remained unquantified until an award was made, there was no reason why a demand could not be used as a set-off merely because it was unquantified. If a defendant claimed unliquidated damages and *bona fide* claimed that they would exceed the amount of the plaintiff's claim, he was entitled to a set-off amounting to a complete defence.

(2) At common law there could be what amounted to a set-off against a claim for rent if the tenant paid money on repairs which the landlord had failed in breach of covenant to carry out or if the tenant had paid money at the landlord's

request to fulfil the latter's obligations in respect of the land, the payment being regarded as a payment *pro tanto* of the rent; but such a defence only applied if, in the case of money paid for repairs, the tenant had given prior notice of want of repair, and in any event only applied if the amount claimed to be set off was certain and could not be disputed or challenged as to quantum. It followed that because the defendants had not in fact paid out anything and because their claim was for an unliquidated amount rather than a sum certain, they could not avail themselves of any common law right of set-off against rent.

(3) The existence of the common law right amounting to set-off against rent did not, however, preclude the defendants from relying on the doctrine of equitable set-off, since, except in cases of distress or replevin, equity had never refused to interfere to protect a tenant whose landlord was bringing proceedings based on non-payment of rent if the tenant had a *bona fide* cross-claim for unliquidated damages against the landlord, provided the tenant had no common law remedy and fulfilled the preconditions for the application of the equitable doctrine.

(4) In order to rely on the doctrine of equitable set-off the defendants had to show, *inter alia*, that their counterclaim was so directly or closely connected with the plaintiffs' claim as to go to the foundation of that claim, and they were unable to do that either from the lease itself or directly from the relationship of landlord and tenant created by the lease, because the plaintiffs had not breached any covenant in the lease.

(5) However, it was not essential for the application of the doctrine for the claim and counterclaim to arise out of the same contract: it was sufficient if the defendants' counterclaim arose out of a transaction so closely connected with the lease that it would be manifestly unjust not to allow a set-off. Since the defendants' counterclaim arose out of alleged breaches of the agreement of June 7, 1973 which had rendered the warehouses unfit in part for the purposes for which they were leased, and because it would be manifestly unjust to allow the plaintiffs to recover rent without taking into account damages caused by the plaintiffs' failure to perform their part of the agreement, the defendants had established a sufficiently close connection between the transactions for them to raise their counterclaim as a set-off against the plaintiffs' claim.

Forbes J said (in part)

... *Taylor v Beal* (1591) Cro Eliz 222 is authority for the proposition that there are at least two sets of circumstances in which at common law there can be a set-off against rent, one where the tenant expends money on repairs to the demised premises which the landlord has covenanted to carry out, but in breach has failed to do so (at any rate where the breach significantly affects the use of the premises), and the other where the tenant has paid money at the request of the landlord in respect of some obligation of the landlord connected with the land demised. To this proposition there must be added two riders. First, that as the landlord's obligation to repair premises demised does not arise until the tenant has notified him of want of repair, such notification must have been given before the set-off can arise; and secondly that the set-off must be for a sum which is not to be regarded as unliquidated damages, that is, it is a sum certain which has actually been paid and in addition its quantum has either been acknowledged by the landlord or in some other way can no longer be disputed by him, as, for instance, if it is the subject of an award on a submission to arbitration. The latest expression of opinion about this matter is in *Lee-Parker v Izzet* [1971] 3 All ER 1099. In that case Goff J was dealing among other things with a claim to a lien, the basis of which was laid on an argument that the tenants were entitled to treat a payment of the cost of repairs, for which the landlord was liable, as a payment of rent and reliance was placed on *Taylor v Beal*. Goff J discussed the principle of *Taylor v Beal* and said this:

> "I do not think this is bound up with technical rules of set-off. It is an ancient common-law right. I therefore declare that so far as the repairs are within the express or implied covenants of the lessor the third and fourth defendants are entitled to recoup themselves out of future rents and defend any action for payment thereof. It does not follow however that the full amount expended by the third and fourth defendants on such repairs can properly be treated as payment of rents. It is a question of fact in every case whether and to what extent the expenditure was proper."

I do not think that there is any difference between the principle as seen by Goff J and that which I have set out above save for this. Goff J took the view that it was money properly expended which could form a subject of this right. My view is that the right is slightly more restricted, namely that it can only be exercised when the sum is certain and its amount cannot really be disputed by the landlord. This restriction which I think should be made arises from a consideration of the judgment of Lord Kenyon CJ in *Weigall v Waters* (1795) 6 Term Rep 488 which was not quoted to Goff J. In that case the tenant had in fact paid £30 but Lord Kenyon CJ still regarded the cross-claim as one for uncertain damages. It seems the quantum of the sum must have been either unchallenged or unchallengeable before it could be regarded as deductible.

Case 107 Melville v Grapelodge Developments Ltd (1978) 254 EG 1193 Neill J

The plaintiffs were the mesne landlords of premises the third floor of which was occupied by the defendants for the purposes of their trade as printers and stationers. The plantiffs claimed arrears of rent alleged to be due under the lease for the four quarters of 1977. The defendants alleged that the occupied premises was subject to disrepair and that the landlords had not carried out a promise to decorate and repair the entrance hall.

Held (1) The obligation of the tenants under the lease to pay the rent and the obligation of the landlords to carry out repairs were separate, albeit closely linked, obligations.

(2) The claim for unliquidated damages was capable of being set-off against the claim for rent in view of the close connection between the two claims.

Neill J said (in part)

I can deal very shortly with the plaintiffs' contention that their obligations under the undertaking were put into suspension by the failure of the defendants to pay the rent due on March 25 1977. I am satisfied that this argument is wrong. The undertaking was given in consideration of the defendants' "completing this matter today." The defendants did duly complete the matter by signing the lease. The obligation of the defendants under the lease to pay the rent and the obligations of the plaintiffs under the undertaking to carry out the repairs are to my mind separate, albeit closely linked, obligations. I am reinforced in this view by the decision of du Parcq J in *Taylor v Webb* [1937] 2 KB 283. The decision of du Parcq J was reversed by the Court of Appeal, but there is nothing in the judgments of the Court of Appeal to throw any doubt on the views of du Parcq J on this point. It is further to be noted that the decision in *Taylor v Webb* in the Court of Appeal was itself overruled by the House of Lords in *Regis Property Co Ltd v Dudley* [1959] AC 370.

I am also satisfied that there is no sound basis for the defendants' argument that their obligation to pay rent was suspended because of the plaintiffs' breach of the undertaking. By the lease dated March 21 the defendants undertook an obligation to pay rent in accordance with the terms of the lease, and in my view the obligation was not removed or altered by any breach by the plaintiffs of the undertaking. Furthermore I would find it impossible on the present evidence to come to the conclusion that the plaintiffs were in breach of that undertaking by March 25 1977. Discussions about repairs to the roof had been continuing since December 1976, and it seems to me to be quite unrealistic to treat the plaintiffs as in breach of the undertaking by reason of the fact that they had not started work by March 25. In any event, however, I consider that the obligation to carry out the repairs was subject to the words "but in any event such works to commence not later than three months from today."

I turn therefore to the second main argument put forward by [counsel] on behalf of the plaintiffs. He argued that even if the obligation to carry out the repairs continued, the defendants are not entitled as a matter of law to set off any claim for damages for breach of the undertaking against the claim for rent. In support of this submission [counsel] referred me to the decision of Goff J (as he then was) in *Lee-Parker v Izzet* [1971] 1 WLR 1688. In that case Goff J held that where a landlord has failed to comply with his obligations to carry out repairs under the terms of a tenancy agreement and the tenant has carried out the work himself, the tenant is entitled to treat the expenditure as a payment of rent. The learned judge referred to the old case of *Taylor v Beal* (1591) Cro Eliz 222 as authority for the proposition that the right to recoup the expenditure out of future rents was an old common law right. [Counsel] submitted that it was implicit in the decision of Goff J that unless the tenant had actually expended money on repairs in fulfilment of the landlord's obligation, there was no right to any set-off against his obligation to pay the rent. With respect to [counsel], I do not consider that one can make any such deduction from Goff J's judgment. Indeed he said in terms at p. 1693 that the ancient common law right of recoupment had nothing to do with technical rules of set-off. Counsel were unable to refer me to any cases which threw light on the right to claim a set-off against a claim for rent and therefore, as the question of set-off was a matter of some general application, I thought it right in the circumstances to reserve my judgment.

It might be argued that the obligation to pay rent is an obligation of a special nature and that the ordinary rules of equitable set-off as explained by Morris LJ in *Hanak v Green* [1958] 2 QB 9 do not apply. It is certainly a matter for surprise that, certainly as far as the searches of counsel can find, there does not seem to be any reported authority since the Judicature Acts in which a claim for damages for breach of a repairing covenant has been allowed by way of set-off for an action for rent. Indeed in *Hart v Rogers* [1916] 1 KB 646 Scrutton J held that a cross-claim by a tenant for breach of an implied covenant to repair did not constitute a defence to a claim by the landlord for unpaid rent of the premises. It is to be noted, however, that in that case Scrutton J was not referred to the principles underlying the doctrine of equitable set-off; in particular he was not referred to the decision in *Beasley v D'Arcy* ((1800) noted in 2 Sch & Lef 403) in which the court in Ireland granted relief in a case of ejectment by way of injunction where the tenant was able to set up a claim for unliquidated damages against the landlord for breach of covenant. The report of the decision in *Beasley v D'Arcy* appears as a note to the report of *O'Mahoney v Dickson* (1805) 2 Sch & Lef 400, a case decided before Lord Redesdale.

It can be further argued in this case that the claim for damages arises not under the lease itself but under a separate contract constituted by the undertaking contained in the letter of March 21. Accordingly, it could be said, the decision in *Beasley v D'Arcy* is distinguishable.

I have come to the conclusion that at the present day there are no adequate grounds for treating an obligation to pay rent as an obligation which is different in kind from that imposed by other contracts. It follows therefore that in my view a claim for unliquidated damages is *capable* of being set off in equity against a claim for rent provided there is a sufficiently close connection between the two claims.

Note:

(i) See also *Asco Developments Ltd v Gordon* [1978] EGD 376.

6.9 Tenant's remedy: Specific Performance

Case 108 Jeune v Queens Cross Properties Ltd [1974] 1 Ch 97 Pennycuick VC

Each of the underleases, under which four tenants were respectively in possession of four flats comprised in the property, contained a covenant by the lessors, the predecessors-in-title of the landlord company, to maintain, repair and renew the structure of the property, including the external walls thereof. The tenants alleged that the landlord, in breach of the repairing covenants, had failed to reinstate a balcony at the front of the property at first floor level in the form in which it existed prior to its partial collapse on May 13, 1972. The balcony was not included in any of the underleases. The tenants issued a writ claiming an order that the landlord should forthwith reinstate the balcony in the form in which it existed prior to its partial collapse. The landlord entered appearance but did not serve a defence.

On motion for judgment in default of defence:

Held (1) That the court had power, which should be carefully exercised, to make an order in an appropriate case against a landlord to do some specific work under a covenant to repair; that, where there had been a plain breach of a covenant to repair and there was no doubt as to what was required to be done to remedy the breach, an order for carrying out the required work ought to be made; and that, accordingly, the landlord should be ordered to reinstate the balcony forthwith.

Pennycuick VC said (in part)

Again in the present case there is no difficulty about that because the defendant would know what has to be done.

The difficulty arises from something which was said by Lord Eldon LC in *Hill v Barclay* (1810) 16 Ves Jun 402. The facts should be looked at but I will not take time reading them now. Lord Eldon LC considered whether this was a case in which forfeiture should be decreed against the plaintiff tenant and in the course of his judgment said, at p. 405:

"The situation of the landlord is however very different as to rent and as to these other covenants. He may bring an ejectment upon non-payment of rent: but he may also compel the tenant to pay rent. He cannot have that specific relief with regard to repairs. He may bring an action for damages; but there is a wide distinction between damages and the actual expenditure upon repairs, specifically done. Even after damages recovered the landlord cannot compel the tenant to repair: but may bring another action. The tenant therefore, standing those actions, may keep the premises until the last year of the term; and from the reasoning of one of the cases [*Hack v Leonard* (1724) 9 Mod 91] the conclusion is, that the most beneficial course for the landlord would be, that the tenant, refraining from doing the repairs until the last year of the term, should then be compelled to do them. The difficulty upon this doctrine of a court of equity is, that there is no mutuality in it. The tenant cannot be compelled to repair."

Now that decision is, I think, an authority laying down the principle that a landlord cannot obtain against his tenant an order for specific performance of a covenant to repair. It does not however apply to a landlord's covenant to repair, although it is said that there may be some other explanation for the words "The difficulty upon this doctrine of a court of equity is, that there is no mutuality in it". . . .

There is nothing at all there inconsistent with a power in the court to make an order on a landlord to do specific work under a covenant to repair. I cannot myself see any reason in principle, why, in an appropriate case, an order should not be made against a landlord to do some specific work pursuant to his covenant to repair. Obviously, it is a jurisdiction which should be carefully exercised. But in a case such as the present where there has been a plain breach of a covenant to repair and there is no doubt at all what is required to be done to remedy the breach, I cannot see why an order for specific performance should not be made.

Note:

(i) There would seem to be no reason in principle why specific performance would not be available to enforce a tenant's repairing obligations despite the ruling in *Hill v Barclay*.

Case 109 *Francis v Cowcliffe Ltd* (1976) 33 P & CR 368 HH Judge Rubin (sitting as a deputy High Court Judge)

The plaintiff, a 70 year old widow, was a tenant of a third floor flat in the defendants' building. She had lived there for 40 years. On October 16, 1969, the defendants' predecessors-in-title granted her a new lease for five years from September 29, 1969. By clause 3(4) the landlord covenanted to provide the services set out in the schedule to the lease. Paragraph 2 of the schedule provided that where facilities existed a lift for the tenants in the building would be supplied and maintained. Until February 1972 a hydraulic lift was in operation but by then it needed repairs and could not be operated for lack of the supply of water under pressure. Without the lift the plaintiff suffered difficulties in that her own access to her flat became inconvenient and her friends were reluctant to visit her. That difficulty continued. The defendants, after buying the property with advances from mortgagees, got into financial difficulties because their plans to redevelop their property went wrong. They were insolvent and were unable to meet their debts without obtaining further advances which they failed to get in spite of trying. In their attempts to make a lift operational again, they obtained expert advice and bought another lift but could not have it installed for lack of funds. On February 14, 1975, the plaintiff brought an action seeking an order for specific performance of the covenant and damages for breach of covenant in lieu of or in addition to the order.

On the defendants, not disputing that there was a breach of covenant on their part but contending that since it had become impossible for them to provide a lift their obligations under the covenant had been frustrated:

Held (1) That accepting that where in a lease a covenant created a continuing or future obligation the doctrine of frustration applied, and applying the tests laid down in *Davis Contractors Ltd v Fareham Urban District Council* [1956] AC 696 namely, first, frustration depended on whether on its true construction the conctract, in the light of its nature and of the relevant surrounding circumstances when it was made, was wide enough to apply to the new situation and if it was not, then it was at an end; and secondly, frustration occurred whenever the law recognised that, without default of either party, a contractual obligation had become incapable of being performed because the circumstances in which performance was called for would render it a thing radically different from that which was undertaken by the contract and it was not hardship or inconvenience or material loss itself which called the principle of frustration into play,—the defendants' contention of frustration failed because the covenant was wide enough to cover the present situation and their present obligation was not in any way different from that contracted for.

(2) That since the work was sufficiently defined by the contract, the plaintiff had a substantial interest in its performance and the defendants were in possession of the building, the plaintiff was entitled to a decree of specific performance since the performance of the covenant would have been no hardship to the covenantors when the covenant was made and the fact that it would cause hardship to the defendants now was of their own making, no one but themselves being responsible for their present financial difficulties; and, accordingly, the decree should be made.

HH Judge Rubin said (in part)

In support of her claim for specific performance the plaintiff in respect of the repairing covenant relies on section 125 of the Housing Act 1974. The defendants say their default is not a breach of clause 3 (2) as the lift is not a part of the building not subject to any lease. The argument is that not being fixed it cannot be part of the building. It seems to me that it is as much part of a building as a door which swings on its hinges.

As far as the other covenant is concerned the plaintiff relies upon the general principle that in an appropriate case the court will decree specific performance of an agreement to build if certain conditions are satisfied. In *Jeune v Queens Cross Properties Ltd* [1974] 1 Ch 97 Pennycuick V-C adopted the statement of these conditions now to be found in *Snell's Principles of Equity* (27th ed, 1973), p. 581:

"The rule has now become settled that the court will order specific performance of an agreement to build if—
  (i) the building work is sufficiently defined by the contract, e.g. by reference to detailed plans;
 (ii) the plaintiff has a substantial interest in the performance of the contract of such a nature that damages would not compensate him for the defendant's failure to build; and
(iii) the defendant is in possession of the land so that the plaintiff cannot employ another person to build without committing a trespass."

The defendants do not dispute that the first and third conditions are satisfied. In my judgment on my finding of fact the second condition is also satisfied.

Prima facie therefore the plaintiff is entitled to specific performance, but as the remedy is equitable and discretionary the court will not grant it where it would inflict great hardship on a defendant. *Snell*, at p. 598, puts the matter in this way:

"To constitute a defence, however, the hardship must have existed at the date of the contract; specific performance will not be refused merely because, owing to events which have happened since the contract was made, the completion of the contract will cause hardship. Financial inability to complete is not hardship, . . ."

This last proposition receives support from *Nicholas v Ingram* [1958] NZLR 972 a decision of the Supreme Court in New Zealand. In *Fry on Specific Performance*, (6th ed., 1921), para. 426, p. 203, the proposition is stated as follows:

"The cases which have been already quoted as showing that the hardship must be judged of at the time of the contract also illustrate another obvious principle, namely, that where the hardship has been brought upon the defendant by himself, it shall not be allowed to furnish any defence against the specific performance of the contract, ..."

In this case there was no hardship at all at the time of the contract. If ever there was a case in which the defendants has brought the hardship on itself, this must be it. The defendants chose to purchase and embark upon an expensive scheme for development of the property without any or any adequate finance and without making any but the most speculative arrangements for such finance.

Accordingly, for these reasons I propose to make the order for specific performance which the plaintiff seeks.

Note:

(i) In *Peninsular Maritime Ltd v Padseal Ltd* (1981) 259 EG 860 an order was made granting an interlocutory mandatory injunction by which the landlords were enjoined to use their best endeavours to put a lift in good working condition until after the trial of the action or further order. In this case there had been a forfeiture and proceedings for relief were pending.

Under the Landlord and Tenant Act 1985 specific performance of a landlord's repairing obligations in any tenancy (other than one to which the Landlord and Tenant Act 1954 Pt II applies) is provided for.

Statute 10: Landlord and Tenant Act 1985. Section 17

Specific performance of landlord's repairing obligations
17.—(1) In proceedings in which a tenant of a dwelling alleges a breach on the part of his landlord of a repairing covenant relating to any part of the premises in which the dwelling is comprised, the court may order specific performance of the covenant whether or not the breach relates to a part of the premises let to the tenant and notwithstanding any equitable rule restricting the scope of the remedy, whether on the basis of a lack of mutuality or otherwise.

(2) In this section:

(a) "tenant" includes a statutory tenant,

(b) in relation to a statutory tenant the reference to the premises let to him is to the premises of which he is a statutory tenant,

(c) "landlord", in relation to a tenant, includes any person against whom the tenant has a right to enforce a repairing covenant, and

(d) "repairing covenant" means a covenant to repair, maintain, renew, construct or replace any property.

Section 125 of the Housing Act 1974 (the predecessor to section 17) was considered in the complex case of *Gordon v Selico Co Ltd*.

Case 110 *Gordon v Selico Co Ltd* [1986] 1 EGLR 71; (1986) 278 EG 53 Court of Appeal

The plaintiffs were the tenants of a flat in a block of flats owned by the first defendants and managed by the second defendants. The demised flat (and the block in general) was in a poor state when the plaintiffs purchased the flat in 1979, but their surveyor indicated that certain works needed to be carried out on the structure and that there was a damp problem in the flat. The tenants' surveyor warned that he could not state that there was no dry rot in any of the other parts of the building. Dry rot was discovered between the tenants' flat and the one above, but they completed the purchase on having advice that they were bound to do so. Upon the service of a dangerous structure notice the dry rot was remedied by works undertaken by builders instructed by the local authority.

The tenants claimed under four heads, namely: (i) deceit or fraudulent misrepresentation; (ii) breach of express obligations in the lease; (iii) breach of implied obligations; and (iv) negligence and nuisance. Goulding J held that the allegation of fraudulent misrepresentation was proved, as evidence was adduced that a builder employed by the managing agents had deliberately or recklessly covered up clear signs of dry rot when decorating the flat prior to the sale to the tenants. The learned judge also found the landlords in breach of express obligations in the lease as they had failed to carry out the scheme of maintenance. Considering the claims of breach of implied obligations and negligence together, the learned judge held the defendants liable but found that an exemption clause in the lease provided a defence to claims under these heads as well as for the claim in nuisance. Goulding J also ordered specific performance of the landlord's obligations by requiring them to put so much of the block as was in their possession or control into such reasonable condition as not to cause damage to the tenants or their flat by the incursion of water, penetration of dry rot etc.

Held (1) The finding of deceit would be upheld but the management company was, through its main shareholder, a party to the deceit. As the lessors had entrusted the company with sufficiently wide authority they were "vicariously" liable for the fraudulent misrepresentation.

(2) Both the lessors and the agents had been guilty of breaches of covenant and breaches of trust under the lease.

(3) The lessors should pay the lessees damages for deceit and for breaches of contractual obligations under the lease.

(4) Specific performance would be ordered of the lessors' covenants to keep certain parts of the block in good repair.

Slade LJ said (in part)
... in his judgment the learned judge considered the relief to be given to the plaintiffs on their claim. He ruled out the possibility of rescission and pointed out the obvious difficulties which, on the face of it, specific performance would present. However, he drew attention to section 125 of the Housing Act 1974, which empowers the court, in proceedings in which a tenant of a dwelling alleges a breach on the part of his landlord of a "repairing covenant", to order specific performance of the covenant "whether or not the breach relates to a part of the premises let to the tenant and notwithstanding any equitable rules restricting the scope of that remedy ...". With the support of that section, the learned judge decided in effect to grant specific performance not of the express covenants on the part of the landlord contained in the lease but of the *implied* obligation which he considered to fall upon Selico, arising from its retention of property whose proper maintenance was necessary for the protection of safe enjoyment of the demised premises. Having delivered his judgment, he gave the parties the opportunity to address further argument to him as to the precise form of the order on a later occasion. We have already indicated the form which his order eventually took. As he explained in his judgment, the thought behind his awards of nominal damages against both defendants was that the plaintiffs must look to their damages in tort as compensation for their past and present loss,

while the order for specific performance would protect them for the immediate future.

6.10 Tenant's remedy: Appointment of a receiver of rents

If a landlord fails to comply with his repairing obligation the High Court has power to grant an injunction or appoint a receiver in all cases in which it appears just and convenient to do so.

Case 111 *Hart v Elmkirk Ltd* (1982) 267 EG 946 Goulding J

The demised premises consisted of two blocks of flats which had seriously deteriorated due to the landlord's failure to comply with his covenant to keep in repair and insure the premises. During the previous two or three years the rents and service charges had not been collected. The plaintiffs were the tenants of the flats and the defendants were a company which sold the reversionary interest in 1979 to a purchaser who had neither registered his title nor exercised any rights attached to his reversion. The plaintiffs brought an action against the defendants seeking a mandatory injunction to compel compliance with the covenants. The present motion was for the appointment, pending the trial, of an independent surveyor to receive the rents of the flats (and other moneys payable) and to manage the blocks of flats in accordance with the landlord's obligations.

Held (1) In the exercise of the court's power under section 37 of the Supreme Court Act 1981 to "appoint a receiver [where] it appears to the court to be just and convenient to do so" and its power to invest the receiver with such powers as the court, in its discretion, thinks necessary for the preservation of property, the court may appoint a receiver to receive and give a good receipt for the rents, profits and all other moneys payable under a lease of a property and to manage the property in accordance with the rights and obligations of the reversioner in a case where the landlord refuses or neglects to collect the rents due under the lease and refuses or neglects to perform the covenants in the lease to repair and insure the property.

Goulding J said (in part)

The action is brought to obtain a mandatory injunction against the defendant company to comply with the landlord's covenants and also for damages, and counsel for the defendant company tells me that third party proceedings are likely. But what I am asked to do today by the plaintiffs in each of the two actions dealing with adjoining blocks of flats is to appoint a named surveyor to receive the rents and profits of each property and all other moneys payable under the lease or any part thereof and to manage the property in accordance with the rights and obligations of the reversioner until trial or further order. I am asked to say that the person so appointed may give a good receipt for certain sums of money which one of the plaintiffs in each case has received as representing (or apparently representing) what remains of a reserve fund, intended under the leases to be built up by tenants' contributions, and that he (the receiver) may have to resort to those funds in course of management.

Now, I know of no precedent for such relief, but I also know of no authority that forbids it under the provisions of the Judicature Acts now represented by the Supreme Court Act 1981, section 37:

> "The High Court may by order (whether interlocutory or final) ... appoint a receiver in all cases in which it appears to the court to be just and convenient to do so ..."

It clearly appears to me to be just to appoint a receiver in this case because it is done to support the enforcement by the court of covenants affecting property: compare *Riches v Owent* (1868) 3 Ch App 820. It is also convenient because, as I said, the properties are in a condition that demands urgent action.

I propose, therefore, in each action to appoint the nominated surveyor, in respect of whom an affidavit of fitness has been provided. I am assuming, of course, that his formal consent to act will be forthcoming. I will appoint him to receive the rents and profits and other moneys payable under the leases in the form of the notice of motion and to manage, in accordance with the rights and obligations of the reversioner, again as stated in the notice of motion, until trial or further order. I think the court has a wide jurisdiction to invest a receiver with such powers as the court, in its discretion, thinks necessary for the preservation of the property, the income of which he is to receive.

Case 112 *Daiches v Bluelake Investments Ltd* [1985] 2 EGLR 67; (1985) 275 EG 462 Harman J

A long leaseholder brought an action seeking the appointment of a receiver to carry out repairs urgently required to a block of flats. The landlords had not complied with their covenant to maintain, decorate and renew the structure and there was substantial disrepair in respect of common parts, external walls, roofs etc. The leaseholders paid a fixed ground rent plus a service charge to meet the costs, *inter alia*, of repairing the structure, roofs and so forth. Although there was a provision for a sinking fund, no such fund had been established in recent years.

Held (1) A receiver and manager would be appointed in the place of the lessors to receive the rents and exercise the powers, duties and authorities of the lessors in managing the block.

Harman J said (in part)

The trouble appears to be that the money to do . . . a major set of works is not there. The evidence before me shows that the present reversioner, the first defendant, which is the reversioner although no notice of its reversion has been given to the tenants, has effectively no assets at all. The only evidence before me as to its accounts shows £100 paid-up share capital, effectively no reserves and a transfer pursuant to a charge for all moneys to a licensed deposit-taker, a secondary banking institution. The ability of the first defendant to provide sums of money, whether of £300,000 or nearer £1 million, is plainly in the highest degree dubious. The second defendant, which now has no interest in the property save that it owns the shares in the first defendant, has large mortgages and all moneys charges and appears to have had a fairly poor financial record; its last accounts were heavily qualified by its auditors. Again, there appears to be little prospect of its having access, certainly not from its own funds, to any such sums of money as would be needed to put in hand such a programme as is needed here.

In those circumstances, says Mr Daiches, the work is urgently needed, the premises are dangerous and deteriorating, and the enjoyment by himself and by each of those he represents of the property (being the leasehold estate which each of them holds) is seriously imperilled and made far less desirable than it should be. He points to the decision of Goulding J in *Hart v Emelkirk Ltd* [1983] 1 WLR 1289 and says that the essence of that decision appears at p. 1291, paras F to H, where the learned judge said:

"I know of no precedent for such a relief,"

being very similar relief—a receiver—to that sought here,

"but I also know of no authority that forbids it under the provisions of the Judicature Acts, now represented by the Supreme Court Act 1981," of which he reads section 37, which I have already read. The learned judge goes on:

"It clearly appears to me to be just to appoint a receiver in this case because it is done to support the enforcement by the court of covenants affecting property: cf *Riches v Owen* (1868) LR 3 Ch App 820. It is also convenient because . . . the properties are in a condition that demands urgent action."

. . . [Counsel] has observed to me that *Hart v Emelkirk* is a case which he described as a vacuum case, a case where the property was in effect abandoned by the lessors who were not complying with their insurance covenant and were not collecting their rents but appear simply to have walked away and left the properties. [Counsel] is entirely correct. That does appear to have been the case. It seems to me, however, that Mr Daiches' answer to that observation is right. Although it may be easy in a vacuum case to persuade the court that someone should step in, and although this is not a vacuum case, since in this case the lessor is performing some of his duties and some of them well, yet the essence of the decision and the ratio decidendi is in the phrase between G and H, "It [is] just to appoint a receiver . . . to support the enforcement . . . of covenants" and "It is also convenient because . . . the properties are in a condition that demands urgent action." I agree that that is in truth the ratio and, on the facts I have recited, is satisfied in this case.

As it seems to me, it is not for me to determine fundamental questions of construction and law upon this application. It is for me to consider whether, interlocutorily, I should exercise the discretion vested in me under section 37. [Counsel] expressly conceded to me, in my view correctly, that there was jurisdiction to exercise such a power. He merely urged me upon discretionary grounds not to do so.

. . . As it seems to me, the test in section 37, as expressed by Goulding J is entirely satisfied here. The fact that the plaintiffs will, they say, finance the receiver in beginning his works and placing the contracts for the repairs is a fact which is of assistance to the court in considering the exercise of its discretion, though not itself determinative. It does mean that there will be a source of money not apparently available to the lessor, although there is nothing that binds the plaintiffs at the present time so to provide.

Thus, as it seems to me, I should simply, upon the question "Is it just and convenient?", consider the evidence as a whole of the works, the probability of their being done, the need for their being done and the obligation to do them. On that I conclude that the only convenient way is to appoint a receiver.

Case 113 Parker v London Borough of Camden [1985] 17 HLR 380 Court of Appeal

The plaintiffs were all tenants of the respondent authority, living on estates provided under Part V, Housing Act 1957, with oil or gas-fired central heating, and which included sheltered accommodation for the elderly. The tenancies were held on standard terms, which included an undertaking by the respondent authority to provide such services as might be considered necessary and, so far as reasonably practicable, efficiently to maintain them. The respondent authority were not to be liable for any failure in such services beyond their reasonable control. In addition, they undertook to keep in repair the services for space heating or heating water.

On February 25, 1985, 75 boilermen employed by the respondent authority came out on strike. The boilers broke down on the estates in which the plaintiffs lived, leaving the plaintiffs and other tenants without heating or hot water. In all, some 3,000 of the respondent authority's 36,000 tenants were affected. The respondent authority were concerned about the position, but would not employ outside contractors to repair and restart the boilers, for fear of escalating the dispute. Instead, they had purchased and were selectively distributing electric heaters, and had undertaken that their tenants' heating charges would be reduced at a future date to compensate for the extra cost of using electricity. These heaters were, however, an inadequate substitute for central heating, and evidence was given of dangers, particularly to the elderly.

Representative proceedings were commenced separately, by Mrs Newman in respect of the Denton Estate and Mrs Joyce in respect of the Malden Lane Estate, and by Mrs Parker in respect of Dudley Court. In each case, the relief included a claim for an injunction to restore the heating and hot water, and for the appointment of a receiver and manager, as a means of achieving the restoration of space heating and hot water. Mrs Parker's proceedings came on for hearing first, before Scott J and Mrs Newman's and Mrs Joyce's proceedings second, before Walton J. The respondent authority did not deny that they were in breach of their contractual obligations, but disputed their enforcement by the appointment of a receiver, or by injunctive relief.

Scott J refused to order the respondent authority to restore space heating and hot water, but appointed a receiver and manager to receive the rents and heating charges and to manage Dudley Court, and authorised the receiver to repair the heating and hot water system. Walton J refused to order the respondent authority to restore space heating and hot water, and refused to appoint a receiver and manager to receive the rents and heating charges and to manage the Denton Estate and the Malden Lane Estate. The respondent authority appealed against the order of Scott J and Mrs Newman and Mrs Joyce against the order of Mr Justice Walton. The appeals were brought on together.

Held (allowing the appeal against the order of Scott J to appoint a receiver and manager, dismissing the appeal against the order of Walton J refusing to appoint a receiver and manager; granting the applications for injunctive relief) (1) The jurisdiction to grant relief contained in section 37 of the Supreme Court Act 1981, is quite general and in terms unlimited; however, when Parliament expressly confers powers and imposes duties and responsibilities of an important kind upon a particular body, it is improper for the court by the appointment of a receiver and manager itself to assume those powers and duties; Parliament had conferred the management of accommodation held under Part V of the Housing Act 1957 on local authorities (Housing Act 1957, s. 111), and the court could accordingly not appoint a receiver and manager of such property

(2) Although there is jurisdiction under s. 125, Housing Act 1974, to make an order for specific performance as a remedy for breach of a landlord's repairing obligation, only in rare cases will a mandatory injunction be issued at an interlocutory stage; the present case was, however, sufficiently exceptional to justify the making of a mandatory order.

Sir John Donaldson MR said (in part)

[Counsel appearing for the tenants], draws attention to the fact that the power to appoint a receiver and manager now derives from section 37 of the Supreme Court Act 1981 as does the power to make injunctive orders. He says, as is correct, that the section is completely general in its terms, providing, as it does, that: "The High Court may by order (whether interlocutory or final) grant an injunction or appoint a receiver in all cases in which it appears just and convenient to do so."

[Opposing counsel] retorted by referring to *Harris v Beauchamp* [1894] 1 QB 801 and submitting that it was only permissible to appoint a receiver in circumstances in which the Court of Chancery would have done so prior to 1873. For my part I do not accept that the pre-Judicature Act practices of the Court of Chancery or any other court still rule us from their graves. In any event that decision relates to equitable execution of a judgment and is not a matter with which we are concerned.

For my part I would accept that the jurisdiction, as a jurisdiction, is quite general and, in terms, unlimited. Nevertheless it has to be exercised judicially and with due regard to authorities which are binding upon this court. One such authority, in my judgment, is *Gardner v London Chatham and Dover Railway Co.* [1867] 2 Ch. App. Cas. 201. There Cairns LJ ruled at page 212 that when Parliament expressly confers powers and imposes duties and responsibilities of an important kind upon a particular body, it is, as he put it, improper for the court by the appointment of a receiver and manager, who is of course the agent of the court, itself to assume those powers and duties. That ruling clearly could be looked at again and, if necessary, overruled by the House of Lords, but its reasoning does not depend upon pre-1873 Chancery practices but on a clear view that parliamentary intentions so expressed should be respected. I think that it applies in this case, bearing in mind that Parliament has charged local authorities with the duty of maintaining Part V housing accommodation under section 111 of the Housing Act 1957. I am therefore driven to the conclusion, with quite unconcealed reluctance, that Scott J was wrong to appoint a receiver and manager for Dudley Court and that Walton J was right to refuse to do so, so far as the Denton and Malden Lane estates were concerned.

6.11 Tenant's remedy: the "Right to Repair".

Statute 11: Housing Act 1985. Section 96

Right to carry out repairs

96.—(1) The Secretary of State may by regulations make a scheme for entitling secure tenants, subject to and in accordance with the provisions of the scheme:

  (a) to carry out to the dwelling-houses of which they are secure tenants repairs which their landlords are obliged by repairing covenants to carry out, and

(b) after carrying out the repairs, to recover from their land-lords such sums as may be determined by or under the scheme.

Under the Secure Tenancies (Right to Repair Scheme) Regulations 1985 the scheme entitles secure tenants to carry out repairs to their dwelling-houses which their landlords are obliged by repairing covenants to carry out and, after carrying out the repairs, to recover sums from their landlords.

A secure tenant who wishes to carry out a qualifying repair must serve on the landlord a notice in the prescribed form and the landlord then has 21 days in which to refuse or accept the claim (with or without modifications). The grounds for refusal are divided into mandatory and discretionary grounds. The mandatory grounds are:

   (i) The landlord's costs would be less than £20.

  (ii) The works specified in the tenant's repair claim do not constitute a qualifying repair.

 (iii) The works specified in the tenant's repair claim, if carried out using the materials specified therein, would not in the landlord's opinion satisfactorily remedy the lack of repair to which they relate.

The discretionary grounds are:

 (vi) The landlord's costs would be more than £200.

  (v) The landlord intends to carry out the landlord's works within 28 days of the service on it of the tenant's repair claim.

 (vi) The works specified in the tenant's repair claim are not, in the landlord's opinion, reasonably necessary for the personal comfort or safety of the tenant or any other person living in the dwelling-house and the landlord intends to carry out the landlord's works, within one year of the service on it of the tenant's repair claim, as part of a planned programme of repair or maintenance.

 (vii) Carrying out of works specified in the tenant's repair claim would infringe the terms of any guarantee of which the landlord has the benefit in respect of any work already done or materials supplied.

(viii) The landlord reasonably requires access to the dwelling-house in order to inspect the site of the works specified in the tenant's repair claim but the tenant has failed to provide such access, although he has been given a reasonable opportunity to do so by the landlord.

If the landlord wishes to accept the tenant's claim he must serve on the tenant a notice accepting the tenant's repair claim within 21 days. In this prescribed form the landlord must advise the tenant how much the work would have cost him and what percentage he will pay the tenant (which must be at least 75% but not more than 100% of the landlord's costs). The landlord can specify modifications to the tenant's proposals and in some circumstances can specify who should do the works; for example, if the works cannot be done without risk to the tenant or others. On completion the tenant claims payment and the landlord must respond in writing, within 21 days, accepting or rejecting the claim. Payment can be refused upon one of the following grounds:

   (i) The works have not been properly carried out or are incomplete.

  (ii) The tenant was not entitled to carry out the works.

 (iii) Authorised materials have not been used.

 (iv) Access for inspection has been denied.

  (v) A specified contractor has not been used.

 (vi) Claim for payment has not been made in time.

It should be noted that grounds (i) and (ii) are discretionary.

Any question arising under the scheme may be referred by the landlord or tenant for determination in the county court.

7 OTHER RIGHTS, OBLIGATIONS AND REMEDIES

7.1 Tenant's duty not to commit waste

A tenant is under an implied duty not to commit waste and to use the premises in a tenant-like manner. The committing of waste may amount to a breach of covenant and a tort.

Case 114 Marsden v Edward Heyes [1927] 2 KB 1 Court of Appeal

In 1914 the plaintiff became the owner of the reversion in certain premises consisting of a dwelling-house and shop let to the defendants on an oral tenancy from year to year. In the same year the defendants removed a partition wall, staircase and fireplaces, and converted the premises into one large shop. In 1923 they assigned their tenancy to third persons. In 1925 the plaintiff brought an action against the defendants for waste and for breach of obligations which, as she contended, were implied by law to use the premises in a tenant-like and proper manner, and having so used them to yield them up at the end of the term. The defendants pleaded the Statute of Limitations:

Held (1) A tenant from year to year is under an implied obligation to use the demised premises in a tenant-like manner and to yield them up so used at the end of the tenancy. The obligation continues as long as he continues tenant. If he alters the character of the premises he commits a breach of the obligation and is liable in damages for the injury to the reversion.

(2) That the defendants were under an implied obligation to use the premises in a tenant-like manner; that they had committed a breach of this obligation; that the breach was continuing in 1923, and that the plaintiff was entitled to damages for injury to the reversion.

Bankes LJ said (in part)

When the tests laid down in *West Ham Central Charity Board v East London Waterworks Co* [1900] 1 CL 624 and *Hyman v Rose* [1912] AC 623 are applied it is clear that this was voluntary waste. I would cite the words of Lord Loreburn in the House of Lords suggesting as a matter to be considered the question whether what has been done is inconsistent with the terms of the letting. He says:

"It is a question of fact whether such an act changes the nature of the thing demised, and regard must be had to the user of the demised premises which is permissible under the lease."

In the court below two points were taken: first, that the plaintiff had no vested interest in the reversion in the premises at the time when the acts of waste were committed. That point is not insisted on here. Secondly, that the waste, assuming it to have been wrongful, was committed more than six years before action brought. To this contention [counsel] answers that it is not conclusive, if sound; because apart from any tort the law recognises a contractual obligation upon the defendants as tenants towards their landlord in reference to the user to which the premises were to be put and the extent to which they were to be maintained and repaired. It is not necessary to define the extent of the obligation. It is enough to say that the facts of this case lead to the clear conclusion that there was a breach of that obligation. In *Horsefall v Mather* Holt NP 7 in an action of assumpsit against a tenant at will of a dwelling-house Gibbs CJ held that the defendant was not bound to repair generally, but said: "He is bound to use the premises in a husband-like manner; the law implies this duty and no more." In *Ferguson v Anon* 2 Esp S 90 Lord Kenyon said:

"A tenant from year to year is bound to commit no waste, and to make fair and tenantable repairs, such as putting in windows or doors that have been broken by him, so as to prevent waste and decay of the premises"

indicating thereby that if a tenant commits waste he must do such repairs to the premises as will enable them to exclude wind and water. It may be that he must restore them to the state they would be in if he had committed no waste, or deliver up premises as they were demised to him, fair wear and tear excepted. But at any rate he must deliver up premises of the same character as those which were demised to him; for example, a tenant who takes a dwelling-house cannot at the end of the tenancy yield up a storehouse, or a stable, or cowhouse, however elaborately constructed. But it is not necessary further to define the obligation, because it cannot be contended that a tenant from year to year, who completely alters the premises, does not commit a breach of his implied obligation in respect of the premises. [Counsel] properly admitted that if there was a continuing breach the Statute of Limitations would not assist the defendants. It follows that on June 25, 1923, the plaintiff had a cause of action for damages. The parties have agreed that the cost of repairs is the measure of the damages. The appeal will therefore be allowed and judgment will be entered for the plaintiff for £215 6s. 7d.

Case 115 *Whitham v Kershaw* (1886) 16 QBD 613 Court of Appeal

The defendants were the owners in fee of an allotment of moorland, situate at Blackmoor, near Bradford. The plaintiffs were the owners in fee of an adjoining allotment, subject to a lease thereof to the defendants for a term of fourteen years from the 7th of May, 1879. Both the allotments consisted of very poor land, there being only a slight depth of earth lying upon rock. The defendants had removed a large quantity of earth from the surface of the plaintiffs' allotment, and had placed it on their own allotment. The action was brought to recover damages for this act of waste. The action was tried before Mathew J without a jury, at Leeds, on the 30th of April, 1885. He held that the proper measure of damages was the sum which it would cost the plaintiffs to replace the soil which the defendants had removed. He held on the evidence that the defendants had removed 600 cartloads of soil, and that it would cost 2s. 6d. per load to replace the soil. This made £75, and he deducted a discount of £15 in respect of the time which would elapse before the reversion would fall into possession. There was evidence that the land when in cultivation would be worth from £30 to £35 per acre, and that it would cost from £10 to £15 per acre to bring it into cultivation. The defendants had removed the surface from a quarter of an acre altogether.

Held (1) A covenant by a tenant not to commit waste on the demised property is not with regard to the measure of damages for the breach of it the same thing as a covenant to deliver up the property at the end of the term in the same state as that in which the tenant received it.

(2) In an action by the reversioner against the tenant for waste, the measure of damages is not necessarily the sum which it would cost to restore the property to its condition before the waste; the true measure of damages is the diminution in the value of the reversion, less a discount for immediate payment.

Lord Esher MR said (in part)

At the trial evidence was given of what it would cost to replace on the plaintiff's land as much valuable earth as the defendant had taken away. The judge arrived at the amount of damages in this way: supposing the land to remain in the condition in which the defendant had wrongfully put it up to the end of the lease, it will be worth nothing, unless the plaintiff restores it to the state in which it was before the removal. The plaintiff cannot go on to the defendant's land in order to do this, because he would be a trespasser there. He must go elsewhere to get the earth, and it would cost a considerable sum to bring the earth up to the land, which is on the top of a hill. Having arrived at the sum which it would cost to do this, the learned judge deducted a discount for immediate payment, and gave the plaintiff £60 damages. The question is whether that is the right mode of measuring the damages in an action of waste by a landlord against his tenant. I confess that at first I was inclined to think that the learned judge had adopted the right measure of damages, but upon further consideration I have come to the conclusion that he has made a mistake. I think the mistake is this—he has treated the implied covenant in the lease not to commit waste as equivalent to, and producing the same result as, a covenant to deliver up the demised property at the end of the term in the same condition as that in which the tenant received it. There is an implied covenant on the part of the tenant not to commit waste, but that is a covenant not to do any act of such a permanent nature as will affect the value of the property. Besides the difference of the time at which the action may be brought, there is a great difference as to the measure of damages between such a covenant and a covenant to restore the property to the same condition as that in which the tenant originally received it. The landlord might have a favourite house on the property which was of great value to him, as a matter of sentiment, though it might not add anything to the pecuniary value of the property. If the house was allowed by the tenant to go to ruin, it would not follow that the landlord's reversion would be injured to the extent of the cost of restoring the house to its original condition. The value of the reversion might be diminished, but the question of how much injured would be a question of value, and the proper way to ascertain the damages would be to ask skilled valuers to say how much the property has been diminished in value. It would be wrong to say that the reversionary value had necessarily been diminished by the cost of restoring the property to its original condition. Whereas in the like case, if there were a covenant to leave the premises in the same condition as when taken, the damages in an action which could only be brought after the termination of the lease would obviously be the cost of replacing the house by a house of equal value. I think, therefore, that the learned judge adopted a wrong mode of estimating the damages. The parties have agreed that we shall now decide the amount of damages, and we think that it ought to be £10.

Case 116 *Manchester Bonded Warehouse Company Ltd v Carr* (1880) 5 CPD 507

The plaintiffs demised certain floors in a warehouse to the defendant at a rent. He covenanted to repair, maintain, and keep the inside of the premises in good and tenantable repair and condition, and to deliver them up at the end of the term, damage by fire, storm, or tempest, or other inevitable accident, and reasonable wear and tear only excepted. The plaintiffs covenanted to keep the walls, roof, and main timbers of the premises in good and substantial repair and condition. The lease also contained a provision for the suspension of the rent in the event of the premises being burnt down, or damaged by fire, storm, or tempest.

Sub-lessees of the defendant overloaded a floor with flour, in consequence of which the whole building fell. The plaintiffs rebuilt it and sued for rent during the time the building was unoccupied, and for damages. The defendant denied liability, and claimed damages from the plaintiffs.

Held (1) That, notwithstanding the fall, the defendant was liable to pay the rent;

(2) That there was no implied warranty by the plaintiffs that the building was fit for the purpose for which it was to be used;

(3) That, in the absence of notice to them of any damage or want of repair, the plaintiffs were not liable on their express covenant to keep the walls, roof, and main timbers of the building in repair;

(4) That on the authority of *Saner v Bilton* 7 Ch D 815 the destruction of the building, if caused, by using the property demised in what was apparently a reasonable and proper manner, having regard to its character and to the purposes for which it was intended to be used, was not waste, and therefore the tenant would not be liable to pay damages for it;

(5) That as the case was not within the exceptions in his express covenant to repair, he was liable under it to the cost of putting the inside of the floors demised, and the fixtures therein in good and tenantable repair.

Lord Coleridge CJ said (in part)

First, we are of opinion that notwithstanding the fall of the building, the defendant is liable to pay rent for it as if it had never fallen. This covenant to pay rent is qualified, but the proviso qualifying it does not include such a case as has actually happened. As applied to the facts of this case the defendant's covenant to pay rent is express and without qualification, and he must pay rent accordingly: see *Saner v Bilton* 7 Ch D 815, and the cases there cited.

Secondly, we are of opinion that the plaintiffs are not liable to damages by reason of any implied covenant or warranty by them that the building was fit for the purpose for which it was to be used. No authority has been found which decides that there is any such warranty; what authority there is on the point is against its existence: *Hart v Windsor* 12 M & W 68; *Sutton v Temple* 12 M & W 68, and we are of opinion that no such warranty can be implied. There are, it is true, some cases relating to furnished apartments and houses which tend to show that a person who lets them impliedly warrants that they are fit for residential purposes: *Smith v Marrable* 11 M & W 5 and *Wilson v Finch-Hatton* 2 Ex D 336; but we are not prepared to extend these decisions to ordinary leases of lands, houses, or warehouses, as we must if we are to hold the plaintiffs liable for the fall of this warehouse by reason of any implied covenant or warranty.

Thirdly, we are of opinion that the plaintiffs are not liable to pay any damages to the defendant by reason of the express covenant binding the plaintiffs to keep the walls, roof and main timbers of the building in repair. Before the building fell the plaintiffs had no notice of any danger or want of repair, and such notice is essential to render them liable to be sued on their covenant: *Makin v Watkinson* Law Rep 6 Ex 25, approved and followed in *London and South Western Ry Co v Flower* 1 CPD 77. If we are correct in this respect it will follow that neither before or after the fall of the building was there any breach by the plaintiffs of their express covenant to keeps its walls, &c, in repair. If, indeed, the defendant can show unreasonable delay in the rebuilding by the plaintiffs, he will be entitled to such damages, if any, as such delay may have caused him, and if the case is re-tried this point will be open to him.

Fourthly. We have to consider whether the defendant is liable for the fall of the building. This covenant to repair the demised premises clearly is not extensive enough to render him liable to rebuild the whole warehouse; but it was contended that as he or his undertenants in fact overloaded the building and caused its fall, he is liable to rebuild it, although there may be no express covenant on his part binding him so to do. It was contended that he was liable for waste and destruction, and it was argued that whenever a tenant actually destroys the property demised he must restore it or compensate his landlord for its loss, unless, of course, in cases where destruction is contemplated, as in mines and quarries. We have no doubt that his contention is well founded where the destruction is wilful or negligent; but there is no authority to show that it applies to destruction by using the property demised in what was apparently a reasonable and proper manner, having regard to its character and to the purposes for which it was intended to be used. On the other hand, this very question had to be considered by Mr Justice Fry in *Saner v Bilton (supra)*, and he came to the conclusion that in such a case the tenant was not liable for the destruction of the property. The question in these cases is whether it is the tenant's duty to ascertain what he can do with safety to the property, or whether he is not entitled to assume that it is fit to be used for the purposes for which it is let and for which it is apparently fit. We are of opinion that the latter is the true view, and that, in the absence of an express agreement to that effect, a tenant is not liable for the destruction of the property let to him if such destruction is in fact due to nothing more than a reasonable use of the property, and any use of it is in our opinion reasonable provided it is for a purpose for which the property was intended to be used, and provided the mode and extent of the user was apparently proper having regard to the nature of the property and to what the tenant knew of it and to what as an ordinary business man he ought to have known of it. To hold a tenant liable for the destruction of the property by its reasonable use as above explained, would be to hold him liable for latent faults and defects in the property demised. We are of opinion that he is not liable for such faults and defects, in the absence of some express agreement on his part imposing such liability upon him. We are, however, of opinion, that *prima facie* a tenant is bound to restore the property demised to him, and that if such property is destroyed by the acts of himself or his undertenants, the presumption is against him, and he must in order to exonerate himself show that the destruction was owing to causes for which he was not responsible. If, therefore, this case should go back for trial, the jury should be directed in accordance with the above principles, and should be asked whether the loading of the warehouse in this case was reasonable or unreasonable; and the jury should be told that the question cannot be decided simply by the fact that the warehouse fell from the overloading, but that they must inquire further and see whether there was, before the overloading took place, any reason for supposing that the goods put into the warehouse were too heavy in kind or quantity for its apparent strength or for its strength as known to the defendant, or as he ought as a business man to have known it.

Fifthly and lastly, we have to consider what liability, if any, the defendant is under by virtue of his express covenant to repair the inside of those parts of the warehouse which were demised to him. The inside does not in this case include the walls, roof, or main timbers, for these are to be kept in repair by the landlord. The defendant's covenant, however, extends to the rest of the inside of the floors demised to him; but this covenant is, we think, subject to the exception in case of damage by fire, storm, or tempest, or other inevitable accident, and reasonable wear and tear. Fire, storm, and tempest are out of the question; and we agree with Fry J, in thinking that inevitable accident means some accident ejusdem generis, and does not extend to use of the property by the tenant: see *Saner v Bilton (supra)*. It only remains to consider whether reasonable wear and tear can include destruction by reasonable use. These words, no doubt, include destruction to some extent, e.g., destruction of surface by ordinary friction, but we do not think they include total destruction by a catastrophe which was never contemplated by either party. It follows that the defendant is liable under his express covenant to make good the cost of putting the inside of the floors demised to him and the fixtures therein in good and tenantable repair. We were told that there were no main timbers as distinguished from iron beams; whether this is so or not we are of opinion that iron beams are main timbers within the meaning of the lessor's covenant to repair, and that the tenant is not bound under his covenant to replace them. This we believe disposes of all the legal questions raised before us, and the case must now go back to be tried if the parties cannot agree about the facts, if any still in dispute, or on the measure of the defendant's liability under his express covenant.

7.2 Landlord's liability under the Defective Premises Act 1972

Statute 12: Defective Premises Act 1972. Section 4

Landlord's duty of care in virtue of obligation or right to repair premises demised

4.—(1) Where premises are let under a tenancy which puts on the landlord an obligation to the tenant for the maintenance or repair of the premises, the landlord owes to all persons who might reasonably be expected to be affected by defects in the state of the premises a duty to take such care as is reasonable in all the circumstances to see that they are reasonably safe from personal injury or from damage to their property caused by a relevant defect.

(2) The said duty is owed if the landlord knows (whether as the result of being notified by the tenant or otherwise) or if he ought in all the circumstances to have known of the relevant defect.

(3) In this section "relevant defect" means a defect in the state of the premises existing at or after the material time and arising from, or continuing because of, an act or omission by the landlord which constitutes or would if he had notice of the defect, have constituted a failure by him to carry out his obligation to the tenant for the maintenance or repair of the premises; and for the purposes of the foregoing provision "the material time" means:

(a) where the tenancy commenced before this Act, the commencement of this Act; and

(b) in all other cases, the earliest of the following times, that is to say:
   (i) the time when the tenancy commences;
   (ii) the time when the tenancy agreement is entered into;
   (iii) the time when possession is taken of the premises in contemplation of the letting.

(4) Where premises are let under a tenancy which expressly or impliedly gives the landlord the right to enter the premises to carry out any description of maintenance or repair of the premises, then, as from the time when he first is, or by notice or otherwise can put himself, in a position to exercise the right and so long as he is or can put himself in that position, he shall be treated for the purposes of subsections (1) to (3) above (but for no other purpose) as if he were under an obligation to the tenant for that description of maintenance or repair of the premises; but the landlord shall not owe the tenant any duty by virtue of this subsection in repsect of any defect in the state of the premises arising from, or continuing because of, a failure to carry out an obligation expressly imposed on the tenant by the tenancy.

(5) For the purposes of this section obligations imposed or rights given by any enactment in virtue of a tenancy shall be treated as imposed or given by the tenancy.

(6) This section applies to a right of occupation given by contract or any enactment and not amounting to a tenancy as if the right were a tenancy, and "tenancy" and cognate expressions shall be construed accordingly.

Case 117 *Smith v Bradford Metropolitan Council* (1982) 44 P & CR 171 Court of Appeal

Condition 6 of a weekly tenancy under which the plaintiff occupied the defendant council's house provided, *inter alia*, "The tenant shall ... (ii) give the council officers agents, contractors and workmen reasonable facilities for inspecting the premises and their state or repair and for carrying out repairs." Condition 9 defined "premises" as "the dwelling-house or flat let to the tenant and where the context so admits shall include any garage, out-building, garden or yard let to the tenant." There was a concrete yard called the "patio" at the back of the house and then, at a lower level reaching to the backfence, there was a grassed area. By the beginning of 1979 the patio needed repair and was in a potentially dangerous state. The plaintiff had made complaints to the council. On June 26, 1979, the plaintiff was hanging out the washing on the line when he slipped and fell because concrete under him crumbled and gave way. He broke a bone in his right leg. He brought an action against the council for damages for personal injuries. The judge found that the plaintiff sustained injuries because of the condition of the patio, but decided that as the council were not caught by section 4 (4) of the Defective Premises Act 1972, it was not liable to the plaintiff for damages for personal injuries.

On the plaintiff's appeal:

Held, Allowing the appeal, (1) that where a right was given to, not a duty imposed on, a landlord by a contract of tenancy to enter premises let by him to carry out maintenance or repair, section 4 (4) of the 1972 Act imposed an obligation upon him for maintenance or repair and so a duty of care under section 4 (1) towards the tenant, unless the defect arose from or was continued because of the tenant's own failure to carry out his express contractual obligations.

(2) That in the Act "premises" meant the premises let—the whole premises, land and buildings and it needed clear language to restrict the premises let to the plaintiff so as to exclude the patio which was obviously part of them; that although the definition of the word "premises" in condition

9 appeared to cut down its meaning in the context of condition 6 (ii) the patio was admitted as part of the garden or yard let to the plaintiff and, accordingly, it was part of the premises over which the council obtained the right given by condition 6 (ii) and fell within section 4 (4) of the Act and the council was liable to the plaintiff pursuant to section 4 (1).

Stephenson LJ said (in part)

Section 4 (4) deals with the position where the landlord is not under any obligation to repair the demised premises, but has a right to enter them for the purposes of repair . . .

So if the landlord has a contractual right, express or implied, to enter the premises he has let to carry out maintenance or repair of them, he is treated under subsection (4) and if he were under an obligation to the tenant for maintenance and repair of the premises under subsection (1); and so, just like the landlord who is under an obligation to repair, apart from the statute, he comes under the duty of care imposed by subsection (1). But there is this proviso: he does not come under the duty if the relevant defect which has caused the injury or damage on which the plaintiff bases his claim for breach of statutory duty arises from, or is continued because of, the tenant's own failure to carry out an express contractual obligation of his own.

What, then, were the terms of the tenancy under which these premises were let to the plaintiff? They are contained in written conditions which, the judge was told, are common form with local authorities. It is not alleged that any of those conditions imposed upon the council an obligation to repair; what is alleged is that one of those conditions conferred upon the council a right to enter and carry out repairs. Nor is it alleged, certainly so far as the council's pleaded defence is concerned, that the conditions of the tenancy imposed upon the plaintiff an express obligation to repair this defective patio.

Condition 6 provides:

"The tenant shall . . .

(ii) give the council's officers, agents, contractors and workmen reasonable facilities for inspecting the premises and their state of repair and for carrying out repairs . . .
(iii) maintain any garden, including hedges, let to the tenant in a neat and tidy condition to the reasonable satisfaction of the council."

It is to be noticed that the concluding words of section 4 (4) of the 1972 Act referred to an obligation expressly imposed upon the tenant by the tenancy, and do not limit it to an obligation to repair. The judge found that paragraph (iii) did not impose upon the tenant any obligation to repair; indeed, that was not suggested. It might be argued that an obligation to keep tidy nevertheless does fall within the concluding words of subsection (4); but it seems to me that if that matter had been pursued, there would have been room for evidence and argument as to whether the failure to keep the garden tidy was the cause of the defect in the patio, and furthermore it may be that the matter was not pursued because the paragraph only requires the tenant to maintain the garden in a state of tidiness—not to put the garden into a state of tidiness—and evidence would have been required on any view, I should have thought, as to the state of the patio at the time when the plaintiff entered into possession in 1976, to see whether he had discharged his liability to maintain it in the condition in which it was when he took it over.

That leaves condition 6 (ii) which, on the face of it, would appear to give the council the necessary right to enter the premises to carry out maintenance or repair of them, unless there is something in the true meaning of the word "premises" which excludes the patio. The Act contains no definition of "premises," but the conditions of tenancy do. Condition 9 provides: "In these conditions the word 'premises' shall mean the dwelling-house or flat let to the tenant and where the context so admits shall include any garage, out-building, garden or yard let to the tenant."

The judge held that the context of condition 6 (ii) did not admit the inclusion of the patio, whether as garden or yard, in the word "premises" as it occurs in that paragraph. But he gave no reasons, and one asks inevitably: why does the context not admit of its inclusion?

It was conceded before the judge that the patio was not part of the dwelling-house and it was contended, as it has been contended by [counsel] in this court, and as the judge held, that it is part of the garden, although pleaded in the statement of claim as the rear concrete yard. That restriction on the options open to those who try to ascertain the meaning of the word "premises" in that condition is derived from the decision of this court in *Hopwood v Cannock Chase District Council* [1975] 1 WLR 373. That is a case where a concrete back yard was held by this court not to be part of the structure and exterior of a dwelling-house (including drains, gutters and external pipes) within section 32 (1) of the Housing Act 1961.

"Premises" seems to me to be a wide word. In this Act I would regard it as meaning the premises let—the letting—the subject of the tenancy—all of it; the whole letting, land and buildings; and it would need clear language to restrict the premises let to the plaintiff so as to exclude what was obviously part of them, namely, the patio. But condition 9 does appear to cut down the word to mean the dwelling-house or flat let, and to treat any garage, outbuilding, garden or yard as not within the word "premises" unless the context admits the extension.

Again I ask: why does the context not admit the extension? It does not have to require the extension to include the garden or yard; it only has to admit it. As it seems to me, it would be surprising if the council was obtaining by condition 6 (ii) facilities for inspecting and repairing the premises inside the house but stopping at the back door. I can find nothing in the decision in *Hopwood v Cannock Chase District Council* to prevent this court from holding as a question of fact and degree that the patio was part of this dwelling-house, though there may be more difficulty in getting round or over the ratio decidendi of this court in *Brown v Liverpool Corporation* [1969] 3 All ER 1345, which was distinguished in *Hopwood v Cannock Chase District Council*.

But, however that may be, the context of condition 6 (ii) admits, in my judgment, of the patio being part of the garden or yard let to the tenant, and it matters not which; whether it was part of the garden or part of the yard, it was, in my judgment, part of the premises over which the council obtained the right given by condition 6 (ii) and so part of the premises within the provisions of the statute.

7.3 Occupiers' Liability Acts 1957 and 1984

Statute 13: Occupiers' Liability Act 1957. Sections 1–3

Preliminary

1.—(1) The rules enacted by the two next following sections shall have effect, in place of the rules of the common law, to regulate the duty which an occupier of premises owes to his visitors in respect of dangers due to the state of the premises or to things done or omitted to be done on them.

(2) The rules so enacted shall regulate the nature of the duty imposed by law in consequence of a person's occupation or control or premises and of any invitation or permission he gives (or is to be treated as giving) to another to enter or use the premises, but they shall not alter the rules of the common law

as to the persons on whom a duty is so imposed or to whom it is owed; and accordingly for the purpose of the rules so enacted the persons who are to be treated as an occupier and as his visitors are the same (subject to subsection (4) of this section) as the persons who would at common law be treated as an occupier and as his invitees or licensees.

(3) The rules so enacted in relation to an occupier of premises and his visitors shall also apply, in like manner and to the like extent as the principles applicable at common law to an occupier of premises and his invitees or licensees would apply, to regulate:

(a) the obligations of a person occupying or having control over any fixed or moveable structure, including any vessel, vehicle or aircraft; and

(b) the obligations of a person occupying or having control over any premises or structure in respect of damage to property, including the property of persons who are not themselves his visitors.

(4) A person entering any premises in exercise of rights conferred by virtue of an access agreement or order under the National Parks and Access to the Countryside Act, 1949, is not, for the purposes of this Act, a visitor of the occupier of those premises.

Extent of occupier's ordinary duty

2.—(1) An occupier of premises owes the same duty, the "common duty of care", to all his visitors, except in so far as he is free to and does extend, restrict, modify or exclude his duty to any visitor or visitors by agreement or otherwise.

(2) The common duty of care is a duty to take such care as in all the circumstances of the case is reasonable to see that the visitor will be reasonably safe in using the premises for the purposes for which he is invited or permitted by the occupier to be there.

(3) The circumstances relevant for the present purpose include the degree of care, and of want of care, which would ordinarily be looked for in such a visitor, so that (for example) in proper cases:

(a) an occupier must be prepared for children to be less careful than adults; and

(b) an occupier may expect that a person, in the exercises of his calling, will appreciate and guard against any special risks ordinarily incident to it, so far as the occupier leaves him free to do so.

(4) In determining whether the occupier or premises has discharged the common duty of care to a visitor, regard is to be had to all the circumstances, so that (for example):

(a) where damage is caused to a visitor by a danger of which he had been warned by the occupier, the warning is not to be treated without more as absolving the occupier from liability, unless in all circumstances it was enough to enable the visitor to be reasonably safe; and

(b) where damage is caused to a visitor by a danger due to the faulty execution of any work of construction, maintenance or repair by an independent contractor employed by the occupier, the occupier is not to be treated without more as answerable for the danger if in all the circumstances he had acted reasonably in entrusting the work to an independent contractor and had taken such steps (if any) as he reasonably ought in order to satisfy himself that the contractor was competent and that the work had been properly done.

(5) The common duty of care does not impose on an occupier any obligation to a visitor in respect of risks willingly accepted as his by the visitor (the question whether a risk was so accepted to be decided on the same principles as in other cases in which one person owes a duty of care to another).

(6) For the purpose of this section, persons who enter premises for any purpose in the exercise of a right conferred by law are to be treated as permitted by the occupier to be there for that purpose, whether they in fact have his permission or not.

Effect of contract on occupier's liability to third party

3.—(1) Where an occupier of premises is bound by contract to permit persons who are strangers to the contract to enter or use the premises, the duty of care which he owes to them as his visitors cannot be restricted or excluded by that contract, but (subject to any provision of the contract to the contrary) shall include the duty to perform his obligations under the contract, whether undertaken for their protection or not, in so far as those obligations go beyond the obligations otherwise involved in that duty.

(2) A contract shall not by virtue of this section have the effect, unless it expressly so provides, of making an occupier who has taken all reasonable care answerable to strangers to the contract for dangers due to the faulty execution of any work of construction, maintenance or repair or other like operation by persons other than himself, his servants and persons acting under his direction and control.

(3) In this section "stranger to the contract" means a person not for the time being entitled to the benefit of the contract as a party to it or as the successor by assignment or otherwise of a party to it, and accordingly includes a party to the contract who has ceased to be so entitled.

(4) Where by the terms or conditions governing any tenancy (including a statutory tenancy which does not in law amount to a tenancy) either the landlord or the tenant is bound, though not by contract, to permit persons to enter or use premises of which he is the occupier, this section shall apply as if the tenancy were a contract between the landlord and the tenant.

(5) This section, in so far as it prevents the common duty of care from being restricted or excluded, applies to contracts entered into and tenancies created before the commencement of this Act, as well as to those entered into or created after its commencement; but, in so far as it enlarges the duty owed by an occupier beyond the common duty of care, it shall have effect in relation to obligations which are undertaken after that commencement or which are renewed by agreement (whether express or implied) after that commencement.

Statute 14: Occupiers' Liability Act 1984. Section 1

Duty of occupier to persons other than his visitors

1.—(1) The rules enacted by this section shall have effect, in place of the rules of the common law, to determine:

- (a) whether any duty is owed by a person as occupier of premises to persons other than his visitors in respect of any risk of their suffering injury on the premises by reason of any danger due to the state of the premises or to things done or omitted to be done on them; and
- (b) if so, what that duty is.

(2) For the purposes of this section, the persons who are to be treated respectively as an occupier of any premises (which, for those purposes, include any fixed or movable structure) and as his visitors are:

- (a) any person who owes in relation to the premises the duty referred to in section 2 of the Occupiers' Liability Act 1957 (the common duty of care), and
- (b) those who are his visitors for the purposes of that duty.

(3) An occupier of premises owes a duty to another (not being his visitor) in respect of any such risk as is referred to in subsection (1) above if:

- (a) he is aware of the danger or has reasonable grounds to believe that it exists;

(b) he knows or has reasonable grounds to believe that the other is in the vicinity of the danger concerned or that he may come into the vicinity of the danger (in either case, whether the other has lawful authority for being in that vicinity or not); and

(c) the risk is one against which, in all the circumstances of the case, he may reasonably be expected to offer the other some protection.

(4) Where, by virtue of this section, an occupier or premises owes a duty to another in respect of such a risk, the duty is to take such care as is reasonable in all the circumstances of the case to see that he does not suffer injury on the premises by reason of the danger concerned.

(5) Any duty owed by virtue of this section in respect of a risk may, in an appropriate case, be discharged by taking such steps as are reasonable in all the circumstances of the case to give warning of the danger concerned or to discourage persons from incurring the risk.

(6) No duty is owed by virtue of this section to any person in respect of risks willingly accepted as his by that person (the question whether a risk was so accepted to be decided on the same principles as in other cases in which one person owes a duty of care to another).

(7) No duty is owed by virtue of this section to persons using the highway, and this section does not affect any duty owed to such persons.

(8) Where a person owes a duty by virtue of this section, he does not, by reason of any breach of the duty, incur any liability in respect of any loss of or damage to property.

(9) In this section:

"highway" means any part of a highway other than a ferry or waterway;

"injury" means anything resulting in death or personal injury, including any disease and any impairment of physical or mental condition; and

"movable structure" includes any vessel, vehicle or aircraft.

7.4 The operation of the Public Health Act 1936

Statute 15: Public Health Act 1936. Sections 92–95, 99

Statutory nuisances

92.—(1) Without prejudice to the exercise by a local authority of any other powers vested in them by or under this Act, the following matters may, subject to the provisions of this Part of this Act, be dealt with summarily, and are in this Part of this Act referred to as "statutory nuisances," that is to say:

(a) any premises in such a state as to be prejudicial to health or a nuisance;

(b) any animal kept in such a place or manner as to be prejudicial to health or a nuisance;

(c) any accumulation or deposit which is prejudicial to health or a nuisance;

(d) any dust or effluvia caused by any trade, business, manufacture or process and [injurious, or likely to cause injury, to the public health or a nuisance];

(e) any [. . .] workplace, which is not provided with sufficient means of ventilation, or in which sufficient ventilation is not maintained, or which is not kept clean or not kept free from noxious effluvia, or which is so overcrowded while work is carried on as to be prejudicial to the health of those employed therein;

(f) any other matter declared by any provision of this Act to be a statutory nuisance.

(2) A local authority shall not without the consent of the Minister institute summary proceedings under this Part of this Act in respect of any such nuisance as is mentioned in paragraph (c) or paragraph (d) of the preceding subsection if proceedings in respect thereof might be instituted under the Alkali, &c. Works Regulation Act, 1906 or for a failure to discharge the duty under section 5 of the Health and Safety at Work etc. Act 1974.

Service of abatement notice

93. Where a local authority are satisfied of the existence of a statutory nuisance, they shall serve a notice (hereafter in this Act referred to as "an abatement notice") on the person by whose act, default or sufference the nuisance arises or continues, or, if that person cannot be found, on the owner or occupier of the premises on which the nuisance arises, requiring him to abate the nuisance and to execute such works and take such steps as may be necessary for that purpose:

Provided that:

(a) where the nuisance arises from any defect of a structural character, the notice shall be served on the owner of the premises;

(b) where the person causing the nuisance cannot be found and it is clear that the nuisance does not arise or continue by the act, default or sufferance of the owner or the occupier of the premises, the local authority may themselves